Cover Image Credit/Copyright Attribution: IIIerlok_Xolms/Shutterstock

Frank Hutter • Lars Kotthoff • Joaquin Vanschoren
Editors

Automated Machine Learning

Methods, Systems, Challenges

Editors
Frank Hutter
Department of Computer Science
University of Freiburg
Freiburg, Germany

Lars Kotthoff
University of Wyoming
Laramie, WY, USA

Joaquin Vanschoren
Eindhoven University of Technology
Eindhoven, The Netherlands

https://doi.org/10.1007/978-3-030-05318-5

To Sophia and Tashia. – F.H.

To Kobe, Elias, Ada, and Veerle. – J.V.

To the AutoML community, for being awesome. – F.H., L.K., and J.V.

Foreword

"*I'd like to use machine learning, but I can't invest much time.*" That is something you hear all too often in industry and from researchers in other disciplines. The resulting demand for hands-free solutions to machine learning has recently given rise to the field of automated machine learning (AutoML), and I'm delighted that with this book, there is now the first comprehensive guide to this field.

I have been very passionate about automating machine learning myself ever since our Automatic Statistician project started back in 2014. I want us to be really ambitious in this endeavor; we should try to automate all aspects of the entire machine learning and data analysis pipeline. This includes automating data collection and experiment design; automating data cleanup and missing data imputation; automating feature selection and transformation; automating model discovery, criticism, and explanation; automating the allocation of computational resources; automating hyperparameter optimization; automating inference; and automating model monitoring and anomaly detection. This is a huge list of things, and we'd optimally like to automate all of it.

There is a caveat of course. While *full* automation can motivate scientific research and provide a long-term engineering goal, in practice, we probably want to *semiautomate* most of these and gradually remove the human in the loop as needed. Along the way, what is going to happen if we try to do all this automation is that we are likely to develop powerful tools that will help make the practice of machine learning, first of all, *more systematic* (since it's very ad hoc these days) and also *more efficient*.

These are worthy goals even if we did not succeed in the final goal of automation, but as this book demonstrates, current AutoML methods can already surpass human machine learning experts in several tasks. This trend is likely only going to intensify as we're making progress and as computation becomes ever cheaper, and AutoML is therefore clearly one of the topics that is here to stay. It is a great time to get involved in AutoML, and this book is an excellent starting point.

This book includes very up-to-date overviews of the bread-and-butter techniques we need in AutoML (hyperparameter optimization, meta-learning, and neural architecture search), provides in-depth discussions of existing AutoML systems, and thoroughly evaluates the state of the art in AutoML in a series of competitions that ran since 2015. As such, I highly recommend this book to any machine learning researcher wanting to get started in the field and to any practitioner looking to understand the methods behind all the AutoML tools out there.

San Francisco, USA
Professor, University of Cambridge and
Chief Scientist, Uber
October 2018

Zoubin Ghahramani

Preface

The past decade has seen an explosion of machine learning research and applications; especially, deep learning methods have enabled key advances in many application domains, such as computer vision, speech processing, and game playing. However, the performance of many machine learning methods is very sensitive to a plethora of design decisions, which constitutes a considerable barrier for new users. This is particularly true in the booming field of deep learning, where human engineers need to select the right neural architectures, training procedures, regularization methods, and hyperparameters of all of these components in order to make their networks do what they are supposed to do with sufficient performance. This process has to be repeated for every application. Even experts are often left with tedious episodes of trial and error until they identify a good set of choices for a particular dataset.

The field of automated machine learning (AutoML) aims to make these decisions in a data-driven, objective, and automated way: the user simply provides data, and the AutoML system automatically determines the approach that performs best for this particular application. Thereby, AutoML makes state-of-the-art machine learning approaches accessible to domain scientists who are interested in applying machine learning but do not have the resources to learn about the technologies behind it in detail. This can be seen as a *democratization* of machine learning: with AutoML, customized state-of-the-art machine learning is at everyone's fingertips.

As we show in this book, AutoML approaches are already mature enough to rival and sometimes even outperform human machine learning experts. Put simply, AutoML can lead to improved performance while saving substantial amounts of time and money, as machine learning experts are both hard to find and expensive. As a result, commercial interest in AutoML has grown dramatically in recent years, and several major tech companies are now developing their own AutoML systems. We note, though, that the purpose of democratizing machine learning is served much better by open-source AutoML systems than by proprietary paid black-box services.

This book presents an overview of the fast-moving field of AutoML. Due to the community's current focus on deep learning, some researchers nowadays mistakenly equate AutoML with the topic of neural architecture search (NAS);

but of course, if you're reading this book, you know that – while NAS is an excellent example of AutoML – there is a lot more to AutoML than NAS. This book is intended to provide some background and starting points for researchers interested in developing their own AutoML approaches, highlight available systems for practitioners who want to apply AutoML to their problems, and provide an overview of the state of the art to researchers already working in AutoML. The book is divided into three parts on these different aspects of AutoML.

Part I presents an overview of AutoML methods. This part gives both a solid overview for novices and serves as a reference to experienced AutoML researchers.

Chap. 1 discusses the problem of hyperparameter optimization, the simplest and most common problem that AutoML considers, and describes the wide variety of different approaches that are applied, with a particular focus on the methods that are currently most efficient.

Chap. 2 shows how to *learn to learn*, i.e., how to use experience from evaluating machine learning models to inform how to approach new learning tasks with new data. Such techniques mimic the processes going on as a human transitions from a machine learning novice to an expert and can tremendously decrease the time required to get good performance on completely new machine learning tasks.

Chap. 3 provides a comprehensive overview of methods for NAS. This is one of the most challenging tasks in AutoML, since the design space is extremely large and a single evaluation of a neural network can take a very long time. Nevertheless, the area is very active, and new exciting approaches for solving NAS appear regularly.

Part II focuses on actual AutoML systems that even novice users can use. If you are most interested in applying AutoML to your machine learning problems, this is the part you should start with. All of the chapters in this part evaluate the systems they present to provide an idea of their performance in practice.

Chap. 4 describes Auto-WEKA, one of the first AutoML systems. It is based on the well-known WEKA machine learning toolkit and searches over different classification and regression methods, their hyperparameter settings, and data preprocessing methods. All of this is available through WEKA's graphical user interface at the click of a button, without the need for a single line of code.

Chap. 5 gives an overview of Hyperopt-Sklearn, an AutoML framework based on the popular scikit-learn framework. It also includes several hands-on examples for how to use system.

Chap. 6 describes Auto-sklearn, which is also based on scikit-learn. It applies similar optimization techniques as Auto-WEKA and adds several improvements over other systems at the time, such as meta-learning for warmstarting the optimization and automatic ensembling. The chapter compares the performance of Auto-sklearn to that of the two systems in the previous chapters, Auto-WEKA and Hyperopt-Sklearn. In two different versions, Auto-sklearn is the system that won the challenges described in Part III of this book.

Chap. 7 gives an overview of Auto-Net, a system for automated deep learning that selects both the architecture and the hyperparameters of deep neural networks. An early version of Auto-Net produced the first automatically tuned neural network that won against human experts in a competition setting.

Chap. 8 describes the TPOT system, which automatically constructs and optimizes tree-based machine learning pipelines. These pipelines are more flexible than approaches that consider only a set of fixed machine learning components that are connected in predefined ways.

Chap. 9 presents the Automatic Statistician, a system to automate data science by generating fully automated reports that include an analysis of the data, as well as predictive models and a comparison of their performance. A unique feature of the Automatic Statistician is that it provides natural-language descriptions of the results, suitable for non-experts in machine learning.

Finally, Part III and Chap. 10 give an overview of the AutoML challenges, which have been running since 2015. The purpose of these challenges is to spur the development of approaches that perform well on practical problems and determine the best overall approach from the submissions. The chapter details the ideas and concepts behind the challenges and their design, as well as results from past challenges.

To the best of our knowledge, this is the first comprehensive compilation of all aspects of AutoML: the methods behind it, available systems that implement AutoML in practice, and the challenges for evaluating them. This book provides practitioners with background and ways to get started developing their own AutoML systems and details existing state-of-the-art systems that can be applied immediately to a wide range of machine learning tasks. The field is moving quickly, and with this book, we hope to help organize and digest the many recent advances. We hope you enjoy this book and join the growing community of AutoML enthusiasts.

Acknowledgments

We wish to thank all the chapter authors, without whom this book would not have been possible. We are also grateful to the European Union's Horizon 2020 research and innovation program for covering the open access fees for this book through Frank's ERC Starting Grant (grant no. 716721).

Freiburg, Germany
Laramie, WY, USA
Eindhoven, The Netherlands
October 2018

Frank Hutter
Lars Kotthoff
Joaquin Vanschoren

Contents

Part I
AutoML Methods

Chapter 1
Hyperparameter Optimization

Matthias Feurer and Frank Hutter

Abstract Recent interest in complex and computationally expensive machine learning models with many hyperparameters, such as automated machine learning (AutoML) frameworks and deep neural networks, has resulted in a resurgence of research on hyperparameter optimization (HPO). In this chapter, we give an overview of the most prominent approaches for HPO. We first discuss blackbox function optimization methods based on model-free methods and Bayesian optimization. Since the high computational demand of many modern machine learning applications renders pure blackbox optimization extremely costly, we next focus on modern multi-fidelity methods that use (much) cheaper variants of the blackbox function to approximately assess the quality of hyperparameter settings. Lastly, we point to open problems and future research directions.

1.1 Introduction

Every machine learning system has hyperparameters, and the most basic task in automated machine learning (AutoML) is to automatically set these hyperparameters to optimize performance. Especially recent deep neural networks crucially depend on a wide range of hyperparameter choices about the neural network's architecture, regularization, and optimization. Automated hyperparameter optimization (HPO) has several important use cases; it can

- reduce the human effort necessary for applying machine learning. This is particularly important in the context of AutoML.

M. Feurer (✉)
Department of Computer Science, University of Freiburg, Freiburg, Baden-Württemberg, Germany
e-mail: feurerm@informatik.uni-freiburg.de

F. Hutter
Department of Computer Science, University of Freiburg, Freiburg, Germany

F. Hutter et al. (eds.), *Automated Machine Learning*, The Springer Series on Challenges in Machine Learning, https://doi.org/10.1007/978-3-030-05318-5_1

- improve the performance of machine learning algorithms (by tailoring them to the problem at hand); this has led to new state-of-the-art performances for important machine learning benchmarks in several studies (e.g. [105, 140]).
- improve the reproducibility and fairness of scientific studies. Automated HPO is clearly more reproducible than manual search. It facilitates fair comparisons since different methods can only be compared fairly if they all receive the same level of tuning for the problem at hand [14, 133].

The problem of HPO has a long history, dating back to the 1990s (e.g., [77, 82, 107, 126]), and it was also established early that different hyperparameter configurations tend to work best for different datasets [82]. In contrast, it is a rather new insight that HPO can be used to adapt general-purpose pipelines to specific application domains [30]. Nowadays, it is also widely acknowledged that tuned hyperparameters improve over the default setting provided by common machine learning libraries [100, 116, 130, 149].

Because of the increased usage of machine learning in companies, HPO is also of substantial commercial interest and plays an ever larger role there, be it in company-internal tools [45], as part of machine learning cloud services [6, 89], or as a service by itself [137].

HPO faces several challenges which make it a hard problem in practice:

- Function evaluations can be extremely expensive for large models (e.g., in deep learning), complex machine learning pipelines, or large datesets.
- The configuration space is often complex (comprising a mix of continuous, categorical and conditional hyperparameters) and high-dimensional. Furthermore, it is not always clear which of an algorithm's hyperparameters need to be optimized, and in which ranges.
- We usually don't have access to a gradient of the loss function with respect to the hyperparameters. Furthermore, other properties of the target function often used in classical optimization do not typically apply, such as convexity and smoothness.
- One cannot directly optimize for generalization performance as training datasets are of limited size.

We refer the interested reader to other reviews of HPO for further discussions on this topic [64, 94].

This chapter is structured as follows. First, we define the HPO problem formally and discuss its variants (Sect. 1.2). Then, we discuss blackbox optimization algorithms for solving HPO (Sect. 1.3). Next, we focus on modern multi-fidelity methods that enable the use of HPO even for very expensive models, by exploiting approximate performance measures that are cheaper than full model evaluations (Sect. 1.4). We then provide an overview of the most important hyperparameter optimization systems and applications to AutoML (Sect. 1.5) and end the chapter with a discussion of open problems (Sect. 1.6).

1.2 Problem Statement

Let $\mathcal{A}$ denote a machine learning algorithm with N hyperparameters. We denote the domain of the n-th hyperparameter by Λ_n and the overall *hyperparameter configuration space* as $\mathbf{\Lambda} = \Lambda_1 \times \Lambda_2 \times \dots \Lambda_N$. A vector of hyperparameters is denoted by $\boldsymbol{\lambda} \in \mathbf{\Lambda}$, and $\mathcal{A}$ with its hyperparameters instantiated to $\boldsymbol{\lambda}$ is denoted by $\mathcal{A}_{\boldsymbol{\lambda}}$.

The domain of a hyperparameter can be real-valued (e.g., learning rate), integer-valued (e.g., number of layers), binary (e.g., whether to use early stopping or not), or categorical (e.g., choice of optimizer). For integer and real-valued hyperparameters, the domains are mostly bounded for practical reasons, with only a few exceptions [12, 113, 136].

Furthermore, the configuration space can contain *conditionality*, i.e., a hyperparameter may only be relevant if another hyperparameter (or some combination of hyperparameters) takes on a certain value. Conditional spaces take the form of directed acyclic graphs. Such conditional spaces occur, e.g., in the automated tuning of machine learning pipelines, where the choice between different preprocessing and machine learning algorithms is modeled as a categorical hyperparameter, a problem known as *Full Model Selection* (FMS) or *Combined Algorithm Selection and Hyperparameter optimization problem* (CASH) [30, 34, 83, 149]. They also occur when optimizing the architecture of a neural network: e.g., the number of layers can be an integer hyperparameter and the per-layer hyperparameters of layer i are only active if the network depth is at least i [12, 14, 33].

Given a data set $\mathcal{D}$, our goal is to find

$$\boldsymbol{\lambda}^* = \operatorname*{argmin}_{\boldsymbol{\lambda} \in \mathbf{\Lambda}} \mathbb{E}_{(D_{train}, D_{valid}) \sim \mathcal{D}} \mathbf{V}(\mathcal{L}, \mathcal{A}_{\boldsymbol{\lambda}}, D_{train}, D_{valid}), \tag{1.1}$$

where $\mathbf{V}(\mathcal{L}, \mathcal{A}_{\boldsymbol{\lambda}}, D_{train}, D_{valid})$ measures the loss of a model generated by algorithm $\mathcal{A}$ with hyperparameters $\boldsymbol{\lambda}$ on training data D_{train} and evaluated on validation data D_{valid}. In practice, we only have access to finite data $D \sim \mathcal{D}$ and thus need to approximate the expectation in Eq. 1.1.

Popular choices for the validation protocol $\mathbf{V}(\cdot, \cdot, \cdot, \cdot)$ are the holdout and cross-validation error for a user-given loss function (such as misclassification rate); see Bischl et al. [16] for an overview of validation protocols. Several strategies for reducing the evaluation time have been proposed: It is possible to only test machine learning algorithms on a subset of folds [149], only on a subset of data [78, 102, 147], or for a small amount of iterations; we will discuss some of these strategies in more detail in Sect. 1.4. Recent work on multi-task [147] and multi-source [121] optimization introduced further cheap, auxiliary tasks, which can be queried instead of Eq. 1.1. These can provide cheap information to help HPO, but do not necessarily train a machine learning model on the dataset of interest and therefore do not yield a usable model as a side product.

1.2.1 Alternatives to Optimization: Ensembling and Marginalization

Solving Eq. 1.1 with one of the techniques described in the rest of this chapter usually requires fitting the machine learning algorithm $\mathcal{A}$ with multiple hyperparameter vectors $\boldsymbol{\lambda}_t$. Instead of using the argmin-operator over these, it is possible to either construct an ensemble (which aims to minimize the loss for a given validation protocol) or to integrate out all the hyperparameters (if the model under consideration is a probabilistic model). We refer to Guyon et al. [50] and the references therein for a comparison of frequentist and Bayesian model selection.

Only choosing a single hyperparameter configuration can be wasteful when many good configurations have been identified by HPO, and combining them in an ensemble can improve performance [109]. This is particularly useful in AutoML systems with a large configuration space (e.g., in *FMS* or *CASH*), where good configurations can be very diverse, which increases the potential gains from ensembling [4, 19, 31, 34]. To further improve performance, *Automatic Frankensteining* [155] uses HPO to train a stacking model [156] on the outputs of the models found with HPO; the 2nd level models are then combined using a traditional ensembling strategy.

The methods discussed so far applied ensembling after the HPO procedure. While they improve performance in practice, the base models are not optimized for ensembling. It is, however, also possible to directly optimize for models which would maximally improve an existing ensemble [97].

Finally, when dealing with Bayesian models it is often possible to integrate out the hyperparameters of the machine learning algorithm, for example using *evidence maximization* [98], *Bayesian model averaging* [56], *slice sampling* [111] or *empirical Bayes* [103].

1.2.2 Optimizing for Multiple Objectives

In practical applications it is often necessary to trade off two or more objectives, such as the performance of a model and resource consumption [65] (see also Chap. 3) or multiple loss functions [57]. Potential solutions can be obtained in two ways.

First, if a limit on a secondary performance measure is known (such as the maximal memory consumption), the problem can be formulated as a constrained optimization problem. We will discuss constraint handling in Bayesian optimization in Sect. 1.3.2.4.

Second, and more generally, one can apply multi-objective optimization to search for the Pareto front, a set of configurations which are optimal tradeoffs between the objectives in the sense that, for each configuration on the Pareto front, there is no other configuration which performs better for at least one and at least as well for all other objectives. The user can then choose a configuration from the Pareto front. We refer the interested reader to further literature on this topic [53, 57, 65, 134].

1.3 Blackbox Hyperparameter Optimization

In general, every blackbox optimization method can be applied to HPO. Due to the non-convex nature of the problem, global optimization algorithms are usually preferred, but some locality in the optimization process is useful in order to make progress within the few function evaluations that are usually available. We first discuss model-free blackbox HPO methods and then describe blackbox Bayesian optimization methods.

1.3.1 Model-Free Blackbox Optimization Methods

Grid search is the most basic HPO method, also known as full factorial design [110]. The user specifies a finite set of values for each hyperparameter, and grid search evaluates the Cartesian product of these sets. This suffers from the curse of dimensionality since the required number of function evaluations grows exponentially with the dimensionality of the configuration space. An additional problem of grid search is that increasing the resolution of discretization substantially increases the required number of function evaluations.

A simple alternative to grid search is random search [13].[1] As the name suggests, random search samples configurations at random until a certain budget for the search is exhausted. This works better than grid search when some hyperparameters are much more important than others (a property that holds in many cases [13, 61]). Intuitively, when run with a fixed budget of B function evaluations, the number of different values grid search can afford to evaluate for each of the N hyperparameters is only $B^{1/N}$, whereas random search will explore B different values for each; see Fig. 1.1 for an illustration.

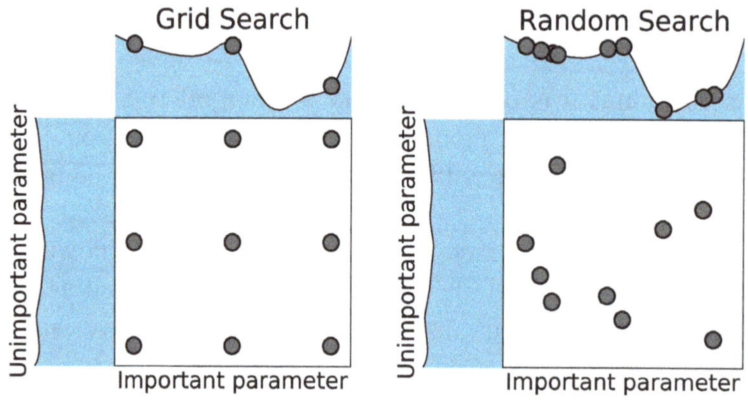

Fig. 1.1 Comparison of grid search and random search for minimizing a function with one important and one unimportant parameter. This figure is based on the illustration in Fig. 1 of Bergstra and Bengio [13]

[1]In some disciplines this is also known as *pure* random search [158].

Further advantages over grid search include easier parallelization (since workers do not need to communicate with each other and failing workers do not leave holes in the design) and flexible resource allocation (since one can add an arbitrary number of random points to a random search design to still yield a random search design; the equivalent does not hold for grid search).

Random search is a useful baseline because it makes no assumptions on the machine learning algorithm being optimized, and, given enough resources, will, in expectation, achieves performance arbitrarily close to the optimum. Interleaving random search with more complex optimization strategies therefore allows to guarantee a minimal rate of convergence and also adds exploration that can improve model-based search [3, 59]. Random search is also a useful method for initializing the search process, as it explores the entire configuration space and thus often finds settings with reasonable performance. However, it is no silver bullet and often takes far longer than guided search methods to identify one of the best performing hyperparameter configurations: e.g., when sampling without replacement from a configuration space with N Boolean hyperparameters with a good and a bad setting each and no interaction effects, it will require an expected 2^{N-1} function evaluations to find the optimum, whereas a guided search could find the optimum in $N + 1$ function evaluations as follows: starting from an arbitrary configuration, loop over the hyperparameters and change one at a time, keeping the resulting configuration if performance improves and reverting the change if it doesn't. Accordingly, the guided search methods we discuss in the following sections usually outperform random search [12, 14, 33, 90, 153].

Population-based methods, such as *genetic algorithms*, *evolutionary algorithms*, *evolutionary strategies*, and *particle swarm optimization* are optimization algorithms that maintain a population, i.e., a set of configurations, and improve this population by applying local perturbations (so-called mutations) and combinations of different members (so-called crossover) to obtain a new generation of better configurations. These methods are conceptually simple, can handle different data types, and are embarrassingly parallel [91] since a population of N members can be evaluated in parallel on N machines.

One of the best known population-based methods is the covariance matrix adaption evolutionary strategy (CMA-ES [51]); this simple evolutionary strategy samples configurations from a multivariate Gaussian whose mean and covariance are updated in each generation based on the success of the population's individuals. CMA-ES is one of the most competitive blackbox optimization algorithms, regularly dominating the *Black-Box Optimization Benchmarking* (BBOB) challenge [11].

For further details on population-based methods, we refer to [28, 138]; we discuss applications to hyperparameter optimization in Sect. 1.5, applications to neural architecture search in Chap. 3, and genetic programming for AutoML pipelines in Chap. 8.

1.3.2 Bayesian Optimization

Bayesian optimization is a state-of-the-art optimization framework for the global optimization of expensive blackbox functions, which recently gained traction in HPO by obtaining new state-of-the-art results in tuning deep neural networks for image classification [140, 141], speech recognition [22] and neural language modeling [105], and by demonstrating wide applicability to different problem settings. For an in-depth introduction to Bayesian optimization, we refer to the excellent tutorials by Shahriari et al. [135] and Brochu et al. [18].

In this section we first give a brief introduction to Bayesian optimization, present alternative surrogate models used in it, describe extensions to conditional and constrained configuration spaces, and then discuss several important applications to hyperparameter optimization.

Many recent advances in Bayesian optimization do not treat HPO as a blackbox any more, for example multi-fidelity HPO (see Sect. 1.4), Bayesian optimization with meta-learning (see Chap. 2), and Bayesian optimization taking the pipeline structure into account [159, 160]. Furthermore, many recent developments in Bayesian optimization do not directly target HPO, but can often be readily applied to HPO, such as new acquisition functions, new models and kernels, and new parallelization schemes.

1.3.2.1 Bayesian Optimization in a Nutshell

Bayesian optimization is an iterative algorithm with two key ingredients: a probabilistic surrogate model and an acquisition function to decide which point to evaluate next. In each iteration, the surrogate model is fitted to all observations of the target function made so far. Then the acquisition function, which uses the predictive distribution of the probabilistic model, determines the utility of different candidate points, trading off exploration and exploitation. Compared to evaluating the expensive blackbox function, the acquisition function is cheap to compute and can therefore be thoroughly optimized.

Although many acquisition functions exist, the *expected improvement* (EI) [72]:

$$\mathbb{E}[\mathbb{I}(\boldsymbol{\lambda})] = \mathbb{E}[\max(f_{min} - y, 0)] \tag{1.2}$$

is common choice since it can be computed in closed form if the model prediction y at configuration $\boldsymbol{\lambda}$ follows a normal distribution:

$$\mathbb{E}[\mathbb{I}(\boldsymbol{\lambda})] = (f_{min} - \mu(\boldsymbol{\lambda}))\,\Phi\left(\frac{f_{min} - \mu(\boldsymbol{\lambda})}{\sigma}\right) + \sigma\phi\left(\frac{f_{min} - \mu(\boldsymbol{\lambda})}{\sigma}\right), \tag{1.3}$$

where $\phi(\cdot)$ and $\Phi(\cdot)$ are the standard normal density and standard normal distribution function, and f_{min} is the best observed value so far.

Fig. 1.2 illustrates Bayesian optimization optimizing a toy function.

1.3.2.2 Surrogate Models

Traditionally, Bayesian optimization employs Gaussian processes [124] to model the target function because of their expressiveness, smooth and well-calibrated

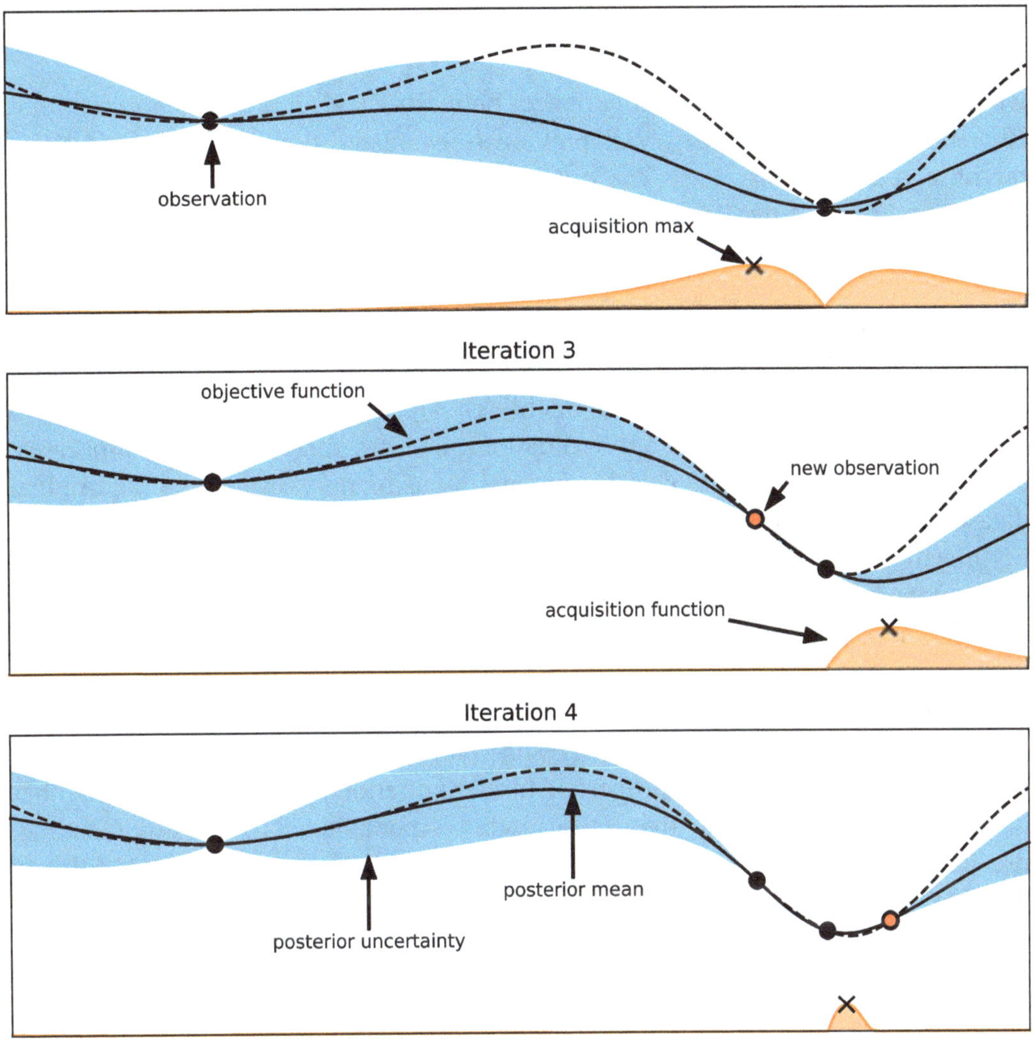

Fig. 1.2 Illustration of Bayesian optimization on a 1-d function. Our goal is to minimize the dashed line using a Gaussian process surrogate (predictions shown as black line, with blue tube representing the uncertainty) by maximizing the acquisition function represented by the lower orange curve. (Top) The acquisition value is low around observations, and the highest acquisition value is at a point where the predicted function value is low and the predictive uncertainty is relatively high. (Middle) While there is still a lot of variance to the left of the new observation, the predicted mean to the right is much lower and the next observation is conducted there. (Bottom) Although there is almost no uncertainty left around the location of the true maximum, the next evaluation is done there due to its expected improvement over the best point so far

uncertainty estimates and closed-form computability of the predictive distribution. A Gaussian process $\mathcal{G}\left(m(\boldsymbol{\lambda}), k(\boldsymbol{\lambda}, \boldsymbol{\lambda}')\right)$ is fully specified by a mean $m(\boldsymbol{\lambda})$ and a covariance function $k(\boldsymbol{\lambda}, \boldsymbol{\lambda}')$, although the mean function is usually assumed to be constant in Bayesian optimization. Mean and variance predictions $\mu(\cdot)$ and $\sigma^2(\cdot)$ for the noise-free case can be obtained by:

$$\mu(\boldsymbol{\lambda}) = \mathbf{k}_*^T \mathbf{K}^{-1} \mathbf{y}, \sigma^2(\boldsymbol{\lambda}) = k(\boldsymbol{\lambda}, \boldsymbol{\lambda}) - \mathbf{k}_*^T \mathbf{K}^{-1} \mathbf{k}_*, \tag{1.4}$$

where $\mathbf{k}_*$ denotes the vector of covariances between $\boldsymbol{\lambda}$ and all previous observations, $\mathbf{K}$ is the covariance matrix of all previously evaluated configurations and $\mathbf{y}$ are the observed function values. The quality of the Gaussian process depends solely on the covariance function. A common choice is the Mátern 5/2 kernel, with its hyperparameters integrated out by Markov Chain Monte Carlo [140].

One downside of standard Gaussian processes is that they scale cubically in the number of data points, limiting their applicability when one can afford many function evaluations (e.g., with many parallel workers, or when function evaluations are cheap due to the use of lower fidelities). This cubic scaling can be avoided by scalable Gaussian process approximations, such as sparse Gaussian processes. These approximate the full Gaussian process by using only a subset of the original dataset as *inducing points* to build the kernel matrix $\mathbf{K}$. While they allowed Bayesian optimization with GPs to scale to tens of thousands of datapoints for optimizing the parameters of a randomized SAT solver [62], there are criticism about the calibration of their uncertainty estimates and their applicability to standard HPO has not been tested [104, 154].

Another downside of Gaussian processes with standard kernels is their poor scalability to high dimensions. As a result, many extensions have been proposed to efficiently handle intrinsic properties of configuration spaces with large number of hyperparameters, such as the use of random embeddings [153], using Gaussian processes on partitions of the configuration space [154], cylindric kernels [114], and additive kernels [40, 75].

Since some other machine learning models are more scalable and flexible than Gaussian processes, there is also a large body of research on adapting these models to Bayesian optimization. Firstly, (deep) neural networks are a very flexible and scalable models. The simplest way to apply them to Bayesian optimization is as a feature extractor to preprocess inputs and then use the outputs of the final hidden layer as basis functions for Bayesian linear regression [141]. A more complex, fully Bayesian treatment of the network weights, is also possible by using a Bayesian neural network trained with stochastic gradient Hamiltonian Monte Carlo [144]. Neural networks tend to be faster than Gaussian processes for Bayesian optimization after ~250 function evaluations, which also allows for large-scale parallelism. The flexibility of deep learning can also enable Bayesian optimization on more complex tasks. For example, a variational auto-encoder can be used to embed complex inputs (such as the structured configurations of the automated statistician, see Chap. 9) into a real-valued vector such that a regular Gaussian process can handle it [92]. For multi-source Bayesian optimization, a neural network architecture built on *factorization machines* [125] can include information on previous tasks [131] and has also been extended to tackle the CASH problem [132].

Another alternative model for Bayesian optimization are random forests [59]. While GPs perform better than random forests on small, numerical configuration spaces [29], random forests natively handle larger, categorical and conditional configuration spaces where standard GPs do not work well [29, 70, 90]. Furthermore, the computational complexity of random forests scales far better to many data points: while the computational complexity of fitting and predicting variances with GPs for n data points scales as $O(n^3)$ and $O(n^2)$, respectively, for random forests, the scaling in n is only $O(n \log n)$ and $O(\log n)$, respectively. Due to these advantages, the SMAC framework for Bayesian optimization with random forests [59] enabled the prominent AutoML frameworks Auto-WEKA [149] and Auto-sklearn [34] (which are described in Chaps. 4 and 6).

Instead of modeling the probability $p(\mathbf{y}|\boldsymbol{\lambda})$ of observations $\mathbf{y}$ given the configurations $\boldsymbol{\lambda}$, the *Tree Parzen Estimator* (TPE [12, 14]) models density functions $p(\boldsymbol{\lambda}|\mathbf{y} < \alpha)$ and $p(\boldsymbol{\lambda}|\mathbf{y} \geq \alpha)$. Given a percentile α (usually set to 15%), the observations are divided in good observations and bad observations and simple 1-d Parzen windows are used to model the two distributions. The ratio $\frac{p(\boldsymbol{\lambda}|\mathbf{y}<\alpha)}{p(\boldsymbol{\lambda}|\mathbf{y}\geq\alpha)}$ is related to the expected improvement acquisition function and is used to propose new hyperparameter configurations. TPE uses a tree of Parzen estimators for conditional hyperparameters and demonstrated good performance on such structured HPO tasks [12, 14, 29, 33, 143, 149, 160], is conceptually simple, and parallelizes naturally [91]. It is also the workhorse behind the AutoML framework Hyperopt-sklearn [83] (which is described in Chap. 5).

Finally, we note that there are also surrogate-based approaches which do not follow the Bayesian optimization paradigm: Hord [67] uses a deterministic RBF surrogate, and Harmonica [52] uses a compressed sensing technique, both to tune the hyperparameters of deep neural networks.

1.3.2.3 Configuration Space Description

Bayesian optimization was originally designed to optimize box-constrained, real-valued functions. However, for many machine learning hyperparameters, such as the learning rate in neural networks or regularization in support vector machines, it is common to optimize the exponent of an exponential term to describe that changing it, e.g., from 0.001 to 0.01 is expected to have a similarly high impact as changing it from 0.1 to 1. A technique known as *input warping* [142] allows to automatically learn such transformations during the optimization process by replacing each input dimension with the two parameters of a Beta distribution and optimizing these.

One obvious limitation of the box-constraints is that the user needs to define these upfront. To avoid this, it is possible to dynamically expand the configuration space [113, 136]. Alternatively, the estimation-of-distribution-style algorithm TPE [12] is able to deal with infinite spaces on which a (typically Gaussian) prior is placed.

Integers and categorical hyperparameters require special treatment but can be integrated fairly easily into regular Bayesian optimization by small adaptations of the kernel and the optimization procedure (see Sect. 12.1.2 of [58], as well as [42]). Other models, such as factorization machines and random forests, can also naturally handle these data types.

Conditional hyperparameters are still an active area of research (see Chaps. 5 and 6 for depictions of conditional configuration spaces in recent AutoML systems). They can be handled natively by tree-based methods, such as random forests [59] and tree Parzen estimators (TPE) [12], but due to the numerous advantages of Gaussian processes over other models, multiple kernels for structured configuration spaces have also been proposed [4, 12, 63, 70, 92, 96, 146].

1.3.2.4 Constrained Bayesian Optimization

In realistic scenarios it is often necessary to satisfy constraints, such as memory consumption [139, 149], training time [149], prediction time [41, 43], accuracy of a compressed model [41], energy usage [43] or simply to not fail during the training procedure [43].

Constraints can be *hidden* in that only a binary observation (success or failure) is available [88]. Typical examples in AutoML are memory and time constraints to allow training of the algorithms in a shared computing system, and to make sure that a single slow algorithm configuration does not use all the time available for HPO [34, 149] (see also Chaps. 4 and 6).

Constraints can also merely be *unknown*, meaning that we can observe and model an auxiliary constraint function, but only know about a constraint violation after evaluating the target function [46]. An example of this is the prediction time of a support vector machine, which can only be obtained by training it as it depends on the number of support vectors selected during training.

The simplest approach to model violated constraints is to define a penalty value (at least as bad as the worst possible observable loss value) and use it as the observation for failed runs [34, 45, 59, 149]. More advanced approaches model the probability of violating one or more constraints and actively search for configurations with low loss values that are unlikely to violate any of the given constraints [41, 43, 46, 88].

Bayesian optimization frameworks using information theoretic acquisition functions allow decoupling the evaluation of the target function and the constraints to dynamically choose which of them to evaluate next [43, 55]. This becomes advantageous when evaluating the function of interest and the constraints require vastly different amounts of time, such as evaluating a deep neural network's performance and memory consumption [43].

1.4 Multi-fidelity Optimization

Increasing dataset sizes and increasingly complex models are a major hurdle in HPO since they make blackbox performance evaluation more expensive. Training a single hyperparameter configuration on large datasets can nowadays easily exceed several hours and take up to several days [85].

A common technique to speed up manual tuning is therefore to probe an algorithm/hyperparameter configuration on a small subset of the data, by training it only for a few iterations, by running it on a subset of features, by only using one or a few of the cross-validation folds, or by using down-sampled images in computer vision. Multi-fidelity methods cast such manual heuristics into formal algorithms, using so-called low fidelity approximations of the actual loss function to minimize. These approximations introduce a tradeoff between optimization performance and runtime, but in practice, the obtained speedups often outweigh the approximation error.

First, we review methods which model an algorithm's learning curve during training and can stop the training procedure if adding further resources is predicted to not help. Second, we discuss simple selection methods which only choose one of a finite set of given algorithms/hyperparameter configurations. Third, we discuss multi-fidelity methods which can actively decide which fidelity will provide most information about finding the optimal hyperparameters. We also refer to Chap. 2 (which discusses how multi-fidelity methods can be used across datasets) and Chap. 3 (which describes low-fidelity approximations for neural architecture search).

1.4.1 Learning Curve-Based Prediction for Early Stopping

We start this section on multi-fidelity methods in HPO with methods that evaluate and model learning curves during HPO [82, 123] and then decide whether to add further resources or stop the training procedure for a given hyperparameter configuration. Examples of learning curves are the performance of the same configuration trained on increasing dataset subsets, or the performance of an iterative algorithm measured for each iteration (or every i-th iteration if the calculation of the performance is expensive).

Learning curve extrapolation is used in the context of *predictive termination* [26], where a learning curve model is used to extrapolate a partially observed learning curve for a configuration, and the training process is stopped if the configuration is predicted to not reach the performance of the best model trained so far in the optimization process. Each learning curve is modeled as a weighted combination of 11 parametric functions from various scientific areas. These functions' parameters and their weights are sampled via Markov chain Monte Carlo to minimize the loss of fitting the partially observed learning curve. This yields a predictive distribution, which allows to stop training based on the probability of not beating the best known model. When combined with Bayesian optimization, the predictive termination criterion enabled lower error rates than off-the-shelve blackbox Bayesian optimization for optimizing neural networks. On average, the method sped up the optimization by a factor of two and was able to find a (then) state-of-the-art neural network for CIFAR-10 (without data augmentation) [26].

While the method above is limited by not sharing information across different hyperparameter configurations, this can be achieved by using the basis functions as the output layer of a Bayesian neural network [80]. The parameters and weights of the basis functions, and thus the full learning curve, can thereby be predicted for arbitrary hyperparameter configurations. Alternatively, it is possible to use previous learning curves as basis function extrapolators [21]. While the experimental results are inconclusive on whether the proposed method is superior to pre-specified parametric functions, not having to manually define them is a clear advantage.

Freeze-Thaw Bayesian optimization [148] is a full integration of learning curves into the modeling and selection process of Bayesian optimization. Instead of terminating a configuration, the machine learning models are trained iteratively for a few iterations and then *frozen*. Bayesian optimization can then decide to *thaw* one of the frozen models, which means to continue training it. Alternatively, the method can also decide to start a new configuration. Freeze-Thaw models the performance of a converged algorithm with a regular Gaussian process and introduces a special covariance function corresponding to exponentially decaying functions to model the learning curves with per-learning curve Gaussian processes.

1.4.2 Bandit-Based Algorithm Selection Methods

In this section, we describe methods that try to determine the best algorithm out of a given finite set of algorithms based on low-fidelity approximations of their performance; towards its end, we also discuss potential combinations with adaptive configuration strategies. We focus on variants of the bandit-based strategies *successive halving* and *Hyperband*, since these have shown strong performance, especially for optimizing deep learning algorithms. Strictly speaking, some of the methods which we will discuss in this subsection also model learning curves, but they provide no means of selecting new configurations based on these models.

First, however, we briefly describe the historical evolution of multi-fidelity algorithm selection methods. In 2000, Petrak [120] noted that simply testing various algorithms on a small subset of the data is a powerful and cheap mechanism to select an algorithm. Later approaches used iterative algorithm elimination schemes to drop hyperparameter configurations if they perform badly on subsets of the data [17], if they perform significantly worse than a group of top-performing configurations [86], if they perform worse than the best configuration by a user-specified factor [143], or if even an optimistic performance bound for an algorithm is worse than the best known algorithm [128]. Likewise, it is possible to drop hyperparameter configurations if they perform badly on one or a few cross-validation folds [149]. Finally, Jamieson and Talwalkar [69] proposed to use the *successive halving* algorithm originally introduced by Karnin et al. [76] for HPO.

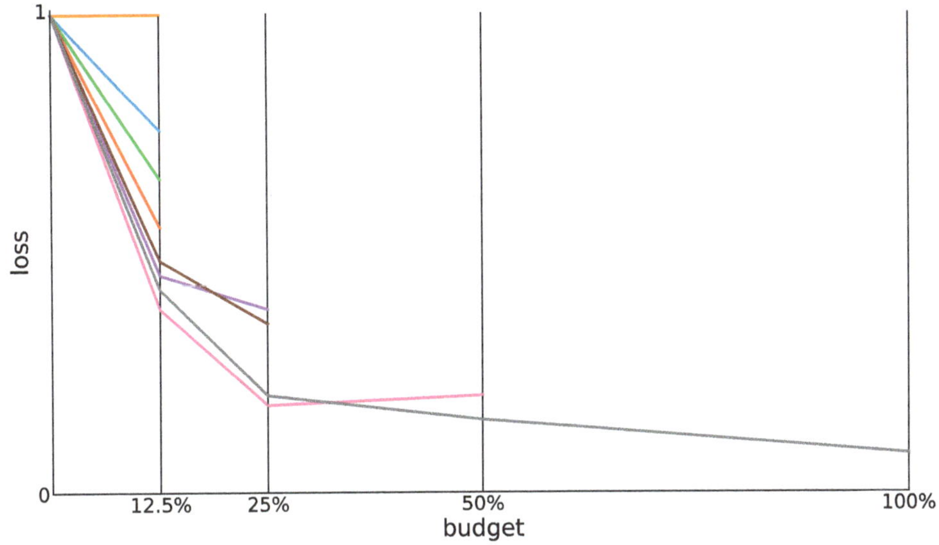

Fig. 1.3 Illustration of successive halving for eight algorithms/configurations. After evaluating all algorithms on $\frac{1}{8}$ of the total budget, half of them are dropped and the budget given to the remaining algorithms is doubled

Successive halving is an extremely simple, yet powerful, and therefore popular strategy for multi-fidelity algorithm selection: for a given initial budget, query all algorithms for that budget; then, remove the half that performed worst, double the budget [2] and successively repeat until only a single algorithm is left. This process is illustrated in Fig. 1.3. Jamieson and Talwalkar [69] benchmarked several common bandit methods and found that successive halving performs well both in terms of the number of required iterations and in the required computation time, that the algorithm theoretically outperforms a uniform budget allocation strategy if the algorithms converge favorably, and that it is preferable to many well-known bandit strategies from the literature, such as *UCB* and *EXP3*.

While successive halving is an efficient approach, it suffers from the budget-vs-number of configurations trade off. Given a total budget, the user has to decide beforehand whether to try many configurations and only assign a small budget to each, or to try only a few and assign them a larger budget. Assigning too small a budget can result in prematurely terminating good configurations, while assigning too large a budget can result in running poor configurations too long and thereby wasting resources.

[2]More precisely, drop the worst fraction $\frac{\eta-1}{\eta}$ of algorithms and multiply the budget for the remaining algorithms by η, where η is a hyperparameter. Its default value was changed from 2 to 3 with the introduction of HyperBand [90].

HyperBand [90] is a hedging strategy designed to combat this problem when selecting from randomly sampled configurations. It divides the total budget into several combinations of number of configurations vs. budget for each, to then call successive halving as a subroutine on each set of random configurations. Due to the hedging strategy which includes running some configurations only on the maximal budget, in the worst case, HyperBand takes at most a constant factor more time than vanilla random search on the maximal budget. In practice, due to its use of cheap low-fidelity evaluations, HyperBand has been shown to improve over vanilla random search and blackbox Bayesian optimization for data subsets, feature subsets and iterative algorithms, such as stochastic gradient descent for deep neural networks.

Despite HyperBand's success for deep neural networks it is very limiting to not adapt the configuration proposal strategy to the function evaluations. To overcome this limitation, the recent approach BOHB [33] combines Bayesian optimization and HyperBand to achieve the best of both worlds: strong anytime performance (quick improvements in the beginning by using low fidelities in HyperBand) and strong final performance (good performance in the long run by replacing HyperBand's random search by Bayesian optimization). BOHB also uses parallel resources effectively and deals with problem domains ranging from a few to many dozen hyperparameters. BOHB's Bayesian optimization component resembles TPE [12], but differs by using multidimensional kernel density estimators. It only fits a model on the highest fidelity for which at least $|\mathbf{\Lambda}| + 1$ evaluations have been performed (the number of hyperparameters, plus one). BOHB's first model is therefore fitted on the lowest fidelity, and over time models trained on higher fidelities take over, while still using the lower fidelities in successive halving. Empirically, BOHB was shown to outperform several state-of-the-art HPO methods for tuning support vector machines, neural networks and reinforcement learning algorithms, including most methods presented in this section [33]. Further approaches to combine HyperBand and Bayesian optimization have also been proposed [15, 151].

Multiple fidelity evaluations can also be combined with HPO in other ways. Instead of switching between lower fidelities and the highest fidelity, it is possible to perform HPO on a subset of the original data and extract the best-performing configurations in order to use them as an initial design for HPO on the full dataset [152]. To speed up solutions to the CASH problem, it is also possible to iteratively remove entire algorithms (and their hyperparameters) from the configuration space based on poor performance on small dataset subsets [159].

1.4.3 Adaptive Choices of Fidelities

All methods in the previous subsection follow a predefined schedule for the fidelities. Alternatively, one might want to actively choose which fidelities to evaluate given previous observations to prevent a misspecification of the schedule.

Multi-task Bayesian optimization [147] uses a multi-task Gaussian process to model the performance of related tasks and to automatically learn the tasks' correlation during the optimization process. This method can dynamically switch between cheaper, low-fidelity tasks and the expensive, high-fidelity target task based on a cost-aware information-theoretic acquisition function. In practice, the proposed method starts exploring the configuration space on the cheaper task and only switches to the more expensive configuration space in later parts of the optimization, approximately halving the time required for HPO. Multi-task Bayesian optimization can also be used to transfer information from previous optimization tasks, and we refer to Chap. 2 for further details.

Multi-task Bayesian optimization (and the methods presented in the previous subsection) requires an upfront specification of a set of fidelities. This can be suboptimal since these can be misspecified [74, 78] and because the number of fidelities that can be handled is low (usually five or less). Therefore, and in order to exploit the typically smooth dependence on the fidelity (such as, e.g., size of the data subset used), it often yields better results to treat the fidelity as continuous (and, e.g., choose a continuous percentage of the full data set to evaluate a configuration on), trading off the information gain and the time required for evaluation [78]. To exploit the domain knowledge that performance typically improves with more data, with diminishing returns, a special kernel can be constructed for the data subsets [78]. This generalization of multi-task Bayesian optimization improves performance and can achieve a 10–100 fold speedup compared to blackbox Bayesian optimization.

Instead of using an information-theoretic acquisition function, Bayesian optimization with the *Upper Confidence Bound* (UCB) acquisition function can also be extended to multiple fidelities [73, 74]. While the first such approach, MF-GP-UCB [73], required upfront fidelity definitions, the later BOCA algorithm [74] dropped that requirement. BOCA has also been applied to optimization with more than one continuous fidelity, and we expect HPO for more than one continuous fidelity to be of further interest in the future.

Generally speaking, methods that can adaptively choose their fidelity are very appealing and more powerful than the conceptually simpler bandit-based methods discussed in Sect. 1.4.2, but in practice we caution that strong models are required to make successful choices about the fidelities. When the models are not strong (since they do not have enough training data yet, or due to model mismatch), these methods may spend too much time evaluating higher fidelities, and the more robust fixed budget schedules discussed in Sect. 1.4.2 might yield better performance given a fixed time limit.

1.5 Applications to AutoML

In this section, we provide a historical overview of the most important hyperparameter optimization systems and applications to automated machine learning.

Grid search has been used for hyperparameter optimization since the 1990s [71, 107] and was already supported by early machine learning tools in 2002 [35]. The first adaptive optimization methods applied to HPO were greedy depth-first search [82] and pattern search [109], both improving over default hyperparameter configurations, and pattern search improving over grid search, too. Genetic algorithms were first applied to tuning the two hyperparameters C and γ of an RBF-SVM in 2004 [119] and resulted in improved classification performance in less time than grid search. In the same year, an evolutionary algorithm was used to learn a composition of three different kernels for an SVM, the kernel hyperparameters and to jointly select a feature subset; the learned combination of kernels was able to outperform every single optimized kernel. Similar in spirit, also in 2004, a genetic algorithm was used to select both the features used by and the hyperparameters of either an SVM or a neural network [129].

CMA-ES was first used for hyperparameter optimization in 2005 [38], in that case to optimize an SVM's hyperparameters C and γ, a kernel lengthscale l_i for each dimension of the input data, and a complete rotation and scaling matrix. Much more recently, CMA-ES has been demonstrated to be an excellent choice for parallel HPO, outperforming state-of-the-art Bayesian optimization tools when optimizing 19 hyperparameters of a deep neural network on 30 GPUs in parallel [91].

In 2009, Escalante et al. [30] extended the HPO problem to the *Full Model Selection* problem, which includes selecting a preprocessing algorithm, a feature selection algorithm, a classifier and all their hyperparameters. By being able to construct a machine learning pipeline from multiple off-the-shelf machine learning algorithms using HPO, the authors empirically found that they can apply their method to any data set as no domain knowledge is required, and demonstrated the applicability of their approach to a variety of domains [32, 49]. Their proposed method, particle swarm model selection (PSMS), uses a modified particle swarm optimizer to handle the conditional configuration space. To avoid overfitting, PSMS was extended with a custom ensembling strategy which combined the best solutions from multiple generations [31]. Since particle swarm optimization was originally designed to work on continuous configuration spaces, PSMS was later also extended to use a genetic algorithm to optimize the pipeline structure and only use particle swarm optimization to optimize the hyperparameters of each pipeline [145].

To the best of our knowledge, the first application of Bayesian optimization to HPO dates back to 2005, when Frohlich and Zell [39] used an online Gaussian process together with EI to optimize the hyperparameters of an SVM, achieving speedups of factor 10 (classification, 2 hyperparameters) and 100 (regression, 3 hyperparameters) over grid search. Tuned Data Mining [84] proposed to tune the hyperparameters of a full machine learning pipeline using Bayesian optimization; specifically, this used a single fixed pipeline and tuned the hyperparameters of the classifier as well as the per-class classification threshold and class weights.

In 2011, Bergstra et al. [12] were the first to apply Bayesian optimization to tune the hyperparameters of a deep neural network, outperforming both manual and random search. Furthermore, they demonstrated that TPE resulted in better performance than a Gaussian process-based approach. TPE, as well as Bayesian optimization with random forests, were also successful for joint neural architecture search and hyperparameter optimization [14, 106].

Another important step in applying Bayesian optimization to HPO was made by Snoek et al. in the 2012 paper *Practical Bayesian Optimization of Machine Learning Algorithms* [140], which describes several tricks of the trade for Gaussian process-based HPO implemented in the Spearmint system and obtained a new state-of-the-art result for hyperparameter optimization of deep neural networks.

Independently of the Full Model Selection paradigm, Auto-WEKA [149] (see also Chap. 4) introduced the *Combined Algorithm Selection and Hyperparameter Optimization* (CASH) problem, in which the choice of a classification algorithm is modeled as a categorical variable, the algorithm hyperparameters are modeled as conditional hyperparameters, and the random-forest based Bayesian optimization system SMAC [59] is used for joint optimization in the resulting 786-dimensional configuration space.

In recent years, multi-fidelity methods have become very popular, especially in deep learning. Firstly, using low-fidelity approximations based on data subsets, feature subsets and short runs of iterative algorithms, Hyperband [90] was shown to outperform blackbox Bayesian optimization methods that did not take these lower fidelities into account. Finally, most recently, in the 2018 paper *BOHB: Robust and Efficient Hyperparameter Optimization at Scale*, Falkner et al. [33] introduced a robust, flexible, and parallelizable combination of Bayesian optimization and Hyperband that substantially outperformed both Hyperband and blackbox Bayesian optimization for a wide range of problems, including tuning support vector machines, various types of neural networks, and reinforcement learning algorithms.

At the time of writing, we make the following recommendations for which tools we would use in practical applications of HPO:

- If multiple fidelities are applicable (i.e., if it is possible to define substantially cheaper versions of the objective function of interest, such that the performance for these roughly correlates with the performance for the full objective function of interest), we recommend BOHB [33] as a robust, efficient, versatile, and parallelizable default hyperparameter optimization method.
- If multiple fidelities are not applicable:
  - If all hyperparameters are real-valued and one can only afford a few dozen function evaluations, we recommend the use of a Gaussian process-based Bayesian optimization tool, such as Spearmint [140].
  - For large and conditional configuration spaces we suggest either the random forest-based SMAC [59] or TPE [14], due to their proven strong performance on such tasks [29].
  - For purely real-valued spaces and relatively cheap objective functions, for which one can afford more than hundreds of evaluations, we recommend CMA-ES [51].

1.6 Open Problems and Future Research Directions

We conclude this chapter with a discussion of open problems, current research questions and potential further developments we expect to have an impact on HPO in the future. Notably, despite their relevance, we leave out discussions on hyperparameter importance and configuration space definition as these fall under the umbrella of meta-learning and can be found in Chap. 2.

1.6.1 Benchmarks and Comparability

Given the breadth of existing HPO methods, a natural question is what are the strengths and weaknesses of each of them. In order to allow for a fair comparison between different HPO approaches, the community needs to design and agree upon a common set of benchmarks that expands over time, as new HPO variants, such as multi-fidelity optimization, emerge. As a particular example for what this could look like we would like to mention the COCO platform (short for comparing continuous optimizers), which provides benchmark and analysis tools for continuous optimization and is used as a workbench for the yearly Black-Box Optimization Benchmarking (BBOB) challenge [11]. Efforts along similar lines in HPO have already yielded the hyperparameter optimization library (HPOlib [29]) and a benchmark collection specifically for Bayesian optimization methods [25]. However, neither of these has gained similar traction as the COCO platform.

Additionaly, the community needs clearly defined metrics, but currently different works use different metrics. One important dimension in which evaluations differ is whether they report performance on the validation set used for optimization or on a separate test set. The former helps to study the strength of the optimizer in isolation, without the noise that is added in the evaluation when going from validation to test set; on the other hand, some optimizers may lead to more overfitting than others, which can only be diagnosed by using the test set. Another important dimension in which evaluations differ is whether they report performance after a given number of function evaluations or after a given amount of time. The latter accounts for the difference in time between evaluating different hyperparameter configurations and includes optimization overheads, and therefore reflects what is required in practice; however, the former is more convenient and aids reproducibility by yielding the same results irrespective of the hardware used. To aid reproducibility, especially studies that use time should therefore release an implementation.

We note that it is important to compare against strong baselines when using new benchmarks, which is another reason why HPO methods should be published with an accompanying implementation. Unfortunately, there is no common software library as is, for example, available in deep learning research that implements all the basic building blocks [2, 117]. As a simple, yet effective baseline that can be trivially included in empirical studies, Jamieson and Recht [68] suggest to compare against different parallelization levels of random search to demonstrate the speedups over regular random search. When comparing to other optimization techniques it is important to compare against a solid implementation, since, e.g., simpler versions of Bayesian optimization have been shown to yield inferior performance [79, 140, 142].

1.6.2 Gradient-Based Optimization

In some cases (e.g., least-squares support vector machines and neural networks) it is possible to obtain the gradient of the model selection criterion with respect to some of the model hyperparameters. Different to blackbox HPO, in this case each evaluation of the target function results in an entire hypergradient vector instead of a single float value, allowing for faster HPO.

Maclaurin et al. [99] described a procedure to compute the exact gradients of validation performance with respect to all continuous hyperparameters of a neural network by backpropagating through the entire training procedure of stochastic gradient descent with momentum (using a novel, memory-efficient algorithm). Being able to handle many hyperparameters efficiently through gradient-based methods allows for a new paradigm of hyperparametrizing the model to obtain flexibility over model classes, regularization, and training methods. Maclaurin et al. demonstrated the applicability of gradient-based HPO to many high-dimensional HPO problems, such as optimizing the learning rate of a neural network for each iteration and layer separately, optimizing the weight initialization scale hyperparameter for each layer in a neural network, optimizing the $l2$ penalty for each individual parameter in logistic regression, and learning completely new training datasets. As a small downside, backpropagating through the entire training procedure comes at the price of doubling the time complexity of the training procedure. The described method can also be generalized to work with other parameter update algorithms [36]. To overcome the necessity of backpropagating through the complete training procedure, later work allows to perform hyperparameter updates with respect to a separate validation set interleaved with the training process [5, 10, 36, 37, 93].

Recent examples of gradient-based optimization of simple model's hyperparameters [118] and of neural network structures (see Chap. 3) show promising results, outperforming state-of-the-art Bayesian optimization models. Despite being highly model-specific, the fact that gradient-based hyperparemeter optimization allows tuning several hundreds of hyperparameters could allow substantial improvements in HPO.

1.6.3 Scalability

Despite recent successes in multi-fidelity optimization, there are still machine learning problems which have not been directly tackled by HPO due to their scale, and which might require novel approaches. Here, scale can mean both the size of the configuration space and the expense of individual model evaluations. For example, there has not been any work on HPO for deep neural networks on the ImageNet challenge dataset [127] yet, mostly because of the high cost of training even a simple neural network on the dataset. It will be interesting to see whether methods going beyond the blackbox view from Sect. 1.3, such as the multi-fidelity methods described in Sect. 1.4, gradient-based methods, or meta-learning methods (described in Chap. 2) allow to tackle such problems. Chap. 3 describes first successes in learning neural network building blocks on smaller datasets and applying them to ImageNet, but the hyperparameters of the training procedure are still set manually.

Given the necessity of parallel computing, we are looking forward to new methods that fully exploit large-scale compute clusters. While there exists much work on parallel Bayesian optimization [12, 24, 33, 44, 54, 60, 135, 140], except for the neural networks described in Sect. 1.3.2.2 [141], so far no method has demonstrated scalability to hundreds of workers. Despite their popularity, and with a single exception of HPO applied to deep neural networks [91],[3] population-based approaches have not yet been shown to be applicable to hyperparameter optimization on datasets larger than a few thousand data points.

Overall, we expect that more sophisticated and specialized methods, leaving the blackbox view behind, will be needed to further scale hyperparameter to interesting problems.

1.6.4 Overfitting and Generalization

An open problem in HPO is overfitting. As noted in the problem statement (see Sect. 1.2), we usually only have a finite number of data points available for calculating the validation loss to be optimized and thereby do not necessarily optimize for generalization to unseen test datapoints. Similarly to overfitting a machine learning algorithm to training data, this problem is about overfitting the hyperparameters to the finite validation set; this was also demonstrated to happen experimentally [20, 81].

A simple strategy to reduce the amount of overfitting is to employ a different shuffling of the train and validation split for each function evaluation; this was shown to improve generalization performance for SVM tuning, both with a holdout and a cross-validation strategy [95]. The selection of the final configuration can

[3]See also Chap. 3 where population-based methods are applied to Neural Architecture Search problems.

be further robustified by not choosing it according to the lowest observed value, but according to the lowest predictive mean of the Gaussian process model used in Bayesian optimization [95].

Another possibility is to use a separate holdout set to assess configurations found by HPO to avoid bias towards the standard validation set [108, 159]. Different approximations of the generalization performance can lead to different test performances [108], and there have been reports that several resampling strategies can result in measurable performance differences for HPO of support vector machines [150].

A different approach to combat overfitting might be to find *stable optima* instead of *sharp optima* of the objective function [112]. The idea is that for stable optima, the function value around an optimum does not change for slight perturbations of the hyperparameters, whereas it *does* change for sharp optima. Stable optima lead to better generalization when applying the found hyperparameters to a new, unseen set of datapoints (i.e., the test set). An acquisition function built around this was shown to only slightly overfit for support vector machine HPO, while regular Bayesian optimization exhibited strong overfitting [112].

Further approaches to combat overfitting are the ensemble methods and Bayesian methods presented in Sect. 1.2.1. Given all these different techniques, there is no commonly agreed-upon technique for how to best avoid overfitting, though, and it remains up to the user to find out which strategy performs best on their particular HPO problem. We note that the best strategy might actually vary across HPO problems.

1.6.5 Arbitrary-Size Pipeline Construction

All HPO techniques we discussed so far assume a finite set of components for machine learning pipelines or a finite maximum number of layers in neural networks. For machine learning pipelines (see the AutoML systems covered in Part II of this book) it might be helpful to use more than one feature preprocessing algorithm and dynamically add them if necessary for a problem, enlarging the search space by a hyperparameter to select an appropriate preprocessing algorithm and its own hyperparameters. While a search space for standard blackbox optimization tools could easily include several extra such preprocessors (and their hyperparameters) as conditional hyperparameters, an unbounded number of these would be hard to support.

One approach for handling arbitrary-sized pipelines more natively is the tree-structured pipeline optimization toolkit (TPOT [115], see also Chap. 8), which uses genetic programming and describes possible pipelines by a grammar. TPOT uses multi-objective optimization to trade off pipeline complexity with performance to avoid generating unnecessarily complex pipelines.

A different pipeline creation paradigm is the usage of hierarchical planning; the recent ML-Plan [101, 108] uses hierarchical task networks and shows competitive performance compared to Auto-WEKA [149] and Auto-sklearn [34].

So far these approaches are not consistently outperforming AutoML systems with a fixed pipeline length, but larger pipelines may provide more improvement. Similarly, neural architecture search yields complex configuration spaces and we refer to Chap. 3 for a description of methods to tackle them.

Acknowledgements We would like to thank Luca Franceschi, Raghu Rajan, Stefan Falkner and Arlind Kadra for valuable feedback on the manuscript.

Bibliography

1. Proceedings of the International Conference on Learning Representations (ICLR'18) (2018), published online: iclr.cc
2. Abadi, M., Agarwal, A., Barham, P., Brevdo, E., Chen, Z., Citro, C., Corrado, G., Davis, A., Dean, J., Devin, M., Ghemawat, S., Goodfellow, I., Harp, A., Irving, G., Isard, M., Jia, Y., Jozefowicz, R., Kaiser, L., Kudlur, M., Levenberg, J., Mané, D., Monga, R., Moore, S., Murray, D., Olah, C., Schuster, M., Shlens, J., Steiner, B., Sutskever, I., Talwar, K., Tucker, P., Vanhoucke, V., Vasudevan, V., Viégas, F., Vinyals, O., Warden, P., Wattenberg, M., Wicke, M., Yu, Y., Zheng, X.: TensorFlow: Large-scale machine learning on heterogeneous systems (2015), https://www.tensorflow.org/
3. Ahmed, M., Shahriari, B., Schmidt, M.: Do we need "harmless" Bayesian optimization and "first-order" Bayesian optimization. In: NeurIPS Workshop on Bayesian Optimization (BayesOpt'16) (2016)
4. Alaa, A., van der Schaar, M.: AutoPrognosis: Automated Clinical Prognostic Modeling via Bayesian Optimization with Structured Kernel Learning. In: Dy and Krause [27], pp. 139–148
5. Almeida, L.B., Langlois, T., Amaral, J.D., Plakhov, A.: Parameter Adaptation in Stochastic Optimization, p. 111–134. Cambridge University Press (1999)
6. Amazon: Automatic model tuning (2018), https://docs.aws.amazon.com/sagemaker/latest/dg/automatic-model-tuning.html
7. Bach, F., Blei, D. (eds.): Proceedings of the 32nd International Conference on Machine Learning (ICML'15), vol. 37. Omnipress (2015)
8. Balcan, M., Weinberger, K. (eds.): Proceedings of the 33rd International Conference on Machine Learning (ICML'17), vol. 48. Proceedings of Machine Learning Research (2016)
9. Bartlett, P., Pereira, F., Burges, C., Bottou, L., Weinberger, K. (eds.): Proceedings of the 26th International Conference on Advances in Neural Information Processing Systems (NeurIPS'12) (2012)
10. Baydin, A.G., Cornish, R., Rubio, D.M., Schmidt, M., Wood, F.: Online Learning Rate Adaption with Hypergradient Descent. In: Proceedings of the International Conference on Learning Representations (ICLR'18) [1], published online: iclr.cc
11. BBOBies: Black-box Optimization Benchmarking (BBOB) workshop series (2018), http://numbbo.github.io/workshops/index.html
12. Bergstra, J., Bardenet, R., Bengio, Y., Kégl, B.: Algorithms for hyper-parameter optimization. In: Shawe-Taylor, J., Zemel, R., Bartlett, P., Pereira, F., Weinberger, K. (eds.) Proceedings of the 25th International Conference on Advances in Neural Information Processing Systems (NeurIPS'11). pp. 2546–2554 (2011)
13. Bergstra, J., Bengio, Y.: Random search for hyper-parameter optimization. Journal of Machine Learning Research 13, 281–305 (2012)

14. Bergstra, J., Yamins, D., Cox, D.: Making a science of model search: Hyperparameter optimization in hundreds of dimensions for vision architectures. In: Dasgupta and McAllester [23], pp. 115–123
15. Bertrand, H., Ardon, R., Perrot, M., Bloch, I.: Hyperparameter optimization of deep neural networks: Combining hyperband with Bayesian model selection. In: Conférence sur l'Apprentissage Automatique (2017)
16. Bischl, B., Mersmann, O., Trautmann, H., Weihs, C.: Resampling methods for meta-model validation with recommendations for evolutionary computation. Evolutionary Computation 20(2), 249–275 (2012)
17. Van den Bosch, A.: Wrapped progressive sampling search for optimizing learning algorithm parameters. In: Proceedings of the sixteenth Belgian-Dutch Conference on Artificial Intelligence. pp. 219–226 (2004)
18. Brochu, E., Cora, V., de Freitas, N.: A tutorial on Bayesian optimization of expensive cost functions, with application to active user modeling and hierarchical reinforcement learning. arXiv:1012.2599v1 [cs.LG] (2010)
19. Bürger, F., Pauli, J.: A Holistic Classification Optimization Framework with Feature Selection, Preprocessing, Manifold Learning and Classifiers., pp. 52–68. Springer (2015)
20. Cawley, G., Talbot, N.: On Overfitting in Model Selection and Subsequent Selection Bias in Performance Evaluation. Journal of Machine Learning Research 11 (2010)
21. Chandrashekaran, A., Lane, I.: Speeding up Hyper-parameter Optimization by Extrapolation of Learning Curves using Previous Builds. In: Ceci, M., Hollmen, J., Todorovski, L., Vens, C., Džeroski, S. (eds.) Machine Learning and Knowledge Discovery in Databases (ECML/PKDD'17). Lecture Notes in Computer Science, vol. 10534. Springer (2017)
22. Dahl, G., Sainath, T., Hinton, G.: Improving deep neural networks for LVCSR using rectified linear units and dropout. In: Adams, M., Zhao, V. (eds.) International Conference on Acoustics, Speech and Signal Processing (ICASSP'13). pp. 8609–8613. IEEE Computer Society Press (2013)
23. Dasgupta, S., McAllester, D. (eds.): Proceedings of the 30th International Conference on Machine Learning (ICML'13). Omnipress (2014)
24. Desautels, T., Krause, A., Burdick, J.: Parallelizing exploration-exploitation tradeoffs in Gaussian process bandit optimization. Journal of Machine Learning Research 15, 4053–4103 (2014)
25. Dewancker, I., McCourt, M., Clark, S., Hayes, P., Johnson, A., Ke, G.: A stratified analysis of Bayesian optimization methods. arXiv:1603.09441v1 [cs.LG] (2016)
26. Domhan, T., Springenberg, J.T., Hutter, F.: Speeding up automatic hyperparameter optimization of deep neural networks by extrapolation of learning curves. In: Yang, Q., Wooldridge, M. (eds.) Proceedings of the 25th International Joint Conference on Artificial Intelligence (IJCAI'15). pp. 3460–3468 (2015)
27. Dy, J., Krause, A. (eds.): Proceedings of the 35th International Conference on Machine Learning (ICML'18), vol. 80. Proceedings of Machine Learning Research (2018)
28. Eberhart, R., Shi, Y.: Comparison between genetic algorithms and particle swarm optimization. In: Porto, V., Saravanan, N., Waagen, D., Eiben, A. (eds.) 7th International conference on evolutionary programming. pp. 611–616. Springer (1998)
29. Eggensperger, K., Feurer, M., Hutter, F., Bergstra, J., Snoek, J., Hoos, H., Leyton-Brown, K.: Towards an empirical foundation for assessing Bayesian optimization of hyperparameters. In: NeurIPS Workshop on Bayesian Optimization in Theory and Practice (BayesOpt'13) (2013)
30. Escalante, H., Montes, M., Sucar, E.: Particle Swarm Model Selection. Journal of Machine Learning Research 10, 405–440 (2009)
31. Escalante, H., Montes, M., Sucar, E.: Ensemble particle swarm model selection. In: Proceedings of the 2010 IEEE International Joint Conference on Neural Networks (IJCNN). pp. 1–8. IEEE Computer Society Press (2010)
32. Escalante, H., Montes, M., Villaseñor, L.: Particle swarm model selection for authorship verification. In: Bayro-Corrochano, E., Eklundh, J.O. (eds.) Progress in Pattern Recognition, Image Analysis, Computer Vision, and Applications. pp. 563–570 (2009)

33. Falkner, S., Klein, A., Hutter, F.: BOHB: Robust and Efficient Hyperparameter Optimization at Scale. In: Dy and Krause [27], pp. 1437–1446
34. Feurer, M., Klein, A., Eggensperger, K., Springenberg, J.T., Blum, M., Hutter, F.: Efficient and robust automated machine learning. In: Cortes, C., Lawrence, N., Lee, D., Sugiyama, M., Garnett, R. (eds.) Proceedings of the 29th International Conference on Advances in Neural Information Processing Systems (NeurIPS'15). pp. 2962–2970 (2015)
35. Fischer, S., Klinkenberg, R., Mierswa, I., Ritthoff, O.: Yale: Yet another learning environment – tutorial. Tech. rep., University of Dortmund (2002)
36. Franceschi, L., Donini, M., Frasconi, P., Pontil, M.: Forward and Reverse Gradient-Based Hyperparameter Optimization. In: Precup and Teh [122], pp. 1165–1173
37. Franceschi, L., Frasconi, P., Salzo, S., Grazzi, R., Pontil, M.: Bilevel Programming for Hyperparameter Optimization and Meta-Learning. In: Dy and Krause [27], pp. 1568–1577
38. Friedrichs, F., Igel, C.: Evolutionary tuning of multiple SVM parameters. Neurocomputing 64, 107–117 (2005)
39. Frohlich, H., Zell, A.: Efficient parameter selection for support vector machines in classification and regression via model-based global optimization. In: Prokhorov, D., Levine, D., Ham, F., Howell, W. (eds.) Proceedings of the 2005 IEEE International Joint Conference on Neural Networks (IJCNN). pp. 1431–1436. IEEE Computer Society Press (2005)
40. Gardner, J., Guo, C., Weinberger, K., Garnett, R., Grosse, R.: Discovering and Exploiting Additive Structure for Bayesian Optimization. In: Singh, A., Zhu, J. (eds.) Proceedings of the Seventeenth International Conference on Artificial Intelligence and Statistics (AISTATS). vol. 54, pp. 1311–1319. Proceedings of Machine Learning Research (2017)
41. Gardner, J., Kusner, M., Xu, Z., Weinberger, K., Cunningham, J.: Bayesian Optimization with Inequality Constraints. In: Xing and Jebara [157], pp. 937–945
42. Garrido-Merchán, E., Hernández-Lobato, D.: Dealing with integer-valued variables in Bayesian optimization with Gaussian processes. arXiv:1706.03673v2 [stats.ML] (2017)
43. Gelbart, M., Snoek, J., Adams, R.: Bayesian optimization with unknown constraints. In: Zhang, N., Tian, J. (eds.) Proceedings of the 30th conference on Uncertainty in Artificial Intelligence (UAI'14). AUAI Press (2014)
44. Ginsbourger, D., Le Riche, R., Carraro, L.: Kriging Is Well-Suited to Parallelize Optimization. In: Computational Intelligence in Expensive Optimization Problems, pp. 131–162. Springer (2010)
45. Golovin, D., Solnik, B., Moitra, S., Kochanski, G., Karro, J., Sculley, D.: Google Vizier: A service for black-box optimization. In: Matwin, S., Yu, S., Farooq, F. (eds.) Proceedings of the 23rd ACM SIGKDD International Conference on Knowledge Discovery and Data Mining (KDD). pp. 1487–1495. ACM Press (2017)
46. Gramacy, R., Lee, H.: Optimization under unknown constraints. Bayesian Statistics 9(9), 229–246 (2011)
47. Gretton, A., Robert, C. (eds.): Proceedings of the Seventeenth International Conference on Artificial Intelligence and Statistics (AISTATS), vol. 51. Proceedings of Machine Learning Research (2016)
48. Guyon, I., von Luxburg, U., Bengio, S., Wallach, H., Fergus, R., Vishwanathan, S., Garnett, R. (eds.): Proceedings of the 31st International Conference on Advances in Neural Information Processing Systems (NeurIPS'17) (2017)
49. Guyon, I., Saffari, A., Dror, G., Cawley, G.: Analysis of the IJCNN 2007 agnostic learning vs. prior knowledge challenge. Neural Networks 21(2), 544–550 (2008)
50. Guyon, I., Saffari, A., Dror, G., Cawley, G.: Model Selection: Beyond the Bayesian/Frequentist Divide. Journal of Machine Learning Research 11, 61–87 (2010)
51. Hansen, N.: The CMA evolution strategy: A tutorial. arXiv:1604.00772v1 [cs.LG] (2016)
52. Hazan, E., Klivans, A., Yuan, Y.: Hyperparameter optimization: A spectral approach. In: Proceedings of the International Conference on Learning Representations (ICLR'18) [1], published online: iclr.cc
53. Hernandez-Lobato, D., Hernandez-Lobato, J., Shah, A., Adams, R.: Predictive Entropy Search for Multi-objective Bayesian Optimization. In: Balcan and Weinberger [8], pp. 1492–1501

54. Hernández-Lobato, J., Requeima, J., Pyzer-Knapp, E., Aspuru-Guzik, A.: Parallel and distributed Thompson sampling for large-scale accelerated exploration of chemical space. In: Precup and Teh [122], pp. 1470–1479
55. Hernández-Lobato, J., Gelbart, M., Adams, R., Hoffman, M., Ghahramani, Z.: A general framework for constrained Bayesian optimization using information-based search. The Journal of Machine Learning Research 17(1), 5549–5601 (2016)
56. Hoeting, J., Madigan, D., Raftery, A., Volinsky, C.: Bayesian model averaging: a tutorial. Statistical science pp. 382–401 (1999)
57. Horn, D., Bischl, B.: Multi-objective parameter configuration of machine learning algorithms using model-based optimization. In: Likas, A. (ed.) 2016 IEEE Symposium Series on Computational Intelligence (SSCI). pp. 1–8. IEEE Computer Society Press (2016)
58. Hutter, F.: Automated Configuration of Algorithms for Solving Hard Computational Problems. Ph.D. thesis, University of British Columbia, Department of Computer Science, Vancouver, Canada (2009)
59. Hutter, F., Hoos, H., Leyton-Brown, K.: Sequential model-based optimization for general algorithm configuration. In: Coello, C. (ed.) Proceedings of the Fifth International Conference on Learning and Intelligent Optimization (LION'11). Lecture Notes in Computer Science, vol. 6683, pp. 507–523. Springer (2011)
60. Hutter, F., Hoos, H., Leyton-Brown, K.: Parallel algorithm configuration. In: Hamadi, Y., Schoenauer, M. (eds.) Proceedings of the Sixth International Conference on Learning and Intelligent Optimization (LION'12). Lecture Notes in Computer Science, vol. 7219, pp. 55–70. Springer (2012)
61. Hutter, F., Hoos, H., Leyton-Brown, K.: An efficient approach for assessing hyperparameter importance. In: Xing and Jebara [157], pp. 754–762
62. Hutter, F., Hoos, H., Leyton-Brown, K., Murphy, K.: Time-bounded sequential parameter optimization. In: Blum, C. (ed.) Proceedings of the Fourth International Conference on Learning and Intelligent Optimization (LION'10). Lecture Notes in Computer Science, vol. 6073, pp. 281–298. Springer (2010)
63. Hutter, F., Osborne, M.: A kernel for hierarchical parameter spaces. arXiv:1310.5738v1 [stats.ML] (2013)
64. Hutter, F., Lücke, J., Schmidt-Thieme, L.: Beyond Manual Tuning of Hyperparameters. KI - Künstliche Intelligenz 29(4), 329–337 (2015)
65. Igel, C.: Multi-objective Model Selection for Support Vector Machines. In: Coello, C., Aguirre, A., Zitzler, E. (eds.) Evolutionary Multi-Criterion Optimization. pp. 534–546. Springer (2005)
66. Ihler, A., Janzing, D. (eds.): Proceedings of the 32nd conference on Uncertainty in Artificial Intelligence (UAI'16). AUAI Press (2016)
67. Ilievski, I., Akhtar, T., Feng, J., Shoemaker, C.: Efficient Hyperparameter Optimization for Deep Learning Algorithms Using Deterministic RBF Surrogates. In: Sierra, C. (ed.) Proceedings of the 27th International Joint Conference on Artificial Intelligence (IJCAI'17) (2017)
68. Jamieson, K., Recht, B.: The news on auto-tuning (2016), http://www.argmin.net/2016/06/20/hypertuning/
69. Jamieson, K., Talwalkar, A.: Non-stochastic best arm identification and hyperparameter optimization. In: Gretton and Robert [47], pp. 240–248
70. Jenatton, R., Archambeau, C., González, J., Seeger, M.: Bayesian Optimization with Tree-structured Dependencies. In: Precup and Teh [122], pp. 1655–1664
71. John, G.: Cross-Validated C4.5: Using Error Estimation for Automatic Parameter Selection. Tech. Rep. STAN-CS-TN-94-12, Stanford University, Stanford University (1994)
72. Jones, D., Schonlau, M., Welch, W.: Efficient global optimization of expensive black box functions. Journal of Global Optimization 13, 455–492 (1998)
73. Kandasamy, K., Dasarathy, G., Oliva, J., Schneider, J., Póczos, B.: Gaussian Process Bandit Optimisation with Multi-fidelity Evaluations. In: Lee et al. [87], pp. 992–1000

74. Kandasamy, K., Dasarathy, G., Schneider, J., Póczos, B.: Multi-fidelity Bayesian Optimisation with Continuous Approximations. In: Precup and Teh [122], pp. 1799–1808
75. Kandasamy, K., Schneider, J., Póczos, B.: High Dimensional Bayesian Optimisation and Bandits via Additive Models. In: Bach and Blei [7], pp. 295–304
76. Karnin, Z., Koren, T., Somekh, O.: Almost optimal exploration in multi-armed bandits. In: Dasgupta and McAllester [23], pp. 1238–1246
77. King, R., Feng, C., Sutherland, A.: Statlog: comparison of classification algorithms on large real-world problems. Applied Artificial Intelligence an International Journal 9(3), 289–333 (1995)
78. Klein, A., Falkner, S., Bartels, S., Hennig, P., Hutter, F.: Fast bayesian hyperparameter optimization on large datasets. In: Electronic Journal of Statistics. vol. 11 (2017)
79. Klein, A., Falkner, S., Mansur, N., Hutter, F.: RoBO: A flexible and robust Bayesian optimization framework in Python. In: NeurIPS workshop on Bayesian Optimization (BayesOpt'17) (2017)
80. Klein, A., Falkner, S., Springenberg, J.T., Hutter, F.: Learning curve prediction with Bayesian neural networks. In: Proceedings of the International Conference on Learning Representations (ICLR'17) (2017), published online: iclr.cc
81. Koch, P., Konen, W., Flasch, O., Bartz-Beielstein, T.: Optimizing support vector machines for stormwater prediction. Tech. Rep. TR10-2-007, Technische Universität Dortmund (2010)
82. Kohavi, R., John, G.: Automatic Parameter Selection by Minimizing Estimated Error. In: Prieditis, A., Russell, S. (eds.) Proceedings of the Twelfth International Conference on Machine Learning, pp. 304–312. Morgan Kaufmann Publishers (1995)
83. Komer, B., Bergstra, J., Eliasmith, C.: Hyperopt-sklearn: Automatic hyperparameter configuration for scikit-learn. In: Hutter, F., Caruana, R., Bardenet, R., Bilenko, M., Guyon, I., Kégl, B., Larochelle, H. (eds.) ICML workshop on Automated Machine Learning (AutoML workshop 2014) (2014)
84. Konen, W., Koch, P., Flasch, O., Bartz-Beielstein, T., Friese, M., Naujoks, B.: Tuned data mining: a benchmark study on different tuners. In: Krasnogor, N. (ed.) Proceedings of the 13th Annual Conference on Genetic and Evolutionary Computation (GECCO'11). pp. 1995–2002. ACM (2011)
85. Krizhevsky, A., Sutskever, I., Hinton, G.: Imagenet classification with deep convolutional neural networks. In: Bartlett et al. [9], pp. 1097–1105
86. Krueger, T., Panknin, D., Braun, M.: Fast cross-validation via sequential testing. Journal of Machine Learning Research (2015)
87. Lee, D., Sugiyama, M., von Luxburg, U., Guyon, I., Garnett, R. (eds.): Proceedings of the 30th International Conference on Advances in Neural Information Processing Systems (NeurIPS'16) (2016)
88. Lee, H., Gramacy, R.: Optimization Subject to Hidden Constraints via Statistical Emulation. Pacific Journal of Optimization 7(3), 467–478 (2011)
89. Li, F.F., Li, J.: Cloud AutoML: Making AI accessible to every business (2018), https://www.blog.google/products/google-cloud/cloud-automl-making-ai-accessible-every-business/
90. Li, L., Jamieson, K., DeSalvo, G., Rostamizadeh, A., Talwalkar, A.: Hyperband: A novel bandit-based approach to hyperparameter optimization. Journal of Machine Learning Research 18(185), 1–52 (2018)
91. Loshchilov, I., Hutter, F.: CMA-ES for hyperparameter optimization of deep neural networks. In: International Conference on Learning Representations Workshop track (2016), published online: iclr.cc
92. Lu, X., Gonzalez, J., Dai, Z., Lawrence, N.: Structured Variationally Auto-encoded Optimization. In: Dy and Krause [27], pp. 3273–3281
93. Luketina, J., Berglund, M., Greff, K., Raiko, T.: Scalable Gradient-Based Tuning of Continuous Regularization Hyperparameters. In: Balcan and Weinberger [8], pp. 2952–2960
94. Luo, G.: A review of automatic selection methods for machine learning algorithms and hyperparameter values. Network Modeling Analysis in Health Informatics and Bioinformatics 5(1) (2016)

95. Lévesque, J.C.: Bayesian Hyperparameter Optimization: Overfitting, Ensembles and Conditional Spaces. Ph.D. thesis, Université Laval (2018)
96. Lévesque, J.C., Durand, A., Gagné, C., Sabourin, R.: Bayesian optimization for conditional hyperparameter spaces. In: Howell, B. (ed.) 2017 International Joint Conference on Neural Networks (IJCNN). pp. 286–293. IEEE (2017)
97. Lévesque, J.C., Gagné, C., Sabourin, R.: Bayesian Hyperparameter Optimization for Ensemble Learning. In: Ihler and Janzing [66], pp. 437–446
98. MacKay, D.: Hyperparameters: Optimize, or Integrate Out?, pp. 43–59. Springer (1996)
99. Maclaurin, D., Duvenaud, D., Adams, R.: Gradient-based Hyperparameter Optimization through Reversible Learning. In: Bach and Blei [7], pp. 2113–2122
100. Mantovani, R., Horvath, T., Cerri, R., Vanschoren, J., Carvalho, A.: Hyper-Parameter Tuning of a Decision Tree Induction Algorithm. In: 2016 5th Brazilian Conference on Intelligent Systems (BRACIS). pp. 37–42. IEEE Computer Society Press (2016)
101. Marcel Wever, F.M., Hüllermeier, E.: ML-Plan for unlimited-length machine learning pipelines. In: Garnett, R., Vanschoren, F.H.J., Brazdil, P., Caruana, R., Giraud-Carrier, C., Guyon, I., Kégl, B. (eds.) ICML workshop on Automated Machine Learning (AutoML workshop 2018) (2018)
102. Maron, O., Moore, A.: The racing algorithm: Model selection for lazy learners. Artificial Intelligence Review 11(1–5), 193–225 (1997)
103. McInerney, J.: An Empirical Bayes Approach to Optimizing Machine Learning Algorithms. In: Guyon et al. [48], pp. 2712–2721
104. McIntire, M., Ratner, D., Ermon, S.: Sparse Gaussian Processes for Bayesian Optimization. In: Ihler and Janzing [66]
105. Melis, G., Dyer, C., Blunsom, P.: On the state of the art of evaluation in neural language models. In: Proceedings of the International Conference on Learning Representations (ICLR'18) [1], published online: iclr.cc
106. Mendoza, H., Klein, A., Feurer, M., Springenberg, J., Hutter, F.: Towards automatically-tuned neural networks. In: ICML 2016 AutoML Workshop (2016)
107. Michie, D., Spiegelhalter, D., Taylor, C., Campbell, J. (eds.): Machine Learning, Neural and Statistical Classification. Ellis Horwood (1994)
108. Mohr, F., Wever, M., Höllermeier, E.: ML-Plan: Automated machine learning via hierarchical planning. Machine Learning 107(8–10), 1495–1515 (2018)
109. Momma, M., Bennett, K.: A Pattern Search Method for Model Selection of Support Vector Regression. In: Proceedings of the 2002 SIAM International Conference on Data Mining, pp. 261–274 (2002)
110. Montgomery, D.: Design and analysis of experiments. John Wiley & Sons, Inc, eighth edn. (2013)
111. Murray, I., Adams, R.: Slice sampling covariance hyperparameters of latent Gaussian models. In: Lafferty, J., Williams, C., Shawe-Taylor, J., Zemel, R., Culotta, A. (eds.) Proceedings of the 24th International Conference on Advances in Neural Information Processing Systems (NeurIPS'10). pp. 1732–1740 (2010)
112. Nguyen, T., Gupta, S., Rana, S., Venkatesh, S.: Stable Bayesian Optimization. In: Kim, J., Shim, K., Cao, L., Lee, J.G., Lin, X., Moon, Y.S. (eds.) Advances in Knowledge Discovery and Data Mining (PAKDD'17). Lecture Notes in Artificial Intelligence, vol. 10235, pp. 578–591 (2017)
113. Nguyen, V., Gupta, S., Rana, S., Li, C., Venkatesh, S.: Filtering Bayesian optimization approach in weakly specified search space. Knowledge and Information Systems (2018)
114. Oh, C., Gavves, E., Welling, M.: BOCK: Bayesian Optimization with Cylindrical Kernels. In: Dy and Krause [27], pp. 3865–3874
115. Olson, R., Bartley, N., Urbanowicz, R., Moore, J.: Evaluation of a Tree-based Pipeline Optimization Tool for Automating Data Science. In: Friedrich, T. (ed.) Proceedings of the Genetic and Evolutionary Computation Conference (GECCO'16). pp. 485–492. ACM (2016)
116. Olson, R., La Cava, W., Mustahsan, Z., Varik, A., Moore, J.: Data-driven advice for applying machine learning to bioinformatics problems. In: Proceedings of the Pacific Symposium in Biocomputing 2018. pp. 192–203 (2018)

117. Paszke, A., Gross, S., Chintala, S., Chanan, G., Yang, E., DeVito, Z., Lin, Z., Desmaison, A., Antiga, L., Lerer, A.: Automatic differentiation in PyTorch. In: NeurIPS Autodiff Workshop (2017)
118. Pedregosa, F.: Hyperparameter optimization with approximate gradient. In: Balcan and Weinberger [8], pp. 737–746
119. Peng-Wei Chen, Jung-Ying Wang, Hahn-Ming Lee: Model selection of SVMs using GA approach. In: Proceedings of the 2004 IEEE International Joint Conference on Neural Networks (IJCNN). vol. 3, pp. 2035–2040. IEEE Computer Society Press (2004)
120. Petrak, J.: Fast subsampling performance estimates for classification algorithm selection. Technical Report TR-2000-07, Austrian Research Institute for Artificial Intelligence (2000)
121. Poloczek, M., Wang, J., Frazier, P.: Multi-Information Source Optimization. In: Guyon et al. [48], pp. 4288–4298
122. Precup, D., Teh, Y. (eds.): Proceedings of the 34th International Conference on Machine Learning (ICML'17), vol. 70. Proceedings of Machine Learning Research (2017)
123. Provost, F., Jensen, D., Oates, T.: Efficient progressive sampling. In: Fayyad, U., Chaudhuri, S., Madigan, D. (eds.) The 5th ACM SIGKDD International Conference on Knowledge Discovery and Data Mining (KDD'99). pp. 23–32. ACM Press (1999)
124. Rasmussen, C., Williams, C.: Gaussian Processes for Machine Learning. The MIT Press (2006)
125. Rendle, S.: Factorization machines. In: Webb, G., Liu, B., Zhang, C., Gunopulos, D., Wu, X. (eds.) Proceedings of the 10th IEEE International Conference on Data Mining (ICDM'06). pp. 995–1000. IEEE Computer Society Press (2010)
126. Ripley, B.D.: Statistical aspects of neural networks. Networks and chaos—statistical and probabilistic aspects 50, 40–123 (1993)
127. Russakovsky, O., Deng, J., Su, H., Krause, J., Satheesh, S., Ma, S., Huang, Z., Karpathy, A., Khosla, A., Bernstein, M., Berg, A., Fei-Fei, L.: Imagenet large scale visual recognition challenge. International Journal of Computer Vision 115(3), 211–252 (2015)
128. Sabharwal, A., Samulowitz, H., Tesauro, G.: Selecting Near-Optimal Learners via Incremental Data Allocation. In: Schuurmans, D., Wellman, M. (eds.) Proceedings of the Thirtieth National Conference on Artificial Intelligence (AAAI'16). AAAI Press (2016)
129. Samanta, B.: Gear fault detection using artificial neural networks and support vector machines with genetic algorithms. Mechanical Systems and Signal Processing 18(3), 625–644 (2004)
130. Sanders, S., Giraud-Carrier, C.: Informing the Use of Hyperparameter Optimization Through Metalearning. In: Gottumukkala, R., Ning, X., Dong, G., Raghavan, V., Aluru, S., Karypis, G., Miele, L., Wu, X. (eds.) 2017 IEEE International Conference on Big Data (Big Data). IEEE Computer Society Press (2017)
131. Schilling, N., Wistuba, M., Drumond, L., Schmidt-Thieme, L.: Hyperparameter optimization with factorized multilayer perceptrons. In: Appice, A., Rodrigues, P., Costa, V., Gama, J., Jorge, A., Soares, C. (eds.) Machine Learning and Knowledge Discovery in Databases (ECML/PKDD'15). Lecture Notes in Computer Science, vol. 9285, pp. 87–103. Springer (2015)
132. Schilling, N., Wistuba, M., Drumond, L., Schmidt-Thieme, L.: Joint Model Choice and Hyperparameter Optimization with Factorized Multilayer Perceptrons. In: 2015 IEEE 27th International Conference on Tools with Artificial Intelligence (ICTAI). pp. 72–79. IEEE Computer Society Press (2015)
133. Sculley, D., Snoek, J., Wiltschko, A., Rahimi, A.: Winner's curse? on pace, progress, and empirical rigor. In: International Conference on Learning Representations Workshop track (2018), published online: iclr.cc
134. Shah, A., Ghahramani, Z.: Pareto Frontier Learning with Expensive Correlated Objectives. In: Balcan and Weinberger [8], pp. 1919–1927
135. Shahriari, B., Swersky, K., Wang, Z., Adams, R., de Freitas, N.: Taking the human out of the loop: A review of Bayesian optimization. Proceedings of the IEEE 104(1), 148–175 (2016)
136. Shahriari, B., Bouchard-Cote, A., de Freitas, N.: Unbounded Bayesian optimization via regularization. In: Gretton and Robert [47], pp. 1168–1176

137. SIGOPT: Improve ML models 100x faster (2018), https://sigopt.com/
138. Simon, D.: Evolutionary optimization algorithms. John Wiley & Sons (2013)
139. Snoek, J.: Bayesian optimization and semiparametric models with applications to assistive technology. PhD Thesis, University of Toronto (2013)
140. Snoek, J., Larochelle, H., Adams, R.: Practical Bayesian optimization of machine learning algorithms. In: Bartlett et al. [9], pp. 2960–2968
141. Snoek, J., Rippel, O., Swersky, K., Kiros, R., Satish, N., Sundaram, N., Patwary, M., Prabhat, Adams, R.: Scalable Bayesian optimization using deep neural networks. In: Bach and Blei [7], pp. 2171–2180
142. Snoek, J., Swersky, K., Zemel, R., Adams, R.: Input warping for Bayesian optimization of non-stationary functions. In: Xing and Jebara [157], pp. 1674–1682
143. Sparks, E., Talwalkar, A., Haas, D., Franklin, M., Jordan, M., Kraska, T.: Automating model search for large scale machine learning. In: Balazinska, M. (ed.) Proceedings of the Sixth ACM Symposium on Cloud Computing - SoCC '15. pp. 368–380. ACM Press (2015)
144. Springenberg, J., Klein, A., Falkner, S., Hutter, F.: Bayesian optimization with robust Bayesian neural networks. In: Lee et al. [87]
145. Sun, Q., Pfahringer, B., Mayo, M.: Towards a Framework for Designing Full Model Selection and Optimization Systems. In: Multiple Classifier Systems, vol. 7872, pp. 259–270. Springer (2013)
146. Swersky, K., Duvenaud, D., Snoek, J., Hutter, F., Osborne, M.: Raiders of the lost architecture: Kernels for Bayesian optimization in conditional parameter spaces. In: NeurIPS Workshop on Bayesian Optimization in Theory and Practice (BayesOpt'14) (2014)
147. Swersky, K., Snoek, J., Adams, R.: Multi-task Bayesian optimization. In: Burges, C., Bottou, L., Welling, M., Ghahramani, Z., Weinberger, K. (eds.) Proceedings of the 27th International Conference on Advances in Neural Information Processing Systems (NeurIPS'13). pp. 2004–2012 (2013)
148. Swersky, K., Snoek, J., Adams, R.: Freeze-thaw Bayesian optimization arXiv:1406.3896v1 [stats.ML] (2014)
149. Thornton, C., Hutter, F., Hoos, H., Leyton-Brown, K.: Auto-WEKA: combined selection and hyperparameter optimization of classification algorithms. In: Dhillon, I., Koren, Y., Ghani, R., Senator, T., Bradley, P., Parekh, R., He, J., Grossman, R., Uthurusamy, R. (eds.) The 19th ACM SIGKDD International Conference on Knowledge Discovery and Data Mining (KDD'13). pp. 847–855. ACM Press (2013)
150. Wainer, J., Cawley, G.: Empirical Evaluation of Resampling Procedures for Optimising SVM Hyperparameters. Journal of Machine Learning Research 18, 1–35 (2017)
151. Wang, J., Xu, J., Wang, X.: Combination of hyperband and Bayesian optimization for hyperparameter optimization in deep learning. arXiv:1801.01596v1 [cs.CV] (2018)
152. Wang, L., Feng, M., Zhou, B., Xiang, B., Mahadevan, S.: Efficient Hyper-parameter Optimization for NLP Applications. In: Proceedings of the 2015 Conference on Empirical Methods in Natural Language Processing. pp. 2112–2117. Association for Computational Linguistics (2015)
153. Wang, Z., Hutter, F., Zoghi, M., Matheson, D., de Feitas, N.: Bayesian optimization in a billion dimensions via random embeddings. Journal of Artificial Intelligence Research 55, 361–387 (2016)
154. Wang, Z., Gehring, C., Kohli, P., Jegelka, S.: Batched Large-scale Bayesian Optimization in High-dimensional Spaces. In: Storkey, A., Perez-Cruz, F. (eds.) Proceedings of the 21st International Conference on Artificial Intelligence and Statistics (AISTATS). vol. 84. Proceedings of Machine Learning Research (2018)
155. Wistuba, M., Schilling, N., Schmidt-Thieme, L.: Automatic Frankensteining: Creating Complex Ensembles Autonomously. In: Proceedings of the 2017 SIAM International Conference on Data Mining (2017)
156. Wolpert, D.: Stacked generalization. Neural Networks 5(2), 241–259 (1992)
157. Xing, E., Jebara, T. (eds.): Proceedings of the 31th International Conference on Machine Learning, (ICML'14). Omnipress (2014)

158. Zabinsky, Z.: Pure Random Search and Pure Adaptive Search. In: Stochastic Adaptive Search for Global Optimization, pp. 25–54. Springer (2003)
159. Zeng, X., Luo, G.: Progressive sampling-based Bayesian optimization for efficient and automatic machine learning model selection. Health Information Science and Systems 5(1) (2017)
160. Zhang, Y., Bahadori, M.T., Su, H., Sun, J.: FLASH: Fast Bayesian Optimization for Data Analytic Pipelines. In: Krishnapuram, B., Shah, M., Smola, A., Aggarwal, C., Shen, D., Rastogi, R. (eds.) Proceedings of the 22nd ACM SIGKDD International Conference on Knowledge Discovery and Data Mining (KDD). pp. 2065–2074. ACM Press (2016)

Chapter 2
Meta-Learning

Joaquin Vanschoren

Abstract Meta-learning, or *learning to learn*, is the science of systematically observing how different machine learning approaches perform on a wide range of learning tasks, and then learning from this experience, or *meta-data*, to learn new tasks much faster than otherwise possible. Not only does this dramatically speed up and improve the design of machine learning pipelines or neural architectures, it also allows us to replace hand-engineered algorithms with novel approaches learned in a data-driven way. In this chapter, we provide an overview of the state of the art in this fascinating and continuously evolving field.

2.1 Introduction

When we learn new skills, we rarely – if ever – start from scratch. We start from skills learned earlier in related tasks, reuse approaches that worked well before, and focus on what is likely worth trying based on experience [82]. With every skill learned, learning new skills becomes easier, requiring fewer examples and less trial-and-error. In short, we *learn how to learn* across tasks. Likewise, when building machine learning models for a specific task, we often build on experience with related tasks, or use our (often implicit) understanding of the behavior of machine learning techniques to help make the right choices.

The challenge in meta-learning is to learn from prior experience in a systematic, data-driven way. First, we need to collect *meta-data* that describe prior learning tasks and previously learned models. They comprise the exact *algorithm configurations* used to train the models, including hyperparameter settings, pipeline compositions and/or network architectures, the resulting *model evaluations*, such as accuracy and training time, the learned model parameters, such as the trained weights of a neural net, as well as measurable properties of the task itself, also

J. Vanschoren (✉)
Department of Mathematics and Computer Science, TU Eindhoven, Eindhoven, North Brabant, The Netherlands
e-mail: j.vanschoren@tue.nl

F. Hutter et al. (eds.), *Automated Machine Learning*, The Springer Series on Challenges in Machine Learning, https://doi.org/10.1007/978-3-030-05318-5_2

known as *meta-features*. Second, we need to *learn* from this prior meta-data, to extract and transfer knowledge that guides the search for optimal models for new tasks. This chapter presents a concise overview of different meta-learning approaches to do this effectively.

The term *meta-learning* covers any type of learning based on prior experience with other tasks. The more *similar* those previous tasks are, the more types of meta-data we can leverage, and defining task similarity will be a key overarching challenge. Perhaps needless to say, there is no free lunch [57, 188]. When a new task represents completely unrelated phenomena, or random noise, leveraging prior experience will not be effective. Luckily, in real-world tasks, there are plenty of opportunities to learn from prior experience.

In the remainder of this chapter, we categorize meta-learning techniques based on the type of meta-data they leverage, from the most general to the most task-specific. First, in Sect. 2.2, we discuss how to *learn purely from model evaluations*. These techniques can be used to recommend generally useful configurations and configuration search spaces, as well as transfer knowledge from *empirically similar* tasks. In Sect. 2.3, we discuss how we can *characterize* tasks to more explicitly express task similarity and build meta-models that learn the relationships between data characteristics and learning performance. Finally, Sect. 2.4 covers how we can *transfer trained model parameters* between tasks that are inherently similar, e.g. sharing the same input features, which enables transfer learning [111] and few-shot learning [126] among others.

Note that while *multi-task learning* [25] (learning multiple related tasks simultaneously) and *ensemble learning* [35] (building multiple models on the same task), can often be meaningfully combined with meta-learning systems, they do not in themselves involve learning from prior experience on other tasks.

This chapter is based on a very recent survey article [176].

2.2 Learning from Model Evaluations

Consider that we have access to prior tasks $t_j \in T$, the set of all known tasks, as well as a set of learning algorithms, fully defined by their *configurations* $\theta_i \in \Theta$; here Θ represents a discrete, continuous, or mixed configuration space which can cover hyperparameter settings, pipeline components and/or network architecture components. $\mathbf{P}$ is the set of all prior scalar evaluations $P_{i,j} = P(\theta_i, t_j)$ of configuration θ_i on task t_j, according to a predefined evaluation measure, e.g. accuracy, and model evaluation technique, e.g. cross-validation. $\mathbf{P}_{new}$ is the set of known evaluations $P_{i,new}$ on a new task t_{new}. We now want to train a *meta-learner* L that predicts recommended configurations Θ^*_{new} for a new task t_{new}. The meta-learner is trained on meta-data $\mathbf{P} \cup \mathbf{P}_{new}$. $\mathbf{P}$ is usually gathered beforehand, or extracted from meta-data repositories [174, 177]. $\mathbf{P}_{new}$ is learned by the meta-learning technique itself in an iterative fashion, sometimes *warm-started* with an initial $\mathbf{P}'_{new}$ generated by another method.

2.2.1 Task-Independent Recommendations

First, imagine not having access to any evaluations on t_{new}, hence $\mathbf{P}_{new} = \varnothing$. We can then still learn a function $f : \Theta \times T \rightarrow \{\theta_k^*\}$, $k = 1..K$, yielding a set of recommended configurations *independent* of t_{new}. These θ_k^* can then be evaluated on t_{new} to select the best one, or to warm-start further optimization approaches, such as those discussed in Sect. 2.2.3.

Such approaches often produce a ranking, i.e. an *ordered* set θ_k^*. This is typically done by discretizing Θ into a set of candidate configurations θ_i, also called a *portfolio*, evaluated on a large number of tasks t_j. We can then build a ranking per task, for instance using *success rates*, *AUC*, or *significant wins* [21, 34, 85]. However, it is often desirable that equally good but faster algorithms are ranked higher, and multiple methods have been proposed to trade off accuracy and training time [21, 134]. Next, we can aggregate these single-task rankings into a *global ranking*, for instance by computing the average rank [1, 91] across all tasks. When there is insufficient data to build a global ranking, one can recommend *subsets of configurations* based on the best known configurations for each prior task [70, 173], or return *quasi-linear rankings* [30].

To find the best θ^* for a task t_{new}, never before seen, a simple anytime method is to select the top-K configurations [21], going down the list and evaluating each configuration on t_{new} in turn. This evaluation can be halted after a predefined value for K, a time budget, or when a sufficiently accurate model is found. In time-constrained settings, it has been shown that multi-objective rankings (including training time) converge to near-optimal models much faster [1, 134], and provide a strong baseline for algorithm comparisons [1, 85].

A very different approach to the one above is to first fit a differentiable function $f_j(\theta_i) = P_{i,j}$ on all prior evaluations of a specific task t_j, and then use gradient descent to find an optimized configuration θ_j^* per prior task [186]. Assuming that some of the tasks t_j will be similar to t_{new}, those θ_j^* will be useful for warm-starting Bayesian optimization approaches.

2.2.2 Configuration Space Design

Prior evaluations can also be used to learn a better *configuration space* Θ^*. While again independent from t_{new}, this can radically speed up the search for optimal models, since only the more relevant regions of the configuration space are explored. This is critical when computational resources are limited, and has proven to be an important factor in practical comparisons of AutoML systems [33].

First, in the functional ANOVA [67] approach, hyperparameters are deemed important if they explain most of the variance in algorithm performance on a given task. In [136], this was explored using 250,000 OpenML experiments with 3 algorithms across 100 datasets.

An alternative approach is to first *learn* an optimal hyperparameter default setting, and then define hyperparameter importance as the *performance gain* that can be achieved by tuning the hyperparameter instead of leaving it at that default value. Indeed, even though a hyperparameter may cause a lot of variance, it may also have one specific setting that always results in good performance. In [120], this was done using about 500,000 OpenML experiments on 6 algorithms and 38 datasets. Default values are learned *jointly* for all hyperparameters of an algorithm by first training surrogate models for that algorithm for a large number of tasks. Next, many configurations are sampled, and the configuration that minimizes the average risk across all tasks is the recommended default configuration. Finally, the importance (or *tunability*) of each hyperparameter is estimated by observing how much improvement can still be gained by tuning it.

In [183], defaults are learned *independently* from other hyperparameters, and defined as the configurations that occur most frequently in the top-K configurations for every task. In the case that the optimal default value depends on meta-features (e.g. the number of training instances or features), simple functions are learned that include these meta-features. Next, a statistical test defines whether a hyperparameter can be safely left at this default, based on the *performance loss* observed when *not* tuning a hyperparameter (or a set of hyperparameters), while all other parameters are tuned. This was evaluated using 118,000 OpenML experiments with 2 algorithms (SVMs and Random Forests) across 59 datasets.

2.2.3 Configuration Transfer

If we want to provide recommendations for a specific task t_{new}, we need additional information on how similar t_{new} is to prior tasks t_j. One way to do this is to evaluate a number of recommended (or potentially random) configurations on t_{new}, yielding new evidence $\mathbf{P}_{new}$. If we then observe that the evaluations $P_{i,new}$ are similar to $P_{i,j}$, then t_j and t_{new} can be considered intrinsically similar, based on empirical evidence. We can include this knowledge to train a meta-learner that predicts a recommended set of configurations Θ^*_{new} for t_{new}. Moreover, every selected θ^*_{new} can be evaluated and included in $\mathbf{P}_{new}$, repeating the cycle and collecting more empirical evidence to learn which tasks are similar to each other.

2.2.3.1 Relative Landmarks

A first measure for task similarity considers the relative (pairwise) performance differences, also called *relative landmarks*, $RL_{a,b,j} = P_{a,j} - P_{b,j}$ between two configurations θ_a and θ_b on a particular task t_j [53]. *Active testing* [85] leverages these as follows: it warm-starts with the globally best configuration (see Sect. 2.2.1), calls it θ_{best}, and proceeds in a tournament-style fashion. In each round, it selects the 'competitor' θ_c that most convincingly outperforms θ_{best} on similar tasks. It deems tasks to be similar if the relative landmarks of all evaluated configurations are similar, i.e., if the configurations perform similarly on both t_j and t_{new} then the tasks are deemed similar. Next, it evaluates the competitor θ_c, yielding $P_{c,new}$, updates the task similarities, and repeats. A limitation of this method is that it can only consider configurations θ_i that were evaluated on many prior tasks.

2.2.3.2 Surrogate Models

A more flexible way to transfer information is to build *surrogate models* $s_j(\theta_i) = P_{i,j}$ for all prior tasks t_j, trained using all available **P**. One can then define task similarity in terms of the error between $s_j(\theta_i)$ and $P_{i,new}$: if the surrogate model for t_j can generate accurate predictions for t_{new}, then those tasks are intrinsically similar. This is usually done in combination with Bayesian optimization (see Chap. 1) to determine the next θ_i.

Wistuba et al. [187] train surrogate models based on Gaussian Processes (GPs) for every prior task, plus one for t_{new}, and combine them into a weighted, normalized sum, with the (new) predicted mean μ defined as the weighted sum of the individual μ_j's (obtained from prior tasks t_j). The weights of the μ_j's are computed using the Nadaraya-Watson kernel-weighted average, where each task is represented as a vector of relative landmarks, and the Epanechnikov quadratic kernel [104] is used to measure the similarity between the relative landmark vectors of t_j and t_{new}. The more similar t_j is to t_{new}, the larger the weight s_j, increasing the influence of the surrogate model for t_j.

Feurer et al. [45] propose to combine the predictive distributions of the individual Gaussian processes, which makes the combined model a Gaussian process again. The weights are computed following the agnostic Bayesian ensemble of Lacoste et al. [81], which weights predictors according to an estimate of their generalization performance.

Meta-data can also be transferred in the acquisition function rather than the surrogate model [187]. The surrogate model is only trained on $P_{i,new}$, but the next θ_i to evaluate is provided by an acquisition function which is the weighted average of the expected improvement [69] on $P_{i,new}$ and the predicted improvements on all prior $P_{i,j}$. The weights of the prior tasks can again be defined via the accuracy of the surrogate model or via relative landmarks. The weight of the expected improvement component is gradually increased with every iteration as more evidence $P_{i,new}$ is collected.

2.2.3.3 Warm-Started Multi-task Learning

Another approach to relate prior tasks t_j is to learn a joint task representation using **P** prior evaluations. In [114], task-specific Bayesian linear regression [20] surrogate models $s_j(\theta_i^z)$ are trained in a novel configuration θ^z learned by a feedforward Neural Network $NN(\theta_i)$ which learns a suitable basis expansion θ^z of the original configuration θ in which linear surrogate models can accurately predict $P_{i,new}$. The surrogate models are pre-trained on OpenML meta-data to provide a warm-start for optimizing $NN(\theta_i)$ in a multi-task learning setting. Earlier work on multi-task learning [166] assumed that we already have a set of 'similar' source tasks t_j. It transfers information between these t_j and t_{new} by building a joint GP model for Bayesian optimization that learns and exploits the exact relationship between the tasks. Learning a joint GP tends to be less scalable than building one GP per task, though. Springenberg et al. [161] also assumes that the tasks are related and similar, but learns the relationship between tasks during the optimization process using Bayesian Neural Networks. As such, their method is somewhat of a hybrid of the previous two approaches. Golovin et al. [58] assume a sequence order (e.g., time) across tasks. It builds a stack of GP regressors, one per task, training each GP on the residuals relative to the regressor below it. Hence, each task uses the tasks before it to define its priors.

2.2.3.4 Other Techniques

Multi-armed bandits [139] provide yet another approach to find the source tasks t_j most related to t_{new} [125]. In this analogy, each t_j is one arm, and the (stochastic) reward for selecting (pulling) a particular prior task (arm) is defined in terms of the error in the predictions of a GP-based Bayesian optimizer that models the prior evaluations of t_j as noisy measurements and combines them with the existing evaluations on t_{new}. The cubic scaling of the GP makes this approach less scalable, though.

Another way to define task similarity is to take the existing evaluations $P_{i,j}$, use Thompson Sampling [167] to obtain the optima distribution ρ^j_{max}, and then measure the KL-divergence [80] between ρ^j_{max} and ρ^{new}_{max} [124]. These distributions are then merged into a mixture distribution based on the similarities and used to build an acquisition function that predicts the next most promising configuration to evaluate. It is so far only evaluated to tune 2 SVM hyperparameters using 5 tasks.

Finally, a complementary way to leverage **P** is to recommend which configurations should *not* be used. After training surrogate models per task, we can look up which t_j are most similar to t_{new}, and then use $s_j(\theta_i)$ to discover regions of Θ where performance is predicted to be poor. Excluding these regions can speed up the search for better-performing ones. Wistuba et al. [185], do this using a task similarity measure based on the Kendall tau rank correlation coefficient [73] between the ranks obtained by ranking configurations θ_i using $P_{i,j}$ and $P_{i,new}$, respectively.

2.2.4 Learning Curves

We can also extract meta-data about the training process itself, such as how fast model performance improves as more training data is added. If we divide the training in steps s_t, usually adding a fixed number of training examples every step, we can measure the performance $P(\theta_i, t_j, s_t) = P_{i,j,t}$ of configuration θ_i on task t_j after step s_t, yielding a *learning curve* across the time steps s_t. As discussed in Chap. 1, learning curves are also used to speed up hyperparameter optimization on a given task. In meta-learning, learning curve information is transferred across tasks.

While evaluating a configuration on new task t_{new}, we can halt the training after a certain number of iterations $r < t$, and use the partially observed learning curve to predict how well the configuration will perform on the full dataset based on prior experience with other tasks, and decide whether to continue the training or not. This can significantly speed up the search for good configurations.

One approach is to assume that similar tasks yield similar learning curves. First, define a distance between tasks based on how similar the partial learning curves are: $dist(t_a, t_b) = f(P_{i,a,t}, P_{i,b,t})$ with $t = 1, \ldots, r$. Next, find the k most similar tasks $t_{1\ldots k}$ and use their complete learning curves to predict how well the configuration will perform on the new complete dataset. Task similarity can be measured by comparing the shapes of the partial curves across all configurations tried, and the prediction is made by adapting the 'nearest' complete curve(s) to the new partial curve [83, 84]. This approach was also successful in combination with active testing [86], and can be sped up further by using multi-objective evaluation measures that include training time [134].

Interestingly, while several methods aim to predict learning curves during neural architecture search (see Chap. 3), as of yet none of this work leverages learning curves previously observed on other tasks.

2.3 Learning from Task Properties

Another rich source of meta-data are characterizations (meta-features) of the task at hand. Each task $t_j \in T$ is described with a vector $m(t_j) = (m_{j,1}, \ldots, m_{j,K})$ of K meta-features $m_{j,k} \in M$, the set of all known meta-features. This can be used to define a task similarity measure based on, for instance, the Euclidean distance between $m(t_i)$ and $m(t_j)$, so that we can transfer information from the most similar tasks to the new task t_{new}. Moreover, together with prior evaluations $\mathbf{P}$, we can train a *meta-learner* L to predict the performance $P_{i,new}$ of configurations θ_i on a new task t_{new}.

2.3.1 Meta-Features

Table 2.1 provides a concise overview of the most commonly used meta-features, together with a short rationale for why they are indicative of model performance. Where possible, we also show the formulas to compute them. More complete surveys can be found in the literature [26, 98, 130, 138, 175].

To build a meta-feature vector $m(t_j)$, one needs to select and further process these meta-features. Studies on OpenML meta-data have shown that the optimal set of meta-features depends on the application [17]. Many meta-features are computed on single features, or combinations of features, and need to be aggregated by summary statistics (min,max,μ,σ,quartiles,$q_{1...4}$) or histograms [72]. One needs to systematically extract and aggregate them [117]. When computing task similarity, it is also important to normalize all meta-features [9], perform feature selection [172], or employ dimensionality reduction techniques (e.g. PCA) [17]. When learning meta-models, one can also use relational meta-learners [173] or case-based reasoning methods [63, 71, 92].

Beyond these general-purpose meta-features, many more specific ones were formulated. For streaming data one can use streaming landmarks [135, 137], for time series data one can compute autocorrelation coefficients or the slope of regression models [7, 121, 147], and for unsupervised problems one can cluster the data in different ways and extract properties of these clusters [159]. In many applications, domain-specific information can be leveraged as well [109, 156].

2.3.2 Learning Meta-Features

Instead of manually defining meta-features, we can also *learn* a joint representation for groups of tasks. One approach is to build meta-models that generate a landmark-like meta-feature representation M' given other task meta-features M and trained on performance meta-data **P**, or $f : M \mapsto M'$. Sun and Pfahringer [165] do this by evaluating a predefined set of configurations θ_i on all prior tasks t_j, and generating a binary metafeature $m_{j,a,b} \in M'$ for every pairwise combination of configurations θ_a and θ_b, indicating whether θ_a outperformed θ_b or not, thus $m'(t_j) = (m_{j,a,b}, m_{j,a,c}, m_{j,b,c}, \ldots)$. To compute $m_{new,a,b}$, *meta-rules* are learned for every pairwise combination (a,b), each predicting whether θ_a will outperform θ_b on task t_j, given its other meta-features $m(t_j)$.

We can also learn a joint representation based entirely on the available **P** meta-data, i.e. $f : \mathbf{P} \times \Theta \mapsto M'$. We previously discussed how to do this with feed-forward neural nets [114] in Sect. 2.2.3. If the tasks share the same input space, e.g., they are images of the same resolution, one can also use deep metric learning to learn a meta-feature representation, for instance, using Siamese networks [75].

Table 2.1 Overview of commonly used meta-features. Groups from top to bottom: simple, statistical, information-theoretic, complexity, model-based, and landmarkers. Continuous features X and target Y have mean μ_X, stdev σ_X, variance σ_X^2. Categorical features $\mathtt{X}$ and class $\mathtt{C}$ have categorical values π_i, conditional probabilities $\pi_{i|j}$, joint probabilities $\pi_{i,j}$, marginal probabilities $\pi_{i+} = \sum_j \pi_{ij}$, entropy $H(\mathtt{X}) = -\sum_i \pi_{i+} log_2(\pi_{i+})$

Name	Formula	Rationale	Variants
Nr instances	n	Speed, Scalability [99]	p/n, $log(n)$, $log(n/p)$
Nr features	p	Curse of dimensionality [99]	$log(p)$, % categorical
Nr classes	c	Complexity, imbalance [99]	ratio min/maj class
Nr missing values	m	Imputation effects [70]	% missing
Nr outliers	o	Data noisiness [141]	o/n
Skewness	$\frac{E(X-\mu_X)^3}{\sigma_X^3}$	Feature normality [99]	min,max,μ,σ,q_1, q_3
Kurtosis	$\frac{E(X-\mu_X)^4}{\sigma_X^4}$	Feature normality [99]	min,max,μ,σ,q_1, q_3
Correlation	$\rho_{X_1 X_2}$	Feature interdependence [99]	min,max,μ,σ,ρ_{XY}[158]
Covariance	$cov_{X_1 X_2}$	Feature interdependence [99]	min,max,μ,σ,cov_{XY}
Concentration	$\tau_{X_1 X_2}$	Feature interdependence [72]	min,max,μ,σ,τ_{XY}
Sparsity	sparsity(X)	Degree of discreteness [143]	min,max,μ,σ
Gravity	gravity(X)	Inter-class dispersion [5]	
ANOVA p-value	$p_{val_{\mathtt{X}_1 \mathtt{X}_2}}$	Feature redundancy [70]	$p_{val_{XY}}$[158]
Coeff. of variation	$\frac{\sigma_Y}{\mu_Y}$	Variation in target [158]	
PCA ρ_{λ_1}	$\sqrt{\frac{\lambda_1}{1+\lambda_1}}$	Variance in first PC [99]	$\frac{\lambda_1}{\sum_i \lambda_i}$[99]
PCA skewness		Skewness of first PC [48]	PCA kurtosis [48]
PCA 95%	$\frac{dim_{95\%var}}{p}$	Intrinsic dimensionality [9]	
Class probability	$P(\mathtt{C})$	Class distribution [99]	min,max,μ,σ
Class entropy	$H(\mathtt{C})$	Class imbalance [99]	
Norm. entropy	$\frac{H(\mathtt{X})}{log_2 n}$	Feature informativeness [26]	min,max,μ,σ
Mutual inform.	$MI(\mathtt{C},\mathtt{X})$	Feature importance [99]	min,max,μ,σ
Uncertainty coeff.	$\frac{MI(\mathtt{C},\mathtt{X})}{H(\mathtt{C})}$	Feature importance [3]	min,max,μ,σ
Equiv. nr. feats	$\frac{H(C)}{\overline{MI(C,X)}}$	Intrinsic dimensionality [99]	
Noise-signal ratio	$\frac{\overline{H(X)}-\overline{MI(C,X)}}{\overline{MI(C,X)}}$	Noisiness of data [99]	
Fisher's discrimin.	$\frac{(\mu_{c1}-\mu_{c2})^2}{\sigma_{c1}^2-\sigma_{c2}^2}$	Separability classes c_1, c_2 [64]	See [64]
Volume of overlap		Class distribution overlap [64]	See [64]
Concept variation		Task complexity [180]	See [179, 180]
Data consistency		Data quality [76]	See [76]
Nr nodes, leaves	$\|\eta\|$, $\|\psi\|$	Concept complexity [113]	Tree depth
Branch length		Concept complexity [113]	min,max,μ,σ
Nodes per feature	$\|\eta_X\|$	Feature importance [113]	min,max,μ,σ
Leaves per class	$\frac{\|\psi_c\|}{\|\psi\|}$	Class complexity [49]	min,max,μ,σ
Leaves agreement	$\frac{n_{\psi_i}}{n}$	Class separability [16]	min,max,μ,σ
Information gain		Feature importance [16]	min,max,μ,σ, gini

(continued)

Table 2.1 (continued)

Name	Formula	Rationale	Variants
Landmarker(1NN)	$P(\theta_{1NN}, t_j)$	Data sparsity [115]	Elite 1NN [115]
Landmarker(Tree)	$P(\theta_{Tree}, t_j)$	Data separability [115]	Stump,RandomTree
Landmarker(Lin)	$P(\theta_{Lin}, t_j)$	Linear separability [115]	Lin.Disciminant
Landmarker(NB)	$P(\theta_{NB}, t_j)$	Feature independence [115]	More models [14, 88]
Relative LM	$P_{a,j} - P_{b,j}$	Probing performance [53]	
Subsample LM	$P(\theta_i, t_j, s_t)$	Probing performance [160]	

These are trained by feeding the data of two different tasks to two twin networks, and using the differences between the predicted and observed performance $P_{i,new}$ as the error signal. Since the model parameters between both networks are tied in a Siamese network, two very similar tasks are mapped to the same regions in the latent meta-feature space. They can be used for warm starting Bayesian hyperparameter optimization [75] and neural architecture search [2].

2.3.3 Warm-Starting Optimization from Similar Tasks

Meta-features are a very natural way to estimate task similarity and initialize optimization procedures based on promising configurations on similar tasks. This is akin to how human experts start a manual search for good models, given experience on related tasks.

First, starting a *genetic search* algorithm in regions of the search space with promising solutions can significantly speed up convergence to a good solution. Gomes et al. [59] recommend initial configurations by finding the k most similar prior tasks t_j based on the L1 distance between vectors $m(t_j)$ and $m(t_{new})$, where each $m(t_j)$ includes 17 simple and statistical meta-features. For each of the k most similar tasks, the best configuration is evaluated on t_{new}, and used to initialize a genetic search algorithm (Particle Swarm Optimization), as well as Tabu Search. Reif et al. [129] follow a very similar approach, using 15 simple, statistical, and landmarking meta-features. They use a forward selection technique to find the most useful meta-features, and warm-start a standard genetic algorithm (GAlib) with a modified Gaussian mutation operation. Variants of active testing (see Sect. 2.2.3) that use meta-features were also tried [85, 100], but did not perform better than the approaches based on relative landmarks.

Also model-based optimization approaches can benefit greatly from an initial set of promising configurations. SCoT [9] trains a single surrogate ranking model $f : M \times \Theta \rightarrow R$, predicting the rank of θ_i on task t_j. M contains 4 meta-features (3 simple ones and one based on PCA). The surrogate model is trained on all the rankings, including those on t_{new}. Ranking is used because the scale of evaluation values can differ greatly between tasks. A GP regression converts the ranks to probabilities to do Bayesian optimization, and each new $P_{i,new}$ is used to retrain the surrogate model after every step.

Schilling et al. [148] use a modified multilayer perceptron as a surrogate model, of the form $s_j(\theta_i, m(t_j), b(t_j)) = P_{i,j}$ where $m(t_j)$ are the meta-features and $b(t_j)$ is a vector of j binary indications which are 1 if the meta-instance is from t_j and 0 otherwise. The multi-layer perceptron uses a modified activation function based on factorization machines [132] in the first layer, aimed at learning a latent representation for each task to model task similarities. Since this model cannot represent uncertainties, an ensemble of 100 multilayer perceptrons is trained to get predictive means and simulate variances.

Training a single surrogate model on all prior meta-data is often less scalable. Yogatama and Mann [190] also build a single Bayesian surrogate model, but only include tasks similar to t_{new}, where task similarity is defined as the Euclidean distance between meta-feature vectors consisting of 3 simple meta-features. The $P_{i,j}$ values are standardized to overcome the problem of different scales for each t_j. The surrogate model learns a Gaussian process with a specific kernel combination on all instances.

Feurer et al. [48] offer a simpler, more scalable method that warm-starts Bayesian optimization by sorting all prior tasks t_j similar to [59], but including 46 simple, statistical, and landmarking meta-features, as well as $H(\mathtt{C})$. The t best configurations on the d most similar tasks are used to warm-start the surrogate model. They search over many more hyperparameters than earlier work, including preprocessing steps. This warm-starting approach was also used in later work [46], which is discussed in detail in Chap. 6.

Finally, one can also use *collaborative filtering* to recommend promising configurations [162]. By analogy, the tasks t_j (users) provide ratings ($P_{i,j}$) for the configurations θ_i (items), and matrix factorization techniques are used to predict unknown $P_{i,j}$ values and recommend the best configurations for any task. An important issue here is the cold start problem, since the matrix factorization requires at least some evaluations on t_{new}. Yang et al. [189] use a D-optimal experiment design to sample an initial set of evaluations $P_{i,new}$. They predict both the predictive performance and runtime, to recommend a set of warm-start configurations that are both accurate and fast. Misir and Sebag [102, 103] leverage meta-features to solve the cold start problem. Fusi et al. [54] also use meta-features, following the same procedure as [46], and use a probabilistic matrix factorization approach that allows them to perform Bayesian optimization to further optimize their pipeline configurations θ_i. This approach yields useful latent embeddings of both the tasks and configurations, in which the bayesian optimization can be performed more efficiently.

2.3.4 *Meta-Models*

We can also *learn* the complex relationship between a task's meta-features and the utility of specific configurations by building a meta-model L that recommends the most useful configurations Θ^*_{new} given the meta-features M of the new task t_{new}. There exists a rich body of earlier work [22, 56, 87, 94] on building meta-models for algorithm selection [15, 19, 70, 115] and hyperparameter recommendation [4, 79, 108, 158]. Experiments showed that boosted and bagged trees often yielded the best predictions, although much depends on the exact meta-features used [72, 76].

2.3.4.1 Ranking

Meta-models can also generate a *ranking* of the top-K most promising configurations. One approach is to build a k-nearest neighbor (kNN) meta-model to predict which tasks are similar, and then rank the best configurations on these similar tasks [23, 147]. This is similar to the work discussed in Sect. 2.3.3, but without ties to a follow-up optimization approach. Meta-models specifically meant for ranking, such as predictive clustering trees [171] and label ranking trees [29] were also shown to work well. Approximate Ranking Tree Forests (ART Forests) [165], ensembles of fast ranking trees, prove to be especially effective, since they have 'built-in' meta-feature selection, work well even if few prior tasks are available, and the ensembling makes the method more robust. *autoBagging* [116] ranks Bagging workflows including four different Bagging hyperparameters, using an XGBoost-based ranker, trained on 140 OpenML datasets and 146 meta-features. Lorena et al. [93] recommends SVM configurations for regression problems using a kNN meta-model and a new set of meta-features based on data complexity.

2.3.4.2 Performance Prediction

Meta-models can also directly predict the performance, e.g. accuracy or training time, of a configuration on a given task, given its meta-features. This allows us to estimate whether a configuration will be interesting enough to evaluate in any optimization procedure. Early work used linear regression or rule-base regressors to predict the performance of a discrete set of configurations and then rank them accordingly [14, 77]. Guerra et al. [61] train an SVM meta-regressor per classification algorithm to predict its accuracy, under default settings, on a new task t_{new} given its meta-features. Reif et al. [130] train a similar meta-regressor on more meta-data to predict its *optimized* performance. Davis et al. [32] use a MultiLayer Perceptron based meta-learner instead, predicting the performance of a specific algorithm configuration.

Instead of predicting predictive performance, a meta-regressor can also be trained to predict algorithm training/prediction time, for instance, using an SVM regressor trained on meta-features [128], itself tuned via genetic algorithms [119]. Yang et al. [189] predict configuration runtime using polynomial regression, based only on the number of instances and features. Hutter et al. [68] provide a general treatise on predicting algorithm runtime in various domains.

Most of these meta-models generate promising configurations, but don't actually tune these configurations to t_{new} themselves. Instead, the predictions can be used to warm-start or guide any other optimization technique, which allows for all kinds of combinations of meta-models and optimization techniques. Indeed, some of the work discussed in Sect. 2.3.3 can be seen as using a distance-based meta-model to warm-start Bayesian optimization [48, 54] or evolutionary algorithms [59, 129]. In principle, other meta-models could be used here as well.

Instead of learning the relationship between a task's meta-features and configuration performance, one can also build surrogate models predicting the performance of configurations on specific tasks [40]. One can then learn how to combine these per-task predictions to warm-start or guide optimization techniques on a new task t_{new} [45, 114, 161, 187], as discussed in Sect. 2.2.3. While meta-features could also be used to combine per-task predictions based on task similarity, it is ultimately more effective to gather new observations $P_{i,new}$, since these allow us to refine the task similarity estimates with every new observation [47, 85, 187].

2.3.5 *Pipeline Synthesis*

When creating entire machine learning pipelines [153], the number of configuration options grows dramatically, making it even more important to leverage prior experience. One can control the search space by imposing a fixed structure on the pipeline, fully described by a set of hyperparameters. One can then use the most promising pipelines on similar tasks to warm-start a Bayesian optimization [46, 54].

Other approaches give recommendations for certain pipeline steps [118, 163], and can be leveraged in larger pipeline construction approaches, such as planning [55, 74, 105, 184] or evolutionary techniques [110, 164]. Nguyen et al. [105] construct new pipelines using a beam search focussed on components recommended by a meta-learner, and is itself trained on examples of successful prior pipelines. Bilalli et al. [18] predict which pre-processing techniques are recommended for a given classification algorithm. They build a meta-model per target classification algorithm that, given the t_{new} meta-features, predicts which preprocessing technique should be included in the pipeline. Similarly, Schoenfeld et al. [152] build meta-models predicting when a preprocessing algorithm will improve a particular classifier's accuracy or runtime.

AlphaD3M [38] uses a *self-play* reinforcement learning approach in which the current state is represented by the current pipeline, and actions include the addition, deletion, or replacement of pipeline components. A Monte Carlo Tree Search (MCTS) generates pipelines, which are evaluated to train a recurrent neural network (LSTM) that can predict pipeline performance, in turn producing the action probabilities for the MCTS in the next round. The state description also includes meta-features of the current task, allowing the neural network to learn across tasks. Mosaic [123] also generates pipelines using MCTS, but instead uses a bandits-based approach to select promising pipelines.

2.3.6 To Tune or Not to Tune?

To reduce the number of configuration parameters to be optimized, and to save valuable optimization time in time-constrained settings, meta-models have also been proposed to predict whether or not it is worth tuning a given algorithm *given the meta-features of the task at hand* [133] and how much improvement we can expect from tuning a specific algorithm versus the additional time investment [144]. More focused studies on specific learning algorithms yielded meta-models predicting when it is necessary to tune SVMs [96], what are good default hyperparameters for SVMs given the task (including interpretable meta-models) [97], and how to tune decision trees [95].

2.4 Learning from Prior Models

The final type of meta-data we can learn from are prior machine learning models themselves, i.e., their structure and learned model parameters. In short, we want to train a *meta-learner* L that learns how to train a (base-) learner l_{new} for a new task t_{new}, given similar tasks $t_j \in T$ and the corresponding optimized models $l_j \in \mathcal{L}$, where $\mathcal{L}$ is the space of all possible models. The learner l_j is typically defined by its model parameters $W = \{w_k\}, k = 1 \dots K$ and/or its configuration $\theta_i \in \Theta$.

2.4.1 Transfer Learning

In *transfer learning* [170], we take models trained on one or more *source* tasks t_j, and use them as starting points for creating a model on a similar *target* task t_{new}. This can be done by forcing the target model to be structurally or otherwise similar to the source model(s). This is a generally applicable idea, and transfer learning approaches have been proposed for kernel methods [41, 42], parametric Bayesian models [8, 122, 140], Bayesian networks [107], clustering [168] and reinforcement learning [36, 62]. Neural networks, however, are exceptionally suitable for transfer learning because both the structure and the model parameters of the source models can be used as a good initialization for the target model, yielding a *pre-trained* model which can then be further fine-tuned using the available training data on t_{new} [11, 13, 24, 169]. In some cases, the source network may need to be modified before transferring it [155]. We will focus on neural networks in the remainder of this section.

Especially large image datasets, such as ImageNet [78], have been shown to yield pre-trained models that transfer exceptionally well to other tasks [37, 154]. However, it has also been shown that this approach doesn't work well when the target task is not so similar [191]. Rather than hoping that a pre-trained model 'accidentally' transfers well to a new problem, we can purposefully imbue meta-learners with an inductive bias (learned from many similar tasks) that allows them to learn new tasks much faster, as we will discuss below.

2.4.2 Meta-Learning in Neural Networks

An early meta-learning approach is to create recurrent neural networks (RNNs) able to modify their own weights [149, 150]. During training, they use their own weights as additional input data and observe their own errors to learn how to modify these weights in response to the new task at hand. The updating of the weights is defined in a parametric form that is differentiable end-to-end and can jointly optimize both the network and training algorithm using gradient descent, yet is also very difficult to train. Later work used reinforcement learning across tasks to adapt the search strategy [151] or the learning rate for gradient descent [31] to the task at hand.

Inspired by the feeling that backpropagation is an unlikely learning mechanism for our own brains, Bengio et al. [12] replace backpropagation with simple biologically-inspired parametric rules (or evolved rules [27]) to update the synaptic weights. The parameters are optimized, e.g. using gradient descent or evolution, across a set of input tasks. Runarsson and Jonsson [142] replaced these parametric rules with a single layer neural network. Santoro et al. [146] instead use a memory-augmented neural network to learn how to store and retrieve 'memories' of prior classification tasks. Hochreiter et al. [65] use LSTMs [66] as a meta-learner to train multi-layer perceptrons.

Andrychowicz et al. [6] also replace the optimizer, e.g. stochastic gradient descent, with an LSTM trained on multiple prior tasks. The loss of the meta-learner (optimizer) is defined as the sum of the losses of the base-learners (optimizees), and optimized using gradient descent. At every step, the meta-learner chooses the weight update estimated to reduce the optimizee's loss the most, based on the learned model weights $\{w_k\}$ of the previous step as well as the current performance gradient. Later work generalizes this approach by training an optimizer on synthetic functions, using gradient descent [28]. This allows meta-learners to optimize optimizees even if these do not have access to gradients.

In parallel, Li and Malik [89] proposed a framework for learning optimization algorithms from a reinforcement learning perspective. It represents any particular optimization algorithm as a policy, and then learns this policy via guided policy search. Follow-up work [90] shows how to leverage this approach to learn optimization algorithms for (shallow) neural networks.

The field of *neural architecture search* includes many other methods that build a model of neural network performance for a specific task, for instance using Bayesian optimization or reinforcement learning. See Chap. 3 for an in-depth discussion. However, most of these methods do not (yet) generalize across tasks and are therefore not discussed here.

2.4.3 Few-Shot Learning

A particularly challenging meta-learning problem is to train an accurate deep learning model using only a few training examples, given prior experience with very similar tasks for which we have large training sets available. This is called *few-shot learning*. Humans have an innate ability to do this, and we wish to build machine learning agents that can do the same [82]. A particular example of this is 'K-shot N-way' classification, in which we are given many examples (e.g., images) of certain classes (e.g., objects), and want to learn a classifier l_{new} able to classify N new classes using only K examples of each.

Using prior experience, we can, for instance, learn a common feature representation of all the tasks, start training l_{new} with a better model parameter initialization W_{init} and acquire an inductive bias that helps guide the optimization of the model parameters, so that l_{new} can be trained much faster than otherwise possible.

Earlier work on *one-shot* learning is largely based on hand-engineered features [10, 43, 44, 50]. With meta-learning, however, we hope to learn a common feature representation for all tasks in an end-to-end fashion.

Vinyals et al. [181] state that, to learn from very little data, one should look to non-parameteric models (such as k-nearest neighbors), which use a memory component rather than learning many model parameters. Their meta-learner is a Matching Network that applies the idea of a memory component in a neural net. It learns a common representation for the labelled examples, and *matches* each new test instance to the memorized examples using cosine similarity. The network is trained on minibatches with only a few examples of a specific task each.

Snell et al. [157] propose Prototypical Networks, which map examples to a p-dimensional vector space such that examples of a given output class are close together. It then calculates a prototype (mean vector) for every class. New test instances are mapped to the same vector space and a distance metric is used to create a softmax over all possible classes. Ren et al. [131] extend this approach to semi-supervised learning.

Ravi and Larochelle [126] use an LSTM-based meta-learner to learn an update rule for training a neural network learner. With every new example, the learner returns the current gradient and loss to the LSTM meta-learner, which then updates the model parameters $\{w_k\}$ of the learner. The meta-learner is trained across all prior tasks.

Model-Agnostic Meta-Learning (MAML) [51], on the other hand, does not try to learn an update rule, but instead learns a model parameter initialization W_{init} that generalizes better to similar tasks. Starting from a random $\{w_k\}$, it iteratively selects a batch of prior tasks, and for each it trains the learner on K examples to compute the gradient and loss (on a test set). It then backpropagates the *meta-gradient* to update the weights $\{w_k\}$ in the direction in which they would have been easier to update. In other words, after each iteration, the weights $\{w_k\}$ become a better W_{init} to start finetuning any of the tasks. Finn and Levine [52] also argue that MAML is able to approximate any learning algorithm when using a sufficiently deep fully connected ReLU network and certain losses. They also conclude that the MAML initializations are more resilient to overfitting on small samples, and generalize more widely than meta-learning approaches based on LSTMs.

REPTILE [106] is an approximation of MAML that executes stochastic gradient descent for K iterations on a given task, and then gradually moves the initialization weights in the direction of the weights obtained after the K iterations. The intuition is that every task likely has more than one set of optimal weights $\{w_i^*\}$, and the goal is to find a W_{init} that is close to at least one of those $\{w_i^*\}$ for every task.

Finally, we can also derive a meta-learner from a black-box neural network. Santoro et al. [145] propose Memory-Augmented Neural Networks (MANNs), which train a Neural Turing Machine (NTM) [60], a neural network with augmented memory capabilities, as a meta-learner. This meta-learner can then memorize information about previous tasks and leverage that to learn a learner l_{new}. SNAIL [101] is a generic meta-learner architecture consisting of interleaved temporal convolution and causal attention layers. The convolutional networks learn a common feature vector for the training instances (images) to aggregate information from past experiences. The causal attention layers learn which pieces of information to pick out from the gathered experience to generalize to new tasks.

Overall, the intersection of deep learning and meta-learning proves to be particular fertile ground for groundbreaking new ideas, and we expect this field to become more important over time.

2.4.4 *Beyond Supervised Learning*

Meta-learning is certainly not limited to (semi-)supervised tasks, and has been successfully applied to solve tasks as varied as reinforcement learning, active learning, density estimation and item recommendation. The base-learner may be unsupervised while the meta-learner is supervised, but other combinations are certainly possible as well.

Duan et al. [39] propose an end-to-end reinforcement learning (RL) approach consisting of a task-specific *fast* RL algorithm which is guided by a general-purpose *slow* meta-RL algorithm. The tasks are interrelated Markov Decision Processes (MDPs). The meta-RL algorithm is modeled as an RNN, which receives the observations, actions, rewards and termination flags. The activations of the RNN store the state of the fast RL learner, and the RNN's weights are learned by observing the performance of fast learners across tasks.

In parallel, Wang et al. [182] also proposed to use a deep RL algorithm to train an RNN, receiving the actions and rewards of the previous interval in order to learn a base-level RL algorithm for specific tasks. Rather than using relatively unstructured tasks such as random MDPs, they focus on structured task distributions (e.g., dependent bandits) in which the meta-RL algorithm can exploit the inherent task structure.

Pang et al. [112] offer a meta-learning approach to active learning (AL). The base-learner can be any binary classifier, and the meta-learner is a deep RL network consisting of a deep neural network that learns a representation of the AL problem across tasks, and a policy network that learns the optimal policy, parameterized as weights in the network. The meta-learner receives the current state (the unlabeled point set and base classifier state) and reward (the performance of the base classifier), and emits a query probability, i.e. which points in the unlabeled set to query next.

Reed et al. [127] propose a few-shot approach for density estimation (DE). The goal is to learn a probability distribution over a small number of images of a certain concept (e.g., a handwritten letter) that can be used to generate images of that concept, or compute the probability that an image shows that concept. The approach uses autoregressive image models which factorize the joint distribution into per-pixel factors. Usually these are conditioned on (many) examples of the target concept. Instead, a MAML-based few-shot learner is used, trained on examples of many other (similar) concepts.

Finally, Vartak et al. [178] address the cold-start problem in matrix factorization. They propose a deep neural network architecture that learns a (base) neural network whose biases are adjusted based on task information. While the structure and weights of the neural net recommenders remain fixed, the meta-learner learns how to adjust the biases based on each user's item history.

All these recent new developments illustrate that it is often fruitful to look at problems through a *meta-learning lens* and find new, data-driven approaches to replace hand-engineered base-learners.

2.5 Conclusion

Meta-learning opportunities present themselves in many different ways, and can be embraced using a wide spectrum of learning techniques. Every time we try to learn a certain task, whether successful or not, we gain useful experience that we can leverage to learn new tasks. We should never have to start entirely from scratch. Instead, we should systematically collect our 'learning experiences' and learn from them to build AutoML systems that continuously improve over time, helping us tackle new learning problems ever more efficiently. The more new tasks we encounter, and the more similar those new tasks are, the more we can tap into prior experience, to the point that most of the required learning has already been done beforehand. The ability of computer systems to store virtually infinite amounts of prior learning experiences (in the form of meta-data) opens up a wide range of opportunities to use that experience in completely new ways, and we are only starting to learn how to learn from prior experience effectively. Yet, this is a worthy goal: learning how to learn any task empowers us far beyond knowing how to learn any specific task.

Acknowledgements The author would like to thank Pavel Brazdil, Matthias Feurer, Frank Hutter, Raghu Rajan, Erin Grant, Hugo Larochelle, Jan van Rijn and Jane Wang for many invaluable discussions and feedback on the manuscript.

Bibliography

1. Abdulrahman, S., Brazdil, P., van Rijn, J., Vanschoren, J.: Speeding up Algorithm Selection using Average Ranking and Active Testing by Introducing Runtime. Machine Learning 107, 79–108 (2018)
2. Afif, I.N.: Warm-Starting Deep Learning Model Construction using Meta-Learning. Master's thesis, TU Eindhoven (2018)
3. Agresti, A.: Categorical Data Analysis. Wiley Interscience (2002)
4. Ali, S., Smith-Miles, K.A.: Metalearning approach to automatic kernel selection for support vector machines. Neurocomputing 70(1), 173–186 (2006)
5. Ali, S., Smith-Miles, K.A.: On learning algorithm selection for classification. Applied Soft Computing 6(2), 119–138 (2006)
6. Andrychowicz, M., Denil, M., Gomez, S., Hoffman, M.W., Pfau, D., Schaul, T., Shillingford, B., De Freitas, N.: Learning to learn by gradient descent by gradient descent. In: Advances in Neural Information Processing Systems. pp. 3981–3989 (2016)
7. Arinze, B.: Selecting appropriate forecasting models using rule induction. Omega 22(6), 647–658 (1994)
8. Bakker, B., Heskes, T.: Task Clustering and Gating for Bayesian Multitask Learning. Journal of Machine Learning Research 4, 83–999 (2003)
9. Bardenet, R., Brendel, M., Kégl, B., Sebag, M.: Collaborative hyperparameter tuning. In: Proceedings of ICML 2013. pp. 199–207 (2013)
10. Bart, E., Ullman, S.: Cross-generalization: Learning novel classes from a single example by feature replacement. In: Proceedings of CVPR 2005. pp. 672–679 (2005)
11. Baxter, J.: Learning Internal Representations. In: Advances in Neural Information Processing Systems, NeurIPS (1996)
12. Bengio, S., Bengio, Y., Cloutier, J.: On the search for new learning rules for anns. Neural Processing Letters 2(4), 26–30 (1995)
13. Bengio, Y.: Deep learning of representations for unsupervised and transfer learning. In: ICML Workshop on Unsupervised and Transfer Learning. pp. 17–36 (2012)
14. Bensusan, H., Kalousis, A.: Estimating the predictive accuracy of a classifier. Lecture Notes in Computer Science 2167, 25–36 (2001)
15. Bensusan, H., Giraud-Carrier, C.: Discovering task neighbourhoods through landmark learning performances. In: Proceedings of PKDD 2000. pp. 325–330 (2000)
16. Bensusan, H., Giraud-Carrier, C., Kennedy, C.: A higher-order approach to meta-learning. In: Proceedings of ILP 2000. pp. 33–42 (2000)
17. Bilalli, B., Abelló, A., Aluja-Banet, T.: On the predictive power of meta-features in OpenML. International Journal of Applied Mathematics and Computer Science 27(4), 697–712 (2017)
18. Bilalli, B., Abelló, A., Aluja-Banet, T., Wrembel, R.: Intelligent assistance for data pre-processing. Computer Standards and Interfaces 57, 101–109 (2018)
19. Bischl, B., Kerschke, P., Kotthoff, L., Lindauer, M., Malitsky, Y., Fréchette, A., Hoos, H., Hutter, F., Leyton-Brown, K., Tierney, K., Vanschoren, J.: ASLib: A benchmark library for algorithm selection. Artificial Intelligence 237, 41–58 (2016)
20. Bishop, C.M.: Pattern recognition and machine learning. Springer (2006)

21. Brazdil, P., Soares, C., da Costa, J.P.: Ranking learning algorithms: Using IBL and meta-learning on accuracy and time results. Machine Learning 50(3), 251–277 (2003)
22. Brazdil, P., Giraud-Carrier, C., Soares, C., Vilalta, R.: Metalearning: Applications to Data Mining. Springer-Verlag Berlin Heidelberg (2009)
23. Brazdil, P.B., Soares, C., Da Coasta, J.P.: Ranking learning algorithms: Using IBL and meta-learning on accuracy and time results. Machine Learning 50(3), 251–277 (2003)
24. Caruana, R.: Learning many related tasks at the same time with backpropagation. Neural Information Processing Systems pp. 657–664 (1995)
25. Caruana, R.: Multitask Learning. Machine Learning 28(1), 41–75 (1997)
26. Castiello, C., Castellano, G., Fanelli, A.M.: Meta-data: Characterization of input features for meta-learning. In: 2nd International Conference on Modeling Decisions for Artificial Intelligence (MDAI). pp. 457–468 (2005)
27. Chalmers, D.J.: The evolution of learning: An experiment in genetic connectionism. In: Connectionist Models, pp. 81–90. Elsevier (1991)
28. Chen, Y., Hoffman, M.W., Colmenarejo, S.G., Denil, M., Lillicrap, T.P., Botvinick, M., de Freitas, N.: Learning to learn without gradient descent by gradient descent. In: Proceedings of ICML 2017, PMLR 70, pp. 748–756 (2017)
29. Cheng, W., Hühn, J., Hüllermeier, E.: Decision tree and instance-based learning for label ranking. In: Proceedings of ICML 2009. pp. 161–168 (2009)
30. Cook, W.D., Kress, M., Seiford, L.W.: A general framework for distance-based consensus in ordinal ranking models. European Journal of Operational Research 96(2), 392–397 (1996)
31. Daniel, C., Taylor, J., Nowozin, S.: Learning step size controllers for robust neural network training. In: Proceedings of AAAI 2016. pp. 1519–1525 (2016)
32. Davis, C., Giraud-Carrier, C.: Annotative experts for hyperparameter selection. In: AutoML Workshop at ICML 2018 (2018)
33. De Sa, A., Pinto, W., Oliveira, L.O., Pappa, G.: RECIPE: A grammar-based framework for automatically evolving classification pipelines. In: European Conference on Genetic Programming. pp. 246–261 (2017)
34. Demšar, J.: Statistical Comparisons of Classifiers over Multiple Data Sets. Journal of Machine Learning Research 7, 1–30 (2006)
35. Dietterich, T.: Ensemble methods in machine learning. In: International workshop on multiple classifier systems. pp. 1–15 (2000)
36. Dietterich, T., Busquets, D., Lopez de Mantaras, R., Sierra, C.: Action Refinement in Reinforcement Learning by Probability Smoothing. In: 19th International Conference on Machine Learning. pp. 107–114 (2002)
37. Donahue, J., Jia, Y., Vinyals, O., Hoffman, J., Zhang, N., Tzeng, E., Darrell, T.: DeCAF: A deep convolutional activation feature for generic visual recognition. In: Proceedings of ICML 2014. pp. 647–655 (2014)
38. Drori, I., Krishnamurthy, Y., Rampin, R., de Paula Lourenco, R., Ono, J.P., Cho, K., Silva, C., Freire, J.: AlphaD3M: Machine learning pipeline synthesis. In: AutoML Workshop at ICML (2018)
39. Duan, Y., Schulman, J., Chen, X., Bartlett, P.L., Sutskever, I., Abbeel, P.: RL^2: Fast reinforcement learning via slow reinforcement learning. arXiv preprint arXiv:1611.02779 (2016)
40. Eggensperger, K., Lindauer, M., Hoos, H., Hutter, F., Leyton-Brown, K.: Efficient Benchmarking of Algorithm Configuration Procedures via Model-Based Surrogates . Machine Learning 107, 15–41 (2018)
41. Evgeniou, T., Micchelli, C., Pontil, M.: Learning Multiple Tasks with Kernel Methods. Journal of Machine Learning Research 6, 615–637 (2005)
42. Evgeniou, T., Pontil, M.: Regularized multi-task learning. In: Tenth Conference on Knowledge Discovery and Data Mining (2004)
43. Fei-Fei, L.: Knowledge transfer in learning to recognize visual objects classes. In: International Conference on Development and Learning. Art. 51 (2006)
44. Fei-Fei, L., Fergus, R., Perona, P.: One-shot learning of object categories. Pattern analysis and machine intelligence 28(4), 594–611 (2006)

45. Feurer, M., Letham, B., Bakshy, E.: Scalable meta-learning for Bayesian optimization. arXiv 1802.02219 (2018)
46. Feurer, M., Klein, A., Eggensperger, K., Springenberg, J., Blum, M., Hutter, F.: Efficient and robust automated machine learning. In: Advances in Neural Information Processing Systems 28. pp. 2944–2952 (2015)
47. Feurer, M., Letham, B., Bakshy, E.: Scalable meta-learning for Bayesian optimization using ranking-weighted gaussian process ensembles. In: AutoML Workshop at ICML 2018 (2018)
48. Feurer, M., Springenberg, J.T., Hutter, F.: Using meta-learning to initialize Bayesian optimization of hyperparameters. In: International Conference on Metalearning and Algorithm Selection. pp. 3–10 (2014)
49. Filchenkov, A., Pendryak, A.: Dataset metafeature description for recommending feature selection. In: Proceedings of AINL-ISMW FRUCT 2015. pp. 11–18 (2015)
50. Fink, M.: Object classification from a single example utilizing class relevance metrics. In: Advances in Neural information processing systems, NeurIPS 2005. pp. 449–456 (2005)
51. Finn, C., Abbeel, P., Levine, S.: Model-agnostic meta-learning for fast adaptation of deep networks. In: Proceedings of ICML 2017. pp. 1126–1135 (2017)
52. Finn, C., Levine, S.: Meta-learning and universality: Deep representations and Gradient Descent can Approximate any Learning Algorithm. In: Proceedings of ICLR 2018 (2018)
53. Fürnkranz, J., Petrak, J.: An evaluation of landmarking variants. ECML/PKDD 2001 Workshop on Integrating Aspects of Data Mining, Decision Support and Meta-Learning pp. 57–68 (2001)
54. Fusi, N., Sheth, R., Elibol, H.M.: Probabilistic matrix factorization for automated machine learning. In: Advances in Neural information processing systems, NeurIPS 2018, pp. 3352–3361 (2018)
55. Gil, Y., Yao, K.T., Ratnakar, V., Garijo, D., Ver Steeg, G., Szekely, P., Brekelmans, R., Kejriwal, M., Luo, F., Huang, I.H.: P4ML: A phased performance-based pipeline planner for automated machine learning. In: AutoML Workshop at ICML 2018 (2018)
56. Giraud-Carrier, C.: Metalearning-a tutorial. In: Tutorial at the International Conference on Machine Learning and Applications. pp. 1–45 (2008)
57. Giraud-Carrier, C., Provost, F.: Toward a justification of meta-learning: Is the no free lunch theorem a show-stopper. In: Proceedings of the ICML-2005 Workshop on Meta-learning. pp. 12–19 (2005)
58. Golovin, D., Solnik, B., Moitra, S., Kochanski, G., Karro, J., Sculley, D.: Google vizier: A service for black-box optimization. In: Proceedings of ICDM 2017. pp. 1487–1495 (2017)
59. Gomes, T.A., Prudêncio, R.B., Soares, C., Rossi, A.L., Carvalho, A.: Combining meta-learning and search techniques to select parameters for support vector machines. Neurocomputing 75(1), 3–13 (2012)
60. Graves, A., Wayne, G., Danihelka, I.: Neural turing machines. arXiv preprint arXiv:1410.5401 (2014)
61. Guerra, S.B., Prudêncio, R.B., Ludermir, T.B.: Predicting the performance of learning algorithms using support vector machines as meta- regressors. In: Proceedings of ICANN. pp. 523–532 (2008)
62. Hengst, B.: Discovering Hierarchy in Reinforcement Learning with HEXQ. In: International Conference on Machine Learning. pp. 243–250 (2002)
63. Hilario, M., Kalousis, A.: Fusion of meta-knowledge and meta-data for case-based model selection. Lecture Notes in Computer Science 2168, 180–191 (2001)
64. Ho, T.K., Basu, M.: Complexity measures of supervised classification problems. Pattern Analysis and Machine Intelligence. 24(3), 289–300 (2002)
65. Hochreiter, S., Younger, A., Conwell, P.: Learning to learn using gradient descent. In: Lecture Notes on Computer Science, 2130. pp. 87–94 (2001)
66. Hochreiter, S., Schmidhuber, J.: Long short-term memory. Neural computation 9(8), 1735–1780 (1997)
67. Hutter, F., Hoos, H., Leyton-Brown, K.: An Efficient Approach for Assessing Hyperparameter Importance. In: Proceedings of ICML (2014)

68. Hutter, F., Xu, L., Hoos, H., Leyton-Brown, K.: Algorithm runtime prediction: Methods & evaluation. Artificial Intelligence 206, 79–111 (2014)
69. Jones, D.R., Schonlau, M., Welch, W.J.: Efficient global optimization of expensive black-box functions. Journal of Global Optimization 13(4), 455–492 (1998)
70. Kalousis, A.: Algorithm Selection via Meta-Learning. Ph.D. thesis, University of Geneva, Department of Computer Science (2002)
71. Kalousis, A., Hilario, M.: Representational issues in meta-learning. Proceedings of ICML 2003 pp. 313–320 (2003)
72. Kalousis, A., Hilario, M.: Model selection via meta-learning: a compara- tive study. International Journal on Artificial Intelligence Tools 10(4), 525–554 (2001)
73. Kendall, M.G.: A new measure of rank correlation. Biometrika 30(1/2), 81–93 (1938)
74. Kietz, J.U., Serban, F., Bernstein, A., Fischer, S.: Designing KDD-workflows via HTN-planning for intelligent discovery assistance. In: 5th Planning to Learn Workshop at ECAI 2012 (2012)
75. Kim, J., Kim, S., Choi, S.: Learning to warm-start Bayesian hyperparameter optimization. arXiv preprint arXiv:1710.06219 (2017)
76. Köpf, C., Iglezakis, I.: Combination of task description strategies and case base properties for meta-learning. ECML/PKDD Workshop on Integration and Collaboration Aspects of Data Mining pp. 65–76 (2002)
77. Köpf, C., Taylor, C., Keller, J.: Meta-analysis: From data characterization for meta-learning to meta-regression. In: PKDD Workshop on Data Mining, Decision Support, Meta-Learning and ILP. pp. 15–26 (2000)
78. Krizhevsky, A., Sutskever, I., Hinton, G.E.: Imagenet classification with deep convolutional neural networks. In: Advances in neural information processing systems. pp. 1097–1105 (2012)
79. Kuba, P., Brazdil, P., Soares, C., Woznica, A.: Exploiting sampling and meta-learning for parameter setting support vector machines. In: Proceedings of IBERAMIA 2002. pp. 217–225 (2002)
80. Kullback, S., Leibler, R.A.: On information and sufficiency. The annals of mathematical statistics 22(1), 79–86 (1951)
81. Lacoste, A., Marchand, M., Laviolette, F., Larochelle, H.: Agnostic Bayesian learning of ensembles. In: Proceedings of ICML. pp. 611–619 (2014)
82. Lake, B.M., Ullman, T.D., Tenenbaum, J.B., Gershman, S.J.: Building machines that learn and think like people. Behavior and Brain Science 40 (2017)
83. Leite, R., Brazdil, P.: Predicting relative performance of classifiers from samples. Proceedings of ICML pp. 497–504 (2005)
84. Leite, R., Brazdil, P.: An iterative process for building learning curves and predicting relative performance of classifiers. Lecture Notes in Computer Science 4874, 87–98 (2007)
85. Leite, R., Brazdil, P., Vanschoren, J.: Selecting Classification Algorithms with Active Testing. Lecture Notes in Artificial Intelligence 10934, 117–131 (2012)
86. Leite, R., Brazdil, P.: Active testing strategy to predict the best classification algorithm via sampling and metalearning. In: Proceedings of ECAI 2010. pp. 309–314 (2010)
87. Lemke, C., Budka, M., Gabrys, B.: Metalearning: a survey of trends and technologies. Artificial intelligence review 44(1), 117–130 (2015)
88. Ler, D., Koprinska, I., Chawla, S.: Utilizing regression-based landmarkers within a meta-learning framework for algorithm selection. Technical Report 569. University of Sydney pp. 44–51 (2005)
89. Li, K., Malik, J.: Learning to optimize. In: Proceedings of ICLR 2017 (2017)
90. Li, K., Malik, J.: Learning to optimize neural nets. arXiv preprint arXiv:1703.00441 (2017)
91. Lin, S.: Rank aggregation methods. WIREs Computational Statistics 2, 555–570 (2010)
92. Lindner, G., Studer, R.: AST: Support for algorithm selection with a CBR approach. In: ICML Workshop on Recent Advances in Meta-Learning and Future Work. pp. 38–47. J. Stefan Institute (1999)
93. Lorena, A.C., Maciel, A.I., de Miranda, P.B.C., Costa, I.G., Prudêncio, R.B.C.: Data complexity meta-features for regression problems. Machine Learning 107(1), 209–246 (2018)

94. Luo, G.: A review of automatic selection methods for machine learning algorithms and hyper-parameter values. Network Modeling Analysis in Health Informatics and Bioinformatics 5(1), 18 (2016)
95. Mantovani, R.G., Horváth, T., Cerri, R., Vanschoren, J., de Carvalho, A.C.: Hyper-parameter tuning of a decision tree induction algorithm. In: Brazilian Conference on Intelligent Systems. pp. 37–42 (2016)
96. Mantovani, R.G., Rossi, A.L., Vanschoren, J., Bischl, B., Carvalho, A.C.: To tune or not to tune: recommending when to adjust SVM hyper-parameters via meta-learning. In: Proceedings of IJCNN. pp. 1–8 (2015)
97. Mantovani, R.G., Rossi, A.L., Vanschoren, J., Carvalho, A.C.: Meta-learning recommendation of default hyper-parameter values for SVMs in classifications tasks. In: ECML PKDD Workshop on Meta-Learning and Algorithm Selection (2015)
98. Mantovani, R.: Use of meta-learning for hyperparameter tuning of classification problems. Ph.D. thesis, University of Sao Carlos, Brazil (2018)
99. Michie, D., Spiegelhalter, D.J., Taylor, C.C., Campbell, J.: Machine Learning, Neural and Statistical Classification. Ellis Horwood (1994)
100. Miranda, P., Prudêncio, R.: Active testing for SVM parameter selection. In: Proceedings of IJCNN. pp. 1–8 (2013)
101. Mishra, N., Rohaninejad, M., Chen, X., Abbeel, P.: A simple neural attentive meta-learner. In: Proceedings of ICLR (2018)
102. Misir, M., Sebag, M.: Algorithm Selection as a Collaborative Filtering Problem. Research report, INRIA (2013)
103. Mısır, M., Sebag, M.: Alors: An algorithm recommender system. Artificial Intelligence 244, 291–314 (2017)
104. Nadaraya, E.A.: On estimating regression. Theory of Probability & Its Applications 9(1), 141–142 (1964)
105. Nguyen, P., Hilario, M., Kalousis, A.: Using meta-mining to support data mining workflow planning and optimization. Journal of Artificial Intelligence Research 51, 605–644 (2014)
106. Nichol, A., Achiam, J., Schulman, J.: On first-order meta-learning algorithms. arXiv 1803.02999v2 (2018)
107. Niculescu-Mizil, A., Caruana, R.: Learning the Structure of Related Tasks. In: Proceedings of NIPS Workshop on Inductive Transfer (2005)
108. Nisioti, E., Chatzidimitriou, K., Symeonidis, A.: Predicting hyperparameters from meta-features in binary classification problems. In: AutoML Workshop at ICML (2018)
109. Olier, I., Sadawi, N., Bickerton, G., Vanschoren, J., Grosan, C., Soldatova, L., King, R.: Meta-QSAR: learning how to learn QSARs. Machine Learning 107, 285–311 (2018)
110. Olson, R.S., Bartley, N., Urbanowicz, R.J., Moore, J.H.: Evaluation of a tree-based pipeline optimization tool for automating data science. In: Proceedings of GECCO. pp. 485–492 (2016)
111. Pan, S.J., Yang, Q.: A survey on transfer learning. IEEE Transactions on knowledge and data engineering 22(10), 1345–1359 (2010)
112. Pang, K., Dong, M., Wu, Y., Hospedales, T.: Meta-learning transferable active learning policies by deep reinforcement learning. In: AutoML Workshop at ICML (2018)
113. Peng, Y., Flach, P., Soares, C., Brazdil, P.: Improved dataset characterisation for meta-learning. Lecture Notes in Computer Science 2534, 141–152 (2002)
114. Perrone, V., Jenatton, R., Seeger, M., Archambeau, C.: Multiple adaptive Bayesian linear regression for scalable Bayesian optimization with warm start. In: Advances in Neural information processing systems, NeurIPS 2018 (2018)
115. Pfahringer, B., Bensusan, H., Giraud-Carrier, C.G.: Meta-learning by landmarking various learning algorithms. In: 17th International Conference on Machine Learning (ICML). pp. 743–750 (2000)
116. Pinto, F., Cerqueira, V., Soares, C., Mendes-Moreira, J.: autoBagging: Learning to rank bagging workflows with metalearning. arXiv 1706.09367 (2017)
117. Pinto, F., Soares, C., Mendes-Moreira, J.: Towards automatic generation of metafeatures. In: Proceedings of PAKDD. pp. 215–226 (2016)

118. Post, M.J., van der Putten, P., van Rijn, J.N.: Does Feature Selection Improve Classification? A Large Scale Experiment in OpenML. In: Advances in Intelligent Data Analysis XV. pp. 158–170 (2016)
119. Priya, R., De Souza, B.F., Rossi, A., Carvalho, A.: Using genetic algorithms to improve prediction of execution times of ML tasks. In: Lecture Notes in Computer Science. vol. 7208, pp. 196–207 (2012)
120. Probst, P., Bischl, B., Boulesteix, A.L.: Tunability: Importance of hyperparameters of machine learning algorithms. ArXiv 1802.09596 (2018)
121. Prudêncio, R., Ludermir, T.: Meta-learning approaches to selecting time series models. Neurocomputing 61, 121–137 (2004)
122. Raina, R., Ng, A.Y., Koller, D.: Transfer Learning by Constructing Informative Priors. In: Proceedings of ICML (2006)
123. Rakotoarison, H., Sebag, M.: AutoML with Monte Carlo Tree Search. In: ICML Workshop on AutoML 2018 (2018)
124. Ramachandran, A., Gupta, S., Rana, S., Venkatesh, S.: Information-theoretic transfer learning framework for Bayesian optimisation. In: Proceedings of ECMLPKDD (2018)
125. Ramachandran, A., Gupta, S., Rana, S., Venkatesh, S.: Selecting optimal source for transfer learning in Bayesian optimisation. In: Proceedings of PRICAI. pp. 42–56 (2018)
126. Ravi, S., Larochelle, H.: Optimization as a model for few-shot learning. In: Proceedings of ICLR (2017)
127. Reed, S., Chen, Y., Paine, T., Oord, A.v.d., Eslami, S., Rezende, D., Vinyals, O., de Freitas, N.: Few-shot autoregressive density estimation: Towards learning to learn distributions. In: Proceedings of ICLR 2018 (2018)
128. Reif, M., Shafait, F., Dengel, A.: Prediction of classifier training time including parameter optimization. In: Proceedings of GfKI 2011. pp. 260–271 (2011)
129. Reif, M., Shafait, F., Dengel, A.: Meta-learning for evolutionary parameter optimization of classifiers. Machine learning 87(3), 357–380 (2012)
130. Reif, M., Shafait, F., Goldstein, M., Breuel, T., Dengel, A.: Automatic classifier selection for non-experts. Pattern Analysis and Applications 17(1), 83–96 (2014)
131. Ren, M., Triantafillou, E., Ravi, S., Snell, J., Swersky, K., Tenenbaum, J.B., Larochelle, H., Zemel, R.S.: Meta-learning for semi-supervised few- shot classification. In: Proceedings of ICLR 2018 (2018)
132. Rendle, S.: Factorization machines. In: Proceedings of ICDM 2015. pp. 995–1000 (2010)
133. Ridd, P., Giraud-Carrier, C.: Using metalearning to predict when parameter optimization is likely to improve classification accuracy. In: ECAI Workshop on Meta-learning and Algorithm Selection. pp. 18–23 (2014)
134. van Rijn, J., Abdulrahman, S., Brazdil, P., Vanschoren, J.: Fast Algorithm Selection Using Learning Curves. In: Proceedings of IDA (2015)
135. van Rijn, J., Holmes, G., Pfahringer, B., Vanschoren, J.: The Online Performance Estimation Framework. Heterogeneous Ensemble Learning for Data Streams. Machine Learning 107, 149–176 (2018)
136. van Rijn, J.N., Hutter, F.: Hyperparameter importance across datasets. In: Proceedings of KDD. pp. 2367–2376 (2018)
137. van Rijn, J.N., Holmes, G., Pfahringer, B., Vanschoren, J.: Algorithm selection on data streams. In: Discovery Science. pp. 325–336 (2014)
138. Rivolli, A., Garcia, L., Soares, C., Vanschoren, J., de Carvalho, A.: Towards reproducible empirical research in meta-learning. arXiv preprint 1808.10406 (2018)
139. Robbins, H.: Some aspects of the sequential design of experiments. In: Herbert Robbins Selected Papers, pp. 169–177. Springer (1985)
140. Rosenstein, M.T., Marx, Z., Kaelbling, L.P.: To Transfer or Not To Transfer. In: NIPS Workshop on transfer learning (2005)
141. Rousseeuw, P.J., Hubert, M.: Robust statistics for outlier detection. Wiley Interdisciplinary Reviews: Data Mining and Knowledge Discovery 1(1), 73–79 (2011)

142. Runarsson, T.P., Jonsson, M.T.: Evolution and design of distributed learning rules. In: IEEE Symposium on Combinations of Evolutionary Computation and Neural Networks. pp. 59–63 (2000)
143. Salama, M.A., Hassanien, A.E., Revett, K.: Employment of neural network and rough set in meta-learning. Memetic Computing 5(3), 165–177 (2013)
144. Sanders, S., Giraud-Carrier, C.: Informing the use of hyperparameter optimization through metalearning. In: Proceedings of ICDM 2017. pp. 1051–1056 (2017)
145. Santoro, A., Bartunov, S., Botvinick, M., Wierstra, D., Lillicrap, T.: Meta-learning with memory-augmented neural networks. In: International conference on machine learning. pp. 1842–1850 (2016)
146. Santoro, A., Bartunov, S., Botvinick, M., Wierstra, D., Lillicrap, T.: One-shot learning with memory-augmented neural networks. arXiv preprint arXiv:1605.06065 (2016)
147. dos Santos, P., Ludermir, T., Prudêncio, R.: Selection of time series forecasting models based on performance information. 4th International Conference on Hybrid Intelligent Systems pp. 366–371 (2004)
148. Schilling, N., Wistuba, M., Drumond, L., Schmidt-Thieme, L.: Hyperparameter optimization with factorized multilayer perceptrons. In: Proceedings of ECML PKDD. pp. 87–103 (2015)
149. Schmidhuber, J.: Learning to control fast-weight memories: An alternative to dynamic recurrent networks. Neural Computing 4(1), 131–139 (1992)
150. Schmidhuber, J.: A neural network that embeds its own meta-levels. In: Proceedings of ICNN. pp. 407–412 (1993)
151. Schmidhuber, J., Zhao, J., Wiering, M.: Shifting inductive bias with success-story algorithm, adaptive levin search, and incremental self-improvement. Machine Learning 28(1), 105–130 (1997)
152. Schoenfeld, B., Giraud-Carrier, C., Poggeman, M., Christensen, J., Seppi, K.: Feature selection for high-dimensional data: A fast correlation-based filter solution. In: AutoML Workshop at ICML (2018)
153. Serban, F., Vanschoren, J., Kietz, J., Bernstein, A.: A survey of intelligent assistants for data analysis. ACM Computing Surveys 45(3), Art.31 (2013)
154. Sharif Razavian, A., Azizpour, H., Sullivan, J., Carlsson, S.: Cnn features off-the-shelf: an astounding baseline for recognition. In: Proceedings of CVPR 2014. pp. 806–813 (2014)
155. Sharkey, N.E., Sharkey, A.J.C.: Adaptive Generalization. Artificial Intelligence Review 7, 313–328 (1993)
156. Smith-Miles, K.A.: Cross-disciplinary perspectives on meta-learning for algorithm selection. ACM Computing Surveys 41(1), 1–25 (2009)
157. Snell, J., Swersky, K., Zemel, R.: Prototypical networks for few-shot learning. In: Neural Information Processing Systems. pp. 4077–4087 (2017)
158. Soares, C., Brazdil, P., Kuba, P.: A meta-learning method to select the kernel width in support vector regression. Machine Learning 54, 195–209 (2004)
159. Soares, C., Ludermir, T., Carvalho, F.D.: An analysis of meta-learning techniques for ranking clustering algorithms applied to artificial data. Lecture Notes in Computer Science 5768, 131–140 (2009)
160. Soares, C., Petrak, J., Brazdil, P.: Sampling based relative landmarks: Systematically testdriving algorithms before choosing. Lecture Notes in Computer Science 3201, 250–261 (2001)
161. Springenberg, J., Klein, A., Falkner, S., Hutter, F.: Bayesian optimization with robust Bayesian neural networks. In: Advances in Neural Information Processing Systems (2016)
162. Stern, D.H., Samulowitz, H., Herbrich, R., Graepel, T., Pulina, L., Tacchella, A.: Collaborative expert portfolio management. In: Proceedings of AAAI. pp. 179–184 (2010)
163. Strang, B., van der Putten, P., van Rijn, J.N., Hutter, F.: Don't Rule Out Simple Models Prematurely. In: Advances in Intelligent Data Analysis (2018)
164. Sun, Q., Pfahringer, B., Mayo, M.: Towards a Framework for Designing Full Model Selection and Optimization Systems. In: International Workshop on Multiple Classifier Systems. pp. 259–270 (2013)

165. Sun, Q., Pfahringer, B.: Pairwise meta-rules for better meta-learning-based algorithm ranking. Machine Learning 93(1), 141–161 (2013)
166. Swersky, K., Snoek, J., Adams, R.P.: Multi-task Bayesian optimization. In: Advances in neural information processing systems. pp. 2004–2012 (2013)
167. Thompson, W.R.: On the likelihood that one unknown probability exceeds another in view of the evidence of two samples. Biometrika 25(3/4), 285–294 (1933)
168. Thrun, S.: Lifelong Learning Algorithms. In: Learning to Learn, chap. 8, pp. 181–209. Kluwer Academic Publishers, MA (1998)
169. Thrun, S., Mitchell, T.: Learning One More Thing. In: Proceedings of IJCAI. pp. 1217–1223 (1995)
170. Thrun, S., Pratt, L.: Learning to Learn: Introduction and Overview. In: Learning to Learn, pp. 3–17. Kluwer (1998)
171. Todorovski, L., Blockeel, H., Džeroski, S.: Ranking with predictive clustering trees. Lecture Notes in Artificial Intelligence 2430, 444–455 (2002)
172. Todorovski, L., Brazdil, P., Soares, C.: Report on the experiments with feature selection in meta-level learning. PKDD 2000 Workshop on Data mining, Decision support, Meta-learning and ILP pp. 27–39 (2000)
173. Todorovski, L., Dzeroski, S.: Experiments in meta-level learning with ILP. Lecture Notes in Computer Science 1704, 98–106 (1999)
174. Vanschoren, J., van Rijn, J.N., Bischl, B., Torgo, L.: OpenML: networked science in machine learning. ACM SIGKDD Explorations Newsletter 15(2), 49–60 (2014)
175. Vanschoren, J.: Understanding Machine Learning Performance with Experiment Databases. Ph.D. thesis, Leuven Univeristy (2010)
176. Vanschoren, J.: Meta-learning: A survey. arXiv:1810.03548 (2018)
177. Vanschoren, J., Blockeel, H., Pfahringer, B., Holmes, G.: Experiment databases. Machine Learning 87(2), 127–158 (2012)
178. Vartak, M., Thiagarajan, A., Miranda, C., Bratman, J., Larochelle, H.: A meta-learning perspective on cold-start recommendations for items. In: Advances in Neural Information Processing Systems. pp. 6904–6914 (2017)
179. Vilalta, R.: Understanding accuracy performance through concept characterization and algorithm analysis. ICML Workshop on Recent Advances in Meta-Learning and Future Work (1999)
180. Vilalta, R., Drissi, Y.: A characterization of difficult problems in classification. Proceedings of ICMLA (2002)
181. Vinyals, O., Blundell, C., Lillicrap, T., Wierstra, D., et al.: Matching networks for one shot learning. In: Advances in Neural Information Processing Systems. pp. 3630–3638 (2016)
182. Weerts, H., Meuller, M., Vanschoren, J.: Importance of tuning hyperparameters of machine learning algorithms. Technical report, TU Eindhoven (2018)
183. Weerts, H., Meuller, M., Vanschoren, J.: Importance of tuning hyperparameters of machine learning algorithms. Tech. rep., TU Eindhoven (2018)
184. Wever, M., Mohr, F., Hüllermeier, E.: Ml-plan for unlimited-length machine learning pipelines. In: AutoML Workshop at ICML 2018 (2018)
185. Wistuba, M., Schilling, N., Schmidt-Thieme, L.: Hyperparameter search space pruning, a new component for sequential model-based hyperparameter optimization. In: ECML PKDD 2015. pp. 104–119 (2015)
186. Wistuba, M., Schilling, N., Schmidt-Thieme, L.: Learning hyperparameter optimization initializations. In: 2015 IEEE International Conference on Data Science and Advanced Analytics (DSAA). pp. 1–10 (2015)
187. Wolpert, D., Macready, W.: No free lunch theorems for search. Technical Report SFI-TR-95-02-010, The Santa Fe Institute (1996)

188. Yang, C., Akimoto, Y., Kim, D., Udell, M.: OBOE: Collaborative filtering for automl initialization. In: NeurIPS 2018 Workshop on Metalearning (2018)
189. Yang, C., Akimoto, Y., Kim, D., Udell, M.: Oboe: Collaborative filtering for automl initialization. arXiv preprint arXiv:1808.03233 (2018)
190. Yogatama, D., Mann, G.: Efficient transfer learning method for automatic hyperparameter tuning. In: AI and Statistics. pp. 1077–1085 (2014)
191. Yosinski, J., Clune, J., Bengio, Y., Lipson, H.: How transferable are features in deep neural networks? In: Advances in neural information processing systems. pp. 3320–3328 (2014)

Chapter 3
Neural Architecture Search

Thomas Elsken, Jan Hendrik Metzen, and Frank Hutter

Abstract Deep Learning has enabled remarkable progress over the last years on a variety of tasks, such as image recognition, speech recognition, and machine translation. One crucial aspect for this progress are novel neural architectures. Currently employed architectures have mostly been developed manually by human experts, which is a time-consuming and error-prone process. Because of this, there is growing interest in automated *neural architecture search* methods. We provide an overview of existing work in this field of research and categorize them according to three dimensions: search space, search strategy, and performance estimation strategy.

3.1 Introduction

The success of deep learning in perceptual tasks is largely due to its automation of the feature engineering process: hierarchical feature extractors are learned in an end-to-end fashion from data rather than manually designed. This success has been

---

The original version of this chapter was revised: Primary affiliation of the Author "Thomas Elsken" has been updated now. The correction to this chapter is available at
https://doi.org/10.1007/978-3-030-05318-5_11

T. Elsken (✉)
Bosch Center for Artificial Intelligence, Robert Bosch GmbH, Renningen, Baden-Württemberg, Germany

Department of Computer Science, University of Freiburg, Freiburg, Baden-Württemberg, Germany
e-mail: elsken@informatik.uni-freiburg.de; thomas.elsken@de.bosch.com

J. H. Metzen
Bosch Center for Artificial Intelligence, Robert Bosch GmbH, Renningen, Baden-Württemberg, Germany

F. Hutter
Department of Computer Science, University of Freiburg, Freiburg, Germany

F. Hutter et al. (eds.), *Automated Machine Learning*, The Springer Series on Challenges in Machine Learning, https://doi.org/10.1007/978-3-030-05318-5_3

accompanied, however, by a rising demand for *architecture engineering*, where increasingly more complex neural architectures are designed manually. *Neural Architecture Search* (NAS), the process of automating architecture engineering, is thus a logical next step in automating machine learning. NAS can be seen as subfield of AutoML and has significant overlap with hyperparameter optimization and meta-learning (which are described in Chaps. 1 and 2 of this book, respectively). We categorize methods for NAS according to three dimensions: search space, search strategy, and performance estimation strategy:

- **Search Space.** The search space defines which architectures can be represented in principle. Incorporating prior knowledge about properties well-suited for a task can reduce the size of the search space and simplify the search. However, this also introduces a human bias, which may prevent finding novel architectural building blocks that go beyond the current human knowledge.

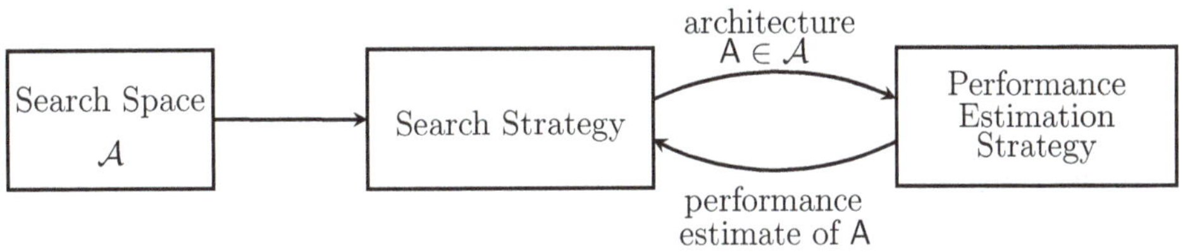

Fig. 3.1 Abstract illustration of Neural Architecture Search methods. A search strategy selects an architecture A from a predefined search space $\mathcal{A}$. The architecture is passed to a performance estimation strategy, which returns the estimated performance of A to the search strategy

- **Search Strategy.** The search strategy details how to explore the search space. It encompasses the classical exploration-exploitation trade-off since, on the one hand, it is desirable to find well-performing architectures quickly, while on the other hand, premature convergence to a region of suboptimal architectures should be avoided.
- **Performance Estimation Strategy.** The objective of NAS is typically to find architectures that achieve high predictive performance on unseen data. *Performance Estimation* refers to the process of estimating this performance: the simplest option is to perform a standard training and validation of the architecture on data, but this is unfortunately computationally expensive and limits the number of architectures that can be explored. Much recent research therefore focuses on developing methods that reduce the cost of these performance estimations.

We refer to Fig. 3.1 for an illustration. The chapter is also structured according to these three dimensions: we start with discussing search spaces in Sect. 3.2, cover search strategies in Sect. 3.3, and outline approaches to performance estimation in Sect. 3.4. We conclude with an outlook on future directions in Sect. 3.5.

This chapter is based on a very recent survey article [23].

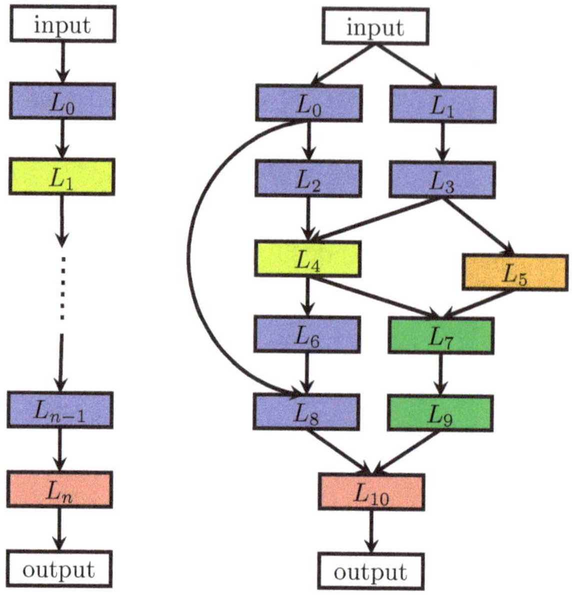

Fig. 3.2 An illustration of different architecture spaces. Each node in the graphs corresponds to a layer in a neural network, e.g., a convolutional or pooling layer. Different layer types are visualized by different colors. An edge from layer L_i to layer L_j denotes that L_j receives the output of L_i as input. Left: an element of a chain-structured space. Right: an element of a more complex search space with additional layer types and multiple branches and skip connections

3.2 Search Space

The search space defines which neural architectures a NAS approach might discover in principle. We now discuss common search spaces from recent works.

A relatively simple search space is the space of *chain-structured neural networks*, as illustrated in Fig. 3.2 (left). A chain-structured neural network architecture A can be written as a sequence of n layers, where the i'th layer L_i receives its input from layer $i - 1$ and its output serves as the input for layer $i + 1$, i.e., $\mathsf{A} = L_n \circ \ldots L_1 \circ L_0$. The search space is then parametrized by: (i) the (maximum) number of layers n (possibly unbounded); (ii) the type of operation every layer can execute, e.g., pooling, convolution, or more advanced layer types like depthwise separable convolutions [13] or dilated convolutions [68]; and (iii) hyperparameters associated with the operation, e.g., number of filters, kernel size and strides for a convolutional layer [4, 10, 59], or simply number of units for fully-connected networks [41]. Note that the parameters from (iii) are conditioned on (ii), hence the parametrization of the search space is not fixed-length but rather a conditional space.

Recent work on NAS [9, 11, 21, 22, 49, 75] incorporate modern design elements known from hand-crafted architectures such as skip connections, which allow to build complex, *multi-branch networks*, as illustrated in Fig. 3.2 (right). In this case the input of layer i can be formally described as a function $g_i(L_{i-1}^{out}, \ldots, L_0^{out})$ combining previous layer outputs. Employing such a function results in significantly more degrees of freedom. Special cases of these multi-branch architectures are (i) the chain-structured networks (by setting $g_i(L_{i-1}^{out}, \ldots, L_0^{out}) = L_{i-1}^{out}$), (ii) Residual Networks [28], where previous layer outputs are summed ($g_i(L_{i-1}^{out}, \ldots, L_0^{out}) = L_{i-1}^{out} + L_j^{out}, j < i$) and (iii) DenseNets [29], where previous layer outputs are concatenated ($g_i(L_{i-1}^{out}, \ldots, L_0^{out}) = concat(L_{i-1}^{out}, \ldots, L_0^{out})$).

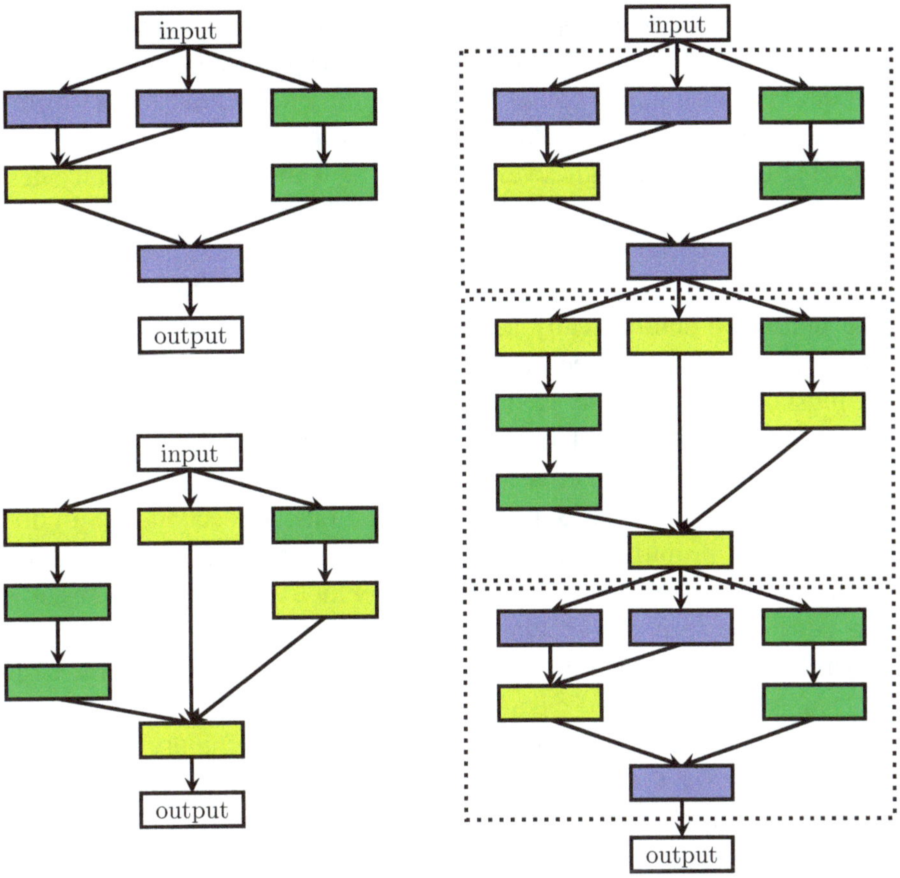

Fig. 3.3 Illustration of the cell search space. Left: Two different cells, e.g., a normal cell (top) and a reduction cell (bottom) [75]. Right: an architecture built by stacking the cells sequentially. Note that cells can also be combined in a more complex manner, such as in multi-branch spaces, by simply replacing layers with cells

Motivated by hand-crafted architectures consisting of repeated motifs [28, 29, 62], Zoph et al. [75] and Zhong et al. [71] propose to search for such motifs, dubbed *cells* or *blocks*, respectively, rather than for whole architectures. Zoph et al. [75] optimize two different kind of cells: a *normal cell* that preservers the dimensionality of the input and a *reduction cell* which reduces the spatial dimension. The final architecture is then built by stacking these cells in a predefined manner, as illustrated in Fig. 3.3. This search space has two major advantages compared to the ones discussed above:

1. The size of the search space is drastically reduced since cells can be comparably small. For example, Zoph et al. [75] estimate a seven-times speed-up compared to their previous work [74] while achieving better performance.
2. Cells can more easily be transferred to other datasets by adapting the number of cells used within a model. Indeed, Zoph et al. [75] transfer cells optimized on CIFAR-10 to ImageNet and achieve state-of-the-art performance.

Consequently, this cell-based search space was also successfully employed by many later works [11, 22, 37, 39, 46, 49, 72]. However, a new design-choice arises when using a cell-based search space, namely how to choose the *meta-architecture*: how many cells shall be used and how should they be connected to build the actual model? For example, Zoph et al. [75] build a sequential model from cells, in which each cell receives the outputs of the two preceding cells as input, while Cai et al. [11] employ the high-level structure of well-known manually designed architectures, such as DenseNet [29], and use their cells within these models. In principle, cells can be combined arbitrarily, e.g., within the multi-branch space described above by simply replacing layers with cells. Ideally, the meta-architecture should be optimized automatically as part of NAS; otherwise one easily ends up doing meta-architecture engineering and the search for the cell becomes overly simple if most of the complexity is already accounted for by the meta-architecture.

One step in the direction of optimizing meta-architectures is the hierarchical search space introduced by Liu et al. [38], which consists of several levels of motifs. The first level consists of the set of primitive operations, the second level of different motifs that connect primitive operations via a direct acyclic graphs, the third level of motifs that encode how to connect second-level motifs, and so on. The cell-based search space can be seen as a special case of this hierarchical search space where the number of levels is three, the second level motifs corresponds to the cells, and the third level is the hard-coded meta-architecture.

The choice of the search space largely determines the difficulty of the optimization problem: even for the case of the search space based on a single cell with fixed meta-architecture, the optimization problem remains (i) non-continuous and (ii) relatively high-dimensional (since more complex models tend to perform better, resulting in more design choices). We note that the architectures in many search spaces can be written as fixed-length vectors; e.g., the search space for each of the two cells by Zoph et al. [75] can be written as a 40-dimensional search space with categorical dimensions, each of which chooses between a small number of different building blocks and inputs. Similarly, unbounded search spaces can be constrained to have a maximal depth, giving rise to fixed-size search spaces with (potentially many) conditional dimensions.

In the next section, we discuss Search Strategies that are well-suited for these kinds of search spaces.

3.3 Search Strategy

Many different search strategies can be used to explore the space of neural architectures, including random search, Bayesian optimization, evolutionary methods, reinforcement learning (RL), and gradient-based methods. Historically, evolutionary algorithms were already used by many researchers to evolve neural architectures (and often also their weights) decades ago [see, e.g., 2, 25, 55, 56]. Yao [67] provides a literature review of work earlier than 2000.

Bayesian optimization celebrated several early successes in NAS since 2013, leading to state-of-the-art vision architectures [7], state-of-the-art performance for CIFAR-10 without data augmentation [19], and the first automatically-tuned neural networks to win competition datasets against human experts [41]. NAS became a mainstream research topic in the machine learning community after Zoph and Le [74] obtained competitive performance on the CIFAR-10 and Penn Treebank benchmarks with a search strategy based on reinforcement learning. While Zoph and Le [74] use vast computational resources to achieve this result (800 GPUs for three to four weeks), after their work, a wide variety of methods have been published in quick succession to reduce the computational costs and achieve further improvements in performance.

To frame NAS as a *reinforcement learning* (RL) problem [4, 71, 74, 75], the generation of a neural architecture can be considered to be the agent's action, with the action space identical to the search space. The agent's reward is based on an estimate of the performance of the trained architecture on unseen data (see Sect. 3.4). Different RL approaches differ in how they represent the agent's policy and how they optimize it: Zoph and Le [74] use a recurrent neural network (RNN) policy to sequentially sample a string that in turn encodes the neural architecture. They initially trained this network with the REINFORCE policy gradient algorithm, but in follow-up work use Proximal Policy Optimization (PPO) instead [75]. Baker et al. [4] use Q-learning to train a policy which sequentially chooses a layer's type and corresponding hyperparameters. An alternative view of these approaches is as sequential decision processes in which the policy samples actions to generate the architecture sequentially, the environment's "state" contains a summary of the actions sampled so far, and the (undiscounted) reward is obtained only after the final action. However, since no interaction with an environment occurs during this sequential process (no external state is observed, and there are no intermediate rewards), we find it more intuitive to interpret the architecture sampling process as the sequential generation of a single action; this simplifies the RL problem to a stateless multi-armed bandit problem.

A related approach was proposed by Cai et al. [10], who frame NAS as a sequential decision process: in their approach the state is the current (partially trained) architecture, the reward is an estimate of the architecture's performance, and the action corresponds to an application of function-preserving mutations, dubbed network morphisms [12, 63], see also Sect. 3.4, followed by a phase of training the network. In order to deal with variable-length network architectures, they use a bi-directional LSTM to encode architectures into a fixed-length representation. Based on this encoded representation, actor networks decide on the sampled action. The combination of these two components constitute the policy, which is trained end-to-end with the REINFORCE policy gradient algorithm. We note that this approach will not visit the same state (architecture) twice so that strong generalization over the architecture space is required from the policy.

An alternative to using RL are *neuro-evolutionary* approaches that use evolutionary algorithms for optimizing the neural architecture. The first such approach for designing neural networks we are aware of dates back almost three decades: Miller et al. [44] use genetic algorithms to propose architectures and use back-propagation to optimize their weights. Many neuro-evolutionary approaches since then [2, 55, 56] use genetic algorithms to optimize both the neural architecture and its weights; however, when scaling to contemporary neural architectures with millions of weights for supervised learning tasks, SGD-based weight optimization methods currently outperform evolutionary ones.[1] More recent neuro-evolutionary approaches [22, 38, 43, 49, 50, 59, 66] therefore again use gradient-based methods for optimizing weights and solely use evolutionary algorithms for optimizing the neural architecture itself. Evolutionary algorithms evolve a population of models, i.e., a set of (possibly trained) networks; in every evolution step, at least one model from the population is sampled and serves as a parent to generate offsprings by applying mutations to it. In the context of NAS, mutations are local operations, such as adding or removing a layer, altering the hyperparameters of a layer, adding skip connections, as well as altering training hyperparameters. After training the offsprings, their fitness (e.g., performance on a validation set) is evaluated and they are added to the population.

Neuro-evolutionary methods differ in how they sample parents, update populations, and generate offsprings. For example, Real et al. [50], Real et al. [49], and Liu et al. [38] use tournament selection [27] to sample parents, whereas Elsken et al. [22] sample parents from a multi-objective Pareto front using an inverse density. Real et al. [50] remove the worst individual from a population, while Real et al. [49] found it beneficial to remove the oldest individual (which decreases greediness), and Liu et al. [38] do not remove individuals at all. To generate offspring, most approaches initialize child networks randomly, while Elsken et al. [22] employ Lamarckian inheritance, i.e, knowledge (in the form of learned weights) is passed on from a parent network to its children by using network morphisms. Real et al. [50] also let an offspring inherit all parameters of its parent that are not affected by the applied mutation; while this inheritance is not strictly function-preserving it might also speed up learning compared to a random initialization. Moreover, they also allow mutating the learning rate which can be seen as a way for optimizing the learning rate schedule during NAS.

Real et al. [49] conduct a case study comparing RL, evolution, and random search (RS), concluding that RL and evolution perform equally well in terms of final test accuracy, with evolution having better anytime performance and finding smaller models. Both approaches consistently perform better than RS in their experiments, but with a rather small margin: RS achieved test errors of approximately 4% on CIFAR-10, while RL and evolution reached approximately 3.5% (after "model augmentation" where depth and number of filters was increased; the difference on the actual, non-augmented search space was approx. 2%). The difference was even smaller for Liu et al. [38], who reported a test error of 3.9% on CIFAR-10 and a top-1 validation error of 21.0% on ImageNet for RS, compared to 3.75% and 20.3% for their evolution-based method, respectively.

[1]Some recent work shows that evolving even millions of weights is competitive to gradient-based optimization when only high-variance estimates of the gradient are available, e.g., for reinforcement learning tasks [15, 51, 57]. Nonetheless, for supervised learning tasks gradient-based optimization is by far the most common approach.

Bayesian Optimization (BO, see, e.g., [53]) is one of the most popular methods for hyperparameter optimization (see also Chap. 1 of this book), but it has not been applied to NAS by many groups since typical BO toolboxes are based on Gaussian processes and focus on low-dimensional continuous optimization problems. Swersky et al. [60] and Kandasamy et al. [31] derive kernel functions for architecture search spaces in order to use classic GP-based BO methods, but so far without achieving new state-of-the-art performance. In contrast, several works use tree-based models (in particular, treed Parzen estimators [8], or random forests [30]) to effectively search very high-dimensional conditional spaces and achieve state-of-the-art performance on a wide range of problems, optimizing both neural architectures and their hyperparameters jointly [7, 19, 41, 69]. While a full comparison is lacking, there is preliminary evidence that these approaches can also outperform evolutionary algorithms [33].

Architectural search spaces have also been explored in a *hierarchical* manner, e.g., in combination with evolution [38] or by sequential model-based optimization [37]. Negrinho and Gordon [45] and Wistuba [65] exploit the tree-structure of their search space and use *Monte Carlo Tree Search*. Elsken et al. [21] propose a simple yet well performing *hill climbing* algorithm that discovers high-quality architectures by greedily moving in the direction of better performing architectures without requiring more sophisticated exploration mechanisms.

In contrast to the gradient-free optimization methods above, Liu et al. [39] propose a continuous relaxation of the search space to enable *gradient-based optimization*: instead of fixing a single operation o_i (e.g., convolution or pooling) to be executed at a specific layer, the authors compute a convex combination from a set of operations $\{o_1, \ldots, o_m\}$. More specifically, given a layer input x, the layer output y is computed as $y = \sum_{i=1}^{m} \lambda_i o_i(x)$, $\lambda_i \geq 0$, $\sum_{i=1}^{m} \lambda_i = 1$, where the convex coefficients λ_i effectively parameterize the network architecture. Liu et al. [39] then optimize both the network weights and the network architecture by alternating gradient descent steps on training data for weights and on validation data for architectural parameters such as λ. Eventually, a discrete architecture is obtained by choosing the operation i with $i = \arg\max_i \lambda_i$ for every layer. Shin et al. [54] and Ahmed and Torresani [1] also employ gradient-based optimization of neural architectures, however they only consider optimizing layer hyperparameters or connectivity patterns, respectively.

3.4 Performance Estimation Strategy

The search strategies discussed in Sect. 3.3 aim at finding a neural architecture A that maximizes some performance measure, such as accuracy on unseen data. To guide their search process, these strategies need to estimate the performance of a given architecture A they consider. The simplest way of doing this is to train A on training data and evaluate its performance on validation data. However, training each architecture to be evaluated from scratch frequently yields computational demands in the order of thousands of GPU days for NAS [49, 50, 74, 75].

To reduce this computational burden, performance can be estimated based on *lower fidelities* of the actual performance after full training (also denoted as proxy metrics). Such lower fidelities include shorter training times [69, 75], training on a subset of the data [34], on lower-resolution images [14], or with less filters per layer [49, 75]. While these low-fidelity approximations reduce the computational cost, they also introduce bias in the estimate as performance will typically be underestimated. This may not be problematic as long as the search strategy only relies on ranking different architectures and the relative ranking remains stable. However, recent results indicate that this relative ranking can change dramatically when the difference between the cheap approximations and the "full" evaluation is too big [69], arguing for a gradual increase in fidelities [24, 35].

Another possible way of estimating an architecture's performance builds upon learning curve extrapolation [5, 19, 32, 48, 61]. Domhan et al. [19] propose to extrapolate initial learning curves and terminate those predicted to perform poorly to speed up the architecture search process. Baker et al. [5], Klein et al. [32], Rawal and Miikkulainen [48], Swersky et al. [61] also consider architectural hyperparameters for predicting which partial learning curves are most promising. Training a surrogate model for predicting the performance of novel architectures is also proposed by Liu et al. [37], who do not employ learning curve extrapolation but support predicting performance based on architectural/cell properties and extrapolate to architectures/cells with larger size than seen during training. The main challenge for predicting the performances of neural architectures is that, in order to speed up the search process, good predictions in a relatively large search space need to be made based on relatively few evaluations.

Another approach to speed up performance estimation is to initialize the weights of novel architectures based on weights of other architectures that have been trained before. One way of achieving this, dubbed *network morphisms* [64], allows modifying an architecture while leaving the function represented by the network unchanged [10, 11, 21, 22]. This allows increasing capacity of networks successively and retaining high performance without requiring training from scratch. Continuing training for a few epochs can also make use of the additional capacity introduced by network morphisms. An advantage of these approaches is that they allow search spaces without an inherent upper bound on the architecture's size [21]; on the other hand, strict network morphisms can only make architectures larger and may thus lead to overly complex architectures. This can be attenuated by employing approximate network morphisms that allow shrinking architectures [22].

One-Shot Architecture Search is another promising approach for speeding up performance estimation, which treats all architectures as different subgraphs of a supergraph (the one-shot model) and shares weights between architectures that have edges of this supergraph in common [6, 9, 39, 46, 52]. Only the weights of a single one-shot model need to be trained (in one of various ways), and architectures (which are just subgraphs of the one-shot model) can then be evaluated without any separate training by inheriting trained weights from the one-shot model. This greatly speeds up performance estimation of architectures, since no training is required (only evaluating performance on validation data). This approach typically incurs a large bias as it underestimates the actual performance of architectures severely; nevertheless, it allows ranking architectures reliably, since the estimated performance correlates strongly with the actual performance [6]. Different one-shot NAS methods differ in how the one-shot model is trained: ENAS [46] learns an RNN controller that samples architectures from the search space and trains the one-shot model based on approximate gradients obtained through REINFORCE. DARTS [39] optimizes all weights of the one-shot model jointly with a continuous relaxation of the search space obtained by placing a mixture of candidate operations on each edge of the one-shot model. Bender et al. [6] only train the one-shot model once and show that this is sufficient when deactivating parts of this model stochastically during training using path dropout. While ENAS and DARTS optimize a distribution over architectures during training, the approach of Bender et al. [6] can be seen as using a fixed distribution. The high performance obtainable by the approach of Bender et al. [6] indicates that the combination of weight sharing and a fixed (carefully chosen) distribution might (perhaps surprisingly) be the only required ingredients for one-shot NAS. Related to these approaches is meta-learning of hypernetworks that generate weights for novel architectures and thus requires only training the hypernetwork but not the architectures themselves [9]. The main difference here is that weights are not strictly shared but generated by the shared hypernetwork (conditional on the sampled architecture).

A general limitation of one-shot NAS is that the supergraph defined a-priori restricts the search space to its subgraphs. Moreover, approaches which require that the entire supergraph resides in GPU memory during architecture search will be restricted to relatively small supergraphs and search spaces accordingly and are thus typically used in combination with cell-based search spaces. While approaches based on weight-sharing have substantially reduced the computational resources required for NAS (from thousands to a few GPU days), it is currently not well understood which biases they introduce into the search if the sampling distribution of architectures is optimized along with the one-shot model. For instance, an initial bias in exploring certain parts of the search space more than others might lead to the weights of the one-shot model being better adapted for these architectures, which in turn would reinforce the bias of the search to these parts of the search space. This might result in premature convergence of NAS and might be one advantage of a fixed sampling distribution as used by Bender et al. [6]. In general, a more systematic analysis of biases introduced by different performance estimators would be a desirable direction for future work.

3.5 Future Directions

In this section, we discuss several current and future directions for research on NAS. Most existing work has focused on NAS for image classification. On the one hand, this provides a challenging benchmark since a lot of manual engineering has been devoted to finding architectures that perform well in this domain and are not easily outperformed by NAS. On the other hand, it is relatively easy to define a well-suited search space by utilizing knowledge from manual engineering. This in turn makes it unlikely that NAS will find architectures that substantially outperform existing ones considerably since the found architectures cannot differ fundamentally. We thus consider it important to go beyond image classification problems by applying NAS to less explored domains. Notable first steps in this direction are applying NAS to language modeling [74], music modeling [48], image restoration [58] and network compression [3]; applications to reinforcement learning, generative adversarial networks, semantic segmentation, or sensor fusion could be further promising future directions.

An alternative direction is developing NAS methods for multi-task problems [36, 42] and for multi-objective problems [20, 22, 73], in which measures of resource efficiency are used as objectives along with the predictive performance on unseen data. Likewise, it would be interesting to extend RL/bandit approaches, such as those discussed in Sect. 3.3, to learn policies that are conditioned on a state that encodes task properties/resource requirements (i.e., turning the setting into a contextual bandit). A similar direction was followed by Ramachandran and Le [47] in extending one-shot NAS to generate different architectures depending on the task or instance on-the-fly. Moreover, applying NAS to searching for architectures that are more robust to adversarial examples [17] is an intriguing recent direction.

Related to this is research on defining more general and flexible search spaces. For instance, while the cell-based search space provides high transferability between different image classification tasks, it is largely based on human experience on image classification and does not generalize easily to other domains where the hard-coded hierarchical structure (repeating the same cells several times in a chain-like structure) does not apply (e.g., semantic segmentation or object detection). A search space which allows representing and identifying more general hierarchical structure would thus make NAS more broadly applicable, see Liu et al. [38] for first work in this direction. Moreover, common search spaces are also based on predefined building blocks, such as different kinds of convolutions and pooling, but do not allow identifying novel building blocks on this level; going beyond this limitation might substantially increase the power of NAS.

The comparison of different methods for NAS is complicated by the fact that measurements of an architecture's performance depend on many factors other than the architecture itself. While most authors report results on the CIFAR-10 dataset, experiments often differ with regard to search space, computational budget, data augmentation, training procedures, regularization, and other factors. For example, for CIFAR-10, performance substantially improves when using a cosine annealing learning rate schedule [40], data augmentation by CutOut [18], by MixUp [70] or by a combination of factors [16], and regularization by Shake-Shake regularization [26] or scheduled drop-path [75]. It is therefore conceivable that improvements in these ingredients have a larger impact on reported performance numbers than the better architectures found by NAS. We thus consider the definition of common benchmarks to be crucial for a fair comparison of different NAS methods. A first step in this direction is the definition of a benchmark for joint architecture and hyperparameter search for a fully connected neural network with two hidden layers [33]. In this benchmark, nine discrete hyperparameters need to be optimized that control both architecture and optimization/regularization. All 62.208 possible hyperparameter combinations have been pre-evaluated such that different methods can be compared with low computational resources. However, the search space is still very simple compared to the spaces employed by most NAS methods. It would also be interesting to evaluate NAS methods not in isolation but as part of a full open-source AutoML system, where also hyperparameters [41, 50, 69], and data augmentation pipeline [16] are optimized along with NAS.

While NAS has achieved impressive performance, so far it provides little insights into why specific architectures work well and how similar the architectures derived in independent runs would be. Identifying common motifs, providing an understanding why those motifs are important for high performance, and investigating if these motifs generalize over different problems would be desirable.

Acknowledgements We would like to thank Esteban Real, Arber Zela, Gabriel Bender, Kenneth Stanley and Thomas Pfeil for feedback on earlier versions of this survey. This work has partly been supported by the European Research Council (ERC) under the European Union's Horizon 2020 research and innovation programme under grant no. 716721.

Bibliography

1. Ahmed, K., Torresani, L.: Maskconnect: Connectivity learning by gradient descent. In: European Conference on Computer Vision (ECCV) (2018)
2. Angeline, P.J., Saunders, G.M., Pollack, J.B.: An evolutionary algorithm that constructs recurrent neural networks. IEEE transactions on neural networks 5 1, 54–65 (1994)
3. Ashok, A., Rhinehart, N., Beainy, F., Kitani, K.M.: N2n learning: Network to network compression via policy gradient reinforcement learning. In: International Conference on Learning Representations (2018)
4. Baker, B., Gupta, O., Naik, N., Raskar, R.: Designing neural network architectures using reinforcement learning. In: International Conference on Learning Representations (2017a)
5. Baker, B., Gupta, O., Raskar, R., Naik, N.: Accelerating Neural Architecture Search using Performance Prediction. In: NIPS Workshop on Meta-Learning (2017b)
6. Bender, G., Kindermans, P.J., Zoph, B., Vasudevan, V., Le, Q.: Understanding and simplifying one-shot architecture search. In: International Conference on Machine Learning (2018)
7. Bergstra, J., Yamins, D., Cox, D.D.: Making a science of model search: Hyperparameter optimization in hundreds of dimensions for vision architectures. In: ICML (2013)
8. Bergstra, J.S., Bardenet, R., Bengio, Y., Kégl, B.: Algorithms for hyper-parameter optimization. In: Shawe-Taylor, J., Zemel, R.S., Bartlett, P.L., Pereira, F., Weinberger, K.Q. (eds.) Advances in Neural Information Processing Systems 24. pp. 2546–2554 (2011)
9. Brock, A., Lim, T., Ritchie, J.M., Weston, N.: SMASH: one-shot model architecture search through hypernetworks. In: NIPS Workshop on Meta-Learning (2017)
10. Cai, H., Chen, T., Zhang, W., Yu, Y., Wang, J.: Efficient architecture search by network transformation. In: Association for the Advancement of Artificial Intelligence (2018a)
11. Cai, H., Yang, J., Zhang, W., Han, S., Yu, Y.: Path-Level Network Transformation for Efficient Architecture Search. In: International Conference on Machine Learning (Jun 2018b)
12. Chen, T., Goodfellow, I.J., Shlens, J.: Net2net: Accelerating learning via knowledge transfer. In: International Conference on Learning Representations (2016)
13. Chollet, F.: Xception: Deep learning with depthwise separable convolutions. arXiv:1610.02357 (2016)
14. Chrabaszcz, P., Loshchilov, I., Hutter, F.: A downsampled variant of imagenet as an alternative to the CIFAR datasets. CoRR abs/1707.08819 (2017)

15. Chrabaszcz, P., Loshchilov, I., Hutter, F.: Back to basics: Benchmarking canonical evolution strategies for playing atari. In: Proceedings of the Twenty-Seventh International Joint Conference on Artificial Intelligence, IJCAI-18. pp. 1419–1426. International Joint Conferences on Artificial Intelligence Organization (Jul 2018)
16. Cubuk, E.D., Zoph, B., Mane, D., Vasudevan, V., Le, Q.V.: AutoAugment: Learning Augmentation Policies from Data. In: arXiv:1805.09501 (May 2018)
17. Cubuk, E.D., Zoph, B., Schoenholz, S.S., Le, Q.V.: Intriguing Properties of Adversarial Examples. In: arXiv:1711.02846 (Nov 2017)
18. Devries, T., Taylor, G.W.: Improved regularization of convolutional neural networks with cutout. arXiv preprint abs/1708.04552 (2017)
19. Domhan, T., Springenberg, J.T., Hutter, F.: Speeding up automatic hyperparameter optimization of deep neural networks by extrapolation of learning curves. In: Proceedings of the 24th International Joint Conference on Artificial Intelligence (IJCAI) (2015)
20. Dong, J.D., Cheng, A.C., Juan, D.C., Wei, W., Sun, M.: Dpp-net: Device-aware progressive search for pareto-optimal neural architectures. In: European Conference on Computer Vision (2018)
21. Elsken, T., Metzen, J.H., Hutter, F.: Simple And Efficient Architecture Search for Convolutional Neural Networks. In: NIPS Workshop on Meta-Learning (2017)
22. Elsken, T., Metzen, J.H., Hutter, F.: Efficient Multi-objective Neural Architecture Search via Lamarckian Evolution. In: International Conference on Learning Representations (2019)
23. Elsken, T., Metzen, J.H., Hutter, F.: Neural architecture search: A survey. arXiv:1808.05377 (2018)
24. Falkner, S., Klein, A., Hutter, F.: BOHB: Robust and efficient hyperparameter optimization at scale. In: Dy, J., Krause, A. (eds.) Proceedings of the 35th International Conference on Machine Learning. Proceedings of Machine Learning Research, vol. 80, pp. 1436–1445. PMLR, Stockholmsmässan, Stockholm Sweden (10–15 Jul 2018)
25. Floreano, D., Dürr, P., Mattiussi, C.: Neuroevolution: from architectures to learning. Evolutionary Intelligence 1(1), 47–62 (2008)
26. Gastaldi, X.: Shake-shake regularization. In: International Conference on Learning Representations Workshop (2017)
27. Goldberg, D.E., Deb, K.: A comparative analysis of selection schemes used in genetic algorithms. In: Foundations of Genetic Algorithms. pp. 69–93. Morgan Kaufmann (1991)
28. He, K., Zhang, X., Ren, S., Sun, J.: Deep Residual Learning for Image Recognition. In: Conference on Computer Vision and Pattern Recognition (2016)
29. Huang, G., Liu, Z., Weinberger, K.Q.: Densely Connected Convolutional Networks. In: Conference on Computer Vision and Pattern Recognition (2017)
30. Hutter, F., Hoos, H., Leyton-Brown, K.: Sequential model-based optimization for general algorithm configuration. In: LION. pp. 507–523 (2011)
31. Kandasamy, K., Neiswanger, W., Schneider, J., Poczos, B., Xing, E.: Neural Architecture Search with Bayesian Optimisation and Optimal Transport. arXiv:1802.07191 (Feb 2018)
32. Klein, A., Falkner, S., Springenberg, J.T., Hutter, F.: Learning curve prediction with Bayesian neural networks. In: International Conference on Learning Representations (2017a)
33. Klein, A., Christiansen, E., Murphy, K., Hutter, F.: Towards reproducible neural architecture and hyperparameter search. In: ICML 2018 Workshop on Reproducibility in ML (RML 2018) (2018)
34. Klein, A., Falkner, S., Bartels, S., Hennig, P., Hutter, F.: Fast Bayesian Optimization of Machine Learning Hyperparameters on Large Datasets. In: Singh, A., Zhu, J. (eds.) Proceedings of the 20th International Conference on Artificial Intelligence and Statistics. Proceedings of Machine Learning Research, vol. 54, pp. 528–536. PMLR, Fort Lauderdale, FL, USA (20–22 Apr 2017b)
35. Li, L., Jamieson, K., DeSalvo, G., Rostamizadeh, A., Talwalkar, A.: Hyperband: bandit-based configuration evaluation for hyperparameter optimization. In: International Conference on Learning Representations (2017)
36. Liang, J., Meyerson, E., Miikkulainen, R.: Evolutionary Architecture Search For Deep Multitask Networks. In: arXiv:1803.03745 (Mar 2018)

37. Liu, C., Zoph, B., Neumann, M., Shlens, J., Hua, W., Li, L.J., Fei-Fei, L., Yuille, A., Huang, J., Murphy, K.: Progressive Neural Architecture Search. In: European Conference on Computer Vision (2018a)
38. Liu, H., Simonyan, K., Vinyals, O., Fernando, C., Kavukcuoglu, K.: Hierarchical Representations for Efficient Architecture Search. In: International Conference on Learning Representations (2018b)
39. Liu, H., Simonyan, K., Yang, Y.: Darts: Differentiable architecture search. In: International Conference on Learning Representations (2019)
40. Loshchilov, I., Hutter, F.: Sgdr: Stochastic gradient descent with warm restarts. In: International Conference on Learning Representations (2017)
41. Mendoza, H., Klein, A., Feurer, M., Springenberg, J., Hutter, F.: Towards Automatically-Tuned Neural Networks. In: International Conference on Machine Learning, AutoML Workshop (Jun 2016)
42. Meyerson, E., Miikkulainen, R.: Pseudo-task Augmentation: From Deep Multitask Learning to Intratask Sharing and Back. In: arXiv:1803.03745 (Mar 2018)
43. Miikkulainen, R., Liang, J., Meyerson, E., Rawal, A., Fink, D., Francon, O., Raju, B., Shahrzad, H., Navruzyan, A., Duffy, N., Hodjat, B.: Evolving Deep Neural Networks. In: arXiv:1703.00548 (Mar 2017)
44. Miller, G., Todd, P., Hedge, S.: Designing neural networks using genetic algorithms. In: 3rd International Conference on Genetic Algorithms (ICGA'89) (1989)
45. Negrinho, R., Gordon, G.: DeepArchitect: Automatically Designing and Training Deep Architectures. arXiv:1704.08792 (2017)
46. Pham, H., Guan, M.Y., Zoph, B., Le, Q.V., Dean, J.: Efficient neural architecture search via parameter sharing. In: International Conference on Machine Learning (2018)
47. Ramachandran, P., Le, Q.V.: Dynamic Network Architectures. In: AutoML 2018 (ICML workshop) (2018)
48. Rawal, A., Miikkulainen, R.: From Nodes to Networks: Evolving Recurrent Neural Networks. In: arXiv:1803.04439 (Mar 2018)
49. Real, E., Aggarwal, A., Huang, Y., Le, Q.V.: Aging Evolution for Image Classifier Architecture Search. In: AAAI Conference on Artificial Intelligence (2019)
50. Real, E., Moore, S., Selle, A., Saxena, S., Suematsu, Y.L., Le, Q.V., Kurakin, A.: Large-scale evolution of image classifiers. International Conference on Machine Learning (2017)
51. Salimans, T., Ho, J., Chen, X., Sutskever, I.: Evolution strategies as a scalable alternative to reinforcement learning. arXiv preprint (2017)
52. Saxena, S., Verbeek, J.: Convolutional neural fabrics. In: Lee, D.D., Sugiyama, M., Luxburg, U.V., Guyon, I., Garnett, R. (eds.) Advances in Neural Information Processing Systems 29, pp. 4053–4061. Curran Associates, Inc. (2016)
53. Shahriari, B., Swersky, K., Wang, Z., Adams, R.P., de Freitas, N.: Taking the human out of the loop: A review of bayesian optimization. Proceedings of the IEEE 104(1), 148–175 (Jan 2016)
54. Shin, R., Packer, C., Song, D.: Differentiable neural network architecture search. In: International Conference on Learning Representations Workshop (2018)
55. Stanley, K.O., D'Ambrosio, D.B., Gauci, J.: A hypercube-based encoding for evolving large-scale neural networks. Artif. Life 15(2), 185–212 (Apr 2009), URL https://doi.org/10.1162/artl.2009.15.2.15202
56. Stanley, K.O., Miikkulainen, R.: Evolving neural networks through augmenting topologies. Evolutionary Computation 10, 99–127 (2002)
57. Such, F.P., Madhavan, V., Conti, E., Lehman, J., Stanley, K.O., Clune, J.: Deep neuroevolution: Genetic algorithms are a competitive alternative for training deep neural networks for reinforcement learning. arXiv preprint (2017)
58. Suganuma, M., Ozay, M., Okatani, T.: Exploiting the potential of standard convolutional autoencoders for image restoration by evolutionary search. In: Dy, J., Krause, A. (eds.) Proceedings of the 35th International Conference on Machine Learning. Proceedings of Machine Learning Research, vol. 80, pp. 4771–4780. PMLR, Stockholmsmässan, Stockholm Sweden (10–15 Jul 2018)

59. Suganuma, M., Shirakawa, S., Nagao, T.: A genetic programming approach to designing convolutional neural network architectures. In: Genetic and Evolutionary Computation Conference (2017)
60. Swersky, K., Duvenaud, D., Snoek, J., Hutter, F., Osborne, M.: Raiders of the lost architecture: Kernels for bayesian optimization in conditional parameter spaces. In: NIPS Workshop on Bayesian Optimization in Theory and Practice (2013)
61. Swersky, K., Snoek, J., Adams, R.P.: Freeze-thaw bayesian optimization (2014)
62. Szegedy, C., Vanhoucke, V., Ioffe, S., Shlens, J., Wojna, Z.: Rethinking the Inception Architecture for Computer Vision. In: Conference on Computer Vision and Pattern Recognition (2016)
63. Wei, T., Wang, C., Chen, C.W.: Modularized morphing of neural networks. arXiv:1701.03281 (2017)
64. Wei, T., Wang, C., Rui, Y., Chen, C.W.: Network morphism. In: International Conference on Machine Learning (2016)
65. Wistuba, M.: Finding Competitive Network Architectures Within a Day Using UCT. In: arXiv:1712.07420 (Dec 2017)
66. Xie, L., Yuille, A.: Genetic CNN. In: International Conference on Computer Vision (2017)
67. Yao, X.: Evolving artificial neural networks. Proceedings of the IEEE 87(9), 1423–1447 (Sept 1999)
68. Yu, F., Koltun, V.: Multi-scale context aggregation by dilated convolutions (2016)
69. Zela, A., Klein, A., Falkner, S., Hutter, F.: Towards automated deep learning: Efficient joint neural architecture and hyperparameter search. In: ICML 2018 Workshop on AutoML (AutoML 2018) (2018)
70. Zhang, H., Cissé, M., Dauphin, Y.N., Lopez-Paz, D.: mixup: Beyond empirical risk minimization. arXiv preprint abs/1710.09412 (2017)
71. Zhong, Z., Yan, J., Wu, W., Shao, J., Liu, C.L.: Practical block-wise neural network architecture generation. In: Proceedings of the IEEE Conference on Computer Vision and Pattern Recognition. pp. 2423–2432 (2018a)
72. Zhong, Z., Yang, Z., Deng, B., Yan, J., Wu, W., Shao, J., Liu, C.L.: Blockqnn: Efficient block-wise neural network architecture generation. arXiv preprint (2018b)
73. Zhou, Y., Ebrahimi, S., Arik, S., Yu, H., Liu, H., Diamos, G.: Resource-efficient neural architect. In: arXiv:1806.07912 (2018)
74. Zoph, B., Le, Q.V.: Neural architecture search with reinforcement learning. In: International Conference on Learning Representations (2017)
75. Zoph, B., Vasudevan, V., Shlens, J., Le, Q.V.: Learning transferable architectures for scalable image recognition. In: Conference on Computer Vision and Pattern Recognition (2018)

Part II
AutoML Systems

Chapter 4
Auto-WEKA: Automatic Model Selection and Hyperparameter Optimization in WEKA

Lars Kotthoff, Chris Thornton, Holger H. Hoos, Frank Hutter, and Kevin Leyton-Brown

Abstract Many different machine learning algorithms exist; taking into account each algorithm's hyperparameters, there is a staggeringly large number of possible alternatives overall. We consider the problem of simultaneously selecting a learning algorithm and setting its hyperparameters. We show that this problem can be addressed by a fully automated approach, leveraging recent innovations in Bayesian optimization. Specifically, we consider feature selection techniques and all machine learning approaches implemented in WEKA's standard distribution, spanning 2 ensemble methods, 10 meta-methods, 28 base learners, and hyperparameter settings for each learner. On each of 21 popular datasets from the UCI repository, the KDD Cup 09, variants of the MNIST dataset and CIFAR-10, we show performance often much better than using standard selection and hyperparameter optimization methods. We hope that our approach will help non-expert users to more effectively identify machine learning algorithms and hyperparameter settings appropriate to their applications, and hence to achieve improved performance.

4.1 Introduction

Increasingly, users of machine learning tools are non-experts who require off-the-shelf solutions. The machine learning community has much aided such users by making available a wide variety of sophisticated learning algorithms and feature

L. Kotthoff (✉)
University of Wyoming, Laramie, WY, USA
e-mail: larsko@uwyo.edu

C. Thornton · K. Leyton-Brown
Department of Computer Science, University of British Columbia, Vancouver, BC, Canada

H. H. Hoos
Leiden Institute for Advanced Computer Science, Leiden University, Leiden, The Netherlands

F. Hutter
Department of Computer Science, University of Freiburg, Freiburg, Germany

F. Hutter et al. (eds.), *Automated Machine Learning*, The Springer Series on Challenges in Machine Learning, https://doi.org/10.1007/978-3-030-05318-5_4

selection methods through open source packages, such as WEKA [15] and mlr [7]. Such packages ask a user to make two kinds of choices: selecting a learning algorithm and customizing it by setting hyperparameters (which also control feature selection, if applicable). It can be challenging to make the right choice when faced with these degrees of freedom, leaving many users to select algorithms based on reputation or intuitive appeal, and/or to leave hyperparameters set to default values. Of course, adopting this approach can yield performance far worse than that of the best method and hyperparameter settings.

This suggests a natural challenge for machine learning: given a dataset, automatically and simultaneously choosing a learning algorithm and setting its hyperparameters to optimize empirical performance. We dub this the *combined algorithm selection and hyperparameter optimization (CASH) problem*; we formally define it in Sect. 4.3. There has been considerable past work separately addressing model selection, e.g., [1, 6, 8, 9, 11, 24, 25, 33], and hyperparameter optimization, e.g., [3–5, 14, 23, 28, 30]. In contrast, despite its practical importance, we are surprised to find only limited variants of the CASH problem in the literature; furthermore, these consider a fixed and relatively small number of parameter configurations for each algorithm, see e.g., [22].

A likely explanation is that it is very challenging to search the combined space of learning algorithms and their hyperparameters: the response function is noisy and the space is high dimensional, involves both categorical and continuous choices, and contains hierarchical dependencies (e.g., , the hyperparameters of a learning algorithm are only meaningful if that algorithm is chosen; the algorithm choices in an ensemble method are only meaningful if that ensemble method is chosen; etc). Another related line of work is on meta-learning procedures that exploit characteristics of the dataset, such as the performance of so-called landmarking algorithms, to predict which algorithm or hyperparameter configuration will perform well [2, 22, 26, 32]. While the CASH algorithms we study in this chapter start from scratch for each new dataset, these meta-learning procedures exploit information from previous datasets, which may not always be available.

In what follows, we demonstrate that CASH can be viewed as a single hierarchical hyperparameter optimization problem, in which even the choice of algorithm itself is considered a hyperparameter. We also show that—based on this problem formulation—recent Bayesian optimization methods can obtain high quality results in reasonable time and with minimal human effort. After discussing some preliminaries (Sect. 4.2), we define the CASH problem and discuss methods for tackling it (Sect. 4.3). We then define a concrete CASH problem encompassing a wide range of learners and feature selectors in the open source package WEKA (Sect. 4.4), and show that a search in the combined space of algorithms and hyperparameters yields better-performing models than standard algorithm selection and hyperparameter optimization methods (Sect. 4.5). More specifically, we show that the recent Bayesian optimization procedures TPE [4] and SMAC [16] often find combinations of algorithms and hyperparameters that outperform existing baseline methods, especially on large datasets.

This chapter is based on two previous papers, published in the *proceedings of KDD 2013* [31] and in the *journal of machine learning research (JMLR)* in 2017 [20].

4.2 Preliminaries

We consider learning a function $f : \mathcal{X} \mapsto \mathcal{Y}$, where $\mathcal{Y}$ is either finite (for classification), or continuous (for regression). A *learning algorithm* A maps a set $\{d_1, \ldots, d_n\}$ of training data points $d_i = (\mathbf{x}_i, y_i) \in \mathcal{X} \times \mathcal{Y}$ to such a function, which is often expressed via a vector of *model parameters*. Most learning algorithms A further expose *hyperparameters* $\boldsymbol{\lambda} \in \boldsymbol{\Lambda}$, which change the way the learning algorithm $A_{\boldsymbol{\lambda}}$ itself works. For example, hyperparameters are used to describe a description-length penalty, the number of neurons in a hidden layer, the number of data points that a leaf in a decision tree must contain to be eligible for splitting, etc. These hyperparameters are typically optimized in an "outer loop" that evaluates the performance of each hyperparameter configuration using cross-validation.

4.2.1 Model Selection

Given a set of learning algorithms $\mathcal{A}$ and a limited amount of training data $\mathcal{D} = \{(\mathbf{x}_1, y_1), \ldots, (\mathbf{x}_n, y_n)\}$, the goal of model selection is to determine the algorithm $A^* \in \mathcal{A}$ with optimal generalization performance. Generalization performance is estimated by splitting $\mathcal{D}$ into disjoint training and validation sets $\mathcal{D}_{\text{train}}^{(i)}$ and $\mathcal{D}_{\text{valid}}^{(i)}$, learning functions f_i by applying A^* to $\mathcal{D}_{\text{train}}^{(i)}$, and evaluating the predictive performance of these functions on $\mathcal{D}_{\text{valid}}^{(i)}$. This allows for the model selection problem to be written as:

$$A^* \in \operatorname*{argmin}_{A \in \mathcal{A}} \frac{1}{k} \sum_{i=1}^{k} \mathcal{L}(A, \mathcal{D}_{\text{train}}^{(i)}, \mathcal{D}_{\text{valid}}^{(i)}),$$

where $\mathcal{L}(A, \mathcal{D}_{\text{train}}^{(i)}, \mathcal{D}_{\text{valid}}^{(i)})$ is the loss achieved by A when trained on $\mathcal{D}_{\text{train}}^{(i)}$ and evaluated on $\mathcal{D}_{\text{valid}}^{(i)}$.

We use k-fold cross-validation [19], which splits the training data into k equal-sized partitions $\mathcal{D}_{\text{valid}}^{(1)}, \ldots, \mathcal{D}_{\text{valid}}^{(k)}$, and sets $\mathcal{D}_{\text{train}}^{(i)} = \mathcal{D} \setminus \mathcal{D}_{\text{valid}}^{(i)}$ for $i = 1, \ldots, k$.[1]

[1]There are other ways of estimating generalization performance; e.g., we also experimented with repeated random subsampling validation [19], and obtained similar results.

4.2.2 Hyperparameter Optimization

The problem of optimizing the hyperparameters $\boldsymbol{\lambda} \in \boldsymbol{\Lambda}$ of a given learning algorithm A is conceptually similar to that of model selection. Some key differences are that hyperparameters are often continuous, that hyperparameter spaces are often high dimensional, and that we can exploit correlation structure between different hyperparameter settings $\boldsymbol{\lambda}_1, \boldsymbol{\lambda}_2 \in \boldsymbol{\Lambda}$. Given n hyperparameters $\lambda_1, \ldots, \lambda_n$ with domains $\Lambda_1, \ldots, \Lambda_n$, the hyperparameter space $\boldsymbol{\Lambda}$ is a subset of the crossproduct of these domains: $\boldsymbol{\Lambda} \subset \Lambda_1 \times \cdots \times \Lambda_n$. This subset is often strict, such as when certain settings of one hyperparameter render other hyperparameters inactive. For example, the parameters determining the specifics of the third layer of a deep belief network are not relevant if the network depth is set to one or two. Likewise, the parameters of a support vector machine's polynomial kernel are not relevant if we use a different kernel instead.

More formally, following [17], we say that a hyperparameter λ_i is *conditional* on another hyperparameter λ_j, if λ_i is only active if hyperparameter λ_j takes values from a given set $V_i(j) \subsetneq \Lambda_j$; in this case we call λ_j a *parent* of λ_i. Conditional hyperparameters can in turn be parents of other conditional hyperparameters, giving rise to a tree-structured space [4] or, in some cases, a directed acyclic graph (DAG) [17]. Given such a structured space $\boldsymbol{\Lambda}$, the (hierarchical) hyperparameter optimization problem can be written as:

$$\boldsymbol{\lambda}^* \in \operatorname*{argmin}_{\boldsymbol{\lambda} \in \boldsymbol{\Lambda}} \frac{1}{k} \sum_{i=1}^{k} \mathcal{L}(A_{\boldsymbol{\lambda}}, \mathcal{D}_{\text{train}}^{(i)}, \mathcal{D}_{\text{valid}}^{(i)}).$$

4.3 Combined Algorithm Selection and Hyperparameter Optimization (CASH)

Given a set of algorithms $\mathcal{A} = \{A^{(1)}, \ldots, A^{(k)}\}$ with associated hyperparameter spaces $\boldsymbol{\Lambda}^{(1)}, \ldots, \boldsymbol{\Lambda}^{(k)}$, we define the combined algorithm selection and hyperparameter optimization problem (CASH) as computing

$$A^*{}_{\boldsymbol{\lambda}^*} \in \operatorname*{argmin}_{A^{(j)} \in \mathcal{A}, \boldsymbol{\lambda} \in \boldsymbol{\Lambda}^{(j)}} \frac{1}{k} \sum_{i=1}^{k} \mathcal{L}(A_{\boldsymbol{\lambda}}^{(j)}, \mathcal{D}_{\text{train}}^{(i)}, \mathcal{D}_{\text{valid}}^{(i)}). \tag{4.1}$$

We note that this problem can be reformulated as a single combined hierarchical hyperparameter optimization problem with parameter space $\boldsymbol{\Lambda} = \boldsymbol{\Lambda}^{(1)} \cup \cdots \cup \boldsymbol{\Lambda}^{(k)} \cup \{\lambda_r\}$, where λ_r is a new root-level hyperparameter that selects between algorithms $A^{(1)}, \ldots, A^{(k)}$. The root-level parameters of each subspace $\boldsymbol{\Lambda}^{(i)}$ are made conditional on λ_r being instantiated to A_i.

In principle, problem (4.1) can be tackled in various ways. A promising approach is Bayesian Optimization [10], and in particular Sequential Model-Based Optimization (SMBO) [16], a versatile stochastic optimization framework that can work with both categorical and continuous hyperparameters, and that can exploit hierarchical structure stemming from conditional parameters. SMBO (outlined in Algorithm 1) first builds a model $\mathcal{M}_\mathcal{L}$ that captures the dependence of loss function $\mathcal{L}$ on hyperparameter settings $\boldsymbol{\lambda}$ (line 1 in Algorithm 1). It then iterates the following steps: use $\mathcal{M}_\mathcal{L}$ to determine a promising candidate configuration of hyperparameters $\boldsymbol{\lambda}$ to evaluate next (line 3); evaluate the loss c of $\boldsymbol{\lambda}$ (line 4); and update the model $\mathcal{M}_\mathcal{L}$ with the new data point $(\boldsymbol{\lambda}, c)$ thus obtained (lines 5–6).

Algorithm 1 SMBO

1: initialise model $\mathcal{M}_L$; $\mathcal{H} \leftarrow \emptyset$
2: **while** time budget for optimization has not been exhausted **do**
3: $\quad \boldsymbol{\lambda} \leftarrow$ candidate configuration from $\mathcal{M}_L$
4: $\quad$ Compute $c = \mathcal{L}(A_{\boldsymbol{\lambda}}, \mathcal{D}^{(i)}_{\text{train}}, \mathcal{D}^{(i)}_{\text{valid}})$
5: $\quad \mathcal{H} \leftarrow \mathcal{H} \cup \{(\boldsymbol{\lambda}, c)\}$
6: $\quad$ Update $\mathcal{M}_L$ given $\mathcal{H}$
7: **end while**
8: **return** $\boldsymbol{\lambda}$ from $\mathcal{H}$ with minimal c

In order to select its next hyperparameter configuration $\boldsymbol{\lambda}$ using model $\mathcal{M}_\mathcal{L}$, SMBO uses a so-called *acquisition function* $a_{\mathcal{M}_\mathcal{L}} : \boldsymbol{\Lambda} \mapsto \mathbb{R}$, which uses the predictive distribution of model $\mathcal{M}_\mathcal{L}$ at arbitrary hyperparameter configurations $\boldsymbol{\lambda} \in \boldsymbol{\Lambda}$ to quantify (in closed form) how useful knowledge about $\boldsymbol{\lambda}$ would be. SMBO then simply maximizes this function over $\boldsymbol{\Lambda}$ to select the most useful configuration $\boldsymbol{\lambda}$ to evaluate next. Several well-studied acquisition functions exist [18, 27, 29]; all aim to automatically trade off exploitation (locally optimizing hyperparameters in regions known to perform well) versus exploration (trying hyperparameters in a relatively unexplored region of the space) in order to avoid premature convergence. In this work, we maximized *positive expected improvement (EI)* attainable over an existing given loss c_{min} [27]. Let $c(\boldsymbol{\lambda})$ denote the loss of hyperparameter configuration $\boldsymbol{\lambda}$. Then, the positive improvement function over c_{min} is defined as

$$I_{c_{min}}(\boldsymbol{\lambda}) := \max\{c_{min} - c(\boldsymbol{\lambda}), 0\}.$$

Of course, we do not know $c(\boldsymbol{\lambda})$. We can, however, compute its expectation with respect to the current model $\mathcal{M}_\mathcal{L}$:

$$\mathbb{E}_{\mathcal{M}_\mathcal{L}}[I_{c_{min}}(\boldsymbol{\lambda})] = \int_{-\infty}^{c_{min}} \max\{c_{min} - c, 0\} \cdot p_{\mathcal{M}_L}(c \mid \lambda)\, dc. \tag{4.2}$$

We briefly review the SMBO approach used in this chapter.

4.3.1 Sequential Model-Based Algorithm Configuration (SMAC)

Sequential model-based algorithm configuration (SMAC) [16] supports a variety of models $p(c \mid \boldsymbol{\lambda})$ to capture the dependence of the loss function c on hyperparameters $\boldsymbol{\lambda}$, including approximate Gaussian processes and random forests. In this chapter we use random forest models, since they tend to perform well with discrete and high-dimensional input data. SMAC handles conditional parameters by instantiating inactive conditional parameters in $\boldsymbol{\lambda}$ to default values for model training and prediction. This allows the individual decision trees to include splits of the kind "is hyperparameter λ_i active?", allowing them to focus on active hyperparameters. While random forests are not usually treated as probabilistic models, SMAC obtains a predictive mean $\mu_{\boldsymbol{\lambda}}$ and variance ${\sigma_{\boldsymbol{\lambda}}}^2$ of $p(c \mid \boldsymbol{\lambda})$ as frequentist estimates over the predictions of its individual trees for $\boldsymbol{\lambda}$; it then models $p_{\mathcal{M}_\mathcal{L}}(c \mid \boldsymbol{\lambda})$ as a Gaussian $\mathcal{N}(\mu_{\boldsymbol{\lambda}}, {\sigma_{\boldsymbol{\lambda}}}^2)$.

SMAC uses the expected improvement criterion defined in Eq. 4.2, instantiating c_{min} to the loss of the best hyperparameter configuration measured so far. Under SMAC's predictive distribution $p_{\mathcal{M}_\mathcal{L}}(c \mid \boldsymbol{\lambda}) = \mathcal{N}(\mu_{\boldsymbol{\lambda}}, {\sigma_{\boldsymbol{\lambda}}}^2)$, this expectation is the closed-form expression

$$\mathbb{E}_{\mathcal{M}_\mathcal{L}}[I_{c_{min}}(\boldsymbol{\lambda})] = \sigma_{\boldsymbol{\lambda}} \cdot [u \cdot \Phi(u) + \varphi(u)],$$

where $u = \frac{c_{\min} - \mu_{\boldsymbol{\lambda}}}{\sigma_{\boldsymbol{\lambda}}}$, and φ and Φ denote the probability density function and cumulative distribution function of a standard normal distribution, respectively [18].

SMAC is designed for robust optimization under noisy function evaluations, and as such implements special mechanisms to keep track of its best known configuration and assure high confidence in its estimate of that configuration's performance. This robustness against noisy function evaluations can be exploited in combined algorithm selection and hyperparameter optimization, since the function to be optimized in Eq. (4.1) is a mean over a set of loss terms (each corresponding to one pair of $\mathcal{D}^{(i)}_{\text{train}}$ and $\mathcal{D}^{(i)}_{\text{valid}}$ constructed from the training set). A key idea in SMAC is to make progressively better estimates of this mean by evaluating these terms one at a time, thus trading off accuracy and computational cost. In order for a new configuration to become a new incumbent, it must outperform the previous incumbent in every comparison made: considering only one fold, two folds, and so on up to the total number of folds previously used to evaluate the incumbent. Furthermore, every time the incumbent survives such a comparison, it is evaluated on a new fold, up to the total number available, meaning that the number of folds used to evaluate the incumbent grows over time. A poorly performing configuration can thus be discarded after considering just a single fold.

Finally, SMAC also implements a diversification mechanism to achieve robust performance even when its model is misled, and to explore new parts of the space: every second configuration is selected at random. Because of the evaluation procedure just described, this requires less overhead than one might imagine.

4.4 Auto-WEKA

To demonstrate the feasibility of an automatic approach to solving the CASH problem, we built Auto-WEKA, which solves this problem for the learners and feature selectors implemented in the WEKA machine learning package [15]. Note that while we have focused on classification algorithms in WEKA, there is no obstacle to extending our approach to other settings. Indeed, another successful system that uses the same underlying technology is auto-sklearn [12].

Fig. 4.1 shows all supported learning algorithms and feature selectors with the number of hyperparameters. algorithms. Meta-methods take a single base classifier and its parameters as an input, and the ensemble methods can take any number of base learners as input. We allowed the meta-methods to use any base learner with any hyperparameter settings, and allowed the ensemble methods to use up to five

Base Learners			
BayesNet	2	NaiveBayes	2
DecisionStump*	0	NaiveBayesMultinomial	0
DecisionTable*	4	OneR	1
GaussianProcesses*	10	PART	4
IBk*	5	RandomForest	7
J48	9	RandomTree*	11
JRip	4	REPTree*	6
KStar*	3	SGD*	5
LinearRegression*	3	SimpleLinearRegression*	0
LMT	9	SimpleLogistic	5
Logistic	1	SMO	11
M5P	4	SMOreg*	13
M5Rules	4	VotedPerceptron	3
MultilayerPerceptron*	8	ZeroR*	0
Ensemble Methods			
Stacking	2	Vote	2
Meta-Methods			
LWL	5	Bagging	4
AdaBoostM1	6	RandomCommittee	2
AdditiveRegression	4		
AttributeSelectedClassifier	2	RandomSubSpace	3
Feature Selection Methods			
BestFirst	2	GreedyStepwise	4

Fig. 4.1 Learners and methods supported by Auto-WEKA, along with number of hyperparameters $|\Lambda|$. Every learner supports classification; starred learners also support regression

learners, again with any hyperparameter settings. Not all learners are applicable on all datasets (e.g., due to a classifier's inability to handle missing data). For a given dataset, our Auto-WEKA implementation automatically only considers the subset of applicable learners. Feature selection is run as a preprocessing phase before building any model.

The algorithms in Fig. 4.1 have a wide variety of hyperparameters, which take values from continuous intervals, from ranges of integers, and from other discrete sets. We associated either a uniform or log uniform prior with each numerical parameter, depending on its semantics. For example, we set a log uniform prior for the ridge regression penalty, and a uniform prior for the maximum depth for a tree in a random forest. Auto-WEKA works with continuous hyperparameter values directly up to the precision of the machine. We emphasize that this combined hyperparameter space is *much* larger than a simple union of the base learners' hyperparameter spaces, since the ensemble methods allow up to 5 *independent* base learners. The meta- and ensemble methods as well as the feature selection contribute further to the total size of AutoWEKA's hyperparameter space.

Auto-WEKA uses the SMAC optimizer described above to solve the CASH problem and is available to the public through the WEKA package manager; the source code can be found at https://github.com/automl/autoweka and the official project website is at http://www.cs.ubc.ca/labs/beta/Projects/autoweka. For the experiments described in this chapter, we used Auto-WEKA version 0.5. The results the more recent versions achieve are similar; we did not replicate the full set of experiments because of the large computational cost.

4.5 Experimental Evaluation

We evaluated Auto-WEKA on 21 prominent benchmark datasets (see Table 4.1): 15 sets from the UCI repository [13]; the 'convex', 'MNIST basic' and 'rotated MNIST with background images' tasks used in [5]; the appentency task from the KDD Cup '09; and two versions of the CIFAR-10 image classification task [21] (CIFAR-10-Small is a subset of CIFAR-10, where only the first 10,000 training data points are used rather than the full 50,000.) Note that in the experimental evaluation, we focus on classification. For datasets with a predefined training/test split, we used that split. Otherwise, we randomly split the dataset into 70% training and 30% test data. We withheld the test data from all optimization method; it was only used once in an offline analysis stage to evaluate the models found by the various optimization methods.

For each dataset, we ran Auto-WEKA with each hyperparameter optimization algorithm with a total time budget of 30 h. For each method, we performed 25 runs of this process with different random seeds and then—in order to simulate parallelization on a typical workstation—used bootstrap sampling to repeatedly select four random runs and report the performance of the one with best cross-validation performance.

Table 4.1 Datasets used; *Num. Discr.* and *Num. Cont.* refer to the number of discrete and continuous attributes of elements in the dataset, respectively

Name	Num Discr.	Num Cont.	Num classes	Num training	Num test
Dexter	20,000	0	2	420	180
GermanCredit	13	7	2	700	300
Dorothea	100,000	0	2	805	345
Yeast	0	8	10	1,038	446
Amazon	10,000	0	49	1,050	450
Secom	0	591	2	1,096	471
Semeion	256	0	10	1,115	478
Car	6	0	4	1,209	519
Madelon	500	0	2	1,820	780
KR-vs-KP	37	0	2	2,237	959
Abalone	1	7	28	2,923	1,254
Wine Quality	0	11	11	3,425	1,469
Waveform	0	40	3	3,500	1,500
Gisette	5,000	0	2	4,900	2,100
Convex	0	784	2	8,000	50,000
CIFAR-10-Small	3,072	0	10	10,000	10,000
MNIST Basic	0	784	10	12,000	50,000
Rot. MNIST + BI	0	784	10	12,000	50,000
Shuttle	9	0	7	43,500	14,500
KDD09-Appentency	190	40	2	35,000	15,000
CIFAR-10	3,072	0	10	50,000	10,000

In early experiments, we observed a few cases in which Auto-WEKA's SMBO method picked hyperparameters that had excellent training performance, but turned out to generalize poorly. To enable Auto-WEKA to detect such overfitting, we partitioned its training set into two subsets: 70% for use inside the SMBO method, and 30% of validation data that we only used after the SMBO method finished.

4.5.1 Baseline Methods

Auto-WEKA aims to aid non-expert users of machine learning techniques. A natural approach that such a user might take is to perform 10-fold cross validation on the training set for each technique with unmodified hyperparameters, and select the classifier with the smallest average misclassification error across folds. We will refer to this method applied to our set of WEKA learners as *Ex-Def*; it is the best choice that can be made for WEKA with default hyperparameters.

For each dataset, the second and third columns in Table 4.2 present the best and worst "oracle performance" of the default learners when prepared given all the training data and evaluated on the test set. We observe that the gap between the best and worst learner was huge, e.g., misclassification rates of 4.93% vs. 99.24% on the Dorothea dataset. This suggests that some form of algorithm selection is essential for achieving good performance.

A stronger baseline we will use is an approach that in addition to selecting the learner, also sets its hyperparameters optimally from a predefined set. More precisely, this baseline performs an exhaustive search over a grid of hyperparameter settings for each of the base learners, discretizing numeric parameters into three points. We refer to this baseline as *grid search* and note that—as an optimization approach in the joint space of algorithms and hyperparameter settings—it is a simple CASH algorithm. However, it is quite expensive, requiring more than 10,000 CPU hours on each of Gisette, Convex, MNIST, Rot MNIST + BI, and both CIFAR variants, rendering it infeasible to use in most practical applications. (In contrast, we gave Auto-WEKA only 120 CPU hours.)

Table 4.2 (columns four and five) shows the best and worst "oracle performance" on the test set across the classifiers evaluated by grid search. Comparing these performances to the default performance obtained using Ex-Def, we note that in most cases, even WEKA's best default algorithm could be improved by selecting better hyperparameter settings, sometimes rather substantially: e.g., , in the CIFAR-10 small task, grid search offered a 13% reduction in error over Ex-Def.

It has been demonstrated in previous work that, holding the overall time budget constant, grid search is outperformed by random search over the hyperparameter space [5]. Our final baseline, *random search*, implements such a method, picking algorithms and hyperparameters sampled at random, and computes their performance on the 10 cross-validation folds until it exhausts its time budget. For each dataset, we first used 750 CPU hours to compute the cross-validation performance of randomly sampled combinations of algorithms and hyperparameters. We then simulated runs of random search by sampling combinations without replacement from these results that consumed 120 CPU hours and returning the sampled combination with the best performance.

4.5.2 Results for Cross-Validation Performance

The middle portion of Table 4.2 reports our main results. First, we note that grid search over the hyperparameters of all base-classifiers yielded better results than Ex-Def in 17/21 cases, which underlines the importance of not only choosing the right algorithm but of also setting its hyperparameters well.

However, we note that we gave grid search a very large time budget (often in excess 10,000 CPU hours for each dataset, in total more than 10 CPU years), meaning that it would often be infeasible to use in practice.

Table 4.2 Performance on both 10-fold cross-validation and test data. Ex-Def and Grid Search are deterministic. Random search had a time budget of 120 CPU hours. For Auto-WEKA, we performed 25 runs of 30 h each. We report results as mean loss across 100,000 bootstrap samples simulating 4 parallel runs. We determined test loss (misclassification rate) by training the selected model/hyperparameters on the entire 70% training data and computing accuracy on the previously unused 30% test data. Bold face indicates the lowest error within a block of comparable methods that was statistically significant

	Oracle Perf. (%)				10-Fold C.V. performance (%)				Test performance (%)			
	Ex-Def		Grid search									
Dataset	Best	Worst	Best	Worst	Ex-Def	Grid search	Rand. search	Auto-WEKA	Ex-Def	Grid search	Rand. search	Auto-WEKA
Dexter	7.78	52.78	**3.89**	63.33	10.20	**5.07**	10.60	5.66	8.89	**5.00**	9.18	7.49
GermanCredit	26.00	38.00	**25.00**	68.00	22.45	20.20	20.15	**17.87**	27.33	**26.67**	29.03	28.24
Dorothea	4.93	99.24	**4.64**	99.24	6.03	6.73	8.11	**5.62**	6.96	5.80	**5.22**	6.21
Yeast	40.00	68.99	**36.85**	69.89	39.43	39.71	38.74	35.51	40.45	42.47	43.15	40.67
Amazon	28.44	99.33	**17.56**	99.33	43.94	**36.88**	59.85	47.34	28.44	**20.00**	41.11	33.99
Secom	7.87	14.26	**7.66**	92.13	6.25	6.12	5.24	**5.24**	8.09	8.09	8.03	**8.01**
Semeion	8.18	92.45	**5.24**	92.45	6.52	4.86	6.06	**4.78**	8.18	6.29	6.10	**5.08**
Car	0.77	29.15	**0.00**	46.14	2.71	0.83	**0.53**	0.61	0.77	0.97	**0.01**	0.40
Madelon	**17.05**	50.26	**17.05**	62.69	25.98	26.46	27.95	**20.70**	21.38	21.15	24.29	**21.12**
KR-vs-KP	0.31	48.96	**0.21**	51.04	0.89	0.64	0.63	**0.30**	0.31	1.15	0.58	**0.31**
Abalone	73.18	84.04	**72.15**	92.90	73.33	72.15	72.03	**71.71**	73.18	73.42	74.88	73.51
Wine Quality	36.35	60.99	**32.88**	99.39	38.94	35.23	35.36	**34.65**	37.51	34.06	34.41	33.95
Waveform	14.27	68.80	**13.47**	68.80	12.73	12.45	12.43	**11.92**	14.40	14.66	14.27	14.42
Gisette	2.52	50.91	**1.81**	51.23	3.62	2.59	4.84	**2.43**	2.81	2.40	4.62	**2.24**
Convex	25.96	50.00	**19.94**	71.49	28.68	**22.36**	33.31	25.93	25.96	23.45	31.20	**23.17**
CIFAR-10-Small	65.91	90.00	**52.16**	90.36	66.59	**53.64**	67.33	58.84	65.91	56.94	66.12	**56.87**
MNIST Basic	5.19	88.75	**2.58**	88.75	5.12	**2.51**	5.05	3.75	5.19	**2.64**	5.05	3.64
Rot. MNIST + BI	63.14	88.88	**55.34**	93.01	66.15	**56.01**	68.62	57.86	63.14	57.59	66.40	**57.04**
Shuttle	0.0138	20.8414	**0.0069**	89.8207	0.0328	0.0361	0.0345	**0.0224**	0.0138	0.0414	0.0157	**0.0130**
KDD09-Appentency	1.7400	6.9733	**1.6332**	54.2400	1.8776	1.8735	1.7510	**1.7038**	1.7405	1.7400	1.7400	**1.7358**
CIFAR-10	64.27	90.00	**55.27**	90.00	65.54	**54.04**	69.46	62.36	64.27	63.13	69.72	**61.15**

In contrast, we gave each of the other methods only 4×30 CPU hours per dataset; nevertheless, they still yielded substantially better performance than grid search, outperforming it in 14/21 cases. Random search outperforms grid search in 9/21 cases, highlighting that even exhaustive grid search with a large time budget is not always the right thing to do. We note that sometimes Auto-WEKA's performance improvements over the baselines were substantial, with relative reductions of the cross-validation loss (in this case the misclassification rate) exceeding 10% in 6/21 cases.

4.5.3 Results for Test Performance

The results just shown demonstrate that Auto-WEKA is effective at optimizing its given objective function; however, this is not sufficient to allow us to conclude that it fits models that generalize well. As the number of hyperparameters of a machine learning algorithm grows, so does its potential for overfitting. The use of cross-validation substantially increases Auto-WEKA's robustness against overfitting, but since its hyperparameter space is much larger than that of standard classification algorithms, it is important to carefully study whether (and to what extent) overfitting poses a problem.

To evaluate generalization, we determined a combination of algorithm and hyperparameter settings A_λ by running Auto-WEKA as before (cross-validating on the training set), trained A_λ on the entire training set, and then evaluated the resulting model on the test set. The right portion of Table 4.2 reports the test performance obtained with all methods.

Broadly speaking, similar trends held as for cross-validation performance: Auto-WEKA outperforms the baselines, with grid search and random search performing better than Ex-Def. However, the performance differences were less pronounced: grid search only yields better results than Ex-Def in 15/21 cases, and random search in turn outperforms grid search in 7/21 cases. Auto-WEKA outperforms the baselines in 15/21 cases. Notably, on 12 of the 13 largest datasets, Auto-WEKA outperforms our baselines; we attribute this to the fact that the risk of overfitting decreases with dataset size. Sometimes, Auto-WEKA's performance improvements over the other methods were substantial, with relative reductions of the test misclassification rate exceeding 16% in 3/21 cases.

As mentioned earlier, Auto-WEKA only used 70% of its training set during the optimization of cross-validation performance, reserving the remaining 30% for assessing the risk of overfitting. At any point in time, Auto-WEKA's SMBO method keeps track of its *incumbent* (the hyperparameter configuration with the lowest cross-validation misclassification rate seen so far). After its SMBO procedure has finished, Auto-WEKA extracts a trajectory of these incumbents from it and computes their generalization performance on the withheld 30% validation data.

It then computes the Spearman rank coefficient between the sequence of training performances (evaluated by the SMBO method through cross-validation) and this generalization performance.

4.6 Conclusion

In this work, we have shown that the daunting problem of combined algorithm selection and hyperparameter optimization (CASH) can be solved by a practical, fully automated tool. This is made possible by recent Bayesian optimization techniques that iteratively build models of the algorithm/hyperparameter landscape and leverage these models to identify new points in the space that deserve investigation.

We built a tool, Auto-WEKA, that draws on the full range of learning algorithms in WEKA and makes it easy for non-experts to build high-quality classifiers for given application scenarios. An extensive empirical comparison on 21 prominent datasets showed that Auto-WEKA often outperformed standard algorithm selection and hyperparameter optimization methods, especially on large datasets.

4.6.1 Community Adoption

Auto-WEKA was the first method to use Bayesian optimization to automatically instantiate a highly parametric machine learning framework at the push of a button. Since its initial release, it has been adopted by many users in industry and academia; the 2.0 line, which integrates with the WEKA package manager, has been downloaded more than 30,000 times, averaging more than 550 downloads a week. It is under active development, with new features added recently and in the pipeline.

Bibliography

1. Adankon, M., Cheriet, M.: Model selection for the LS-SVM. application to handwriting recognition. Pattern Recognition 42(12), 3264–3270 (2009)
2. Bardenet, R., Brendel, M., Kégl, B., Sebag, M.: Collaborative hyperparameter tuning. In: Proc. of ICML-13 (2013)
3. Bengio, Y.: Gradient-based optimization of hyperparameters. Neural Computation 12(8), 1889–1900 (2000)
4. Bergstra, J., Bardenet, R., Bengio, Y., Kégl, B.: Algorithms for Hyper-Parameter Optimization. In: Proc. of NIPS-11 (2011)
5. Bergstra, J., Bengio, Y.: Random search for hyper-parameter optimization. JMLR 13, 281–305 (2012)
6. Biem, A.: A model selection criterion for classification: Application to HMM topology optimization. In: Proc. of ICDAR-03. pp. 104–108. IEEE (2003)

7. Bischl, B., Lang, M., Kotthoff, L., Schiffner, J., Richter, J., Studerus, E., Casalicchio, G., Jones, Z.M.: mlr: Machine Learning in R. Journal of Machine Learning Research 17(170), 1–5 (2016), http://jmlr.org/papers/v17/15-066.html
8. Bozdogan, H.: Model selection and Akaike's information criterion (AIC): The general theory and its analytical extensions. Psychometrika 52(3), 345–370 (1987)
9. Brazdil, P., Soares, C., Da Costa, J.: Ranking learning algorithms: Using IBL and meta-learning on accuracy and time results. Machine Learning 50(3), 251–277 (2003)
10. Brochu, E., Cora, V.M., de Freitas, N.: A tutorial on Bayesian optimization of expensive cost functions, with application to active user modeling and hierarchical reinforcement learning. Tech. Rep. UBC TR-2009-23 and arXiv:1012.2599v1, Department of Computer Science, University of British Columbia (2009)
11. Chapelle, O., Vapnik, V., Bengio, Y.: Model selection for small sample regression. Machine Learning (2001)
12. Feurer, M., Klein, A., Eggensperger, K., Springenberg, J., Blum, M., Hutter, F.: Efficient and robust automated machine learning. In: Cortes, C., Lawrence, N.D., Lee, D.D., Sugiyama, M., Garnett, R. (eds.) Advances in Neural Information Processing Systems 28, pp. 2962–2970. Curran Associates, Inc. (2015), http://papers.nips.cc/paper/5872-efficient-and-robust-automated-machine-learning.pdf
13. Frank, A., Asuncion, A.: UCI machine learning repository (2010), http://archive.ics.uci.edu/ml, uRL: http://archive.ics.uci.edu/ml. University of California, Irvine, School of Information and Computer Sciences
14. Guo, X., Yang, J., Wu, C., Wang, C., Liang, Y.: A novel LS-SVMs hyper-parameter selection based on particle swarm optimization. Neurocomputing 71(16), 3211–3215 (2008)
15. Hall, M., Frank, E., Holmes, G., Pfahringer, B., Reutemann, P., Witten, I.: The WEKA data mining software: an update. ACM SIGKDD Explorations Newsletter 11(1), 10–18 (2009)
16. Hutter, F., Hoos, H., Leyton-Brown, K.: Sequential model-based optimization for general algorithm configuration. In: Proc. of LION-5. pp. 507–523 (2011)
17. Hutter, F., Hoos, H., Leyton-Brown, K., Stützle, T.: ParamILS: an automatic algorithm configuration framework. JAIR 36(1), 267–306 (2009)
18. Jones, D.R., Schonlau, M., Welch, W.J.: Efficient global optimization of expensive black box functions. Journal of Global Optimization 13, 455–492 (1998)
19. Kohavi, R.: A study of cross-validation and bootstrap for accuracy estimation and model selection. In: Proc. of IJCAI-95. pp. 1137–1145 (1995)
20. Kotthoff, L., Thornton, C., Hoos, H.H., Hutter, F., Leyton-Brown, K.: Auto-WEKA 2.0: Automatic model selection and hyperparameter optimization in WEKA. Journal of Machine Learning Research 18(25), 1–5 (2017), http://jmlr.org/papers/v18/16-261.html
21. Krizhevsky, A., Hinton, G.: Learning multiple layers of features from tiny images. Master's thesis, Department of Computer Science, University of Toronto (2009)
22. Leite, R., Brazdil, P., Vanschoren, J.: Selecting classification algorithms with active testing. In: Proc. of MLDM-12. pp. 117–131 (2012)
23. López-Ibáñez, M., Dubois-Lacoste, J., Stützle, T., Birattari, M.: The irace package, iterated race for automatic algorithm configuration. Tech. Rep. TR/IRIDIA/2011-004, IRIDIA, Université Libre de Bruxelles, Belgium (2011), http://iridia.ulb.ac.be/IridiaTrSeries/IridiaTr2011-004.pdf
24. Maron, O., Moore, A.: Hoeffding races: Accelerating model selection search for classification and function approximation. In: Proc. of NIPS-94. pp. 59–66 (1994)
25. McQuarrie, A., Tsai, C.: Regression and time series model selection. World Scientific (1998)
26. Pfahringer, B., Bensusan, H., Giraud-Carrier, C.: Meta-learning by landmarking various learning algorithms. In: Proc. of ICML-00. pp. 743–750 (2000)
27. Schonlau, M., Welch, W.J., Jones, D.R.: Global versus local search in constrained optimization of computer models. In: Flournoy, N., Rosenberger, W., Wong, W. (eds.) New Developments and Applications in Experimental Design, vol. 34, pp. 11–25. Institute of Mathematical Statistics, Hayward, California (1998)

28. Snoek, J., Larochelle, H., Adams, R.P.: Practical bayesian optimization of machine learning algorithms. In: Proc. of NIPS-12 (2012)
29. Srinivas, N., Krause, A., Kakade, S., Seeger, M.: Gaussian process optimization in the bandit setting: No regret and experimental design. In: Proc. of ICML-10. pp. 1015–1022 (2010)
30. Strijov, V., Weber, G.: Nonlinear regression model generation using hyperparameter optimization. Computers & Mathematics with Applications 60(4), 981–988 (2010)
31. Thornton, C., Hutter, F., Hoos, H.H., Leyton-Brown, K.: Auto-WEKA: Combined selection and hyperparameter optimization of classification algorithms. In: KDD (2013)
32. Vilalta, R., Drissi, Y.: A perspective view and survey of meta-learning. Artif. Intell. Rev. 18(2), 77–95 (Oct 2002)
33. Zhao, P., Yu, B.: On model selection consistency of lasso. JMLR 7, 2541–2563 (Dec 2006)

Chapter 5
Hyperopt-Sklearn

Brent Komer, James Bergstra, and Chris Eliasmith

Abstract Hyperopt-sklearn is a software project that provides automated algorithm configuration of the Scikit-learn machine learning library. Following Auto-Weka, we take the view that the choice of classifier and even the choice of preprocessing module can be taken together to represent a single large hyperparameter optimization problem. We use Hyperopt to define a search space that encompasses many standard components (e.g. SVM, RF, KNN, PCA, TFIDF) and common patterns of composing them together. We demonstrate, using search algorithms in Hyperopt and standard benchmarking data sets (MNIST, 20-Newsgroups, Convex Shapes), that searching this space is practical and effective. In particular, we improve on best-known scores for the model space for both MNIST and Convex Shapes at the time of release.

5.1 Introduction

Relative to deep networks, algorithms such as Support Vector Machines (SVMs) and Random Forests (RFs) have a small-enough number of hyperparameters that manual tuning and grid or random search provides satisfactory results. Taking a step back though, there is often no particular reason to use either an SVM or an RF when they are both computationally viable. A model-agnostic practitioner may simply prefer to go with the one that provides greater accuracy. In this light, the choice of classifier can be seen as hyperparameter alongside the C-value in the SVM and the max-tree-depth of the RF. Indeed the choice and configuration of preprocessing components may likewise be seen as part of the model selection/hyperparameter optimization problem.

B. Komer (✉) · J. Bergstra · C. Eliasmith
Center for Theoretical Neuroscience, University of Waterloo, Waterloo, ON, Canada
e-mail: bjkomer@uwaterloo.ca

F. Hutter et al. (eds.), *Automated Machine Learning*, The Springer Series on Challenges in Machine Learning, https://doi.org/10.1007/978-3-030-05318-5_5

The Auto-Weka project [19] was the first to show that an entire library of machine learning approaches (Weka [8]) can be searched within the scope of a single run of hyperparameter tuning. However, Weka is a GPL-licensed Java library, and was not written with scalability in mind, so we feel there is a need for alternatives to Auto-Weka. Scikit-learn [16] is another library of machine learning algorithms. It is written in Python (with many modules in C for greater speed), and is BSD-licensed. Scikit-learn is widely used in the scientific Python community and supports many machine learning application areas.

This chapter introduces Hyperopt-Sklearn: a project that brings the benefits of automated algorithm configuration to users of Python and scikit-learn. Hyperopt-Sklearn uses Hyperopt [3] to describe a search space over possible configurations of scikit-learn components, including preprocessing, classification, and regression modules. One of the main design features of this project is to provide an interface that is familiar to users of scikit-learn. With very little changes, hyperparameter search can be applied to an existing code base. This chapter begins with a background of Hyperopt and the configuration space it uses within scikit-learn, followed by example usage and experimental results with this software.

This chapter is an extended version of our 2014 paper introducing hyperopt-sklearn, presented at the *2014 ICML Workshop on AutoML* [10].

5.2 Background: Hyperopt for Optimization

The Hyperopt library [3] offers optimization algorithms for search spaces that arise in algorithm configuration. These spaces are characterized by a variety of types of variables (continuous, ordinal, categorical), different sensitivity profiles (e.g. uniform vs. log scaling), and conditional structure (when there is a choice between two classifiers, the parameters of one classifier are irrelevant when the other classifier is chosen). To use Hyperopt, a user must define/choose three things:

- A search domain,
- An objective function,
- An optimization algorithm.

The search domain is specified via random variables, whose distributions should be chosen so that the most promising combinations have high prior probability. The search domain can include Python operators and functions that combine random variables into more convenient data structures for the objective function. Any conditional structure is defined within this domain. The objective function maps a joint sampling of these random variables to a scalar-valued score that the optimization algorithm will try to minimize.

An example search domain using Hyperopt is depicted below.

```
from hyperopt import hp

space = hp.choice('my_conditional',
[
    ('case 1', 1 + hp.lognormal('c1', 0, 1)),
    ('case 2', hp.uniform('c2', -10, 10))
    ('case 3', hp.choice('c3', ['a', 'b', 'c']))
])
```

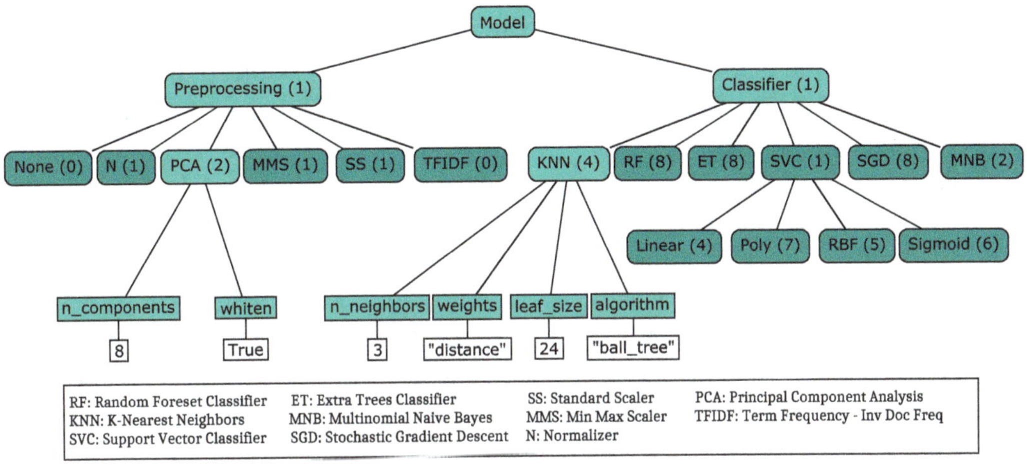

Fig. 5.1 An example hyperopt-sklearn search space consisting of a preprocessing step followed by a classifier. There are six possible preprocessing modules and six possible classifiers. Choosing a model within this configuration space means choosing paths in an ancestral sampling process. The highlighted light blue nodes represent a (PCA, K-Nearest Neighbor) model. The white leaf nodes at the bottom depict example values for their parent hyperparameters. The number of active hyperparameters in a model is the sum of parenthetical numbers in the selected boxes. For the PCA + KNN combination, eight hyperparameters are activated

Here there are four parameters, one for selecting which case is active, and one for each of the three cases. The first case contains a positive valued parameter that is sensitive to log scaling. The second case contains a bounded real valued parameter. The third case contains a categorical parameter with three options.

Having chosen a search domain, an objective function, and an optimization algorithm, Hyperopt's `fmin` function carries out the optimization, and stores results of the search to a database (e.g. either a simple Python list or a MongoDB instance). The `fmin` call carries out the simple analysis of finding the best-performing configuration, and returns that to the caller. The `fmin` call can use multiple workers when using the MongoDB backend, to implement parallel model selection on a compute cluster.

5.3 Scikit-Learn Model Selection as a Search Problem

Model selection is the process of estimating which machine learning model performs best from among a possibly infinite set of options. As an optimization problem, the search domain is the set of valid assignments to the configuration parameters (hyperparameters) of the machine learning model.The objective function is typically the measure of success (e.g. accuracy, F1-Score, etc) on held-out examples. Often the negative degree of success (loss) is used to set up the task as a minimization problem, and cross-validation is applied to produce a more robust final score. Practitioners usually address this optimization by hand, by grid search, or by random search. In this chapter we discuss solving it with the Hyperopt optimization library. The basic approach is to set up a search space with random variable hyperparameters, use scikit-learn to implement the objective function that performs model training and model validation, and use Hyperopt to optimize the hyperparameters.

Scikit-learn includes many algorithms for learning from data (classification or regression), as well as many algorithms for preprocessing data into the vectors expected by these learning algorithms. Classifiers include for example, K-Nearest-Neighbors, Support Vector Machines, and Random Forest algorithms. Preprocessing algorithms include transformations such as component-wise Z-scaling (Normalizer) and Principle Components Analysis (PCA). A full classification algorithm typically includes a series of preprocessing steps followed by a classifier. For this reason, scikit-learn provides a pipeline data structure to represent and use a sequence of preprocessing steps and a classifier as if they were just one component (typically with an API similar to the classifier). Although hyperopt-sklearn does not formally use scikit-learn's pipeline object, it provides related functionality. Hyperopt-sklearn provides a parameterization of a search space over pipelines, that is, of sequences of preprocessing steps and classifiers or regressors.

The configuration space provided at the time of this writing currently includes 24 classifiers, 12 regressors, and 7 preprocessing methods. Being an open-source project, this space is likely to expand in the future as more users contribute. Upon initial release, only a subset of the search space was available, consisting of six classifiers and five preprocessing algorithms. This space was used for initial performance analysis and is illustrated in Fig. 5.1. In total, this parameterization contains 65 hyperparameters: 15 boolean variables, 14 categorical, 17 discrete, and 19 real-valued variables.

Although the total number of hyperparameters in the full configuration space is large, the number of active hyperparameters describing any one model is much smaller: a model consisting of PCA and a RandomForest for example, would have only 12 active hyperparameters (1 for the choice of preprocessing, 2 internal to PCA, 1 for the choice of classifier and 8 internal to the RF). Hyperopt description language allows us to differentiate between conditional hyperparameters (which must always be assigned) and non-conditional hyperparameters (which may remain unassigned when they would be unused). We make use of this mechanism extensively so that Hyperopt's search algorithms do not waste time learning by trial and error that e.g. RF hyperparameters have no effect on SVM performance. Even internally within classifiers, there are instances of conditional parameters: KNN has conditional parameters depending on the distance metric, and LinearSVC has 3 binary parameters (loss, penalty, and dual) that admit only 4 valid joint assignments. Hyperopt-sklearn also includes a blacklist of (preprocessing, classifier) pairs that do not work together, e.g. PCA and MinMaxScaler were incompatible with MultinomialNB, TF-IDF could only be used for text data, and the tree-based classifiers were not compatible with the sparse features produced by the TF-IDF preprocessor. Allowing for a 10-way discretization of real-valued hyperparameters, and taking these conditional hyperparameters into account, a grid search of our search space would still require an infeasible number of evalutions (on the order of 10^{12}).

Finally, the search space becomes an optimization problem when we also define a scalar-valued search objective. By default, Hyperopt-sklearn uses scikit-learn's score method on validation data to define the search criterion. For classifiers, this is the so-called "Zero-One Loss": the number of correct label predictions among data that has been withheld from the data set used for training (and also from the data used for testing after the model selection search process).

5.4 Example Usage

Following Scikit-learn's convention, hyperopt-sklearn provides an Estimator class with a fit method and a predict method. The fit method of this class performs hyperparameter optimization, and after it has completed, the predict method applies the best model to given test data. Each evaluation during optimization performs training on a large fraction of the training set, estimates test set accuracy on a validation set, and returns that validation set score to the optimizer. At the end of search, the best configuration is retrained on the whole data set to produce the classifier that handles subsequent predict calls.

One of the important goals of hyperopt-sklearn is that it is easy to learn and to use. To facilitate this, the syntax for fitting a classifier to data and making predictions is very similar to scikit-learn. Here is the simplest example of using this software.

```
from hpsklearn import HyperoptEstimator

# Load data
train_data, train_label, test_data, test_label =
    load_my_data()

# Create the estimator object
estim = HyperoptEstimator()
```

```
# Search the space of classifiers and preprocessing steps and
    their
# respective hyperparameters in scikit-learn to fit a model
    to the data
estim.fit(train_data, train_label)

# Make a prediction using the optimized model
prediction = estim.predict(test_data)

# Report the accuracy of the classifier on a given set of data
score = estim.score(test_data, test_label)

# Return instances of the classifier and preprocessing steps
model = estim.best_model()
```

The HyperoptEstimator object contains the information of what space to search as well as how to search it. It can be configured to use a variety of hyperparameter search algorithms and also supports using a combination of algorithms. Any algorithm that supports the same interface as the algorithms in hyperopt can be used here. This is also where you, the user, can specify the maximum number of function evaluations you would like to be run as well as a timeout (in seconds) for each run.

```
from hpsklearn import HyperoptEstimator
from hyperopt import tpe
estim = HyperoptEstimator(algo=tpe.suggest,
                          max_evals=150,
                          trial_timeout=60)
```

Each search algorithm can bring its own bias to the search space, and it may not be clear that one particular strategy is the best in all cases. Sometimes it can be helpful to use a mixture of search algorithms.

```
from hpsklearn import HyperoptEstimator
from hyperopt import anneal, rand, tpe, mix
# define an algorithm that searches randomly 5% of the time,
# uses TPE 75% of the time, and uses annealing 20% of the time
mix_algo = partial(mix.suggest, p_suggest=[
        (0.05, rand.suggest),
        (0.75, tpe.suggest),
        (0.20, anneal.suggest)])
estim = HyperoptEstimator(algo=mix_algo,
                          max_evals=150,
                          trial_timeout=60)
```

Searching effectively over the entire space of classifiers available in scikit-learn can use a lot of time and computational resources. Sometimes you might have a particular subspace of models that they are more interested in. With hyperopt-sklearn it is possible to specify a more narrow search space to allow it to be explored in greater depth.

```
from hpsklearn import HyperoptEstimator, svc

# limit the search to only SVC models
estim = HyperoptEstimator(classifier=svc('my_svc'))
```

Combinations of different spaces can also be used.

```
from hpsklearn import HyperoptEstimator, svc, knn
from hyperopt import hp

# restrict the space to contain only random forest,
# k-nearest neighbors, and SVC models.
clf = hp.choice('my_name',
    [random_forest('my_name.random_forest'),
     svc('my_name.svc'),
     knn('my_name.knn')])
estim = HyperoptEstimator(classifier=clf)
```

The support vector machine provided by scikit-learn has a number of different kernels that can be used (linear, rbf, poly, sigmoid). Changing the kernel can have a large effect on the performance of the model, and each kernel has its own unique hyperparameters. To account for this, hyperopt-sklearn treats each kernel choice as a unique model in the search space. If you already know which kernel works best for your data, or you are just interested in exploring models with a particular kernel, you may specify it directly rather than going through the svc.

```
from hpsklearn import HyperoptEstimator, svc_rbf
estim = HyperoptEstimator(classifier=svc_rbf('my_svc'))
```

It is also possible to specify which kernels you are interested in by passing a list to the svc.

```
from hpsklearn import HyperoptEstimator, svc
estim = HyperoptEstimator(
     classifier=svc('my_svc',
                    kernels=['linear',
                             'sigmoid']))
```

In a similar manner to classifiers, the space of preprocessing modules can be fine tuned. Multiple successive stages of preprocessing can be specified through an ordered list. An empty list means that no preprocessing will be done on the data.

```
from hpsklearn import HyperoptEstimator, pca
estim = HyperoptEstimator(preprocessing=[pca('my_pca')])
```

Combinations of different spaces can be used here as well.

```
from hpsklearn import HyperoptEstimator, tfidf, pca
from hyperopt import hp
preproc = hp.choice('my_name',
    [[pca('my_name.pca')],
     [pca('my_name.pca'), normalizer('my_name.norm')]
     [standard_scaler('my_name.std_scaler')],
     []])
estim = HyperoptEstimator(preprocessing=preproc)
```

Some types of preprocessing will only work on specific types of data. For example, the TfidfVectorizer that scikit-learn provides is designed to work with text data and would not be appropriate for other types of data. To address this, hyperopt-sklearn comes with a few pre-defined spaces of classifiers and preprocessing tailored to specific data types.

```
from hpsklearn import HyperoptEstimator, \
                    any_sparse_classifier, \
                    any_text_preprocessing
from hyperopt import tpe
estim = HyperoptEstimator(
     algo=tpe.suggest,
     classifier=any_sparse_classifier('my_clf')
     preprocessing=any_text_preprocessing('my_pp')
     max_evals=200,
     trial_timeout=60)
```

So far in all of these examples, every hyperparameter available to the model is being searched over. It is also possible for you to specify the values of specific hyperparameters, and those parameters will remain constant during the search. This could be useful, for example, if you knew you wanted to use whitened PCA data and a degree-3 polynomial kernel SVM.

```
from hpsklearn import HyperoptEstimator, pca, svc_poly
estim = HyperoptEstimator(
        preprocessing=[pca('my_pca', whiten=True)],
        classifier=svc_poly('my_poly', degree=3))
```

It is also possible to specify ranges of individual parameters. This is done using the standard hyperopt syntax. These will override the defaults defined within hyperopt-sklearn.

```
from hpsklearn import HyperoptEstimator, pca, sgd
from hyperopt import hp
import numpy as np
```

```
sgd_loss = hp.pchoice('loss',
                      [(0.50, 'hinge'),
                       (0.25, 'log'),
                       (0.25, 'huber')])
sgd_penalty = hp.choice('penalty',
                        ['l2', 'elasticnet'])
sgd_alpha = hp.loguniform('alpha',
                          low=np.log(1e-5),
                          high=np.log(1) )
estim = HyperoptEstimator(
        classifier=sgd('my_sgd',
                       loss=sgd_loss,
                       penalty=sgd_penalty,
                       alpha=sgd_alpha) )
```

All of the components available to the user can be found in the `components.py` file. A complete working example of using hyperopt-sklearn to find a model for the 20 newsgroups data set is shown below.

```
from hpsklearn import HyperoptEstimator, tfidf,
    any_sparse_classifier
from sklearn.datasets import fetch_20newsgroups
from hyperopt import tpe
import numpy as np
# Download data and split training and test sets
train = fetch_20newsgroups(subset='train')
test = fetch_20newsgroups(subset='test')
X_train = train.data
y_train = train.target
X_test = test.data
y_test = test.target
estim = HyperoptEstimator(
        classifier=any_sparse_classifier('clf'),
        preprocessing=[tfidf('tfidf')],
        algo=tpe.suggest,
        trial_timeout=180)
estim.fit(X_train, y_train)
print(estim.score(X_test, y_test))
print(estim.best_model())
```

5.5 Experiments

We conducted experiments on three data sets to establish that hyperopt-sklearn can find accurate models on a range of data sets in a reasonable amount of time. Results were collected on three data sets: MNIST, 20-Newsgroups, and Convex Shapes. MNIST is a well-known data set of 70 K 28×28 greyscale images of hand-drawn digits [12]. 20-Newsgroups is a 20-way classification data set of 20 K newsgroup messages ([13], we did not remove the headers for our experiments). Convex Shapes is a binary classification task of distinguishing pictures of convex white-colored regions in small (32 × 32) black-and-white images [11].

Fig. 5.2 (left) shows that there was no penalty for searching broadly. We performed optimization runs of up to 300 function evaluations searching the subset of the space depicted in Fig. 5.1, and compared the quality of solution with specialized searches of specific classifier types (including best known classifiers).

Fig. 5.2 (right) shows that search could find different, good models. This figure was constructed by running hyperopt-sklearn with different initial conditions (number of evaluations, choice of optimization algorithm, and random number seed) and keeping track of what final model was chosen after each run. Although support vector machines were always among the best, the parameters of best SVMs looked very different across data sets. For example, on the image data sets (MNIST and Convex) the SVMs chosen never had a sigmoid or linear kernel, while on 20 newsgroups the linear and sigmoid kernel were often best.

Sometimes researchers not familiar with machine learning techniques may simply use the default parameters of the classifiers available to them. To look at the effectiveness of hyperopt-sklearn as a drop-in replacement for this approach, a comparison between the performance of the default scikit-learn parameters and a small search (25 evaluations) of the default hyperopt-sklearn space was conducted. The results on the 20 Newsgroups dataset are shown in Fig. 5.3. Improved performance over the baseline is observed in all cases, which suggests that this search technique is valuable even with a small computational budget.

5.6 Discussion and Future Work

Table 5.1 lists the test set scores of the best models found by cross-validation, as well as some points of reference from previous work. Hyperopt-sklearn's scores are relatively good on each data set, indicating that with hyperopt-sklearn's parameterization, Hyperopt's optimization algorithms are competitive with human experts.

The model with the best performance on the MNIST Digits data set uses deep artificial neural networks. Small receptive fields of convolutional winner-take-all neurons build up the large network. Each neural column becomes an expert on inputs preprocessed in different ways, and the average prediction of 35 deep neural columns to come up with a single final prediction [4]. This model is much more advanced than those available in scikit-learn. The previously best known model in the scikit-learn search space is a radial-basis SVM on centered data that scores 98.6%, and hyperopt-sklearn matches that performance [15].

Table 5.1 Hyperopt-sklearn scores relative to selections from literature on the three data sets used in our experiments. On MNIST, hyperopt-sklearn is one of the best-scoring methods that does not use image-specific domain knowledge (these scores and others may be found at http://yann.lecun.com/exdb/mnist/). On 20 Newsgroups, hyperopt-sklearn is competitive with similar approaches from the literature (scores taken from [7]). In the 20 Newsgroups data set, the score reported for hyperopt-sklearn is the weighted-average F1 score provided by sklearn. The other approaches shown here use the macro-average F1 score. On Convex Shapes, hyperopt-sklearn outperforms previous automated algorithm configuration approaches [6] and manual tuning [11]

MNIST		20 Newsgroups		Convex shapes	
Approach	Accuracy	Approach	F-Score	Approach	Accuracy
Committee of convnets	99.8%	CFC	0.928	**hyperopt-sklearn**	**88.7%**
hyperopt-sklearn	**98.7%**	**hyperopt-sklearn**	**0.856**	hp-dbnet	84.6%
libSVM grid search	98.6%	SVMTorch	0.848	dbn-3	81.4%
Boosted trees	98.5%	LibSVM	0.843		

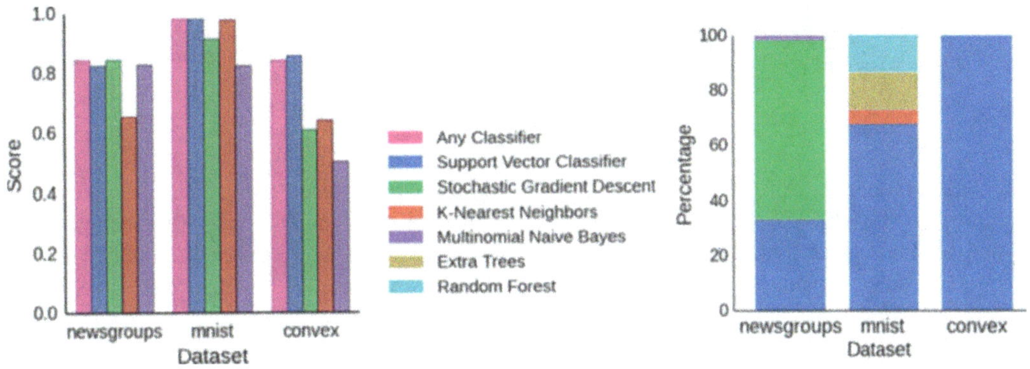

Fig. 5.2 Left: Best model performance. For each data set, searching the full configuration space ("Any Classifier") delivered performance approximately on par with a search that was restricted to the best classifier type. Each bar represents the score obtained from a search restricted to that particular classifier. For the "Any Classifier" case there is no restriction on the search space. In all cases 300 hyperparameter evaluations were performed. Score is F1 for 20 Newsgroups, and accuracy for MNIST and Convex Shapes.
Right: Model selection distribution. Looking at the best models from all optimization runs performed on the full search space (Any Classifier, using different initial conditions, and different optimization algorithms) we see that different data sets are handled best by different classifiers. SVC was the only classifier ever chosen as the best model for Convex Shapes, and was often found to be best on MNIST and 20 Newsgroups, however the best SVC parameters were very different across data sets

The CFC model that performed quite well on the 20 newsgroups document classification data set is a Class-Feature-Centroid classifier. Centroid approaches are typically inferior to an SVM, due to the centroids found during training being far from the optimal location. The CFC method reported here uses a centroid built from the inter-class term index and the inner-class term index. It uses a novel combination of these indices along with a denormalized cosine measure to calculate the similarity score between the centroid and a text vector [7]. This style of model is not currently implemented in hyperopt-sklearn, and our experiments suggest that existing hyperopt-sklearn components cannot be assembled to match its level of performance. Perhaps when it is implemented, Hyperopt may find a set of parameters that provides even greater classification accuracy.

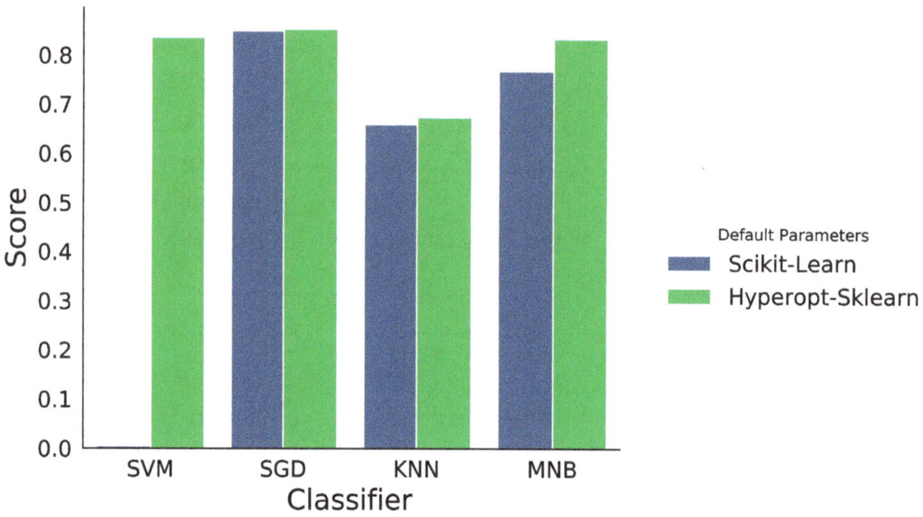

Fig. 5.3 Comparison of F1-Score on the 20 Newsgroups dataset using either the default parameters of scikit-learn or the default search space of hyperopt-sklearn. The results from hyperopt-sklearn were obtained from a single run with 25 evaluations, restricted to either Support Vector Classifier, Stochastic Gradient Descent, K-Nearest Neighbors, or Multinomial Naive Bayes

On the Convex Shapes data set, our Hyperopt-sklearn experiments revealed a more accurate model than was previously believed to exist in any search space, let alone a search space of such standard components. This result underscores the difficulty and importance of hyperparameter search.

Hyperopt-sklearn provides many opportunities for future work: more classifiers and preprocessing modules could be included in the search space, and there are more ways to combine even the existing components. Other types of data require different preprocessing, and other prediction problems exist beyond classification. In expanding the search space, care must be taken to ensure that the benefits of new models outweigh the greater difficulty of searching a larger space. There are some parameters that scikit-learn exposes that are more implementation details than actual hyperparameters that affect the fit (such as `algorithm` and `leaf_size` in the KNN model). Care should be taken to identify these parameters in each model and they may need to be treated differently during exploration.

It is possible for a user to add their own classifier to the search space as long as it fits the scikit-learn interface. This currently requires some understanding of how hyperopt-sklearn's code is structured and it would be nice to improve the support for this so minimal effort is required by the user. It is also possible for the user to specify alternate scoring methods besides the default accuracy or F-measure, as there can be cases where these are not best suited to the particular problem.

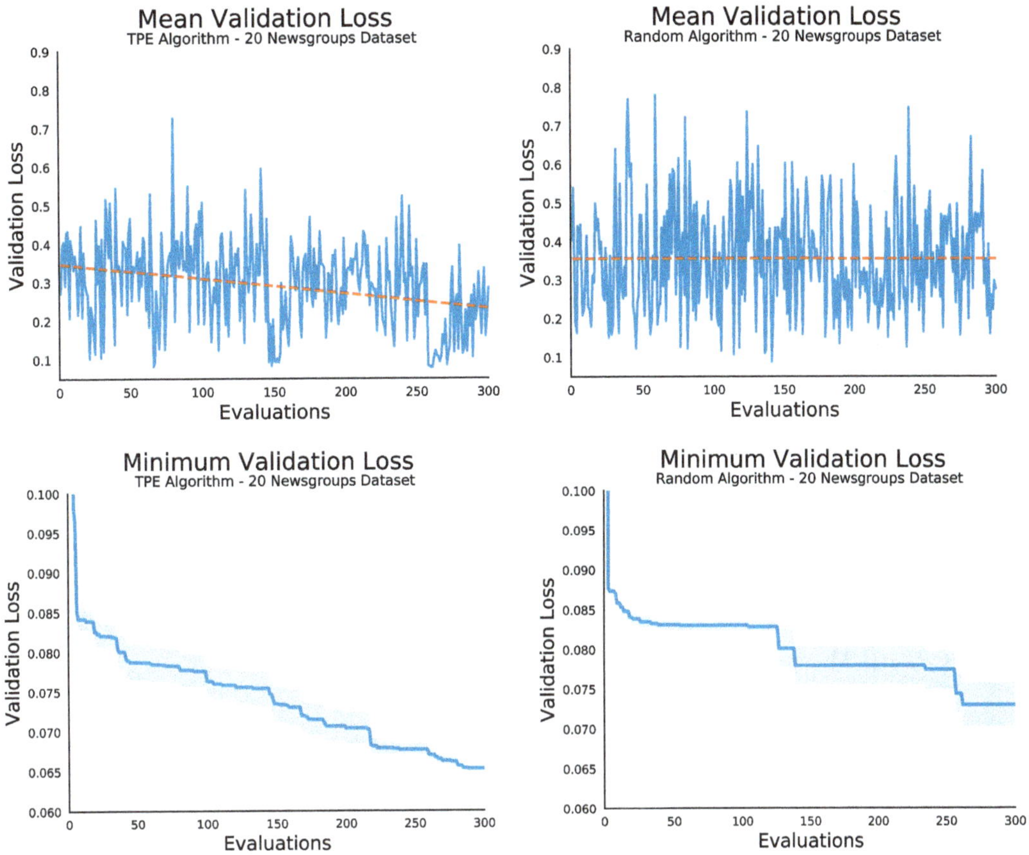

Fig. 5.4 Validation loss of models found for each successive parameter evaluation using the 20 Newsgroups dataset and the Any Classifier search domain. **Upper Left**: Mean validation loss at each step across different random number seeds for the TPE algorithm. Downward trend indicates more promising regions are explored more often over time. **Upper Right**: Mean validation loss for the random algorithm. Flat trend illustrates no learning from previous trials. Large variation in performance across evaluations indicates the problem is very sensitive to hyperparameter tunings. **Lower Left**: Minimum validation loss of models found so far for the TPE algorithm. Gradual progress is made on 20 Newsgroups over 300 iterations and gives no indication of convergence. **Lower Right**: Minimum validation loss for the random algorithm. Progress is initially rapid for the first 40 or so evaluations and then settles for long periods. Improvement still continues, but becomes less likely as time goes on

We have shown here that Hyperopt's random search, annealing search, and TPE algorithms make Hyperopt-sklearn viable, but the slow convergence in Fig. 5.4 suggests that other optimization algorithms might be more call-efficient. The development of Bayesian optimization algorithms is an active research area, and we look forward to looking at how other search algorithms interact with hyperopt-sklearn's search spaces. Hyperparameter optimization opens up a new art of matching the parameterization of search spaces to the strengths of search algorithms.

Computational wall time spent on search is of great practical importance, and hyperopt-sklearn currently spends a significant amount of time evaluating points that are un-promising. Techniques for recognizing bad performers early could speed up search enormously [5, 18].

5.7 Conclusions

This chapter has introduced Hyperopt-sklearn, a Python package for automated algorithm configuration of standard machine learning algorithms provided by Scikit-Learn. Hyperopt-sklearn provides a unified interface to a large subset of the machine learning algorithms available in scikit-learn and with the help of Hyperopt's optimization functions it is able to both rival and surpass human experts in algorithm configuration. We hope that it provides practitioners with a useful tool for the development of machine learning systems, and automated machine learning researchers with benchmarks for future work in algorithm configuration.

Acknowledgements This research was supported by the NSERC Banting Fellowship program, the NSERC Engage Program and by D-Wave Systems. Thanks also to Hristijan Bogoevski for early drafts of a hyperopt-to-scikit-learn bridge.

Bibliography

1. J. Bergstra, R. Bardenet, Y. Bengio, and B. Kegl. Algorithms for hyper-parameter optimization, NIPS, 24:2546–2554, 2011.
2. J. Bergstra, D. Yamins, and D. D. Cox. Making a science of model search: Hyperparameter optimization in hundreds of dimensions for vision architectures, In Proc. ICML, 2013a.
3. J. Bergstra, D. Yamins, and D. D. Cox. Hyperopt: A Python library for optimizing the hyperparameters of machine learning algorithms, SciPy'13, 2013b.
4. D. Ciresan, U. Meier, and J. Schmidhuber. Multi-column Deep Neural Networks for Image Classification, IEEE Conference on Computer Vision and Pattern Recognition (CVPR), 3642–3649. 2012.
5. T. Domhan, T. Springenberg, F. Hutter. Extrapolating Learning Curves of Deep Neural Networks, ICML AutoML Workshop, 2014.
6. K. Eggensperger, M. Feurer, F. Hutter, J. Bergstra, J. Snoek, H. Hoos, and K. Leyton-Brown. Towards an empirical foundation for assessing bayesian optimization of hyperparameters, NIPS workshop on Bayesian Optimization in Theory and Practice, 2013.
7. H. Guan, J. Zhou, and M. Guo. A class-feature-centroid classifier for text categorization, Proceedings of the 18th international conference on World wide web, 201–210. ACM, 2009.
8. M. Hall, E. Frank, G. Holmes, B. Pfahringer, P. Reutemann, and I. H. Witten. The weka data mining software: an update, ACM SIGKDD explorations newsletter, 11(1):10–18, 2009.
9. F. Hutter, H. Hoos, and K. Leyton-Brown. Sequential model-based optimization for general algorithm configuration, LION-5, 2011. Extended version as UBC Tech report TR-2010-10.
10. B. Komer, J. Bergstra, and C. Eliasmith. Hyperopt-sklearn: automatic hyperparameter configuration for scikit-learn, ICML AutoML Workshop, 2014.
11. H. Larochelle, D. Erhan, A. Courville, J. Bergstra, and Y. Bengio. An empirical evaluation of deep architectures on problems with many factors of variation, ICML, 473–480, 2007.
12. Y. LeCun, L. Bottou, Y. Bengio, and P. Haffner. Gradient-based learning applied to document recognition, Proceedings of the IEEE, 86(11):2278–2324, November 1998.
13. T. Mitchell. 20 newsgroups data set, http://qwone.com/jason/20Newsgroups/, 1996.
14. J. Mockus, V. Tiesis, and A. Zilinskas. The application of Bayesian methods for seeking the extremum, L.C.W. Dixon and G.P. Szego, editors, Towards Global Optimization, volume 2, pages 117–129. North Holland, New York, 1978.
15. The MNIST Database of handwritten digits: http://yann.lecun.com/exdb/mnist/

16. F. Pedregosa, G. Varoquaux, A. Gramfort, V. Michel, B. Thirion, O. Grisel, M. Blondel, P. Prettenhofer, R. Weiss, V. Dubourg, J. Vanderplas, A. Passos, D. Cournapeau, M. Brucher, M. Perrot, and E. Duchesnay. Scikit-learn: Machine Learning in Python, Journal of Machine Learning Research, 12:2825–2830, 2011.
17. J. Snoek, H. Larochelle, and R. P. Adams. Practical Bayesian optimization of machine learning algorithms, Neural Information Processing Systems, 2012.
18. K. Swersky, J. Snoek, R.P. Adams. Freeze-Thaw Bayesian Optimization, arXiv:1406.3896, 2014.
19. C. Thornton, F. Hutter, H. H. Hoos, and K. Leyton-Brown. AutoWEKA: Automated selection and hyper-parameter optimization of classification algorithms, KDD 847–855, 2013.

Chapter 6
Auto-sklearn: Efficient and Robust Automated Machine Learning

Matthias Feurer, Aaron Klein, Katharina Eggensperger, Jost Tobias Springenberg, Manuel Blum, and Frank Hutter

Abstract The success of machine learning in a broad range of applications has led to an ever-growing demand for machine learning systems that can be used off the shelf by non-experts. To be effective in practice, such systems need to automatically choose a good algorithm and feature preprocessing steps for a new dataset at hand, and also set their respective hyperparameters. Recent work has started to tackle this *automated machine learning (AutoML)* problem with the help of efficient Bayesian optimization methods. Building on this, we introduce a robust new AutoML system based on the Python machine learning package scikit-learn (using 15 classifiers, 14 feature preprocessing methods, and 4 data preprocessing methods, giving rise to a structured hypothesis space with 110 hyperparameters). This system, which we dub *Auto-sklearn*, improves on existing AutoML methods by automatically taking into account past performance on similar datasets, and by constructing ensembles from the models evaluated during the optimization. Our system won six out of ten phases of the first ChaLearn AutoML challenge, and our comprehensive analysis on over 100 diverse datasets shows that it substantially outperforms the previous state of the art in AutoML. We also demonstrate the performance gains due to each of our contributions and derive insights into the effectiveness of the individual components of Auto-sklearn.

6.1 Introduction

Machine learning has recently made great strides in many application areas, fueling a growing demand for machine learning systems that can be used effectively by novices in machine learning. Correspondingly, a growing number of commercial

---

M. Feurer (✉) · A. Klein · K. Eggensperger · J. T. Springenberg · M. Blum
Department of Computer Science, University of Freiburg, Freiburg, Baden-Württemberg, Germany
e-mail: feurerm@informatik.uni-freiburg.de

F. Hutter
Department of Computer Science, University of Freiburg, Freiburg, Germany

F. Hutter et al. (eds.), *Automated Machine Learning*, The Springer Series on Challenges in Machine Learning, https://doi.org/10.1007/978-3-030-05318-5_6

enterprises aim to satisfy this demand (e.g., BigML.com, Wise.io, H2O.ai, feedzai.com, RapidMiner.com, Prediction.io, DataRobot.com, Microsoft's Azure Machine Learning, Google's Cloud Machine Learning Engine, and Amazon Machine Learning). At its core, every effective machine learning service needs to solve the fundamental problems of deciding which machine learning algorithm to use on a given dataset, whether and how to preprocess its features, and how to set all hyperparameters. This is the problem we address in this work.

More specifically, we investigate automated machine learning (AutoML), the problem of automatically (without human input) producing test set predictions for a new dataset within a fixed computational budget. Formally, this AutoML problem can be stated as follows:

Definition 1 (AutoML problem) For $i = 1, \ldots, n+m$, let $\boldsymbol{x}_i$ denote a feature vector and y_i the corresponding target value. Given a training dataset $D_{train} = \{(\boldsymbol{x}_1, y_1), \ldots, (\boldsymbol{x}_n, y_n)\}$ and the feature vectors $\boldsymbol{x}_{n+1}, \ldots, \boldsymbol{x}_{n+m}$ of a test dataset $D_{test} = \{(\boldsymbol{x}_{n+1}, y_{n+1}), \ldots, (\boldsymbol{x}_{n+m}, y_{n+m})\}$ drawn from the same underlying data distribution, as well as a resource budget b and a loss metric $\mathcal{L}(\cdot,\cdot)$, the AutoML problem is to (automatically) produce accurate test set predictions $\hat{y}_{n+1}, \ldots, \hat{y}_{n+m}$. The loss of a solution $\hat{y}_{n+1}, \ldots, \hat{y}_{n+m}$ to the AutoML problem is given by $\frac{1}{m}\sum_{j=1}^{m} \mathcal{L}(\hat{y}_{n+j}, y_{n+j})$.

In practice, the budget b would comprise computational resources, such as CPU and/or wallclock time and memory usage. This problem definition reflects the setting of the first ChaLearn AutoML challenge [23] (also, see Chap. 10 for a description and analysis of the first AutoML challenge). The AutoML system we describe here won six out of ten phases of that challenge.

Here, we follow and extend the AutoML approach first introduced by Auto-WEKA [42]. At its core, this approach combines a highly parametric machine learning framework F with a Bayesian optimization [7, 40] method for instantiating F well for a given dataset.

The contribution of this paper is to extend this AutoML approach in various ways that considerably improve its *efficiency* and *robustness*, based on principles that apply to a wide range of machine learning frameworks (such as those used by the machine learning service providers mentioned above). First, following successful previous work for low dimensional optimization problems [21, 22, 38], we reason across datasets to identify instantiations of machine learning frameworks that perform well on a new dataset and warmstart Bayesian optimization with them (Sect. 6.3.1). Second, we automatically construct ensembles of the models considered by Bayesian optimization (Sect. 6.3.2). Third, we carefully design a highly parameterized machine learning framework from high-performing classifiers and preprocessors implemented in the popular machine learning framework scikit-learn [36] (Sect. 6.4). Finally, we perform an extensive empirical analysis using a diverse collection of datasets to demonstrate that the resulting Auto-sklearn system outperforms previous state-of-the-art AutoML methods (Sect. 6.5), to show that each of our contributions leads to substantial performance improvements

(Sect. 6.6), and to gain insights into the performance of the individual classifiers and preprocessors used in Auto-sklearn (Sect. 6.7).

This chapter is an extended version of our 2015 paper introducing Auto-sklearn, published in the *proceedings of NeurIPS 2015* [20].

6.2 AutoML as a CASH Problem

We first review the formalization of AutoML as a *Combined Algorithm Selection and Hyperparameter optimization (CASH)* problem used by Auto-WEKA's AutoML approach. Two important problems in AutoML are that (1) no single machine learning method performs best on all datasets and (2) some machine learning methods (e.g., non-linear SVMs) crucially rely on hyperparameter optimization. The latter problem has been successfully attacked using Bayesian optimization [7, 40], which nowadays forms a core component of many AutoML systems. The former problem is intertwined with the latter since the rankings of algorithms depend on whether their hyperparameters are tuned properly. Fortunately, the two problems can efficiently be tackled as a single, structured, joint optimization problem:

Definition 2 (CASH) Let $\mathcal{A} = \{A^{(1)}, \ldots, A^{(R)}\}$ be a set of algorithms, and let the hyperparameters of each algorithm $A^{(j)}$ have domain $\mathbf{\Lambda}^{(j)}$. Further, let $D_{train} = \{(x_1, y_1), \ldots, (x_n, y_n)\}$ be a training set which is split into K cross-validation folds $\{D_{valid}^{(1)}, \ldots, D_{valid}^{(K)}\}$ and $\{D_{train}^{(1)}, \ldots, D_{train}^{(K)}\}$ such that $D_{train}^{(i)} = D_{train} \backslash D_{valid}^{(i)}$ for $i = 1, \ldots, K$. Finally, let $\mathcal{L}(A_{\boldsymbol{\lambda}}^{(j)}, D_{train}^{(i)}, D_{valid}^{(i)})$ denote the loss that algorithm $A^{(j)}$ achieves on $D_{valid}^{(i)}$ when trained on $D_{train}^{(i)}$ with hyperparameters $\boldsymbol{\lambda}$. Then, the *Combined Algorithm Selection and Hyperparameter optimization (CASH)* problem is to find the joint algorithm and hyperparameter setting that minimizes this loss:

$$A^{\star}, \boldsymbol{\lambda}_{\star} \in \underset{A^{(j)} \in \mathcal{A}, \boldsymbol{\lambda} \in \mathbf{\Lambda}^{(j)}}{\operatorname{argmin}} \frac{1}{K} \sum_{i=1}^{K} \mathcal{L}(A_{\boldsymbol{\lambda}}^{(j)}, D_{train}^{(i)}, D_{valid}^{(i)}). \tag{6.1}$$

This CASH problem was first tackled by Thornton et al. [42] in the Auto-WEKA system using the machine learning framework WEKA [25] and tree-based Bayesian optimization methods [5, 27]. In a nutshell, Bayesian optimization [7] fits a probabilistic model to capture the relationship between hyperparameter settings and their measured performance; it then uses this model to select the most promising hyperparameter setting (trading off exploration of new parts of the space vs. exploitation in known good regions), evaluates that hyperparameter setting, updates the model with the result, and iterates. While Bayesian optimization based on Gaussian process models (e.g., Snoek et al. [41]) performs best in low-dimensional problems with numerical hyperparameters, tree-based models have been shown to be more successful in high-dimensional, structured, and partly discrete problems [15]—such as the CASH problem—and are also used in the AutoML system HYPEROPT-SKLEARN [30]. Among the tree-based Bayesian optimization methods, Thornton et al. [42] found the random-forest-based SMAC [27] to outperform the tree Parzen estimator TPE [5], and we therefore use SMAC to solve the CASH problem in this paper. Next to its use of random forests [6], SMAC's main distinguishing feature is that it allows fast cross-validation by evaluating one fold at a time and discarding poorly-performing hyperparameter settings early.

6.3 New Methods for Increasing Efficiency and Robustness of AutoML

We now discuss our two improvements of the AutoML approach. First, we include a meta-learning step to warmstart the Bayesian optimization procedure, which results in a considerable boost in efficiency. Second, we include an automated ensemble construction step, allowing us to use all classifiers that were found by Bayesian optimization.

Fig. 6.1 summarizes the overall AutoML workflow, including both of our improvements. We note that we expect their effectiveness to be greater for flexible ML frameworks that offer many degrees of freedom (e.g., many algorithms, hyperparameters, and preprocessing methods).

6.3.1 Meta-learning for Finding Good Instantiations of Machine Learning Frameworks

Domain experts derive knowledge from previous tasks: They *learn about the performance of machine learning algorithms*. The area of meta-learning (see Chap. 2) mimics this strategy by reasoning about the performance of learning algorithms across datasets. In this work, we apply meta-learning to select instantiations of our given machine learning framework that are likely to perform well on a new dataset. More specifically, for a large number of datasets, we collect both performance data

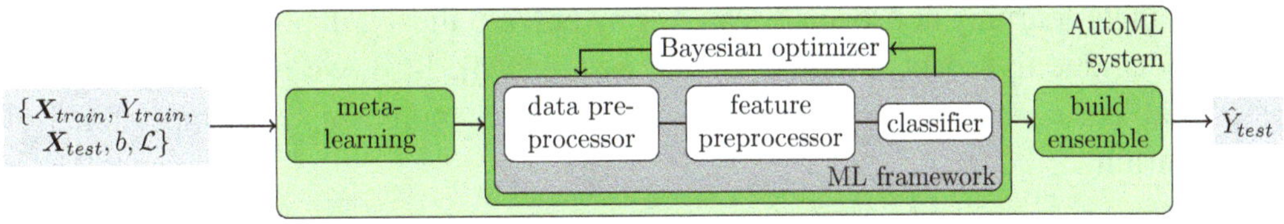

Fig. 6.1 Our improved AutoML approach. We add two components to Bayesian hyperparameter optimization of an ML framework: meta-learning for initializing the Bayesian optimizer and automated ensemble construction from configurations evaluated during optimization

and a set of *meta-features*, i.e., characteristics of the dataset that can be computed efficiently and that help to determine which algorithm to use on a new dataset.

This meta-learning approach is complementary to Bayesian optimization for optimizing an ML framework. Meta-learning can quickly suggest some instantiations of the ML framework that are likely to perform quite well, but it is unable to provide fine-grained information on performance. In contrast, Bayesian optimization is slow to start for hyperparameter spaces as large as those of entire ML frameworks, but can fine-tune performance over time. We exploit this complementarity by selecting k configurations based on meta-learning and use their result to seed Bayesian optimization. This approach of warmstarting optimization by meta-learning has already been successfully applied before [21, 22, 38], but never to an optimization problem as complex as that of searching the space of instantiations of a full-fledged ML framework. Likewise, learning across datasets has also been applied in collaborative Bayesian optimization methods [4, 45]; while these approaches are promising, they are so far limited to very few meta-features and cannot yet cope with the high-dimensional partially discrete configuration spaces faced in AutoML.

More precisely, our meta-learning approach works as follows. In an offline phase, for each machine learning dataset in a dataset repository (in our case 140 datasets from the OpenML [43] repository), we evaluated a set of meta-features (described below) and used Bayesian optimization to determine and store an instantiation of the given ML framework with strong empirical performance for that dataset. (In detail, we ran SMAC [27] for 24 h with 10-fold cross-validation on two thirds of the data and stored the resulting ML framework instantiation which exhibited best performance on the remaining third). Then, given a new dataset $\mathcal{D}$, we compute its meta-features, rank all datasets by their L_1 distance to $\mathcal{D}$ in meta-feature space and select the stored ML framework instantiations for the $k = 25$ nearest datasets for evaluation before starting Bayesian optimization with their results.

To characterize datasets, we implemented a total of 38 meta-features from the literature, including simple, information-theoretic and statistical meta-features [29, 33], such as statistics about the number of data points, features, and classes, as well as data skewness, and the entropy of the targets. All meta-features are listed in Table 1 of the original publication's supplementary material [20]. Notably, we had to exclude the prominent and effective category of landmarking meta-features [37] (which measure the performance of simple base learners), because they were computationally too expensive to be helpful in the online evaluation phase. We note that this meta-learning approach draws its power from the availability of a repository of datasets; due to recent initiatives, such as OpenML [43], we expect the number of available datasets to grow ever larger over time, increasing the importance of meta-learning.

6.3.2 *Automated Ensemble Construction of Models Evaluated During Optimization*

While Bayesian hyperparameter optimization is data-efficient in finding the best-performing hyperparameter setting, we note that it is a very wasteful procedure when the goal is simply to make good predictions: all the models it trains during the course of the search are lost, usually including some that perform almost as well as the best. Rather than discarding these models, we propose to store them and to use an efficient post-processing method (which can be run in a second process on-the-fly) to construct an ensemble out of them. This automatic ensemble construction avoids to commit itself to a single hyperparameter setting and is thus more robust (and less prone to overfitting) than using the point estimate that standard hyperparameter optimization yields. To our best knowledge, we are the first to make this simple observation, which can be applied to improve any Bayesian hyperparameter optimization method.[1]

It is well known that ensembles often outperform individual models [24, 31], and that effective ensembles can be created from a library of models [9, 10]. Ensembles perform particularly well if the models they are based on (1) are individually strong and (2) make uncorrelated errors [6]. Since this is much more likely when the individual models are different in nature, ensemble building is particularly well suited for combining strong instantiations of a flexible ML framework.

However, simply building a uniformly weighted ensemble of the models found by Bayesian optimization does *not* work well. Rather, we found it crucial to adjust these weights using the predictions of all individual models on a hold-out set. We experimented with different approaches to optimize these weights: *stacking* [44], gradient-free numerical optimization, and the method *ensemble selection* [10]. While we found both numerical optimization and stacking to overfit to the validation set and to be computationally costly, ensemble selection was fast and robust. In a nutshell, ensemble selection (introduced by Caruana et al. [10]) is a greedy procedure that starts from an empty ensemble and then iteratively adds the model that minimizes ensemble validation loss (with uniform weight, but allowing for repetitions). We used this technique in all our experiments—building an ensemble of size 50 using selection with replacement [10]. We calculated the ensemble loss using the same validation set that we use for Bayesian optimization.

[1]Since the original publication [20] we have learned that Escalante et al. [16] and Bürger and Pauli [8] applied ensembles as a post-processing step of an AutoML system to improve generalization as well. However, both works combined the learned models with a pre-defined strategy and did not adapt the ensemble construction based on the performance of the individual models.

6.4 A Practical Automated Machine Learning System

To design a robust AutoML system, as our underlying ML framework we chose scikit-learn [36], one of the best known and most widely used machine learning libraries. It offers a wide range of well established and efficiently-implemented ML algorithms and is easy to use for both experts and beginners. Since our AutoML system closely resembles Auto-WEKA, but—like HYPEROPT-SKLEARN—is based on scikit-learn, we dub it Auto-sklearn.

Fig. 6.2 is an illustration Auto-sklearn's machine learning pipeline and its components. It comprises 15 classification algorithms, 14 preprocessing methods, and 4 data preprocessing methods. We parameterized each of them, which resulted in a space of 110 hyperparameters. Most of these are conditional hyperparameters that are only active if their respective component is selected. We note that SMAC [27] can handle this conditionality natively.

All 15 classification algorithms in Auto-sklearn are listed in Table 6.1. They fall into different categories, such as general linear models (2 algorithms), support vector machines (2), discriminant analysis (2), nearest neighbors (1), naïve Bayes (3), decision trees (1) and ensembles (4). In contrast to Auto-WEKA [42] (also, see Chap. 4 for a description of Auto-WEKA), we focused our configuration space on base classifiers and excluded meta-models and ensembles that are themselves parameterized by one or more base classifiers. While such ensembles increased Auto-WEKA's number of hyperparameters by almost a factor of five (to 786), Auto-sklearn "only" features 110 hyperparameters. We instead construct complex ensembles using our post-hoc method from Sect. 6.3.2. Compared to Auto-WEKA, this is much more data-efficient: in Auto-WEKA, evaluating the performance of an ensemble with five components requires the construction and evaluation of five

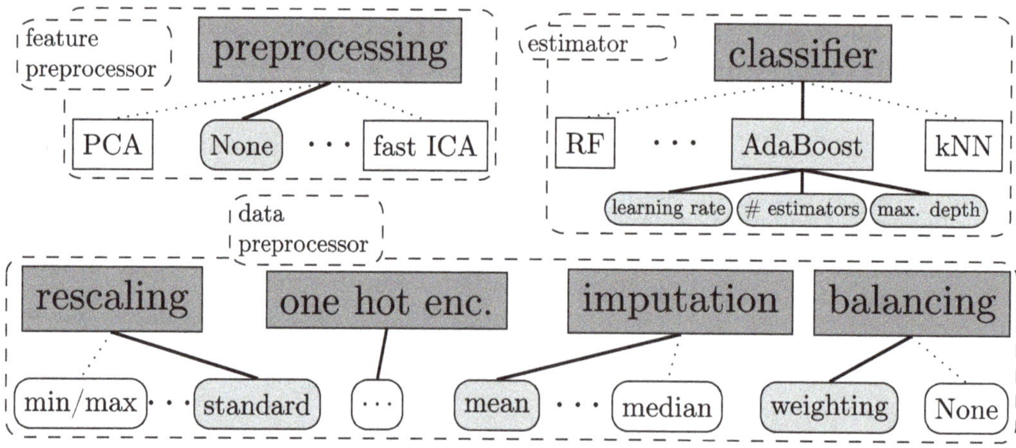

Fig. 6.2 Structured configuration space. Squared boxes denote parent hyperparameters whereas boxes with rounded edges are leaf hyperparameters. Grey colored boxes mark active hyperparameters which form an example configuration and machine learning pipeline. Each pipeline comprises one *feature preprocessor*, *classifier* and up to three *data preprocessor* methods plus respective hyperparameters

Table 6.1 Number of hyperparameters for each classifier (top) and feature preprocessing method (bottom) for a **binary classification** dataset in **dense** representation. Tables for sparse binary classification and sparse/dense multiclass classification datasets can be found in Section E of the original publication's supplementary material [20], Tables 2a, 3a, 4a, 2b, 3b and 4b. We distinguish between categorical (cat) hyperparameters with discrete values and continuous (cont) numerical hyperparameters. Numbers in brackets are conditional hyperparameters, which are only relevant when another hyperparameter has a certain value

Type of Classifier	#λ	cat (cond)	cont (cond)
AdaBoost (AB)	4	1 (–)	3 (–)
Bernoulli naïve Bayes	2	1 (–)	1 (–)
Decision tree (DT)	4	1 (–)	3 (–)
Extremely randomized trees	5	2 (–)	3 (–)
Gaussian naïve Bayes	–	–	–
Gradient boosting (GB)	6	–	6 (–)
k-nearest neighbors (kNN)	3	2 (–)	1 (–)
Linear discriminant analysis (LDA)	4	1 (–)	3 (1)
Linear SVM	4	2 (–)	2 (–)
Kernel SVM	7	2 (-)	5 (2)
Multinomial naïve Bayes	2	1 (–)	1 (–)
Passive aggressive	3	1 (–)	2 (–)
Quadratic discriminant analysis (QDA)	2	–	2 (–)
Random forest (RF)	5	2 (–)	3 (–)
Linear Classifier (SGD)	10	4 (–)	6 (3)

Preprocessing method	#λ	cat (cond)	cont (cond)
Extremely randomized trees preprocessing	5	2 (–)	3 (–)
Fast ICA	4	3 (–)	1 (1)
Feature agglomeration	4	3 ()	1 (–)
Kernel PCA	5	1 (–)	4 (3)
Rand. kitchen sinks	2	–	2 (–)
Linear SVM preprocessing	3	1 (–)	2 (–)
No preprocessing	–	–	–
Nystroem sampler	5	1 (–)	4 (3)
Principal component analysis (PCA)	2	1 (–)	1 (–)
Polynomial	3	2 (–)	1 (–)
Random trees embed.	4	–	4 (–)
Select percentile	2	1 (–)	1 (–)
Select rates	3	2 (–)	1 (–)
One-hot encoding	2	1 (–)	1 (1)
Imputation	1	1 (–)	–
Balancing	1	1 (–)	–
Rescaling	1	1 (–)	–

models; in contrast, in Auto-sklearn, ensembles come largely for free, and it is possible to mix and match models evaluated at arbitrary times during the optimization.

The preprocessing methods for datasets in dense representation in Auto-sklearn are listed in Table 6.1. They comprise data preprocessors (which change the feature values and are always used when they apply) and feature preprocessors (which change the actual set of features, and only one of which [or none] is used). Data preprocessing includes rescaling of the inputs, imputation of missing values, one-hot encoding and balancing of the target classes. The 14 possible feature preprocessing methods can be categorized into feature selection (2), kernel approximation (2), matrix decomposition (3), embeddings (1), feature clustering (1), polynomial feature expansion (1) and methods that use a classifier for feature selection (2). For example, L_1-regularized linear SVMs fitted to the data can be used for feature selection by eliminating features corresponding to zero-valued model coefficients.

For detailed descriptions of the machine learning algorithms used in Auto-sklearn we refer to Sect. A.1 and A.2 of the original paper's supplementary material [20], the scikit-learn documentation [36] and the references therein.

To make the most of our computational power and not get stuck in a very slow run of a certain combination of preprocessing and machine learning algorithm, we implemented several measures to prevent such long runs. First, we limited the time for each evaluation of an instantiation of the ML framework. We also limited the memory of such evaluations to prevent the operating system from swapping or freezing. When an evaluation went over one of those limits, we automatically terminated it and returned the worst possible score for the given evaluation metric. For some of the models we employed an iterative training procedure; we instrumented these to still return their current performance value when a limit was reached before they were terminated. To further reduce the amount of overly long runs, we forbade several combinations of preprocessors and classification methods: in particular, kernel approximation was forbidden to be active in conjunction with non-linear and tree-based methods as well as the KNN algorithm. (SMAC handles such forbidden combinations natively.) For the same reason we also left out feature learning algorithms, such as dictionary learning.

Another issue in hyperparameter optimization is overfitting and data resampling since the training data of the AutoML system must be divided into a dataset for training the ML pipeline (training set) and a dataset used to calculate the loss function for Bayesian optimization (validation set). Here we had to trade off between running a more robust cross-validation (which comes at little additional overhead in SMAC) and evaluating models on all cross-validation folds to allow for ensemble construction with these models. Thus, for the tasks with a rigid time limit of 1 h in Sect. 6.6, we employed a simple train/test split. In contrast, we were able to employ ten-fold crossvalidation in our 24 and 30 h runs in Sects. 6.5 and 6.7.

Finally, not every supervised learning task (for example classification with multiple targets), can be solved by all of the algorithms available in Auto-sklearn. Thus, given a new dataset, Auto-sklearn preselects the methods that are suitable for the dataset's properties. Since scikit-learn methods are restricted to numerical input values, we always transformed data by applying a one-hot encoding to categorical features. In order to keep the number of dummy features low, we configured a percentage threshold and a value occurring more rarely than this percentage was transformed to a special *other* value [35].

6.5 Comparing Auto-sklearn to Auto-WEKA and Hyperopt-Sklearn

As a baseline experiment, we compared the performance of vanilla Auto-sklearn (without our improvements meta-learning and ensemble building) to Auto-WEKA (see Chap. 4) and Hyperopt-Sklearn (see Chap. 5), reproducing the experimental setup with the 21 datasets of the paper introducing Auto-WEKA [42] (see Table 4.1 in Chap. 4 for a description of the datasets). Following the original setup of the Auto-WEKA paper, we used the same train/test splits of the datasets [1], a walltime limit of 30 h, 10-fold cross validation (where the evaluation of each fold was allowed to take 150 min), and 10 independent optimization runs with SMAC on each dataset. As in Auto-WEKA, the evaluation is sped up by SMAC's intensify procedure, which only schedules runs on new cross validation folds if the configuration currently being evaluated is likely to outperform the so far best performing configuration [27]. We did not modify Hyperopt-sklearn which always uses a 80/20 train/test split. All our experiments ran on Intel Xeon E5-2650 v2 eight-core processors with 2.60 GHz and 4 GiB of RAM. We allowed the machine learning framework to use 3 GiB and reserved the rest for SMAC. All experiments used Auto-WEKA 0.5 and scikit-learn 0.16.1.

We present the results of this experiment in Table 6.2. Since our setup followed exactly that of the original Auto-WEKA paper, as a sanity check we compared the numbers we achieved for Auto-WEKA ourselves (first line in Fig. 6.2) to the ones presented by the authors of Auto-WEKA (see Chap. 4) and found that overall the results were reasonable. Furthermore, the table shows that Auto-sklearn performed significantly better than Auto-WEKA in 6/21 cases, tied it in 12 cases, and lost against it in 3. For the three datasets where Auto-WEKA performed best, we found that in more than 50% of its runs the best classifier it chose is not implemented in scikit-learn (trees with a pruning component). So far, Hyperopt-sklearn is more of a proof-of-concept—inviting the user to adapt the configuration space to her own needs—than a full AutoML system. The current version crashes when presented with sparse data and missing values. It also crashes on Cifar-10 due to a memory limit which we set for all optimizers to enable a fair comparison. On the 16 datasets on which it ran, it statistically tied the best competing AutoML system in 9 cases and lost against it in 7.

6.6 Evaluation of the Proposed AutoML Improvements

In order to evaluate the robustness and general applicability of our proposed AutoML system on a broad range of datasets, we gathered 140 binary and multiclass classification datasets from the OpenML repository [43], only selecting

Table 6.2 Test set classification error of Auto-WEKA (AW), vanilla Auto-sklearn (AS) and HYPEROPT-SKLEARN (HS), as in the original evaluation of Auto-WEKA [42] (see also Sect. 4.5). We show median percent test error rate across 100,000 bootstrap samples (based on 10 runs), each sample simulating 4 parallel runs and always picking the best one according to cross-validation performance. Bold numbers indicate the best result. Underlined results are not statistically significantly different from the best according to a bootstrap test with $p = 0.05$

	Abalone	Amazon	Car	Cifar-10	Cifar-10 small	Convex	Dexter	Dorothea	German credit	Gisette	KDD09 appetency
AS	**73.50**	**16.00**	0.39	**51.70**	**54.81**	**17.53**	**5.56**	**5.51**	**27.00**	**1.62**	**1.74**
AW	**73.50**	30.00	**0.00**	56.95	56.20	21.80	8.33	6.38	28.33	2.29	**1.74**
HS	76.21	16.22	0.39	–	57.95	19.18	–	–	27.67	2.29	–

	KR-vs-KP	Madelon	MNIST basic	MRBI	Secom	Semeion	Shuttle	Waveform	Wine quality	Yeast	
AS	0.42	**12.44**	2.84	**46.92**	**7.87**	**5.24**	**0.01**	14.93	33.76	40.67	
AW	**0.31**	18.21	2.84	60.34	8.09	5.24	**0.01**	14.13	**33.36**	**37.75**	
HS	0.42	14.74	**2.82**	55.79	–	5.87	0.05	**14.07**	34.72	38.45	

datasets with at least 1000 data points to allow robust performance evaluations. These datasets cover a diverse range of applications, such as text classification, digit and letter recognition, gene sequence and RNA classification, advertisement, particle classification for telescope data, and cancer detection in tissue samples. We list all datasets in Table 7 and 8 in the supplementary material of the original publication [20] and provide their unique OpenML identifiers for reproducibility. We randomly split each dataset into a two-thirds training and a one-thirds test set. Auto-sklearn could only access the training set, and split this further into two thirds for training and a one third holdout set for computing the validation loss for SMAC. All in all, we used four-ninths of the data to train the machine learning models, two-ninths to calculate their validation loss and the final three-ninths to report the test performance of the different AutoML systems we compared. Since the class distribution in many of these datasets is quite imbalanced we evaluated all AutoML methods using a measure called *balanced classification error rate* (BER). We define balanced error rate as the average of the proportion of wrong classifications in each class. In comparison to standard classification error (the average overall error), this measure (the average of the *class-wise* error) assigns equal weight to all classes. We note that balanced error or accuracy measures are often used in machine learning competitions, such as the AutoML challenge [23], which is described in Chap. 10.

We performed 10 runs of Auto-sklearn both with and without meta-learning and with and without ensemble building on each of the datasets. To study their

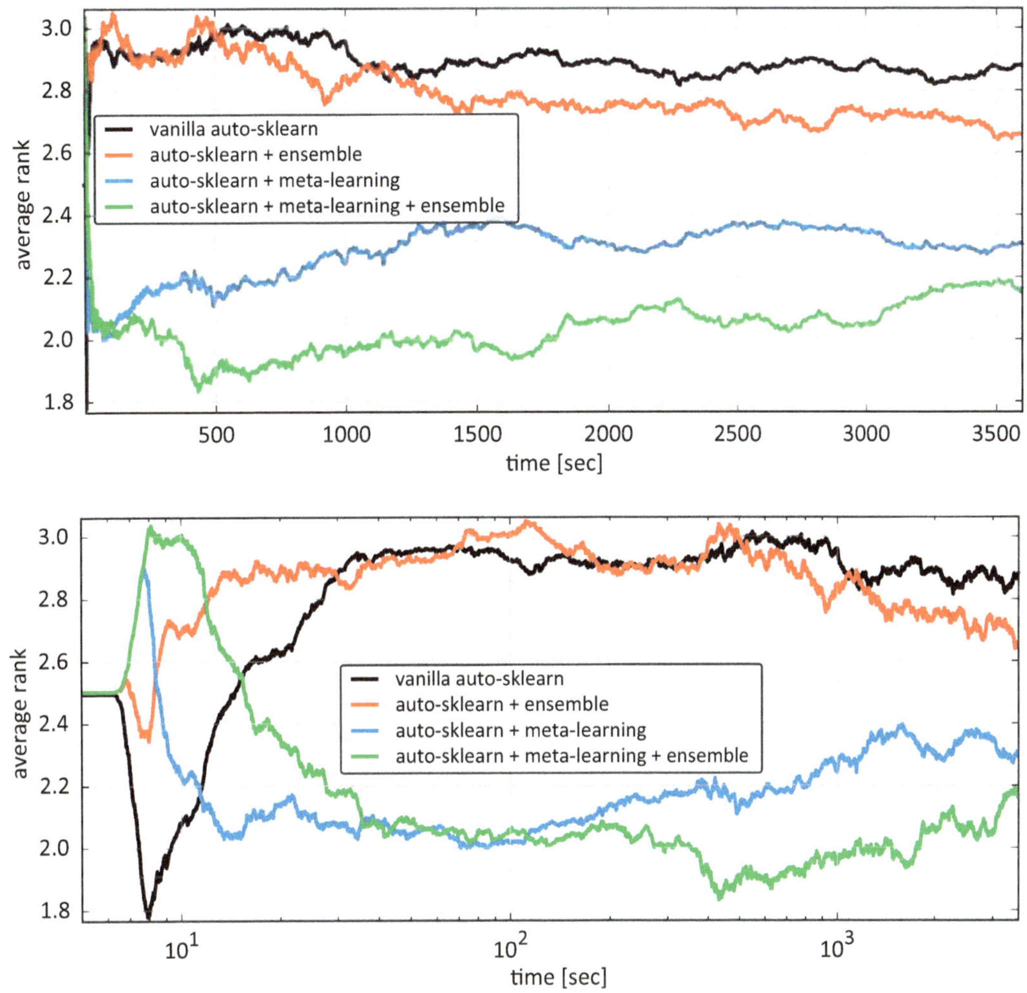

Fig. 6.3 Average rank of all four Auto-sklearn variants (ranked by balanced test error rate (BER)) across 140 datasets. Note that ranks are a relative measure of performance (here, the rank of all methods has to add up to 10), and hence an improvement in BER of one method can worsen the rank of another. (Top) Data plotted on a linear x scale. (Bottom) This is the same data as for the upper plot, but on a log x scale. Due to the small additional overhead that meta-learning and ensemble selection cause, vanilla Auto-sklearn is able to achieve the best rank within the first 10 s as it produces predictions before the other Auto-sklearn variants finish training their first model. After this, meta-learning quickly takes off

performance under rigid time constraints, and also due to computational resource constraints, we limited the CPU time for each run to 1 h; we also limited the runtime for evaluating a single model to a tenth of this (6 min).

To not evaluate performance on data sets already used for meta-learning, we performed a leave-one-dataset-out validation: when evaluating on dataset $\mathcal{D}$, we only used meta-information from the 139 other datasets.

Fig. 6.3 shows the average ranks over time of the four Auto-sklearn versions we tested. We observe that both of our new methods yielded substantial improvements over vanilla Auto-sklearn. The most striking result is that meta-learning yielded drastic improvements starting with the first configuration it selected and lasting until the end of the experiment. We note that the improvement was most pronounced in the beginning and that over time, vanilla Auto-sklearn also found good solutions without meta-learning, letting it catch up on some datasets (thus improving its overall rank).

Moreover, both of our methods complement each other: our automated ensemble construction improved both vanilla Auto-sklearn and Auto-sklearn with meta-learning. Interestingly, the ensemble's influence on the performance started earlier for the meta-learning version. We believe that this is because meta-learning produces better machine learning models earlier, which can be directly combined into a strong ensemble; but when run longer, vanilla Auto-sklearn without meta-learning also benefits from automated ensemble construction.

6.7 Detailed Analysis of Auto-sklearn Components

We now study Auto-sklearn's individual classifiers and preprocessors, compared to jointly optimizing all methods, in order to obtain insights into their peak performance and robustness. Ideally, we would have liked to study all combinations of a single classifier and a single preprocessor in isolation, but with 15 classifiers and 14 preprocessors this was infeasible; rather, when studying the performance of a single classifier, we still optimized over all preprocessors, and vice versa. To obtain a more detailed analysis, we focused on a subset of datasets but extended the configuration budget for optimizing all methods from one hour to one day and to two days for Auto-sklearn. Specifically, we clustered our 140 datasets with g-means [26] based on the dataset meta-features and used one dataset from each of the resulting 13 clusters. We give a basic description of the datasets in Table 6.3. In total, these extensive experiments required 10.7 CPU years.

Table 6.4 compares the results of the various classification methods against Auto-sklearn. Overall, as expected, random forests, extremely randomized trees, AdaBoost, and gradient boosting, showed the most robust performance, and SVMs showed strong peak performance for some datasets. Besides a variety of strong classifiers, there are also several models which could not compete: The decision tree, passive aggressive, kNN, Gaussian NB, LDA and QDA were statistically significantly inferior to the best classifier on most datasets. Finally, the table indicates that no single method was the best choice for all datasets. As shown in the table and also visualized for two example datasets in Fig. 6.4, optimizing the joint configuration space of Auto-sklearn led to the most robust performance. A plot of ranks over time (Fig. 2 and 3 in the supplementary material of the original publication [20]) quantifies this across all 13 datasets, showing that Auto-sklearn starts with reasonable but not optimal performance and effectively searches its more general configuration space to converge to the best overall performance over time.

Table 6.5 compares the results of the various preprocessors against Auto-sklearn. As for the comparison of classifiers above, Auto-sklearn showed the most robust

Table 6.3 Representative datasets for the 13 clusters obtained via g-means clustering of the 140 datasets' meta-feature vectors

ID	Name	#Cont	#Nom	#Class	Sparse	Missing Values	|Training|	|Test|
38	Sick	7	22	2	–	X	2527	1245
46	Splice	0	60	3	–	–	2137	1053
179	Adult	2	12	2	–	X	32,724	16,118
184	KROPT	0	6	18	–	–	18,797	9259
554	MNIST	784	0	10	–	–	46,900	23,100
772	Quake	3	0	2	–	–	1459	719
917	fri_c1_1000_25 (binarized)	25	0	2	–	–	670	330
1049	pc4	37	0	2	–	–	976	482
1111	KDDCup09 Appetency	192	38	2	–	X	33,500	16,500
1120	Magic Telescope	10	0	2	–	–	12,743	6277
1128	OVA Breast	10935	0	2	–	–	1035	510
293	Covertype (binarized)	54	0	2	X	–	389,278	191,734
389	fbis_wc	2000	0	17	X	–	1651	812

performance: It performed best on three of the datasets and was not statistically significantly worse than the best preprocessor on another 8 of 13.

6.8 Discussion and Conclusion

Having presented our experimental validation, we now conclude this chapter with a brief discussion, a simple usage example of Auto-sklearn, a short review of recent extensions, and concluding remarks.

6.8.1 Discussion

We demonstrated that our new AutoML system Auto-sklearn performs favorably against the previous state of the art in AutoML, and that our meta-learning and ensemble improvements for AutoML yield further efficiency and robustness. This finding is backed by the fact that Auto-sklearn won three out of five auto-tracks, including the final two, in ChaLearn's first AutoML challenge. In this paper, we did not evaluate the use of Auto-sklearn for interactive machine learning with an expert in the loop and weeks of CPU power, but we note that mode has led to three first places in the human (aka Final) track of the first ChaLearn AutoML challenge (in

Table 6.4 Median balanced test error rate (BER) of optimizing Auto-sklearn subspaces for each classification method (and all preprocessors), as well as the whole configuration space of Auto-sklearn, on 13 datasets. All optimization runs were allowed to run for 24 h except for Auto-sklearn which ran for 48 h. Bold numbers indicate the best result; underlined results are not statistically significantly different from the best according to a bootstrap test using the same setup as for Table 6.2

OpenML dataset ID	AUTO-SKLEARN	AdaBoost	Bernoulli naïve Bayes	Decision tree	Extreml. rand. trees	Gaussian naïve Bayes	Gradient boosting	kNN	LDA	Linear SVM	Kernel SVM	Multi-nomial naïve Bayes	Passive aggresive	QDA	Random forest	Linear Class. (SGD)
38	2.15	2.68	50.22	2.15	18.06	11.22	**1.77**	50.00	8.55	16.29	17.89	46.99	50.00	8.78	2.34	15.82
46	3.76	4.65	–	5.62	4.74	7.88	**3.49**	7.57	8.67	8.31	5.36	7.55	9.23	7.57	4.20	7.31
179	**16.99**	17.03	19.27	18.31	17.09	21.77	17.00	22.23	18.93	17.30	17.57	18.97	22.29	19.06	17.24	17.01
184	**10.32**	10.52	–	17.46	11.10	64.74	10.42	31.10	35.44	15.76	12.52	27.13	20.01	47.18	10.98	12.76
554	1.55	2.42	–	12.00	2.91	10.52	3.86	2.68	3.34	2.23	**1.50**	10.37	100.00	2.75	3.08	2.50
772	46.85	49.68	47.90	47.75	**45.62**	48.83	48.15	48.00	46.74	48.38	48.66	47.21	48.75	47.67	47.71	47.93
917	10.22	9.11	25.83	11.00	10.22	33.94	10.11	11.11	34.22	18.67	**6.78**	25.50	20.67	30.44	10.83	18.33
1049	12.93	**12.53**	15.50	19.31	17.18	26.23	13.38	23.80	25.12	17.28	21.44	26.40	29.25	21.38	13.75	19.92
1111	23.70	23.16	28.40	24.40	24.47	29.59	**22.93**	50.30	24.11	23.99	23.56	27.67	43.79	25.86	28.06	23.36
1120	13.81	**13.54**	18.81	17.45	13.86	21.50	13.61	17.23	15.48	14.94	14.17	18.33	16.37	15.62	13.70	14.66
1128	4.21	4.89	4.71	9.30	3.89	4.77	4.58	4.59	4.58	4.83	4.59	4.46	5.65	5.59	**3.83**	4.33
293	2.86	4.07	24.30	5.03	3.59	32.44	24.48	4.86	24.40	14.16	100.00	24.20	21.34	28.68	**2.57**	15.54
389	19.65	22.98	–	33.14	19.38	29.18	19.20	30.87	19.68	**17.95**	22.04	20.04	20.14	39.57	20.66	17.99

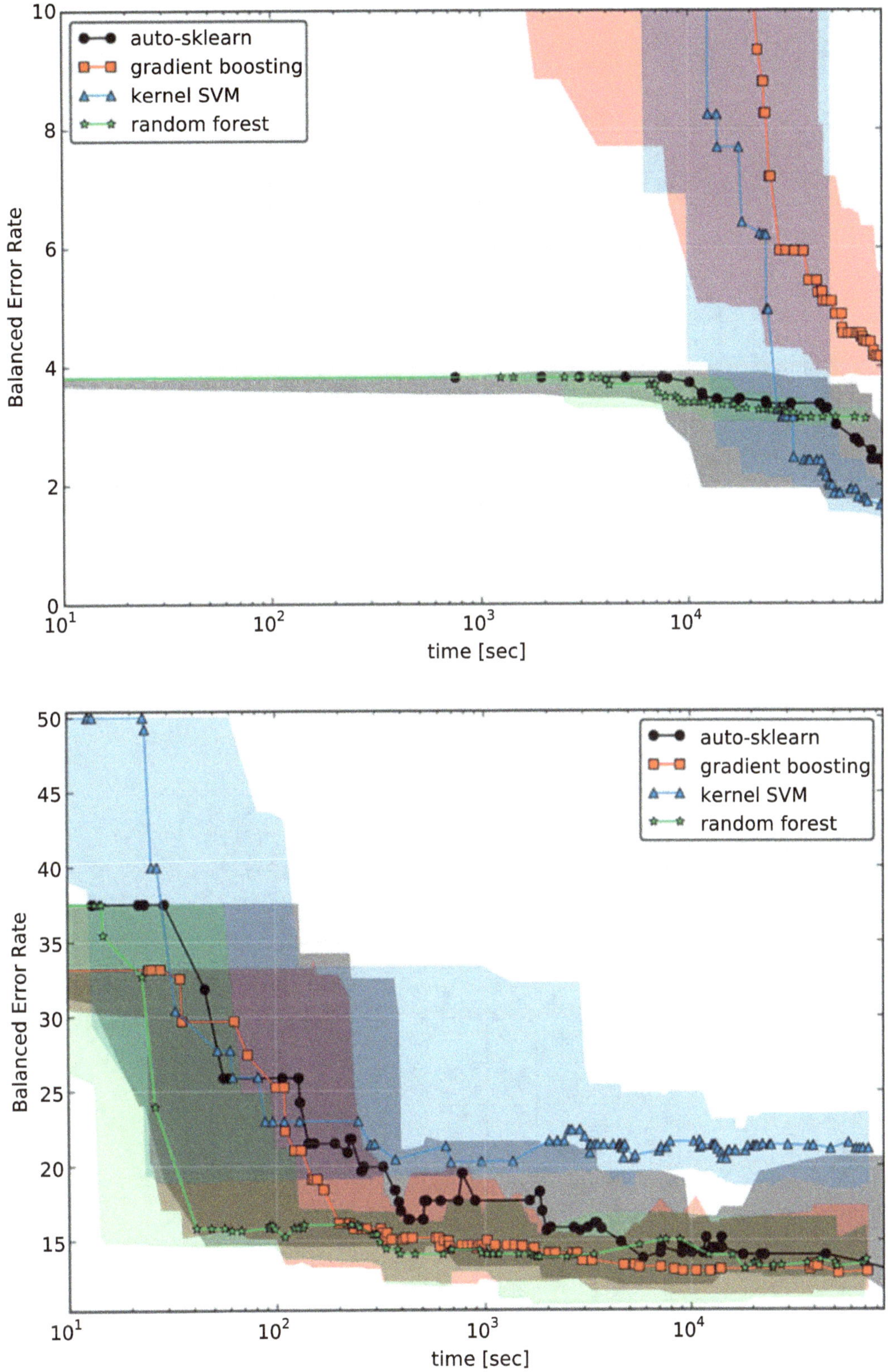

Fig. 6.4 Performance of a subset of classifiers compared to Auto-sklearn over time. (Top) MNIST (OpenML dataset ID 554). (Bottom) Promise pc4 (OpenML dataset ID 1049). We show median test error rate and the fifth and 95th percentile over time for optimizing three classifiers separately with optimizing the joint space. A plot with all classifiers can be found in Fig. 4 in the supplementary material of the original publication [20]. While Auto-sklearn is inferior in the beginning, in the end its performance is close to the best method

Table 6.5 Like Table 6.4, but instead optimizing subspaces for each preprocessing method (and all classifiers)

OpenML dataset ID	AUTO-SKLEARN	Densifier	Extreml. rand. trees prepr.	Fast ICA	Feature agglomeration	Kernel PCA	Rand. kitchen sinks	Linear SVM prepr.	No preproc.	Nystroem sampler	PCA	Polynomial	Random trees embed.	Select percentile classification	Select rates	Truncated-SVD
38	**2.15**	–	4.03	7.27	2.24	5.84	8.57	2.28	2.28	7.70	7.23	2.90	18.50	2.20	2.28	–
46	**3.76**	–	4.98	7.95	4.40	8.74	8.41	4.25	4.52	8.48	8.40	4.21	7.51	4.17	4.68	–
179	16.99	–	17.83	17.24	16.92	100.00	17.34	**16.84**	16.97	17.30	17.64	16.94	17.05	17.09	16.86	–
184	10.32	–	55.78	19.96	11.31	36.52	28.05	**9.92**	11.43	25.53	21.15	10.54	12.68	45.03	10.47	–
554	1.55	–	1.56	2.52	1.65	100.00	100.00	2.21	1.60	2.21	1.65	100.00	3.48	**1.46**	1.70	–
772	**46.85**	–	47.90	48.65	48.62	47.59	47.68	47.72	48.34	48.06	47.30	48.00	47.84	47.56	48.43	–
917	10.22	–	**8.33**	16.06	10.33	20.94	35.44	8.67	9.44	37.83	22.33	9.11	17.67	10.00	10.44	–
1049	12.93	–	20.36	19.92	13.14	19.57	20.06	13.28	15.84	18.96	17.22	12.95	18.52	**11.94**	14.38	–
1111	23.70	–	23.36	24.69	23.73	100.00	25.25	23.43	**22.27**	23.95	23.25	26.94	26.68	23.53	23.33	–
1120	13.81	–	16.29	14.22	13.73	14.57	14.82	14.02	13.85	14.66	14.23	**13.22**	15.03	13.65	13.67	–
1128	4.21	–	4.90	4.96	4.76	4.21	5.08	4.52	4.59	**4.08**	4.59	50.00	9.23	4.33	**4.08**	–
293	2.86	24.40	3.41	–	–	100.00	19.30	3.01	**2.66**	20.94	–	–	8.05	2.86	2.74	4.05
389	19.65	20.63	21.40	–	–	**17.50**	19.66	19.89	20.87	18.46	–	–	44.83	20.17	19.18	21.58

addition to the auto-tracks, in particular Table 10.5, phases Final 0–4). As such, we believe that Auto-sklearn is a promising system for use by both machine learning novices and experts.

Since the publication of the original NeurIPS paper [20], Auto-sklearn has become a standard baseline for new approaches to automated machine learning, such as FLASH [46], RECIPE [39], Hyperband [32], AutoPrognosis [3], ML-PLAN [34], Auto-Stacker [11] and AlphaD3M [13].

6.8.2 Usage

One important outcome of the research on Auto-sklearn is the *auto-sklearn* Python package. It is a drop-in replacement for any scikit-learn classifier or regressor, similar to the classifier provided by HYPEROPT-SKLEARN [30] and can be used as follows:

```
import autosklearn.classification
cls = autosklearn.classification.AutoSklearnClassifier()
cls.fit(X_train, y_train)
predictions = cls.predict(X_test)
```

Auto-sklearn can be used with any loss function and resampling strategy to estimate the validation loss. Furthermore, it is possible to extend the classifiers and preprocessors Auto-sklearn can choose from. Since the initial publication we also added regression support to Auto-sklearn. We develop the package on *https://github.com/automl/auto-sklearn* and it is available via the Python packaging index *pypi.org*. We provide documentation on automl.github.io/auto-sklearn.

6.8.3 Extensions in PoSH Auto-sklearn

While Auto-sklearn as described in this chapter is limited to handling datasets of relatively modest size, in the context of the most recent AutoML challenge (AutoML 2, run in 2018; see Chap. 10), we have extended it towards also handling large datasets effectively. Auto-sklearn was able to handle datasets of several hundred thousand datapoints by using a cluster of 25 CPUs for two days, but not within the 20 min time budget required by the AutoML 2 challenge. As described in detail in a recent workshop paper [18], this implied opening up the methods considered to also include extreme gradient boosting (in particular, XGBoost [12]), using the multi-fidelity approach of successive halving [28] (also described in Chap. 1) to solve the CASH problem, and changing our meta-learning approach. We now briefly describe the resulting system, **PoSH Auto-sklearn** (short for *Portfolio Successive Halving*, combined with Auto-sklearn), which obtained the best performance in the 2018 challenge.

PoSH Auto-sklearn starts by running successive halving with a fixed portfolio of 16 machine learning pipeline configurations, and if there is time left, it uses the outcome of these runs to warmstart a combination of Bayesian optimization and successive halving. The fixed portfolio of 16 pipelines was obtained by running greedy submodular function maximization to select a strong set of complementary configurations to optimize the performance obtained on a set of 421 datasets; the candidate configurations configured for this optimization were the 421 configurations found by running SMAC [27] on each of these 421 datasets.

The combination of Bayesian optimization and successive halving we used to yield robust results within a short time window is an adaptation of the multi-fidelity hyperparameter optimization method BOHB (Bayesian Optimization and HyperBand) [17] discussed in Chap. 1. As budgets for this multifidelity approach, we used the number of iterations for all iterative algorithms, except for the SVM, where we used dataset size as a budget.

Another extension for large datasets that is currently ongoing is our work on automated deep learning; this is discussed in the following chapter on Auto-Net.

6.8.4 Conclusion and Future Work

Following the AutoML approach taken by Auto-WEKA, we introduced Auto-sklearn, which performs favorably against the previous state of the art in AutoML. We also showed that our meta-learning and ensemble mechanisms improve its efficiency and robustness further.

While Auto-sklearn handles the hyperparameter tuning for a user, Auto-sklearn has hyperparameters on its own which influence its performance for a given time budget, such as the time limits discussed in Sects. 6.5, 6.6, and 6.7, or the resampling strategy used to calculate the loss function. We demonstrated in preliminary work that the choice of the resampling strategy and the selection of timeouts can be cast as a meta-learning problem itself [19], but we would like to extend this to other possible design choices Auto-sklearn users face.

Since the time of writing the original paper, the field of meta-learning has progressed a lot, giving access to multiple new methods to include meta information into Bayesian optimization. We expect that using one of the newer methods discussed in Chap. 2 could substantially improve the optimization procedure.

Finally, having a fully automated procedure that can test hundreds of hyperparameter configurations puts us at increased risk of overfitting to the validation set. To avoid this overfitting, we would like to combine Auto-sklearn with one of the techniques discussed in Chap. 1, techniques from differential privacy [14], or other techniques yet to be developed.

Acknowledgements This work was supported by the German Research Foundation (DFG), under Priority Programme Autonomous Learning (SPP 1527, grant HU 1900/3-1), under Emmy Noether grant HU 1900/2-1, and under the BrainLinks-BrainTools Cluster of Excellence (grant number EXC 1086).

Bibliography

1. Auto-WEKA website, http://www.cs.ubc.ca/labs/beta/Projects/autoweka
2. Proc. of NeurIPS'15 (2015)
3. Ahmed, A., van der Schaar, M.: AutoPrognosis: Automated clinical prognostic modeling via Bayesian optimization with structured kernel learning. In: Proc. of ICML'18. pp. 139–148 (2018)
4. Bardenet, R., Brendel, M., Kégl, B., Sebag, M.: Collaborative hyperparameter tuning. In: Proc. of ICML'13. pp. 199–207 (2014)
5. Bergstra, J., Bardenet, R., Bengio, Y., Kégl, B.: Algorithms for hyper-parameter optimization. In: Proc. of NIPS'11. pp. 2546–2554 (2011)
6. Breiman, L.: Random forests. MLJ 45, 5–32 (2001)
7. Brochu, E., Cora, V., de Freitas, N.: A tutorial on Bayesian optimization of expensive cost functions, with application to active user modeling and hierarchical reinforcement learning. arXiv:1012.2599v1 [cs.LG] (2010)
8. Bürger, F., Pauli, J.: A holistic classification optimization framework with feature selection, preprocessing, manifold learning and classifiers. In: Proc. of ICPRAM'15. pp. 52–68 (2015)
9. Caruana, R., Munson, A., Niculescu-Mizil, A.: Getting the most out of ensemble selection. In: Proc. of ICDM'06. pp. 828–833 (2006)
10. Caruana, R., Niculescu-Mizil, A., Crew, G., Ksikes, A.: Ensemble selection from libraries of models. In: Proc. of ICML'04. p. 18 (2004)
11. Chen, B., Wu, H., Mo, W., Chattopadhyay, I., Lipson, H.: Autostacker: A compositional evolutionary learning system. In: Proc. of GECCO'18 (2018)
12. Chen, T., Guestrin, C.: XGBoost: A scalable tree boosting system. In: Proc. of KDD'16. pp. 785–794 (2016)
13. Drori, I., Krishnamurthy, Y., Rampin, R., Lourenco, R., One, J., Cho, K., Silva, C., Freire, J.: AlphaD3M: Machine learning pipeline synthesis. In: ICML AutoML workshop (2018)
14. Dwork, C., Feldman, V., Hardt, M., Pitassi, T., Reingold, O., Roth, A.: Generalization in adaptive data analysis and holdout reuse. In: Proc. of NIPS'15 [2], pp. 2350–2358
15. Eggensperger, K., Feurer, M., Hutter, F., Bergstra, J., Snoek, J., Hoos, H., Leyton-Brown, K.: Towards an empirical foundation for assessing Bayesian optimization of hyperparameters. In: NIPS Workshop on Bayesian Optimization in Theory and Practice (2013)
16. Escalante, H., Montes, M., Sucar, E.: Ensemble particle swarm model selection. In: Proc. of IJCNN'10. pp. 1–8. IEEE (Jul 2010)
17. Falkner, S., Klein, A., Hutter, F.: BOHB: Robust and Efficient Hyperparameter Optimization at Scale. In: Proc. of ICML'18. pp. 1437–1446 (2018)
18. Feurer, M., Eggensperger, K., Falkner, S., Lindauer, M., Hutter, F.: Practical automated machine learning for the automl challenge 2018. In: ICML AutoML workshop (2018)
19. Feurer, M., Hutter, F.: Towards further automation in automl. In: ICML AutoML workshop (2018)
20. Feurer, M., Klein, A., Eggensperger, K., Springenberg, J., Blum, M., Hutter, F.: Efficient and robust automated machine learning. In: Proc. of NIPS'15 [2], pp. 2962–2970
21. Feurer, M., Springenberg, J., Hutter, F.: Initializing Bayesian hyperparameter optimization via meta-learning. In: Proc. of AAAI'15. pp. 1128–1135 (2015)

22. Gomes, T., Prudêncio, R., Soares, C., Rossi, A., Carvalho, A.: Combining meta-learning and search techniques to select parameters for support vector machines. Neurocomputing 75(1), 3–13 (2012)
23. Guyon, I., Bennett, K., Cawley, G., Escalante, H., Escalera, S., Ho, T., N.Macià, Ray, B., Saeed, M., Statnikov, A., Viegas, E.: Design of the 2015 ChaLearn AutoML Challenge. In: Proc. of IJCNN'15 (2015)
24. Guyon, I., Saffari, A., Dror, G., Cawley, G.: Model selection: Beyond the Bayesian/Frequentist divide. JMLR 11, 61–87 (2010)
25. Hall, M., Frank, E., Holmes, G., Pfahringer, B., Reutemann, P., Witten, I.: The WEKA data mining software: An update. ACM SIGKDD Exploratians Newsletter 11(1), 10–18 (2009)
26. Hamerly, G., Elkan, C.: Learning the k in k-means. In: Proc. of NIPS'04. pp. 281–288 (2004)
27. Hutter, F., Hoos, H., Leyton-Brown, K.: Sequential model-based optimization for general algorithm configuration. In: Proc. of LION'11. pp. 507–523 (2011)
28. Jamieson, K., Talwalkar, A.: Non-stochastic best arm identification and hyperparameter optimization. In: Proc. of AISTATS'16. pp. 240–248 (2016)
29. Kalousis, A.: Algorithm Selection via Meta-Learning. Ph.D. thesis, University of Geneve (2002)
30. Komer, B., Bergstra, J., Eliasmith, C.: Hyperopt-sklearn: Automatic hyperparameter configuration for scikit-learn. In: ICML workshop on AutoML (2014)
31. Lacoste, A., Marchand, M., Laviolette, F., Larochelle, H.: Agnostic Bayesian learning of ensembles. In: Proc. of ICML'14. pp. 611–619 (2014)
32. Li, L., Jamieson, K., DeSalvo, G., Rostamizadeh, A., Talwalkar, A.: Hyperband: A novel bandit-based approach to hyperparameter optimization. JMLR 18(185), 1–52 (2018)
33. Michie, D., Spiegelhalter, D., Taylor, C., Campbell, J.: Machine Learning, Neural and Statistical Classification. Ellis Horwood (1994)
34. Mohr, F., Wever, M., Hüllermeier, E.: Ml-plan: Automated machine learning via hierarchical planning. Machine Learning (2018)
35. Niculescu-Mizil, A., Perlich, C., Swirszcz, G., Sindhwani, V., Liu, Y., Melville, P., Wang, D., Xiao, J., Hu, J., Singh, M., Shang, W., Zhu, Y.: Winning the KDD cup orange challenge with ensemble selection. The 2009 Knowledge Discovery in Data Competition pp. 23–34 (2009)
36. Pedregosa, F., Varoquaux, G., Gramfort, A., Michel, V., Thirion, B., Grisel, O., Blondel, M., Prettenhofer, P., Weiss, R., Dubourg, V., Vanderplas, J., Passos, A., Cournapeau, D., Brucher, M., Perrot, M., Duchesnay, E.: Scikit-learn: Machine learning in Python. JMLR 12, 2825–2830 (2011)
37. Pfahringer, B., Bensusan, H., Giraud-Carrier, C.: Meta-learning by landmarking various learning algorithms. In: Proc. of ICML'00. pp. 743–750 (2000)
38. Reif, M., Shafait, F., Dengel, A.: Meta-learning for evolutionary parameter optimization of classifiers. Machine Learning 87, 357–380 (2012)
39. de Sá, A., Pinto, W., Oliveira, L., Pappa, G.: RECIPE: a grammar-based framework for automatically evolving classification pipelines. In: Proc. of ECGP'17. pp. 246–261 (2017)
40. Shahriari, B., Swersky, K., Wang, Z., Adams, R., de Freitas, N.: Taking the human out of the loop: A review of Bayesian optimization. Proceedings of the IEEE 104(1), 148–175 (2016)
41. Snoek, J., Larochelle, H., Adams, R.: Practical Bayesian optimization of machine learning algorithms. In: Proc. of NIPS'12. pp. 2960–2968 (2012)
42. Thornton, C., Hutter, F., Hoos, H., Leyton-Brown, K.: Auto-WEKA: combined selection and hyperparameter optimization of classification algorithms. In: Proc. of KDD'13. pp. 847–855 (2013)

43. Vanschoren, J., van Rijn, J., Bischl, B., Torgo, L.: OpenML: Networked science in machine learning. SIGKDD Explorations 15(2), 49–60 (2013)
44. Wolpert, D.: Stacked generalization. Neural Networks 5, 241–259 (1992)
45. Yogatama, D., Mann, G.: Efficient transfer learning method for automatic hyperparameter tuning. In: Proc. of AISTATS'14. pp. 1077–1085 (2014)
46. Zhang, Y., Bahadori, M., Su, H., Sun, J.: FLASH: Fast Bayesian Optimization for Data Analytic Pipelines. In: Proc. of KDD'16. pp. 2065–2074 (2016)

Chapter 7
Towards Automatically-Tuned Deep Neural Networks

Hector Mendoza, Aaron Klein, Matthias Feurer, Jost Tobias Springenberg, Matthias Urban, Michael Burkart, Maximilian Dippel, Marius Lindauer, and Frank Hutter

Abstract Recent advances in AutoML have led to automated tools that can compete with machine learning experts on supervised learning tasks. In this work, we present two versions of Auto-Net, which provide automatically-tuned deep neural networks without any human intervention. The first version, Auto-Net 1.0, builds upon ideas from the competition-winning system Auto-sklearn by using the Bayesian Optimization method SMAC and uses Lasagne as the underlying deep learning (DL) library. The more recent Auto-Net 2.0 builds upon a recent combination of Bayesian Optimization and HyperBand, called BOHB, and uses PyTorch as DL library. To the best of our knowledge, Auto-Net 1.0 was the first automatically-tuned neural network to win competition datasets against human experts (as part of the first AutoML challenge). Further empirical results show that ensembling Auto-Net 1.0 with Auto-sklearn can perform better than either approach alone, and that Auto-Net 2.0 can perform better yet.

7.1 Introduction

Neural networks have significantly improved the state of the art on a variety of benchmarks in recent years and opened many new promising research avenues [22, 27, 36, 39, 41]. However, neural networks are not easy to use for non-experts since their performance crucially depends on proper settings of a large set of hyperparameters (e.g., learning rate and weight decay) and architecture choices (e.g., number of layers and type of activation functions). Here, we present work

H. Mendoza · A. Klein · M. Feurer · J. T. Springenberg · M. Urban · M. Burkart · M. Dippel
M. Lindauer
Department of Computer Science, University of Freiburg, Freiburg, Baden-Württemberg, Germany
e-mail: fh@informatik.uni-freiburg.de

F. Hutter (✉)
Department of Computer Science, University of Freiburg, Freiburg, Germany

F. Hutter et al. (eds.), *Automated Machine Learning*, The Springer Series on Challenges in Machine Learning, https://doi.org/10.1007/978-3-030-05318-5_7

towards effective off-the-shelf neural networks based on approaches from automated machine learning (AutoML).

AutoML aims to provide effective off-the-shelf learning systems to free experts and non-experts alike from the tedious and time-consuming tasks of selecting the right algorithm for a dataset at hand, along with the right preprocessing method and the various hyperparameters of all involved components. Thornton et al. [43] phrased this AutoML problem as a combined algorithm selection and hyperparameter optimization (CASH) problem, which aims to identify the combination of algorithm components with the best (cross-)validation performance.

One powerful approach for solving this CASH problem treats this cross-validation performance as an expensive blackbox function and uses Bayesian optimization [4, 35] to search for its optimizer. While Bayesian optimization typically uses Gaussian processes [32], these tend to have problems with the special characteristics of the CASH problem (high dimensionality; both categorical and continuous hyperparameters; many conditional hyperparameters, which are only relevant for some instantiations of other hyperparameters). Adapting GPs to handle these characteristics is an active field of research [40, 44], but so far Bayesian optimization methods using tree-based models [2, 17] work best in the CASH setting [9, 43].

Auto-Net is modelled after the two prominent AutoML systems Auto-WEKA [43] and Auto-sklearn [11], discussed in Chaps. 4 and 6 of this book, respectively. Both of these use the random forest-based Bayesian optimization method SMAC [17] to tackle the CASH problem – to find the best instantiation of classifiers in WEKA [16] and scikit-learn [30], respectively. Auto-sklearn employs two additional methods to boost performance. Firstly, it uses meta-learning [3] based on experience on previous datasets to start SMAC from good configurations [12]. Secondly, since the eventual goal is to make the best predictions, it is wasteful to try out dozens of machine learning models and then only use the single best model; instead, Auto-sklearn saves all models evaluated by SMAC and constructs an ensemble of these with the ensemble selection technique [5]. Even though both Auto-WEKA and Auto-sklearn include a wide range of supervised learning methods, neither includes modern neural networks.

Here, we introduce two versions of a system we dub *Auto-Net* to fill this gap. Auto-Net 1.0 is based on Theano and has a relatively simple search space, while the more recent Auto-Net 2.0 is implemented in PyTorch and uses a more complex space and more recent advances in DL. A further difference lies in their respective search procedure: Auto-Net 1.0 automatically configures neural networks with SMAC [17], following the same AutoML approach as Auto-WEKA and Auto-sklearn, while Auto-Net 2.0 builds upon BOHB [10], a combination of Bayesian Optimization (BO) and efficient racing strategies via HyperBand (HB) [23].

Auto-Net 1.0 achieved the best performance on two datasets in the human expert track of the recent *ChaLearn AutoML Challenge* [14]. To the best of our knowledge, this is the first time that a fully-automatically-tuned neural network won a competition dataset against human experts. Auto-Net 2.0 further improves upon Auto-Net 1.0 on large data sets, showing recent progress in the field.

We describe the configuration space and implementation of Auto-Net 1.0 in Sect. 7.2 and of Auto-Net 2.0 in Sect. 7.3. We then study their performance empirically in Sect. 7.4 and conclude in Sect. 7.5. We omit a thorough discussion of related work and refer to Chap. 3 of this book for an overview on the extremely active field of neural architecture search. Nevertheless, we note that several other recent tools follow Auto-Net's goal of automating deep learning, such as Auto-Keras [20], Photon-AI, H2O.ai, DEvol or Google's Cloud AutoML service.

This chapter is an extended version of our 2016 paper introducing Auto-Net, presented at the *2016 ICML Workshop on AutoML* [26].

7.2 Auto-Net 1.0

We now introduce Auto-Net 1.0 and describe its implementation. We chose to implement this first version of Auto-Net as an extension of Auto-sklearn [11] by adding a new classification (and regression) component; the reason for this choice was that it allows us to leverage existing parts of the machine learning pipeline: feature preprocessing, data preprocessing and ensemble construction. Here, we limit Auto-Net to fully-connected feed-forward neural networks, since they apply to a wide range of different datasets; we defer the extension to other types of neural networks, such as convolutional or recurrent neural networks, to future work. To have access to neural network techniques we use the Python deep learning library Lasagne [6], which is built around Theano [42]. However, we note that in general our approach is independent of the neural network implementation.

Following [2] and [7], we distinguish between layer-independent *network hyperparameters* that control the architecture and training procedure and *per-layer hyperparameters* that are set for each layer. In total, we optimize 63 hyperparameters (see Table 7.1), using the same configuration space for all types of supervised learning (binary, multiclass and multilabel classification, as well as regression). Sparse datasets also share the same configuration space. (Since neural networks cannot handle datasets in sparse representation out of the box, we transform the data into a dense representation on a per-batch basis prior to feeding it to the neural network.)

The per-layer hyperparameters of layer k are conditionally dependent on the number of layers being at least k. For practical reasons, we constrain the number of layers to be between one and six: firstly, we aim to keep the training time of a single configuration low,[1] and secondly each layer adds eight per-layer hyperparameters to the configuration space, such that allowing additional layers would further complicate the configuration process.

The most common way to optimize the internal weights of neural networks is via stochastic gradient descent (SGD) using partial derivatives calculated with back-propagation. Standard SGD crucially depends on the correct setting of the learning

[1]We aimed to be able to afford the evaluation of several dozens of configurations within a time budget of two days on a single CPU.

Table 7.1 Configuration space of Auto-Net. The configuration space for the preprocessing methods can be found in [11]

	Name	Range	Default	log scale	Type	Conditional
Network hyperparameters	Batch size	[32, 4096]	32	✓	float	–
	Number of updates	[50, 2500]	200	✓	int	–
	Number of layers	[1, 6]	1	–	int	–
	Learning rate	$[10^{-6}, 1.0]$	10^{-2}	✓	float	–
	L_2 regularization	$[10^{-7}, 10^{-2}]$	10^{-4}	✓	float	–
	Dropout output layer	[0.0, 0.99]	0.5	✓	float	–
	Solver type	{SGD, Momentum, Adam, Adadelta, Adagrad, smorm, Nesterov }	smorm3s	–	cat	–
	lr-policy	{Fixed, Inv, Exp, Step}	Fixed	–	cat	–
Conditioned on solver type	β_1	$[10^{-4}, 10^{-1}]$	10^{-1}	✓	float	✓
	β_2	$[10^{-4}, 10^{-1}]$	10^{-1}	✓	float	✓
	ρ	[0.05, 0.99]	0.95	✓	float	✓
	Momentum	[0.3, 0.999]	0.9	✓	float	✓
Conditioned on lr-policy	γ	$[10^{-3}, 10^{-1}]$	10^{-2}	✓	float	✓
	k	[0.0, 1.0]	0.5	–	float	✓
	s	[2, 20]	2	–	int	✓
Per-layer hyperparameters	Activation-type	{Sigmoid, TanH, ScaledTanH, ELU, ReLU, Leaky, Linear}	ReLU	–	cat	✓
	Number of units	[64, 4096]	128	✓	int	✓
	Dropout in layer	[0.0, 0.99]	0.5	–	float	✓
	Weight initialization	{Constant, Normal, Uniform, Glorot-Uniform, Glorot-Normal, He-Normal, He-Uniform, Orthogonal, Sparse}	He-Normal	–	cat	✓
	Std. normal init.	$[10^{-7}, 0.1]$	0.0005	–	float	✓
	Leakiness	[0.01, 0.99]	$\frac{1}{3}$	–	float	✓
	tanh scale in	[0.5, 1.0]	2/3	–	float	✓
	tanh scale out	[1.1, 3.0]	1.7159	✓	float	✓

rate hyperparameter. To lessen this dependency, various algorithms (solvers) for stochastic gradient descent have been proposed. We include the following well-known methods from the literature in the configuration space of Auto-Net: vanilla stochastic gradient descent (SGD), stochastic gradient descent with momentum (Momentum), Adam [21], Adadelta [48], Nesterov momentum [28] and Adagrad [8]. Additionally, we used a variant of the vSGD optimizer [33], dubbed "smorm", in which the estimate of the Hessian is replaced by an estimate of the squared gradient (calculated as in the RMSprop procedure). Each of these methods comes with a learning rate α and an own set of hyperparameters, for example Adam's momentum vectors β_1 and β_2. Each solver's hyperparameter(s) are only active if the corresponding solver is chosen.

We also decay the learning rate α over time, using the following policies (which multiply the initial learning rate by a factor α_{decay} after each epoch $t = 0 \ldots T$):

- Fixed: $\alpha_{decay} = 1$
- Inv: $\alpha_{decay} = (1 + \gamma t)^{(-k)}$
- Exp: $\alpha_{decay} = \gamma^t$
- Step: $\alpha_{decay} = \gamma^{\lfloor t/s \rfloor}$

Here, the hyperparameters k, s and γ are conditionally dependent on the choice of the policy.

To search for a strong instantiation in this conditional search space of Auto-Net 1.0, as in Auto-WEKA and Auto-sklearn, we used the random-forest based Bayesian optimization method SMAC [17]. SMAC is an anytime approach that keeps track of the best configuration seen so far and outputs this when terminated.

7.3 Auto-Net 2.0

AutoNet 2.0 differs from AutoNet 1.0 mainly in the following three aspects:

- it uses PyTorch [29] instead of Lasagne as a deep learning library
- it uses a larger configuration space including up-to-date deep learning techniques, modern architectures (such as ResNets) and includes more compact representations of the search space, and
- it applies BOHB [10] instead of SMAC to obtain a well-performing neural network more efficiently.

In the following, we will discuss these points in more detail.

Since the development and maintenance of Lasagne ended last year, we chose a different Python library for Auto-Net 2.0. The most popular deep learning libraries right now are PyTorch [29] and Tensorflow [1]. These come with quite similar features and mostly differ in the level of detail they give insight into. For example, PyTorch offers the user the possibility to trace all computations during training. While there are advantages and disadvantages for each of these libraries, we decided to use PyTorch because of its ability to dynamically construct computational graphs. For this reason, we also started referring to Auto-Net 2.0 as Auto-PyTorch.

The search space of AutoNet 2.0 includes both hyperparameters for module selection (e.g. scheduler type, network architecture) and hyperparameters for each of the specific modules. It supports different deep learning modules, such as network type, learning rate scheduler, optimizer and regularization technique, as described below. Auto-Net 2.0 is also designed to be easily extended; users can add their own modules to the ones listed below.

Auto-Net 2.0 currently offers four different network types:

Multi-Layer Perceptrons This is a standard implementation of conventional MLPs extended by dropout layers [38]. Similar as in AutoNet 1.0, each layer of the MLP is parameterized (e.g., number of units and dropout rate).

Residual Neural Networks These are deep neural networks that learn residual functions [47], with the difference that we use fully connected layers instead of convolutional ones. As is standard with ResNets, the architecture consists of M groups, each of which stacks N residual blocks in sequence. While the architecture of each block is fixed, the number M of groups, the number of blocks N per group, as well as the width of each group is determined by hyperparameters, as shown in Table 7.2.

Shaped Multi-Layer Perceptrons To avoid that every layer has its own hyperparameters (which is an inefficient representation to search), in shaped MLPs the overall shape of the layers is predetermined, e.g. as a funnel, long funnel, diamond, hexagon, brick, or triangle. We followed the shapes from https://mikkokotila.github.io/slate/#shapes; Ilya Loshchilov also proposed parameterization by such shapes to us before [25].

Shaped Residual Networks A ResNet where the overall shape of the layers is predetermined (e.g. funnel, long funnel, diamond, hexagon, brick, triangle).

The network types of ResNets and ShapedResNets can also use any of the regularization methods of Shake-Shake [13] and ShakeDrop [46]. MixUp [49] can be used for all networks.

The optimizers currently supported in Auto-Net 2.0 are Adam [21] and SGD with momentum. Moreover, Auto-Net 2.0 currently offers five different schedulers that change the optimizer's learning rate over time (as a function of the number of epochs):

Exponential This multiplies the learning rate with a constant factor in each epoch.

Step This decays the learning rate by a multiplicative factor after a constant number of steps.

Cyclic This modifies the learning rate in a certain range, alternating between increasing and decreasing [37].

Cosine Annealing with Warm Restarts [24] This learning rate schedule implements multiple phases of convergence. It cools down the learning rate to zero following a cosine decay [24], and after each convergence phase heats it up to start a next phase of convergence, often to a better optimum. The network weights

Table 7.2 Configuration space of Auto-Net 2.0. There are 112 hyperparameters in total

	Name	Range	Default	Log scale	Type	Conditional
General hyperparameters	Batch size	$[32, 500]$	32	✓	int	–
	Use mixup	{True, False}	True	–	bool	–
	Mixup alpha	$[0.0, 1.0]$	1.0	–	float	✓
	Network	{MLP, ResNet, ShapedMLP, ShapedResNet}	MLP	–	cat	–
	Optimizer	{Adam, SGD}	Adam	–	cat	–
	Preprocessor	{nystroem, kernel pca, fast ica, kitchen sinks, truncated svd}	Nystroem	–	cat	–
	Imputation	{most frequent, median, mean}	Most frequent	–	cat	–
	Use loss weight strategy	{True, False}	True	–	cat	–
	Learning rate scheduler	{Step, Exponential, OnPlateau, Cyclic, CosineAnnealing}	Step	–	cat	–
Preprocessor						
Nystroem	Coef	$[-1.0, 1.0]$	0.0	–	float	✓
	Degree	$[2, 5]$	3	–	int	✓
	Gamma	$[0.00003, 8.0]$	0.1	✓	float	✓
	Kernel	{poly, rbf, sigmoid, cosine}	rbf	–	cat	✓
	Num components	$[50, 10000]$	100	✓	int	✓
Kitchen sinks	Gamma	$[0.00003, 8.0]$	1.0	✓	float	✓
	Num components	$[50, 10000]$	100	✓	int	✓
Truncated SVD	Target dimension	$[10, 256]$	128	–	int	✓
Kernel PCA	Coef	$[-1.0, 1.0]$	0.0	–	float	✓
	Degree	$[2, 5]$	3	–	int	✓
	Gamma	$[0.00003, 8.0]$	0.1	✓	float	✓
	Kernel	{poly, rbf, sigmoid, cosine}	rbf	–	cat	✓
	Num components	$[50, 10000]$	100	✓	int	✓
Fast ICA	Algorithm	{parallel, deflation}	Parallel	–	cat	✓
	Fun	{logcosh, exp, cube}	Logcosh	–	cat	✓
	Whiten	{True, False}	True	–	cat	✓
	Num components	$[10, 2000]$	1005	–	int	✓
Networks						
MLP	Activation function	{Sigmoid, Tanh, ReLu}	Sigmoid	–	cat	✓
	Num layers	$[1, 15]$	9	–	int	✓
	Num units (for layer i)	$[10, 1024]$	100	✓	int	✓
	Dropout (for layer i)	$[0.0, 0.5]$	0.25	–	int	✓
ResNet	Activation function	{Sigmoid, Tanh, ReLu}	Sigmoid	–	cat	✓
	Residual block groups	$[1, 9]$	4	–	int	✓
	Blocks per group	$[1, 4]$	2	–	int	✓
	Num units (for group i)	$[128, 1024]$	200	✓	int	✓
	Use dropout	{True, False}	True	–	bool	✓
	Dropout (for group i)	$[0.0, 0.9]$	0.5	–	int	✓
	Use shake drop	{True, False}	True	–	bool	✓
	Use shake shake	{True, False}	True	–	bool	✓
	Shake drop β_{max}	$[0.0, 1.0]$	0.5	–	float	✓
ShapedMLP	Activation function	{Sigmoid, Tanh, ReLu}	Sigmoid	–	cat	✓
	Num layers	$[3, 15]$	9	–	int	✓
	Max units per layer	$[10, 1024]$	200	✓	int	✓
	Network shape	{Funnel, LongFunnel, Diamond, Hexagon, Brick, Triangle, Stairs}	Funnel	–	cat	✓
	Max dropout per layer	$[0.0, 0.6$	0.2	–	float	✓
	Dropout shape	{Funnel, LongFunnel, Diamond, Hexagon, Brick, Triangle, Stairs}	Funnel	–	cat	✓
Shaped ResNet	Activation function	{Sigmoid, Tanh, ReLu}	Sigmoid	–	cat	✓
	Num layers	$[3, 9]$	4	–	int	✓
	Blocks per layer	$[1, 4]$	2	–	int	✓
	Use dropout	{True, False}	True	–	bool	✓
	Max units per layer	$[10, 1024]$	200	✓	int	✓
	Network shape	{Funnel, LongFunnel, Diamond, Hexagon, Brick, Triangle, Stairs}	Funnel	–	cat	✓
	Max dropout per layer	$[0.0, 0.6$	0.2	–	float	✓
	Dropout shape	{Funnel, LongFunnel, Diamond, Hexagon, Brick, Triangle, Stairs}	Funnel	–	cat	✓
	Use shake drop	{True, False}	True	–	bool	✓
	Use shake shake	{True, False}	True	–	bool	✓
	Shake drop β_{max}	$[0.0, 1.0]$	0.5	–	float	✓
Optimizers						
Adam	Learning rate	$[0.0001, 0.1]$	0.003	✓	float	✓
	Weight decay	$[0.0001, 0.1]$	0.05	–	float	✓
SGD	Learning rate	$[0.0001, 0.1]$	0.003	✓	float	✓
	Weight decay	$[0.0001, 0.1]$	0.05	–	float	✓
	Momentum	$[0.1, 0.9]$	0.3	✓	float	✓
Schedulers						
Step	γ	$[0.001, 0.9]$	0.4505	–	float	✓
	Step size	$[1, 10]$	6	–	int	✓
Exponential	γ	$[0.8, 0.9999]$	0.89995	–	float	✓
OnPlateau	γ	$[0.05, 0.5]$	0.275	–	float	✓
	Patience	$[3, 10]$	6	–	int	✓
Cyclic	Cycle length	$[3, 10]$	6	–	int	✓
	Max factor	$[1.0, 2.0]$	1.5	–	float	✓
	Min factor	$[0.001, 1.0]$	0.5	–	float	✓
Cosine annealing	T_0	$[1, 20]$	10	–	int	✓
	T_{mult}	$[1.0, 2.0]$	1.5	–	float	✓

are not modified when heating up the learning rate, such that the next phase of convergence is warm-started.

OnPlateau This scheduler[2] changes the learning rate whenever a metric stops improving; specifically, it multiplies the current learning rate with a factor γ if there was no improvement after p epochs.

Similar to Auto-Net 1.0, Auto-Net 2.0 can search over pre-processing techniques. Auto-Net 2.0 currently supports Nyström [45], Kernel principal component analysis [34], fast independent component analysis [18], random kitchen sinks [31] and truncated singular value decomposition [15]. Users can specify a list of pre-processing techniques to be taken into account and can also choose between different balancing and normalization strategies (for balancing strategies only weighting the loss is available, and for normalization strategies, min-max normalization and standardization are supported). In contrast to Auto-Net 1.0, Auto-Net 2.0 does not build an ensemble at the end (although this feature will likely be added soon). All hyperparameters of Auto-Net 2.0 with their respective ranges and default values can be found in Table 7.2.

As optimizer for this highly conditional space, we used BOHB (**B**ayesian **O**ptimization with **H**yper**B**and) [10], which combines conventional Bayesian optimization with the bandit-based strategy Hyperband [23] to substantially improve its efficiency. Like Hyperband, BOHB uses repeated runs of Successive Halving [19] to invest most runtime in promising neural networks and stops training neural networks with poor performance early. Like in Bayesian optimization, BOHB learns which kinds of neural networks yield good results. Specifically, like the BO method TPE [2], BOHB uses a kernel density estimator (KDE) to describe regions of high performance in the space of neural networks (architectures and hyperparameter settings) and trades off exploration versus exploitation using this KDE. One of the advantages of BOHB is that it is easily parallelizable, achieving almost linear speedups with an increasing number of workers [10].

As a budget for BOHB we can either handle epochs or (wallclock) time in minutes; by default we use runtime, but users can freely adapt the different budget parameters. An example usage is shown in Algorithm 1. Similar to Auto-sklearn, Auto-Net is built as a plugin estimator for scikit-learn. Users have to provide a training set and a performance metric (e.g., accuracy). Optionally, they might

Algorithm 1 Example usage of Auto-Net 2.0

```
from autonet import AutoNetClassification

cls = AutoNetClassification(min_budget=5, max_budget=20, max_runtime=120)
cls.fit(X_train, Y_train)
predictions = cls.predict(X_test)
```

[2]Implemented by PyTorch.

specify a validation and testset. The validation set is used during training to get a measure for the performance of the network and to train the KDE models of BOHB.

7.4 Experiments

We now empirically evaluate our methods. Our implementations of Auto-Net run on both CPUs and GPUs, but since neural networks heavily employ matrix operations they run much faster on GPUs. Our CPU-based experiments were run on a compute cluster, each node of which has two eight-core Intel Xeon E5-2650 v2 CPUs, running at 2.6 GHz, and a shared memory of 64 GB. Our GPU-based experiments were run on a compute cluster, each node of which has four GeForce GTX TITAN X GPUs.

7.4.1 Baseline Evaluation of Auto-Net 1.0 and Auto-sklearn

In our first experiment, we compare different instantiations of Auto-Net 1.0 on the five datasets of phase 0 of the AutoML challenge. First, we use the CPU-based and GPU-based versions to study the difference of running NNs on different hardware. Second, we allow the combination of neural networks with the models from Auto-sklearn. Third, we also run Auto-sklearn without neural networks as a baseline. On each dataset, we performed 10 one-day runs of each method, allowing up to 100 min for the evaluation of a single configuration by five-fold cross-validation on the training set. For each time step of each run, following [11] we constructed an ensemble from the models it had evaluated so far and plot the test error of that ensemble over time. In practice, we would either use a separate process to calculate the ensembles in parallel or compute them after the optimization process.

Fig. 7.1 shows the results on two of the five datasets. First, we note that the GPU-based version of Auto-Net was consistently about an order of magnitude faster than the CPU-based version. Within the given fixed compute budget, the CPU-based version consistently performed worst, whereas the GPU-based version performed best on the `newsgroups` dataset (see Fig. 7.1a), tied with Auto-sklearn on 3 of the other datasets, and performed worse on one. Despite the fact that the CPU-based Auto-Net was very slow, in 3/5 cases the combination of Auto-sklearn and CPU-based Auto-Net still improved over Auto-sklearn; this can, for example, be observed for the `dorothea` dataset in Fig. 7.1b.

7.4.2 Results for AutoML Competition Datasets

Having developed Auto-Net 1.0 during the first AutoML challenge, we used a combination of Auto-sklearn and GPU-based Auto-Net for the last two phases

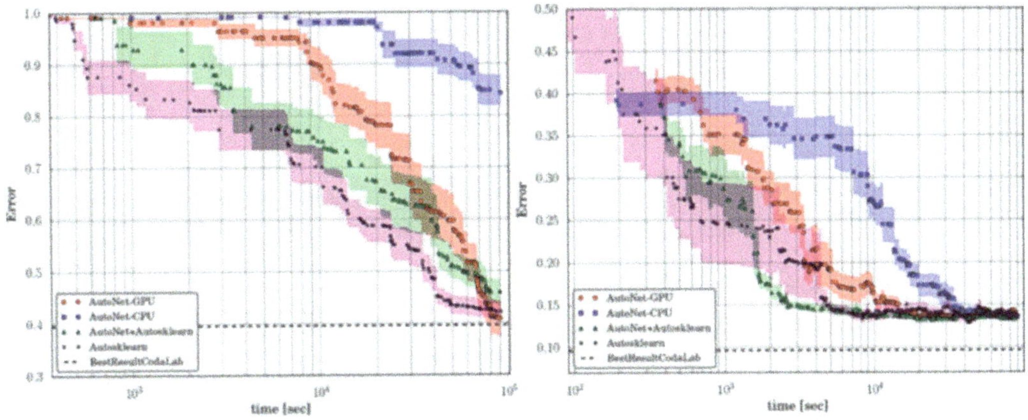

(a) (b)

Fig. 7.1 Results for the four methods on two datasets from *Tweakathon0* of the AutoML challenge. We show errors on the competition's validation set (not the test set since its true labels are not available), with our methods only having access to the training set. To avoid clutter, we plot mean error ± 1/4 standard deviations over the 10 runs of each method. (**a**) `newsgroups` dataset. (**b**) `dorothea` dataset

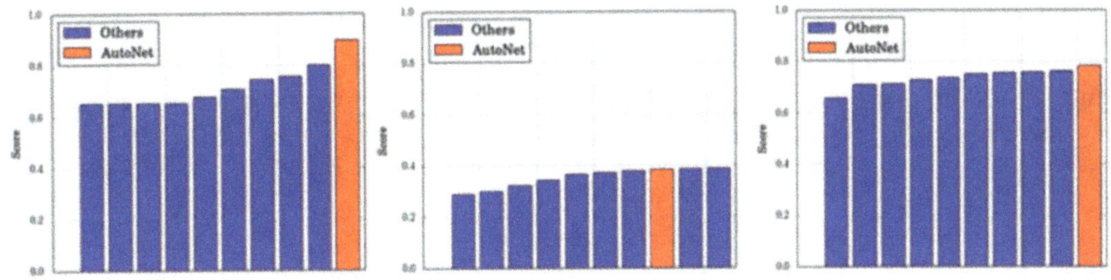

(a) (b) (c)

Fig. 7.2 Official AutoML human expert track competition results for the three datasets for which we used Auto-Net. We only show the top 10 entries. (**a**) `alexis` dataset. (**b**) `yolanda` dataset. (**c**) `tania` dataset

to win the respective human expert tracks. Auto-sklearn has been developed for much longer and is much more robust than Auto-Net, so for 4/5 datasets in the 3rd phase and 3/5 datasets in the 4th phase Auto-sklearn performed best by itself and we only submitted its results. Here, we discuss the three datasets for which we used Auto-Net. Fig. 7.2 shows the official AutoML human expert track competition results for the three datasets for which we used Auto-Net. The `alexis` dataset was part of the 3rd phase ("advanced phase") of the challenge. For this, we ran Auto-Net on five GPUs in parallel (using SMAC in shared-model mode) for 18 h. Our submission included an automatically-constructed ensemble of 39 models and clearly outperformed all human experts, reaching an AUC score of 90%, while the best human competitor (Ideal Intel Analytics) only reached 80%. To our best knowledge, this is the first time an automatically-constructed neural network won a competition dataset. The `yolanda` and `tania` datasets were part of the 4th phase ("expert phase") of the challenge. For `yolanda`, we ran Auto-Net for 48 h

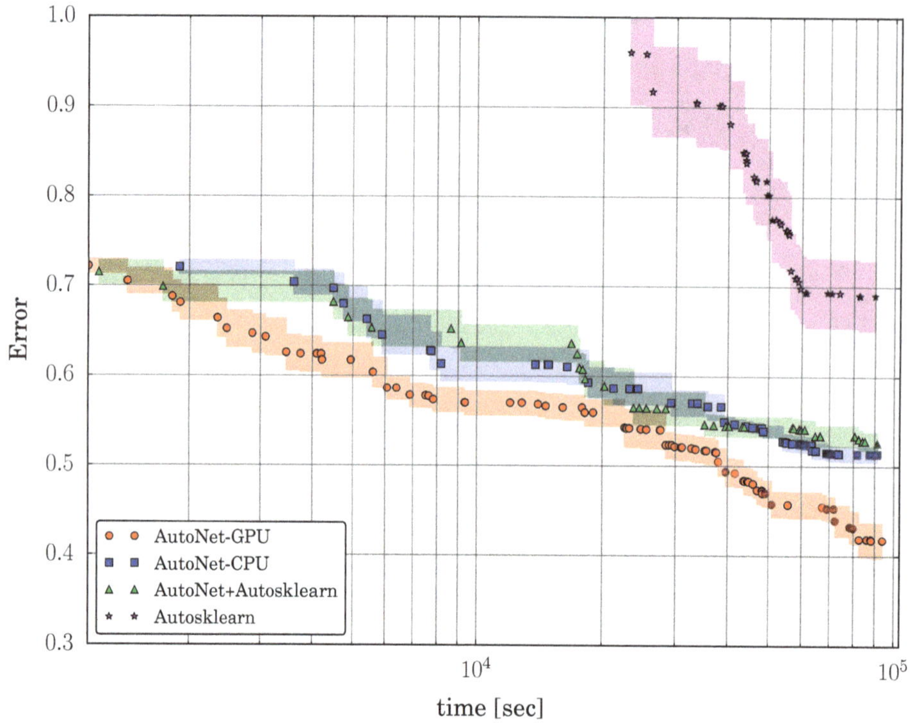

Fig. 7.3 Performance on the `tania` dataset over time. We show cross-validation performance on the training set since the true labels for the competition's validation or test set are not available. To avoid clutter, we plot mean error ± 1/4 standard deviations over the 10 runs of each method

on eight GPUs and automatically constructed an ensemble of five neural networks, achieving a close third place. For `tania`, we ran Auto-Net for 48 h on eight GPUs along with Auto-sklearn on 25 CPUs, and in the end our automated ensembling script constructed an ensemble of eight 1-layer neural networks, two 2-layer neural networks, and one logistic regression model trained with SGD. This ensemble won the first place on the `tania` dataset.

For the `tania` dataset, we also repeated the experiments from Sect. 7.4.1. Fig. 7.3 shows that for this dataset Auto-Net performed clearly better than Auto-sklearn, even when only running on CPUs. The GPU-based variant of Auto-Net performed best.

7.4.3 Comparing AutoNet 1.0 and 2.0

Finally, we show an illustrative comparison between Auto-Net 1.0 and 2.0. We note that Auto-Net 2.0 has a much more comprehensive search space than Auto-Net 1.0, and we therefore expect it to perform better on large datasets given enough time. We also expect that searching the larger space is harder than searching Auto-Net 1.0's smaller space; however, since Auto-Net 2.0 uses the efficient multi-fidelity optimizer BOHB to terminate poorly-performing neural networks early on, it may nevertheless obtain strong anytime performance. On the other hand, Auto-Net 2.0

Table 7.3 Error metric of different Auto-Net versions, run for different times, all on CPU. We compare Auto-Net 1.0, ensembles of Auto-Net 1.0 and Auto-sklearn, Auto-Net 2.0 with one worker, and Auto-Net 2.0 with four workers. All results are means across 10 runs of each system. We show errors on the competition's validation set (not the test set since its true labels are not available), with our methods only having access to the training set

	newsgroups			dorothea		
	10^3 s	10^4 s	1 day	10^3 s	10^4 s	1 day
Auto-Net 1.0	0.99	0.98	0.85	0.38	0.30	0.13
Auto-sklearn + Auto-Net 1.0	0.94	0.76	0.47	0.29	0.13	0.13
Auto-Net 2.0: 1 worker	1.0	0.67	0.55	0.88	0.17	0.16
Auto-Net 2.0: 4 workers	0.89	0.57	0.44	0.22	0.17	0.14

so far does not implement ensembling, and due to this missing regularization component and its larger hypothesis space, it may be more prone to overfitting than Auto-Net 1.0.

In order to test these expectations about performance on different-sized datasets, we used a medium-sized dataset (`newsgroups`, with 13k training data points) and a small one (`dorothea`, with 800 training data points). The results are presented in Table 7.3.

On the medium-sized dataset `newsgroups`, Auto-Net 2.0 performed much better than Auto-Net 1.0, and using four workers also led to strong speedups on top of this, making Auto-Net 2.0 competitive to the ensemble of Auto-sklearn and Auto-Net 1.0. We found that despite Auto-Net 2.0's larger search space its anytime performance (using the multi-fidelity method BOHB) was better than that of Auto-Net 1.0 (using the blackbox optimization method SMAC). On the small dataset `dorothea`, Auto-Net 2.0 also performed better than Auto-Net 1.0 early on, but given enough time Auto-Net 1.0 performed slightly better. We attribute this to the lack of ensembling in Auto-Net 2.0, combined with its larger search space.

7.5 Conclusion

We presented Auto-Net, which provides automatically-tuned deep neural networks without any human intervention. Even though neural networks show superior performance on many datasets, for traditional data sets with manually-defined features they do not always perform best. However, we showed that, even in cases where other methods perform better, combining Auto-Net with Auto-sklearn to an ensemble often leads to an equal or better performance than either approach alone.

Finally, we reported results on three datasets from the AutoML challenge's human expert track, for which Auto-Net won one third place and two first places. We showed that ensembles of Auto-sklearn and Auto-Net can get users the best of both worlds and quite often improve over the individual tools. First experiments on the new Auto-Net 2.0 showed that using a more comprehensive search space, combined with BOHB as an optimizer yields promising results.

In future work, we aim to extend Auto-Net to more general neural network architectures, including convolutional and recurrent neural networks.

Acknowledgements This work has partly been supported by the European Research Council (ERC) under the European Union's Horizon 2020 research and innovation programme under grant no. 716721.

Bibliography

1. Abadi, M., Barham, P., Chen, J., Chen, Z., Davis, A., Dean, J., Devin, M., Ghemawat, S., Irving, G., Isard, M., Kudlur, M., Levenberg, J., Monga, R., Moore, S., Murray, D., Steiner, B., Tucker, P., Vasudevan, V., Warden, P., Wicke, M., Yu, Y., Zheng, X.: Tensorflow: A system for large-scale machine learning. In: 12th USENIX Symposium on Operating Systems Design and Implementation (OSDI 16). pp. 265–283 (2016), https://www.usenix.org/system/files/conference/osdi16/osdi16-abadi.pdf
2. Bergstra, J., Bardenet, R., Bengio, Y., Kégl, B.: Algorithms for hyper-parameter optimization. In: Shawe-Taylor, J., Zemel, R., Bartlett, P., Pereira, F., Weinberger, K. (eds.) Proceedings of the 25th International Conference on Advances in Neural Information Processing Systems (NIPS'11). pp. 2546–2554 (2011)
3. Brazdil, P., Giraud-Carrier, C., Soares, C., Vilalta, R.: Metalearning: Applications to Data Mining. Springer Publishing Company, Incorporated, 1 edn. (2008)
4. Brochu, E., Cora, V., de Freitas, N.: A tutorial on Bayesian optimization of expensive cost functions, with application to active user modeling and hierarchical reinforcement learning. Computing Research Repository (CoRR) abs/1012.2599 (2010)
5. Caruana, R., Niculescu-Mizil, A., Crew, G., Ksikes, A.: Ensemble selection from libraries of models. In: In Proceedings of the 21st International Conference on Machine Learning. pp. 137–144. ACM Press (2004)
6. Dieleman, S., Schlüter, J., Raffel, C., Olson, E., Sønderby, S., Nouri, D., Maturana, D., Thoma, M., Battenberg, E., Kelly, J., Fauw, J.D., Heilman, M., diogo149, McFee, B., Weideman, H., takacsg84, peterderivaz, Jon, instagibbs, Rasul, K., CongLiu, Britefury, Degrave, J.: Lasagne: First release. (Aug 2015), https://doi.org/10.5281/zenodo.27878
7. Domhan, T., Springenberg, J.T., Hutter, F.: Speeding up automatic hyperparameter optimization of deep neural networks by extrapolation of learning curves. In: Yang, Q., Wooldridge, M. (eds.) Proceedings of the 25th International Joint Conference on Artificial Intelligence (IJCAI'15). pp. 3460–3468 (2015)
8. Duchi, J., Hazan, E., Singer, Y.: Adaptive subgradient methods for online learning and stochastic optimization. J. Mach. Learn. Res. 12, 2121–2159 (Jul 2011)
9. Eggensperger, K., Feurer, M., Hutter, F., Bergstra, J., Snoek, J., Hoos, H., Leyton-Brown, K.: Towards an empirical foundation for assessing Bayesian optimization of hyperparameters. In: NIPS Workshop on Bayesian Optimization in Theory and Practice (BayesOpt'13) (2013)
10. Falkner, S., Klein, A., Hutter, F.: Combining hyperband and bayesian optimization. In: NIPS 2017 Bayesian Optimization Workshop (Dec 2017)
11. Feurer, M., Klein, A., Eggensperger, K., Springenberg, J.T., Blum, M., Hutter, F.: Efficient and robust automated machine learning. In: Cortes, C., Lawrence, N., Lee, D., Sugiyama, M., Garnett, R. (eds.) Proceedings of the 29th International Conference on Advances in Neural Information Processing Systems (NIPS'15) (2015)
12. Feurer, M., Springenberg, T., Hutter, F.: Initializing Bayesian hyperparameter optimization via meta-learning. In: Bonet, B., Koenig, S. (eds.) Proceedings of the Twenty-nineth National Conference on Artificial Intelligence (AAAI'15). pp. 1128–1135. AAAI Press (2015)
13. Gastaldi, X.: Shake-shake regularization. CoRR abs/1705.07485 (2017)

14. Guyon, I., Bennett, K., Cawley, G., Escalante, H.J., Escalera, S., Ho, T.K., Macià, N., Ray, B., Saeed, M., Statnikov, A., Viegas, E.: Design of the 2015 chalearn automl challenge. In: 2015 International Joint Conference on Neural Networks (IJCNN). pp. 1–8 (July 2015)
15. Halko, N., Martinsson, P., Tropp, J.: Finding structure with randomness: Stochastic algorithms for constructing approximate matrix decompositions (2009)
16. Hall, M., Frank, E., Holmes, G., Pfahringer, B., Reutemann, P., Witten, I.: The WEKA data mining software: An update. SIGKDD Explorations 11(1), 10–18 (2009)
17. Hutter, F., Hoos, H., Leyton-Brown, K.: Sequential model-based optimization for general algorithm configuration. In: Coello, C. (ed.) Proceedings of the Fifth International Conference on Learning and Intelligent Optimization (LION'11). Lecture Notes in Computer Science, vol. 6683, pp. 507–523. Springer-Verlag (2011)
18. Hyvärinen, A., Oja, E.: Independent component analysis: algorithms and applications. Neural networks 13(4–5), 411–430 (2000)
19. Jamieson, K., Talwalkar, A.: Non-stochastic best arm identification and hyperparameter optimization. In: Gretton, A., Robert, C. (eds.) Proceedings of the 19th International Conference on Artificial Intelligence and Statistics, AISTATS. JMLR Workshop and Conference Proceedings, vol. 51, pp. 240–248. JMLR.org (2016)
20. Jin, H., Song, Q., Hu, X.: Efficient neural architecture search with network morphism. CoRR abs/1806.10282 (2018)
21. Kingma, D., Ba, J.: Adam: A method for stochastic optimization. In: Proceedings of the International Conference on Learning Representations (2015)
22. Krizhevsky, A., Sutskever, I., Hinton, G.: ImageNet classification with deep convolutional neural networks. In: Bartlett, P., Pereira, F., Burges, C., Bottou, L., Weinberger, K. (eds.) Proceedings of the 26th International Conference on Advances in Neural Information Processing Systems (NIPS'12). pp. 1097–1105 (2012)
23. Li, L., Jamieson, K., DeSalvo, G., Rostamizadeh, A., Talwalkar, A.: Hyperband: A novel bandit-based approach to hyperparameter optimization. Journal of Machine Learning Research 18, 185:1–185:52 (2017)
24. Loshchilov, I., Hutter, F.: Sgdr: Stochastic gradient descent with warm restarts. In: International Conference on Learning Representations (ICLR) 2017 Conference Track (2017)
25. Loshchilov, I.: Personal communication (2017)
26. Mendoza, H., Klein, A., Feurer, M., Springenberg, J., Hutter, F.: Towards automatically-tuned neural networks. In: ICML 2016 AutoML Workshop (2016)
27. Mnih, V., Kavukcuoglu, K., Silver, D., Rusu, A.A., Veness, J., Bellemare, M.G., Graves, A., Riedmiller, M., Fidjeland, A.K., Ostrovski, G., Petersen, S., Beattie, C., Sadik, A., Antonoglou, I., King, H., Kumaran, D., Wierstra, D., Legg, S., Hassabis, D.: Human-level control through deep reinforcement learning. Nature 518, 529–533 (2015)
28. Nesterov, Y.: A method of solving a convex programming problem with convergence rate O(1/sqr(k)). Soviet Mathematics Doklady 27, 372–376 (1983)
29. Paszke, A., Gross, S., Chintala, S., Chanan, G., Yang, E., DeVito, Z., Lin, Z., Desmaison, A., Antiga, L., Lerer, A.: Automatic differentiation in pytorch. In: Autodiff Workshop at NIPS (2017)
30. Pedregosa, F., Varoquaux, G., Gramfort, A., Michel, V., Thirion, B., Grisel, O., Blondel, M., Prettenhofer, P., Weiss, R., Dubourg, V., Vanderplas, J., Passos, A., Cournapeau, D., Brucher, M., Perrot, M., Duchesnay, E.: Scikit-learn: Machine learning in Python. Journal of Machine Learning Research 12, 2825–2830 (2011)
31. Rahimi, A., Recht, B.: Weighted sums of random kitchen sinks: Replacing minimization with randomization in learning. In: Advances in neural information processing systems. pp. 1313–1320 (2009)
32. Rasmussen, C., Williams, C.: Gaussian Processes for Machine Learning. The MIT Press (2006)
33. Schaul, T., Zhang, S., LeCun, Y.: No More Pesky Learning Rates. In: Dasgupta, S., McAllester, D. (eds.) Proceedings of the 30th International Conference on Machine Learning (ICML'13). Omnipress (2014)
34. Schölkopf, B., Smola, A., Müller, K.: Kernel principal component analysis. In: International Conference on Artificial Neural Networks. pp. 583–588. Springer (1997)

35. Shahriari, B., Swersky, K., Wang, Z., Adams, R., de Freitas, N.: Taking the human out of the loop: A Review of Bayesian Optimization. Proc. of the IEEE 104(1) (12/2015 2016)
36. Silver, D., Huang, A., Maddison, C.J., Guez, A., Sifre, L., van den Driessche, G., Schrittwieser, J., Antonoglou, I., Panneershelvam, V., Lanctot, M., Dieleman, S., Grewe, D., Nham, J., Kalchbrenner, N., Sutskever, I., Lillicrap, T., Leach, M., Kavukcuoglu, K., Graepel, T., Hassabis, D.: Mastering the game of go with deep neural networks and tree search. Nature 529, 484–503 (2016)
37. Smith, L.N.: Cyclical learning rates for training neural networks. In: Applications of Computer Vision (WACV), 2017 IEEE Winter Conference on. pp. 464–472. IEEE (2017)
38. Srivastava, N., Hinton, G., Krizhevsky, A., Sutskever, I., Salakhutdinov, R.: Dropout: a simple way to prevent neural networks from overfitting. The Journal of Machine Learning Research 15(1), 1929–1958 (2014)
39. Sutskever, I., Vinyals, O., Le, Q.V.: Sequence to sequence learning with neural networks. CoRR abs/1409.3215 (2014), http://arxiv.org/abs/1409.3215
40. Swersky, K., Duvenaud, D., Snoek, J., Hutter, F., Osborne, M.: Raiders of the lost architecture: Kernels for Bayesian optimization in conditional parameter spaces. In: NIPS Workshop on Bayesian Optimization in Theory and Practice (BayesOpt'13) (2013)
41. Taigman, Y., Yang, M., Ranzato, M., Wolf, L.: Deepface: Closing the gap to human-level performance in face verification. In: Proceedings of the International Conference on Computer Vision and Pattern Recognition (CVPR'14). pp. 1701–1708. IEEE Computer Society Press (2014)
42. Theano Development Team: Theano: A Python framework for fast computation of mathematical expressions. Computing Research Repository (CoRR) abs/1605.02688 (may 2016)
43. Thornton, C., Hutter, F., Hoos, H., Leyton-Brown, K.: Auto-WEKA: combined selection and hyperparameter optimization of classification algorithms. In: I.Dhillon, Koren, Y., Ghani, R., Senator, T., Bradley, P., Parekh, R., He, J., Grossman, R., Uthurusamy, R. (eds.) The 19th ACM SIGKDD International Conference on Knowledge Discovery and Data Mining (KDD'13). pp. 847–855. ACM Press (2013)
44. Wang, Z., Hutter, F., Zoghi, M., Matheson, D., de Feitas, N.: Bayesian optimization in a billion dimensions via random embeddings. Journal of Artificial Intelligence Research 55, 361–387 (2016)
45. Williams, C., Seeger, M.: Using the nyström method to speed up kernel machines. In: Advances in neural information processing systems. pp. 682–688 (2001)
46. Yamada, Y., Iwamura, M., Kise, K.: Shakedrop regularization. CoRR abs/1802.02375 (2018)
47. Zagoruyko, S., Komodakis, N.: Wide residual networks. CoRR abs/1605.07146 (2016)
48. Zeiler, M.: ADADELTA: an adaptive learning rate method. CoRR abs/1212.5701 (2012), http://arxiv.org/abs/1212.5701
49. Zhang, H., Cissé, M., Dauphin, Y., Lopez-Paz, D.: mixup: Beyond empirical risk minimization. CoRR abs/1710.09412 (2017)

Chapter 8
TPOT: A Tree-Based Pipeline Optimization Tool for Automating Machine Learning

Randal S. Olson and Jason H. Moore

Abstract As data science becomes increasingly mainstream, there will be an ever-growing demand for data science tools that are more accessible, flexible, and scalable. In response to this demand, automated machine learning (AutoML) researchers have begun building systems that automate the process of designing and optimizing machine learning pipelines. In this chapter we present TPOT v0.3, an open source genetic programming-based AutoML system that optimizes a series of feature preprocessors and machine learning models with the goal of maximizing classification accuracy on a supervised classification task. We benchmark TPOT on a series of 150 supervised classification tasks and find that it significantly outperforms a basic machine learning analysis in 21 of them, while experiencing minimal degradation in accuracy on 4 of the benchmarks—all without any domain knowledge nor human input. As such, genetic programming-based AutoML systems show considerable promise in the AutoML domain.

8.1 Introduction

Machine learning is commonly described as a "field of study that gives computers the ability to learn without being explicitly programmed" [19]. Despite this common claim, experienced machine learning practitioners know that designing effective machine learning pipelines is often a tedious endeavor, and typically requires considerable experience with machine learning algorithms, expert knowledge of the problem domain, and time-intensive brute force search to accomplish [13]. Thus, contrary to what machine learning enthusiasts would have us believe, machine learning still requires considerable explicit programming.

R. S. Olson (✉)
Life Epigenetics, Minneapolis, MN, USA
e-mail: rso@randalolson.com

J. H. Moore
Institute for Biomedical Informatics, University of Pennsylvania, Philadelphia, PA, USA

F. Hutter et al. (eds.), *Automated Machine Learning*, The Springer Series on Challenges in Machine Learning, https://doi.org/10.1007/978-3-030-05318-5_8

In response to this challenge, several automated machine learning methods have been developed over the years [10]. Over the past several years, we have been developing a Tree-based Pipeline Optimization Tool (TPOT) that automatically designs and optimizes machine learning pipelines for a given problem domain [16], without any need for human intervention. In short, TPOT optimizes machine learning pipelines using a version of genetic programming (GP), a well-known evolutionary computation technique for automatically constructing computer programs [1]. Previously, we demonstrated that combining GP with Pareto optimization enables TPOT to automatically construct high-accuracy *and* compact pipelines that consistently outperform basic machine learning analyses [13]. In this chapter, we extend that benchmark to include 150 supervised classification tasks and evaluate TPOT in a wide variety of application domains ranging from genetic analyses to image classification and more.

This chapter is an extended version of our 2016 paper introducing TPOT, presented at the *2016 ICML Workshop on AutoML* [15].

8.2 Methods

In the following sections, we provide an overview of the Tree-based Pipeline Optimization Tool (TPOT) v0.3, including the machine learning operators used as genetic programming (GP) primitives, the tree-based pipelines used to combine the primitives into working machine learning pipelines, and the GP algorithm used to evolve said tree-based pipelines. We follow with a description of the datasets used to evaluate the latest version of TPOT in this chapter. TPOT is an open source project on GitHub, and the underlying Python code can be found at https://github.com/rhiever/tpot.

8.2.1 Machine Learning Pipeline Operators

At its core, TPOT is a wrapper for the Python machine learning package, scikit-learn [17]. Thus, each machine learning pipeline operator (i.e., GP primitive) in TPOT corresponds to a machine learning algorithm, such as a supervised classification model or standard feature scaler. All implementations of the machine learning algorithms listed below are from scikit-learn (except XGBoost), and we refer to the scikit-learn documentation [17] and [9] for detailed explanations of the machine learning algorithms used in TPOT.

Supervised Classification Operators DecisionTree, RandomForest, eXtreme Gradient Boosting Classifier (from XGBoost, [3]), LogisticRegression, and KNearestNeighborClassifier. Classification operators store the classifier's predictions as a new feature as well as the classification for the pipeline.

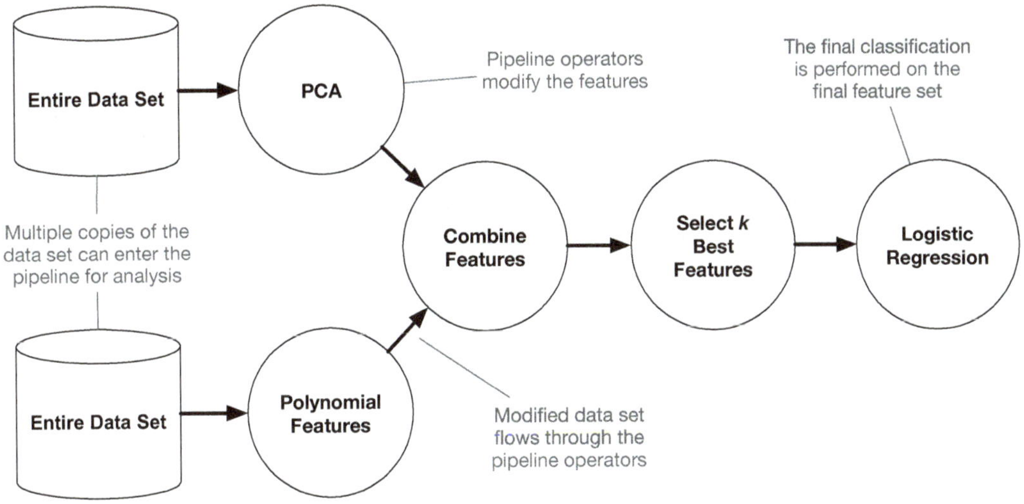

Fig. 8.1 An example tree-based pipeline from TPOT. Each circle corresponds to a machine learning operator, and the arrows indicate the direction of the data flow

Feature Preprocessing Operators StandardScaler, RobustScaler, MinMaxScaler, MaxAbsScaler, RandomizedPCA [12], Binarizer, and PolynomialFeatures. Preprocessing operators modify the dataset in some way and return the modified dataset.

Feature Selection Operators VarianceThreshold, SelectKBest, SelectPercentile, SelectFwe, and Recursive Feature Elimination (RFE). Feature selection operators reduce the number of features in the dataset using some criteria and return the modified dataset.

We also include an operator that combines disparate datasets, as demonstrated in Fig. 8.1, which allows multiple modified variants of the dataset to be combined into a single dataset. Additionally, TPOT v0.3 does not include missing value imputation operators, and therefore does not support datasets with missing data. Lastly, we provide integer and float terminals to parameterize the various operators, such as the number of neighbors k in the k-Nearest Neighbors Classifier.

8.2.2 *Constructing Tree-Based Pipelines*

To combine these operators into a machine learning pipeline, we treat them as GP primitives and construct GP trees from them. Fig. 8.1 shows an example tree-based pipeline, where two copies of the dataset are provided to the pipeline, modified in a successive manner by each operator, combined into a single dataset, and finally used to make classifications. Other than the restriction that every pipeline must have a classifier as its final operator, it is possible to construct arbitrarily shaped machine learning pipelines that can act on multiple copies of the dataset. Thus, GP trees provide an inherently flexible representation of machine learning pipelines.

In order for these tree-based pipelines to operate, we store three additional variables for each record in the dataset. The "class" variable indicates the true label for each record, and is used when evaluating the accuracy of each pipeline. The "guess" variable indicates the pipeline's latest guess for each record, where the predictions from the final classification operator in the pipeline are stored as the "guess". Finally, the "group" variable indicates whether the record is to be used as a part of the internal training or testing set, such that the tree-based pipelines are only trained on the training data and evaluated on the testing data. We note that the dataset provided to TPOT as training data is further split into an internal stratified 75%/25% training/testing set.

8.2.3 Optimizing Tree-Based Pipelines

To automatically generate and optimize these tree-based pipelines, we use a genetic programming (GP) algorithm [1] as implemented in the Python package DEAP [7]. The TPOT GP algorithm follows a standard GP process: To begin, the GP algorithm generates 100 random tree-based pipelines and evaluates their balanced cross-validation accuracy on the dataset. For every generation of the GP algorithm, the algorithm selects the top 20 pipelines in the population according to the NSGA-II selection scheme [4], where pipelines are selected to simultaneously maximize classification accuracy on the dataset while minimizing the number of operators in the pipeline. Each of the top 20 selected pipelines produce five copies (i.e., offspring) into the next generation's population, 5% of those offspring cross over with another offspring using one-point crossover, then 90% of the remaining unaffected offspring are randomly changed by a point, insert, or shrink mutation (1/3 chance of each). Every generation, the algorithm updates a Pareto front of the non-dominated solutions [4] discovered at any point in the GP run. The algorithm repeats this evaluate-select-crossover-mutate process for 100 generations—adding and tuning pipeline operators that improve classification accuracy and pruning operators that degrade classification accuracy—at which point the algorithm selects the highest-accuracy pipeline from the Pareto front as the representative "best" pipeline from the run.

8.2.4 Benchmark Data

We compiled 150 supervised classification benchmarks[1] from a wide variety of sources, including the UCI machine learning repository [11], a large preexisting benchmark repository from [18], and simulated genetic analysis datasets from [20].

[1]Benchmark data at https://github.com/EpistasisLab/penn-ml-benchmarks

These benchmark datasets range from 60 to 60,000 records, few to hundreds of features, and include binary as well as multi-class supervised classification problems. We selected datasets from a wide range of application domains, including genetic analysis, image classification, time series analysis, and many more. Thus, this benchmark—called the Penn Machine Learning Benchmark (PMLB) [14]—represents a comprehensive suite of tests with which to evaluate automated machine learning systems.

8.3 Results

To evaluate TPOT, we ran 30 replicates of it on each of the 150 benchmarks, where each replicate had 8 h to complete 100 generations of optimization (i.e., $100 \times 100 = 10{,}000$ pipeline evaluations). In each replicate, we divided the dataset into a stratified 75%/25% training/testing split and used a distinct random number generator seed for each split and subsequent TPOT run.

In order to provide a reasonable control as a baseline comparison, we similarly evaluated 30 replicates of a Random Forest with 500 trees on the 150 benchmarks, which is meant to represent a basic machine learning analysis that a novice practitioner would perform. We also ran 30 replicates of a version of TPOT that randomly generates and evaluates the same number of pipelines (10,000), which is meant to represent a random search in the TPOT pipeline space. In all cases, we measured accuracy of the resulting pipelines or models as balanced accuracy [21], which corrects for class frequency imbalances in datasets by computing the accuracy on a per-class basis then averaging the per-class accuracies. In the remainder of this chapter, we refer to "balanced accuracy" as simply "accuracy."

Shown in Fig. 8.2, the average performance of TPOT and a Random Forest with 500 trees is similar on most of the datasets. Overall, TPOT discovered pipelines that perform statistically significantly better than a Random Forest on 21 benchmarks, significantly worse on 4 benchmarks, and had no statistically significant difference on 125 benchmarks. (We determined statistical significance using a Wilcoxon rank-sum test, where we used a conservative Bonferroni-corrected p-value threshold of $< 0.000\overline{333}$ ($\frac{0.05}{150}$) for significance.) In Fig. 8.3, we show the distributions of accuracies on the 25 benchmarks that had significant differences, where the benchmarks are sorted by the difference in median accuracy between the two experiments.

Notably, the majority of TPOT's improvements on the benchmarks are quite large, with several ranging from 10% to 60% median accuracy improvement over a Random Forest analysis. In contrast, the 4 benchmarks where TPOT experienced a degradation in median accuracy ranged from only 2–5% accuracy degradation. In some cases, TPOT's improvements were made by discovering useful feature preprocessors that allow the models to better classify the data,[2] e.g., TPOT

[2]Full list: https://gist.github.com/rhiever/578cc9c686ffd873f46bca29406dde1d

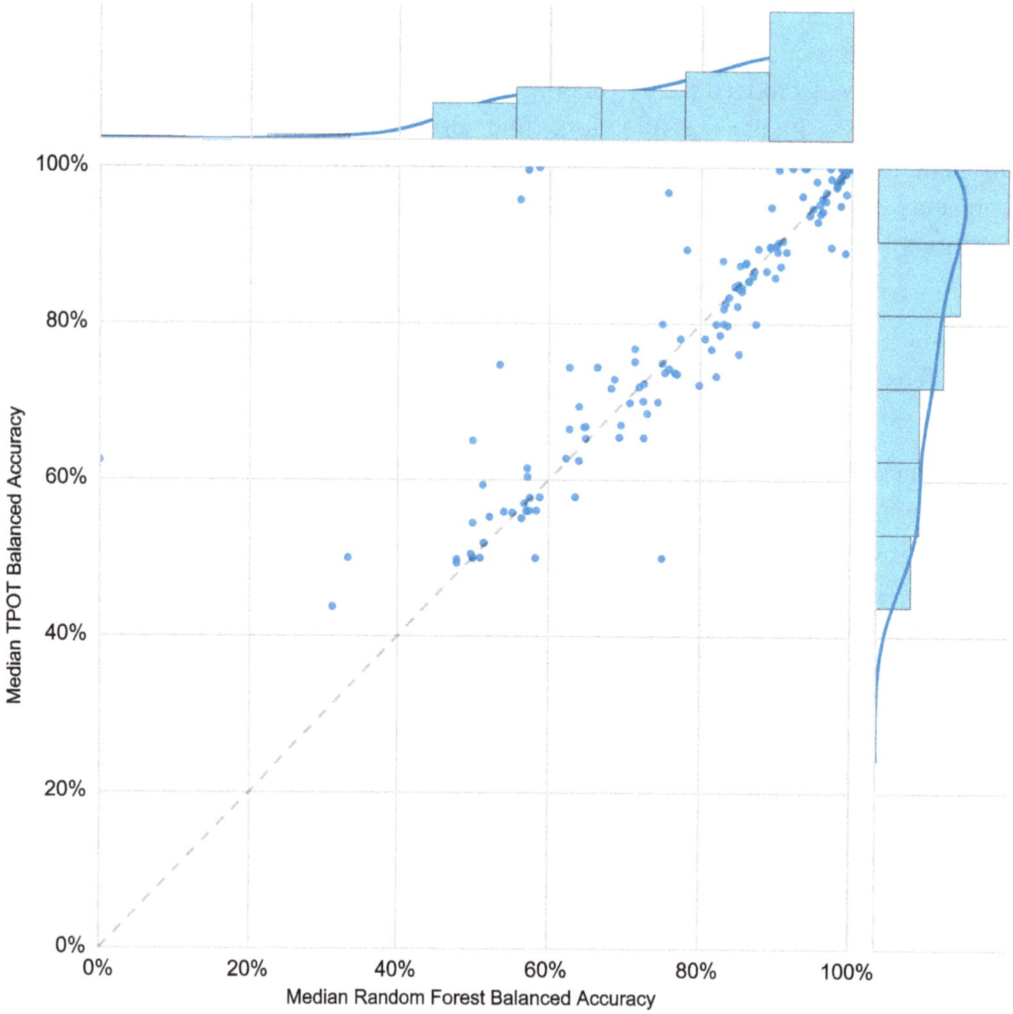

Fig. 8.2 Scatter plot showing the median balanced accuracies of TPOT and a Random Forest with 500 trees on the 150 benchmark datasets. Each dot represents the accuracies on one benchmark dataset, and the diagonal line represents the line of parity (i.e., when both algorithms achieve the same accuracy score). Dots above the line represent datasets where TPOT performed better than the Random Forest, and dots below the line represent datasets where Random Forests performed better

discovered that applying a RandomizedPCA feature preprocessor prior to modeling the "Hill_valley" benchmarks allows Random Forests to classify the dataset with near-perfect accuracy. In other cases, TPOT's improvements were made by applying a different model to the benchmark, e.g., TPOT discovered that a k-nearest-neighbor classifier with $k = 10$ neighbors can classify the "parity5" benchmark, whereas a Random Forest consistently achieved 0% accuracy on the same benchmark.

When we compared TPOT to a version of TPOT that uses random search ("TPOT Random" in Fig. 8.3), we found that random search typically discovered pipelines that achieve comparable accuracy to pipelines discovered by TPOT, except in the "dis" benchmark where TPOT consistently discovered better-performing pipelines. For 17 of the presented benchmarks, none of the random search runs finished within

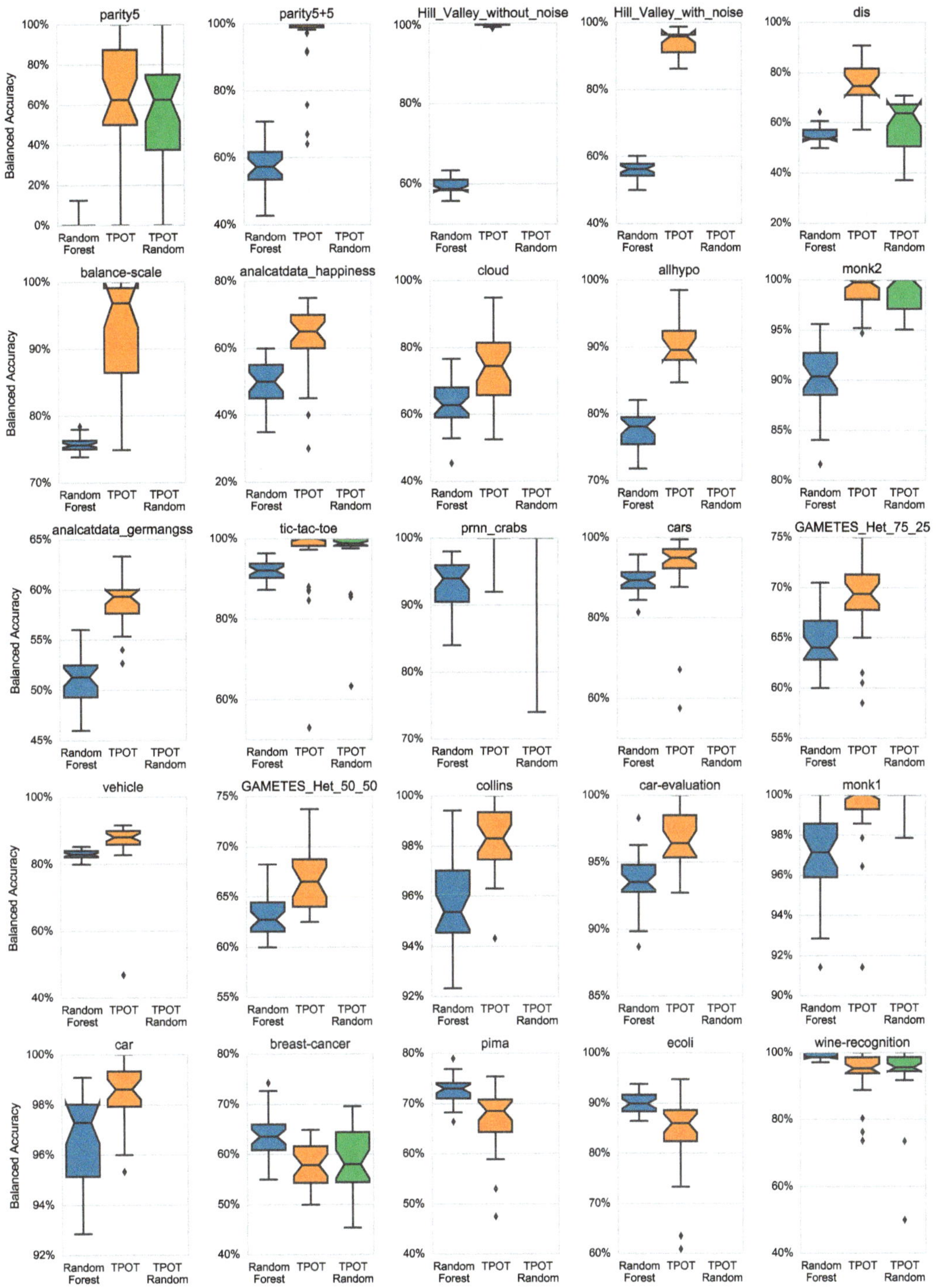

Fig. 8.3 Box plots showing the distribution of balanced accuracies for the 25 benchmarks with a significant difference in median accuracy between TPOT and a Random Forest with 500 trees. Each box plot represents 30 replicates, the inner line shows the median, the notches represent the bootstrapped 95% confidence interval of the median, the ends of the box represent the first and third quartiles, and the dots represent outliers

24 h, which we indicated by leaving the box plot blank in Fig. 8.3. We found that random search often generated needlessly complex pipelines for the benchmark problems, even when a simple pipeline with a tuned model was sufficient to classify the benchmark problem. Thus, even if random search can sometimes perform as well as TPOT in terms of accuracy, performing a guided search for pipelines that achieve high accuracy with as few pipeline operations as possible still offers considerable advantages in terms of search run-time, model complexity, and model interpretability.

8.4 Conclusions and Future Work

We benchmarked the Tree-based Pipeline Optimization Tool (TPOT) v0.3 on 150 supervised classification datasets and found that it discovers machine learning pipelines that can outperform a basic machine learning analysis on several benchmarks. In particular, we note that TPOT discovered these pipelines without any domain knowledge nor human input. As such, TPOT shows considerable promise in the automated machine learning (AutoML) domain and we will continue to refine TPOT until it consistently discovers human-competitive machine learning pipelines. We discuss some of these future refinements below.

First, we will explore methods to provide sensible initialization [8] for genetic programming (GP)-based AutoML systems such as TPOT. For example, we can use meta-learning techniques to intelligently match pipeline configurations that may work well on the particular problem being solved [6]. In brief, meta-learning harnesses information from previous machine learning runs to predict how well each pipeline configuration will work on a particular dataset. To place datasets on a standard scale, meta-learning algorithms compute meta-features from the datasets, such as dataset size, the number of features, and various aspects about the features, which are then used to map dataset meta-features to corresponding pipeline configurations that may work well on datasets with those meta-features. Such an intelligent meta-learning algorithm is likely to improve the TPOT sensible initialization process.

Furthermore, we will attempt to characterize the ideal "shape" of a machine learning pipeline. In auto-sklearn, [5] imposed a short and fixed pipeline structure of a data preprocessor, a feature preprocessor, and a model. In another GP-based AutoML system, [22] allowed the GP algorithm to design arbitrarily-shaped pipelines and found that complex pipelines with several preprocessors and models were useful for signal processing problems. Thus, it may be vital to allow AutoML systems to design arbitrarily-shaped pipelines if they are to achieve human-level competitiveness.

Finally, genetic programming (GP) optimization methods are typically criticized for optimizing a large population of solutions, which can sometimes be slow and wasteful for certain optimization problems. Instead, it is possible to turn GP's purported weakness into a strength by creating an ensemble out of the GP populations. Bhowan et al. [2] explored one such population ensemble method previously with a standard GP algorithm and showed that it significantly improved performance, and it is a natural extension to create ensembles out of TPOT's population of machine learning pipelines.

In conclusion, these experiments demonstrate that there is much to be gained from taking a model-agnostic approach to machine learning and allowing the machine to automatically discover what series of preprocessors and models work best for a given problem domain. As such, AutoML stands to revolutionize data science by automating some of the most tedious—yet most important—aspects of machine learning.

Bibliography

1. Banzhaf, W., Nordin, P., Keller, R.E., Francone, F.D.: Genetic Programming: An Introduction. Morgan Kaufmann, San Meateo, CA, USA (1998)
2. Bhowan, U., Johnston, M., Zhang, M., Yao, X.: Evolving diverse ensembles using genetic programming for classification with unbalanced data. Trans. Evol. Comp 17(3), 368–386 (Jun 2013)
3. Chen, T., Guestrin, C.: Xgboost: A scalable tree boosting system. In: Proceedings of the 22Nd ACM SIGKDD International Conference on Knowledge Discovery and Data Mining. pp. 785–794. KDD '16, ACM, New York, NY, USA (2016)
4. Deb, K., Pratap, A., Agarwal, S., Meyarivan, T.: A fast and elitist multiobjective genetic algorithm: NSGA-II. IEEE Transactions on Evolutionary Computation 6, 182–197 (2002)
5. Feurer, M., Klein, A., Eggensperger, K., Springenberg, J., Blum, M., Hutter, F.: Efficient and robust automated machine learning. In: Cortes, C., Lawrence, N., Lee, D., Sugiyama, M., Garnett, R. (eds.) Advances in Neural Information Processing Systems 28, pp. 2944–2952. Curran Associates, Inc. (2015)
6. Feurer, M., Springenberg, J.T., Hutter, F.: Initializing bayesian hyperparameter optimization via meta-learning. In: Proceedings of the 29th AAAI Conference on Artificial Intelligence, January 25–30, 2015, Austin, Texas, USA. pp. 1128–1135 (2015)
7. Fortin, F.A., De Rainville, F.M., Gardner, M.A., Parizeau, M., Gagné, C.: DEAP: Evolutionary Algorithms Made Easy. Journal of Machine Learning Research 13, 2171–2175 (2012)
8. Greene, C.S., White, B.C., Moore, J.H.: An expert knowledge-guided mutation operator for genome-wide genetic analysis using genetic programming. In: Pattern Recognition in Bioinformatics, pp. 30–40. Springer Berlin Heidelberg (2007)
9. Hastie, T.J., Tibshirani, R.J., Friedman, J.H.: The Elements of Statistical Learning: Data Mining, Inference, and Prediction. Springer, New York, NY, USA (2009)
10. Hutter, F., Lücke, J., Schmidt-Thieme, L.: Beyond Manual Tuning of Hyperparameters. KI - Künstliche Intelligenz 29, 329–337 (2015)
11. Lichman, M.: UCI machine learning repository (2013), http://archive.ics.uci.edu/ml
12. Martinsson, P.G., Rokhlin, V., Tygert, M.: A randomized algorithm for the decomposition of matrices. Applied and Computational Harmonic Analysis 30, 47–68 (2011)
13. Olson, R.S., Bartley, N., Urbanowicz, R.J., Moore, J.H.: Evaluation of a tree-based pipeline optimization tool for automating data science. In: Proceedings of the Genetic and Evolutionary Computation Conference 2016. pp. 485–492. GECCO '16, ACM, New York, NY, USA (2016)
14. Olson, R.S., La Cava, W., Orzechowski, P., Urbanowicz, R.J., Moore, J.H.: PMLB: A Large Benchmark Suite for Machine Learning Evaluation and Comparison. arXiv e-print. https://arxiv.org/abs/1703.00512 (2017)

15. Olson, R.S., Moore, J.H.: Tpot: A tree-based pipeline optimization tool for automating machine learning. In: Hutter, F., Kotthoff, L., Vanschoren, J. (eds.) Proceedings of the Workshop on Automatic Machine Learning. Proceedings of Machine Learning Research, vol. 64, pp. 66–74. PMLR, New York, New York, USA (24 Jun 2016), http://proceedings.mlr.press/v64/olson_tpot_2016.html
16. Olson, R.S., Urbanowicz, R.J., Andrews, P.C., Lavender, N.A., Kidd, L.C., Moore, J.H.: Applications of Evolutionary Computation: 19th European Conference, EvoApplications 2016, Porto, Portugal, March 30 — April 1, 2016, Proceedings, Part I, chap. Automating Biomedical Data Science Through Tree-Based Pipeline Optimization, pp. 123–137. Springer International Publishing (2016)
17. Pedregosa, F., Varoquaux, G., Gramfort, A., Michel, V., Thirion, B., Grisel, O., Blondel, M., Prettenhofer, P., Weiss, R., Dubourg, V., Vanderplas, J., Passos, A., Cournapeau, D., Brucher, M., Perrot, M., Duchesnay, E.: Scikit-learn: Machine learning in Python. Journal of Machine Learning Research 12, 2825–2830 (2011)
18. Reif, M.: A comprehensive dataset for evaluating approaches of various meta-learning tasks. In: First International Conference on Pattern Recognition and Methods (ICPRAM) (2012)
19. Simon, P.: Too big to ignore: the business case for big data. Wiley & SAS Business Series, Wiley, New Delhi (2013)
20. Urbanowicz, R.J., Kiralis, J., Sinnott-Armstrong, N.A., Heberling, T., Fisher, J.M., Moore, J.H.: GAMETES: a fast, direct algorithm for generating pure, strict, epistatic models with random architectures. BioData Mining 5 (2012)
21. Velez, D.R., White, B.C., Motsinger, A.A., Bush, W.S., Ritchie, M.D., Williams, S.M., Moore, J.H.: A balanced accuracy function for epistasis modeling in imbalanced datasets using multifactor dimensionality reduction. Genetic Epidemiology 31(4), 306–315 (2007)
22. Zutty, J., Long, D., Adams, H., Bennett, G., Baxter, C.: Multiple objective vector-based genetic programming using human-derived primitives. In: Proceedings of the 2015 Annual Conference on Genetic and Evolutionary Computation. pp. 1127–1134. GECCO '15, ACM, New York, NY, USA (2015)

Chapter 9
The Automatic Statistician

Christian Steinruecken, Emma Smith, David Janz, James Lloyd, and Zoubin Ghahramani

Abstract The Automatic Statistician project aims to automate data science, producing predictions and human-readable reports from raw datasets with minimal human intervention. Alongside basic graphs and statistics, the generated reports contain a curation of high-level insights about the dataset that are obtained from (1) an automated construction of models for the dataset, (2) a comparison of these models, and (3) a software component that turns these results into natural language descriptions. This chapter describes the common architecture of such Automatic Statistician systems, and discusses some of the design decisions and technical challenges.

9.1 Introduction

Machine Learning (ML) and data science are closely related fields of research, that are focused on the development of algorithms for automated learning from data. These algorithms also underpin many of the recent advances in artificial intelligence (AI), which have had a tremendous impact in industry, ushering in a new golden age of AI. However, many of the current approaches to machine learning, data science, and AI, suffer from a set of important but related limitations.

Firstly, many of the approaches used are complicated black-boxes that are difficult to interpret, understand, debug, and trust. This lack of interpretability hampers the deployment of ML systems. For example, consider the major legal, technical and ethical consequences of using an uninterpretable black-box system that arrives at a prediction or decision related to a medical condition, a criminal justice setting, or in a self-driving car. The realisation that black-box ML methods are severely limited in such settings has led to major efforts to develop "explainable AI", and systems that offer interpretability, trust, and transparency.

C. Steinruecken (✉) · E. Smith · D. Janz · J. Lloyd · Z. Ghahramani
Department of Engineering, University of Cambridge, Cambridge, UK
e-mail: tcs27@cam.ac.uk

F. Hutter et al. (eds.), *Automated Machine Learning*, The Springer Series on Challenges in Machine Learning, https://doi.org/10.1007/978-3-030-05318-5_9

Secondly, the development of ML systems has turned into a cottage industry where ML experts tackle problems by hand-designing solutions that often reflect a set of ad-hoc manual decisions, or the preferences and biases of the expert. It is ironic that machine learning, a field dedicated to building systems that automatically learn from data, is so dependent on human experts and manual tuning of models and learning algorithms. Manual search over possible models and methods can result in solutions that are sub-optimal across any number of metrics. Moreover, the tremendous imbalance between the supply of experts and the demand for data science and ML solutions is likely resulting in many missed opportunities for applications that could have a major benefit for society.

The vision of the Automatic Statistician is to automate many aspects of data analysis, model discovery, and explanation. In a sense, the goal is to develop an *AI for data science* – a system that can reason about patterns in data and explain them to the user. Ideally, given some raw data, such a system should be able to:

- automate the process of feature selection and transformation,
- deal with the messiness of real data, including missing values, outliers, and different types and encodings of variables,
- search over a large space of models so as to automatically discover a good model that captures any reliable patterns in the data,
- find such a model while avoiding both overfitting and underfitting,
- explain the patterns that have been found to the user, ideally by having a conversation with the user about the data, and
- do all of this in a manner that is efficient and robust with respect to constraints on compute time, memory, amount of data, and other relevant resources.

While this agenda is obviously a very ambitious one, the work to date on the Automatic Statistician project has made progress on many of the above desiderata. In particular, the ability to discover plausible models from data and to explain these discoveries in plain English, is one of the distinguishing features of the Automatic Statistician [18]. Such a feature could be useful to almost any field or endeavour that is reliant on extracting knowledge from data.

In contrast to much of the machine learning literature that has been focused on extracting increasing performance improvements on pattern recognition problems (using techniques such as kernel methods, random forests, or deep learning), the Automatic Statistician needs to build models that are composed of interpretable components, and to have a principled way of representing uncertainty about model structures given data. It also needs to be able to give reasonable answers not just for big data sets, but also for small ones.

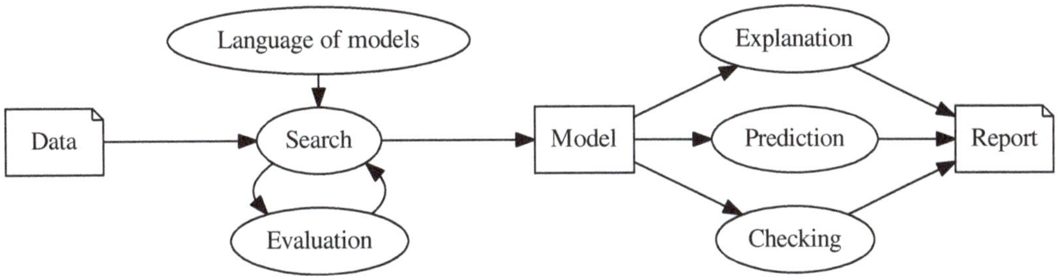

Fig. 9.1 A simplified flow diagram outlining the operation of a report-writing Automatic Statistician. Models for the data are automatically constructed (from the open-ended language of models), and evaluated on the data. This evaluation is done in a way that allows models to be compared to each other. The best models are then inspected to produce a report. Each model can be used to make extrapolations or predictions from the data, and the construction blue-print of the model can be turned into a human-readable description. For some models, it is also possible to generate *model criticism*, and report on where the modelling assumptions do not match the data well

9.2 Basic Anatomy of an Automatic Statistician

At the heart of the Automatic Statistician is the idea that a good solution to the above challenges can be obtained by working in the framework of *model-based machine learning* [2, 9]. In model-based ML, the basic idea is that probabilistic models are explanations for patterns in data, and that the probabilistic framework (or Bayesian Occam's razor) can be used to discover models that avoid both overfitting and underfitting [21]. Bayesian approaches provide an elegant way of trading off the complexity of the model and the complexity of the data, and probabilistic models are compositional and interpretable as described previously. Moreover, the model-based philosophy maintains that tasks such as data pre-processing and transformation are all parts of the model and should ideally all be conducted at once [35].

An Automatic Statistician contains the following key ingredients:

1. **An open-ended language of models** – expressive enough to capture real-world phenomena, and to allow applying the techniques used by human statisticians and data scientists.
2. **A search procedure** to efficiently explore the language of models.
3. **A principled method of evaluating models**, trading off complexity, fit to data, and resource usage.
4. **A procedure to automatically explain the models**, making the assumptions of the models explicit in a way that is simultaneously accurate and intelligible to non-experts.

Fig. 9.1 shows a high-level overview of how these components could be used to produce a basic version of a report-writing Automatic Statistician.

As will be discussed later in this chapter, it is possible to build Automatic Statistician systems that exchange ingredient (4) for procedures that produce other desirable outputs, for example raw predictions or decisions. In such cases, the language, search, and evaluation components may be modified appropriately to prioritise the chosen objective.

9.2.1 Related Work

Important earlier work includes statistical expert systems [11, 37], and equation learning [26, 27]. The *Robot Scientist* [16] integrates machine learning and scientific discovery in a closed loop with an experimental platform in microbiology to automate the design and execution of new experiments. *Auto-WEKA* [17, 33] and *Auto-sklearn* [6] are projects that automate learning classifiers, making heavy use of Bayesian optimisation techniques. Efforts to automate the application of machine learning methods to data have recently gained momentum, and may ultimately result in practical AI systems for data science.

9.3 An Automatic Statistician for Time Series Data

Automatic Statistician systems can be defined for a variety of different objectives, and can be based on different underlying model families. We'll start by describing one such system, and discuss the wider taxonomy later, with notes on common design elements and general architecture.

An early Automatic Statistician for one-dimensional regression tasks was described by Lloyd et al. [18]. Their system, called *Automatic Bayesian Covariance Discovery (ABCD)*, uses an open-ended language of Gaussian process models through a compositional grammar over kernels. A Gaussian process (GP) defines a distribution over functions, and the parameters of the GP – its mean and its kernel – determine the properties of the functions [25]. There is a broad choice of available kernels that induce function distributions with particular properties; for example distributions over functions that are linear, polynomial, periodic, or uncorrelated noise. A pictorial overview of this system is shown in Fig. 9.2.

9.3.1 The Grammar over Kernels

As mentioned above, a grammar over GP kernels makes it possible to represent many interesting properties of functions, and gives a systematic way of constructing distributions over such functions. This grammar over kernels is compositional: it comprises a set of fixed *base kernels*, and *kernel operators* that make it possible to compose new kernels from existing ones. This grammar was carefully chosen to be *interpretable*: each expression in the grammar defines a kernel that can be described with a simple but descriptive set of words in human language.

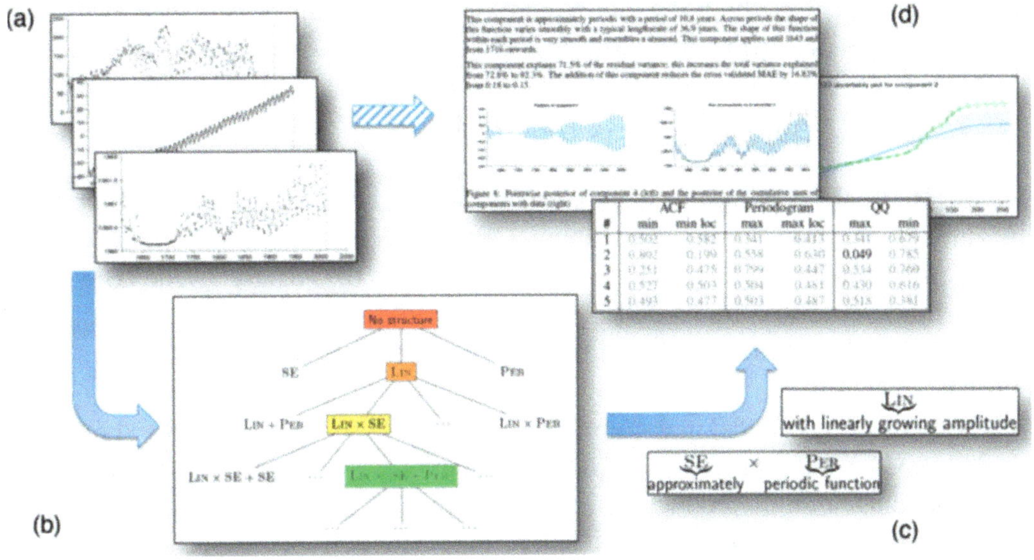

Fig. 9.2 A flow diagram describing a report-writing Automatic Statistician for time-series data. (**a**) The input to the system is data, in this case represented as time series. (**b**) The system searches over a grammar of models to discover a good interpretation of the data, using Bayesian inference to score models. (**c**) Components of the model discovered are translated into English phrases. (**d**) The end result is a report with text, figures and tables, describing in detail what has been inferred about the data, including a section on model checking and criticism [8, 20]

The base kernels in the grammar are: C (constant), LIN (linear), SE (squared exponential), PER (periodic), and WN (white noise). The kernel operators are: + (addition), × (multiplication), and CP (a change point operator), defined as follows:

$$(k_1 + k_2)(x, x') = k_1(x, x') + k_2(x, x')$$
$$(k_1 \times k_2)(x, x') = k_1(x, x') \times k_2(x, x')$$
$$\text{CP}\,(k_1, k_2)\,(x, x') = k_1(x, x')\,\sigma(x)\,\sigma(x') \;+\; k_2(x, x')\,(1 - \sigma(x))\,(1 - \sigma(x'))$$

where $\sigma(x) = \frac{1}{2}\left(1 + \tanh \frac{l-x}{s}\right)$ is a sigmoidal function, and l and s are parameters of the change point. The base kernels can be arbitrarily combined using the above operators to produce new kernels.

The infinite space of kernels defined by this grammar allows a large class of interesting distributions over functions to be searched, evaluated, and described in an automated way. This type of grammar was first described in [10] for matrix factorization problems, and then refined in [5] and [18] for GP models.

9.3.2 *The Search and Evaluation Procedure*

ABCD performs a greedy search over the space of models (as defined by the grammar). The kernel parameters of each proposed model are optimised by a conjugate-gradient method; the model with optimised parameters is then evaluated using the Bayesian Information Criterion [29]:

$$\text{BIC}(M) = -2 \log p(D \mid M) + |M| \log N \tag{9.1}$$

where M is the optimised model, $p(D \mid M)$ is the marginal likelihood of the model integrating out the latent GP function, $|M|$ is the number of kernel parameters in M, and N is the size of the dataset. The Bayesian Information Criterion trades off model complexity and fit to the data, and approximates the full marginal likelihood (which integrates out latent functions and hyperparameters).

The best-scoring model in each round is used to construct new proposed models, either by: (1) expanding the kernel with production rules from the grammar, such as introducing a sum, product, or change point; or (2) mutating the kernel by swapping out a base kernel for a different one. The new set of proposed kernels is then evaluated in the next round. It is possible with the above rules that a kernel expression gets proposed several times, but a well-implemented system will keep records and only ever evaluate each expression once. The search and evaluation procedure stops either when the score of all newly proposed models is worse than the best model from the previous round, or when a pre-defined search depth is exceeded.

This greedy search procedure is not guaranteed to find the best model in the language for any given dataset: a better model might be hiding in one of the subtrees that weren't expanded out. Finding the globally best model isn't usually essential, as long as a good interpretable models is found in a reasonable amount of time. There are other ways of conducting the search and evaluation of models. For example, Malkomes et al. [22] describe a kernel search procedure based on Bayesian optimisation. Janz et al. [14] implemented a kernel search method using particle filtering and Hamiltonian Monte Carlo.

9.3.3 Generating Descriptions in Natural Language

When the search procedure terminates, it produces a list of kernel expressions and their scores on the dataset. The expression with the best score is then used to generate a natural-language description. To convert a kernel to a description in natural language, the kernel is first converted to a canonical form, using the following process:

1. Nested sums and products are flattened into a sum of products form.
2. Some products of kernels can be simplified into base kernels with modified parameters, for example: SE $\times$ SE $\to$ SE*, C $\times$ k $\to$ k^* for any k, and WN $\times$ k $\to$ WN* for any $k \in \{$C, SE, WN, Per$\}$.

After applying these rules, the kernel expression is a sum of product terms, where each product term has the following canonical form:

$$k \times \prod_m \text{LIN}^{(m)} \times \prod_n \boldsymbol{\sigma}^{(n)} \tag{9.2}$$

where $\boldsymbol{\sigma}(x, x') = \sigma(x)\,\sigma(x')$ is a product of two sigmoid functions, and k has one of the following forms: 1, WN, C, SE, $\prod_j \text{PER}^{(j)}$, or SE $\times \prod_j \text{PER}^{(j)}$. The notation $\prod_j k^{(j)}$ stands for products of kernels, each with separate parameters.

In this canonical form, the kernel is a sum of products, and the number of terms in the sum is described first: "The structure search algorithm has identified N additive components in the data." This sentence is then followed by a description of each additive component (i.e. each product in the sum), using the following algorithm:

1. Choose *one* of the kernels in the product to be the noun descriptor. A heuristic recommended by Lloyd et al. [18] is to pick according to the following preference: PER $>$ {C, SE, WN} $> \prod_j \text{LIN}^{(j)} > \prod_j \boldsymbol{\sigma}^{(j)}$, where PER is the most preferred.
2. Convert the chosen kernel type to a string using this table:

WN	"uncorrelated noise"	SE	"smooth function"
PER	"periodic function"	LIN	"linear function"
C	"constant"	$\prod_j \text{LIN}^{(j)}$	"polynomial"

3. The other kernels in the product are converted to *post-modifier* expressions that are appended to the noun descriptor. The post modifiers are converted using this table:

SE	"whose shape changes smoothly"
PER	"modulated by a periodic function"
LIN	"with linearly varying amplitude"
$\prod_j \text{LIN}^{(j)}$	"with polynomially varying amplitude"
$\prod_j \boldsymbol{\sigma}^{(j)}$	"which applies from / until [changepoint]"

4. Further refinements to the description are possible, including insights from kernel parameters, or extra information calculated from the data. Some of these refinements are described in [18].

More details on the translation of kernel expressions to natural language can be found in [18] and [19]. An example extract from a generated report is shown in Fig. 9.3.

This component is approximately periodic with a period of 10.8 years. Across periods the shape of this function varies smoothly with a typical lengthscale of 36.9 years. The shape of this function within each period is very smooth and resembles a sinusoid. This component applies until 1643 and from 1716 onwards.

This component explains 71.5% of the residual variance; this increases the total variance explained from 72.8% to 92.3%. The addition of this component reduces the cross validated MAE by 16.82% from 0.18 to 0.15.

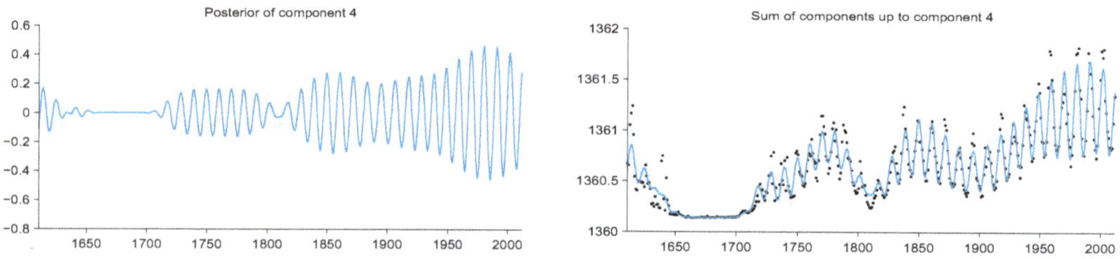

Fig. 9.3 Extract from an automatically generated report that describes the model components discovered by ABCD. This part of the report isolates and describes the approximately 11-year sunspot cycle, also noting its disappearance during the sixteenth century, a time period known as the Maunder minimum. (This figure is reproduced from [18])

9.3.4 Comparison with Humans

An interesting question to consider is to what extent predictions made by an Automated Statistician (such as the ABCD algorithm) are human-like, and how they compare to predictions made with other methods that are also based on Gaussian processes. To answer that question, Schulz et al. [28] presented participants with the task of extrapolating from a given set of data, and choosing a preferred extrapolation from a given set. The results were encouraging for composite kernel search in two ways: Firstly, the participants preferred the extrapolations made by ABCD over those made with Spectral Kernels [36], and over those made with a simple RBF (radial basis function) kernel. Secondly, when human participants were asked to extrapolate the data themselves, their predictions were most similar to those given by ABCD's composite search procedure.

One of the design goals of a report-writing Automatic Statistician is the ability to explain its findings in terms that are understandable by humans. The system described earlier restricts itself to a space of models that can be explained in human language using simple terms, even though this design choice may come at the cost of predictive accuracy. In general, it is not straight-forward to measure the interpretability of machine learning systems; one possible framework is suggested by Doshi-Velez and Kim [4]. We note in passing that not all machine learning systems require such functionality. For example, when the results of a system have little impact on society, especially in terms of social norms and interactions, it is acceptable to optimise for performance or accuracy instead (e.g. recognising post codes for automatic mail sorting).

9.4 Other Automatic Statistician Systems

The ability to generate human-readable reports is perhaps one of the distinguishing features of Automatic Statistician systems. But, as mentioned earlier, software of this nature can serve other purposes as well. For example, users might be interested in raw predictions from the data (with or without explanations), or they might want the system to make data-driven decisions directly on their behalf.

Also, it is possible to build Automatic Statistician systems for model families that are different from Gaussian processes or grammars. For example, we built Automated Statistician systems for regression [5, 18], classification [12, 23], univariate and multivariate data; systems based on various different model classes, and systems with and without intelligent resource control. This section discusses some of the design elements that are shared across many Automatic Statistician systems.

9.4.1 Core Components

One of the key tasks that an Automatic Statistician has to perform is to select, evaluate, and compare models. These types of task can be run concurrently, but they have interdependencies. For example, the evaluation of one set of models might influence the selection of the next set of models.

Most generally, the **selection strategy** component in our system is responsible for choosing models to evaluate: it might choose from a fixed or open-ended family of models, or it might generate and refine models based on the evaluation and comparison of previously chosen models. Sometimes, the *types* of the variables in the dataset (whether inferred from the data or annotated by the user) influence which models might be chosen by the selection strategy. For example, one might want to distinguish continuous and discrete data, and to use different treatments for categorical and ordinal data.

The **model evaluation** task trains a given model on part of the user-supplied dataset, and then produces a score by testing the model on held-out data. Some models do not require a separate training phase and can produce a log-likelihood for the entire dataset directly. Model evaluation is probably one of the most important tasks to parallelise: at any given time, multiple selected models can be evaluated simultaneously, on multiple CPUs or even multiple computers.

The **report curator** component is the piece of software that decides which results to include in the final report. For example, it might include sections that describe the best fitting models, along with extrapolations, graphs, or data tables. Depending on the evaluation results, the report curator might choose to include additional material, such as data falsification/model criticism sections, recommendations, or a summary. In some systems the deliverable might be something other than a report, such as raw predictions, parameter settings, or model source code.

In interactive systems, a **data loading stage** provides an instant summary about the uploaded dataset, and allows the user to correct any assumptions about the format of the data. The user can make type annotations, remove columns from the dataset, choose an output variable (e.g. for classification), and specify the analyses that should be run.

9.4.2 Design Challenges

9.4.2.1 User Interaction

While the aim of an Automatic Statistician is to automate *all* aspects of data handling (from low-level tasks such as formatting and clean-up, to high-level tasks such as model construction, evaluation, and criticism), it is also useful to give users the option to interact with the system and influence the choices it makes. For example, users might want to specify which parts or which aspects of the data they are interested in, and which parts can be ignored. Some users might want to choose the family of models that the system will consider in the model construction or evaluation phase. Finally, the system may want to engage in a dialogue with the user to explore or explain what it found in the data. Such interactivity needs to be supported by the underlying system.

9.4.2.2 Missing and Messy Data

A common problem with real-world datasets is that they may have missing or corrupt entries, unit or formatting inconsistencies, or other kinds of defects. These kinds of defects may require some pre-processing of the data, and while many decisions could be made automatically, some might benefit from interaction with the user. Good models can handle missing data directly, and as long as the missing data is detected correctly by the data loading stage, everything should be fine. But there are some data models that cannot handle missing data natively. In such cases, it might be useful to perform *data imputation* to feed these models a version of the dataset that has the missing values filled in. This imputation task itself is performed by a model that is trained on the data. Examples of such techniques include e.g. MissForest [31], MissPaLasso [30], mice [3], KNNimpute [34], and Bayesian approaches [1, 7].

9.4.2.3 Resource Allocation

Another important aspect of an Automatic Statistician is *resource usage*. For example, a user might only have a limited number of CPU cores available, or might be interested to get the best possible report within a fixed time limit, e.g. before a given deadline. To make good model selection and evaluation choices, an intelligent system might take into account such resource constraints. The ability to do so will affect the overall usability of the system.

Even when there are no direct constraints on computation time, CPU cores, or memory usage, an intelligent system might benefit from allocating resources to models whose evaluation is promising for the chosen deliverable. Such functionality can be implemented for models that support some form of gradual evaluation, for example by training incrementally on increasingly large subsets of the dataset. One of our systems used a variant of Freeze-thaw Bayesian optimisation [32] for this purpose.

9.5 Conclusion

Our society has entered an era of abundant data. Analysis and exploration of the data is essential for harnessing the benefits of this growing resource. Unfortunately, the growth of data currently outpaces our ability to analyse it, especially because this task still largely rests on human experts. But many aspects of machine learning and data analysis can be automated, and one guiding principle in pursuit of this goal is to "apply machine learning to itself".

The Automatic Statistician project aims to automate data science by taking care of all aspects of data analysis, from data pre-processing, modelling and evaluation, to the generation of useful and transparent results. All these tasks should be performed in a way that requires little user expertise, minimises the amount of user interaction, and makes intelligent and controlled use of computational resources.

While this aim is ambitious, and a lot of the work still needs to happen, encouraging progress has been made towards the creation of such automated systems. Multiple Automatic Statistician systems have been built, each with slight differences in purpose and underlying technology, but they all share the same intent and much of the same design philosophy. We hope that the creation of such instruments will bring the ability to gain insights from data to a larger group of people, and help empower society to make great use of our data resources.

Acknowledgements The authors would like to thank Tameem Adel Hesham, Lars Kotthoff, and Frank Hutter for helpful feedback.

Bibliography

1. Allingham, J.U.: Unsupervised automatic dataset repair. Master's thesis in advanced computer science, Computer Laboratory, University of Cambridge (2018)
2. Bishop, C.M.: Pattern recognition and machine learning. Information science and statistics, Springer (2006)
3. van Buuren, S., Groothuis-Oudshoorn, K.: `mice`: Multivariate imputation by chained equations in R. Journal of Statistical Software 45(3) (2011)
4. Doshi-Velez, F., Kim, B.: Towards a rigorous science of interpretable machine learning (Mar 2017), http://arxiv.org/abs/1702.08608

5. Duvenaud, D., Lloyd, J.R., Grosse, R., Tenenbaum, J.B., Ghahramani, Z.: Structure discovery in nonparametric regression through compositional kernel search. In: Proceedings of the 30th International Conference on Machine Learning (Jun 2013)
6. Feurer, M., Klein, A., Eggensperger, K., Springenberg, J., Blum, M., Hutter, F.: Efficient and robust automated machine learning. In: Cortes, C., Lawrence, N.D., Lee, D.D., Sugiyama, M., Garnett, R. (eds.) Advances in Neural Information Processing Systems 28, pp. 2962–2970. Curran Associates, Inc. (2015)
7. Garriga Alonso, A.: Probability density imputation of missing data with Gaussian Mixture Models. MSc thesis, University of Oxford (2017)
8. Gelman, A., Carlin, J.B., Stern, H.S., Dunson, D.B., Vehtari, A., Rubin, D.B.: Bayesian Data Analysis, Third Edition. Chapman & Hall/CRC Texts in Statistical Science. Taylor & Francis (2013)
9. Ghahramani, Z.: Probabilistic machine learning and artificial intelligence. Nature 521, 452–459 (2015)
10. Grosse, R.B., Salakhutdinov, R., Tenenbaum, J.B.: Exploiting compositionality to explore a large space of model structures. In: Uncertainty in Artificial Intelligence (2012)
11. Hand, D.J.: Patterns in statistical strategy. In: Gale, W.A. (ed.) Artificial intelligence and statistics (1986)
12. He, Q.: The Automatic Statistician for Classification. Master's thesis, Department of Engineering, University of Cambridge (May 2016)
13. Hwang, Y., Tong, A., Choi, J.: Automatic construction of nonparametric relational regression models for multiple time series. In: Balcan, M.F., Weinberger, K.Q. (eds.) ICML 2016: Proceedings of the 33rd International Conference on Machine Learning. Proceedings of Machine Learning Research, vol. 48, pp. 3030–3039. PLMR (2016)
14. Janz, D., Paige, B., Rainforth, T., van de Meent, J.W., Wood, F.: Probabilistic structure discovery in time series data (2016), https://arxiv.org/abs/1611.06863
15. Kim, H., Teh, Y.W.: Scaling up the Automatic Statistician: Scalable structure discovery using Gaussian processes. In: Storkey, A., Perez-Cruz, F. (eds.) Proceedings of the 21st International Conference on Artificial Intelligence and Statistics. Proceedings of Machine Learning Research, vol. 84, pp. 575–584. PLMR (2018)
16. King, R.D., Whelan, K.E., Jones, F.M., Reiser, P.G.K., Bryant, C.H., Muggleton, S.H., Kell, D.B., Oliver, S.G.: Functional genomic hypothesis generation and experimentation by a robot scientist. Nature 427(6971), 247–252 (2004)
17. Kotthoff, L., Thornton, C., Hoos, H.H., Hutter, F., Leyton-Brown, K.: Auto-WEKA 2.0: Automatic model selection and hyperparameter optimization in WEKA. Journal of Machine Learning Research 18(25), 1–5 (2017)
18. Lloyd, J.R., Duvenaud, D., Grosse, R., Tenenbaum, J.B., Ghahramani, Z.: Automatic construction and natural-language description of nonparametric regression models. In: Twenty-Eighth AAAI Conference on Artificial Intelligence (AAAI-14) (2014)
19. Lloyd, J.R.: Representation, learning, description and criticism of probabilistic models with applications to networks, functions and relational data. Ph.D. thesis, Department of Engineering, University of Cambridge (Dec 2014)
20. Lloyd, J.R., Ghahramani, Z.: Statistical model criticism using kernel two sample tests. In: Cortes, C., Lawrence, N.D., Lee, D.D., Sugiyama, M., Garnett, R. (eds.) Advances in Neural Information Processing Systems 28. pp. 829–837. Curran Associates, Inc. (2015)
21. MacKay, D.J.C.: Bayesian interpolation. Neural Computation 4(3), 415–447 (1992), see [24] for additional discussion and illustration.
22. Malkomes, G., Schaff, C., Garnett, R.: Bayesian optimization for automated model selection. In: Lee, D.D., Sugiyama, M., von Luxburg, U., Guyon, I., Garnett, R. (eds.) Advances in Neural Information Processing Systems 29, pp. 2900–2908. Curran Associates, Inc. (2016)
23. Mrkšić, N.: Kernel Structure Discovery for Gaussian Process Classification. Master's thesis, Computer Laboratory, University of Cambridge (Jun 2014)
24. Murray, I., Ghahramani, Z.: A note on the evidence and Bayesian Occam's razor. Tech. Rep. GCNU-TR 2005-003, Gatsby Computational Neuroscience Unit, University College London (2005)

25. Rasmussen, C.E., Williams, C.K.I.: Gaussian Processes for Machine Learning. MIT Press (2006), http://www.gaussianprocess.org/gpml/
26. Schmidt, M., Lipson, H.: Distilling free-form natural laws from experimental data. Science 324(5923), 81–85 (2009)
27. Schmidt, M., Lipson, H.: Symbolic regression of implicit equations. In: Riolo, R., O'Reilly, U.M., McConaghy, T. (eds.) Genetic Programming Theory and Practice VII, pp. 73–85. Springer, Boston, MA (2010)
28. Schulz, E., Tenenbaum, J., Duvenaud, D.K., Speekenbrink, M., Gershman, S.J.: Probing the compositionality of intuitive functions. In: Lee, D.D., Sugiyama, M., von Luxburg, U., Guyon, I., Garnett, R. (eds.) Advances in Neural Information Processing Systems 29, pp. 3729–3737. Curran Associates, Inc. (2016)
29. Schwarz, G.: Estimating the dimension of a model. The Annals of Statistics 6(2), 461–464 (1978)
30. Städler, N., Stekhoven, D.J., Bühlmann, P.: Pattern alternating maximization algorithm for missing data in high-dimensional problems. Journal of Machine Learning Research 15, 1903–1928 (Jun 2014)
31. Stekhoven, D.J., Bühlmann, P.: MissForest – non-parametric missing value imputation for mixed-type data. Bioinformatics 28(1), 112–118 (Nov 2011)
32. Swersky, K., Snoek, J., Adams, R.P.: Freeze-thaw Bayesian optimization (Jun 2014), http://arxiv.org/abs/1406.3896
33. Thornton, C., Hutter, F., Hoos, H.H., Leyton-Brown, K.: Auto-WEKA: Combined selection and hyperparameter optimization of classification algorithms. In: Proceedings of the 19th ACM SIGKDD International Conference on Knowledge Discovery and Data Mining. pp. 847–855. KDD '13, ACM, New York, NY, USA (2013)
34. Troyanskaya, O., Cantor, M., Sherlock, G., Brown, P., Hastie, T., Tibshirani, R., Botstein, D., Altman, R.B.: Missing value estimation methods for DNA microarrays. Bioinformatics pp. 520–525 (Jun 2001)
35. Valera, I., Ghahramani, Z.: Automatic discovery of the statistical types of variables in a dataset. In: Precup, D., Teh, Y.W. (eds.) ICML 2017: Proceedings of the 34th International Conference on Machine Learning. Proceedings of Machine Learning Research, vol. 70, pp. 3521–3529. PLMR (2017)
36. Wilson, A.G., Adams, R.P.: Gaussian process kernels for pattern discovery and extrapolation. In: Dasgupta, S., McAllester, D. (eds.) ICML 2013: Proceedings of the 30th International Conference on Machine Learning. JLMR Proceedings, vol. 28, pp. 1067–1075. JLMR.org (Jun 2013)
37. Wolstenholme, D.E., O'Brien, C.M., Nelder, J.A.: GLIMPSE: a knowledge-based front end for statistical analysis. Knowledge-Based Systems 1(3), 173–178 (1988)

Part III
AutoML Challenges

Chapter 10
Analysis of the AutoML Challenge Series 2015–2018

Isabelle Guyon, Lisheng Sun-Hosoya, Marc Boullé, Hugo Jair Escalante, Sergio Escalera, Zhengying Liu, Damir Jajetic, Bisakha Ray, Mehreen Saeed, Michèle Sebag, Alexander Statnikov, Wei-Wei Tu, and Evelyne Viegas

Abstract The ChaLearn AutoML Challenge (The authors are in alphabetical order of last name, except the first author who did most of the writing and the second author who produced most of the numerical analyses and plots.) (NIPS 2015 – ICML 2016) consisted of six rounds of a machine learning competition of progressive difficulty, subject to limited computational resources. It was followed by

I. Guyon (✉)
University of Paris-Sud, Orsay, France

INRIA, University of Paris-Saclay, Paris, France

ChaLearn and ClopiNet, Berkeley, CA, USA
e-mail: guyon@chalearn.org

L. Sun-Hosoya · Z. Liu
Laboratoire de Recherche en Informatique, University of Paris-Sud, Orsay, France

University of Paris-Saclay, Paris, France

M. Boullé
Machine Learning Group, Orange Labs, Lannion, France

H. J. Escalante
Computational Sciences Department, INAOE and ChaLearn, Tonantzintla, Mexico

S. Escalera
Computer Vision Center, University of Barcelona, Barcelona, Spain

D. Jajetic
IN2, Zagreb, Croatia

B. Ray
Langone Medical Center, New York University, New York, NY, USA

M. Saeed
Department of Computer Science, National University of Computer and Emerging Sciences, Islamabad, Pakistan

M. Sebag
Laboratoire de Recherche en Informatique, CNRS, Paris, France

University of Paris-Saclay, Paris, France

F. Hutter et al. (eds.), *Automated Machine Learning*, The Springer Series on Challenges in Machine Learning, https://doi.org/10.1007/978-3-030-05318-5_10

a one-round AutoML challenge (PAKDD 2018). The AutoML setting differs from former model selection/hyper-parameter selection challenges, such as the one we previously organized for NIPS 2006: the participants aim to develop fully automated and computationally efficient systems, capable of being trained and tested without human intervention, with code submission. This chapter analyzes the results of these competitions and provides details about the datasets, which were not revealed to the participants. The solutions of the winners are systematically benchmarked over all datasets of all rounds and compared with canonical machine learning algorithms available in scikit-learn. All materials discussed in this chapter (data and code) have been made publicly available at http://automl.chalearn.org/.

10.1 Introduction

Until about 10 years ago, machine learning (ML) was a discipline little known to the public. For ML scientists, it was a "seller's market": they were producing hosts of algorithms in search for applications and were constantly looking for new interesting datasets. Large internet corporations accumulating massive amounts of data such as Google, Facebook, Microsoft and Amazon have popularized the use of ML and data science competitions have engaged a new generation of young scientists in this wake. Nowadays, government and corporations keep identifying new applications of ML and with the increased availability of open data, we have switched to a "buyer's market": everyone seems to be in need of a learning machine. Unfortunately however, learning machines are not yet fully automatic: it is still difficult to figure out which software applies to which problem, how to horseshoe-fit data into a software and how to select (hyper-)parameters properly. The ambition of the ChaLearn AutoML challenge series is to channel the energy of the ML community to reduce step by step the need for human intervention in applying ML to a wide variety of practical problems.

Full automation is an unbounded problem since there can always be novel settings, which have never been encountered before. Our first challenges AutoML1 were limited to:

- **Supervised learning** problems (classification and regression).
- **Feature vector** representations.
- **Homogeneous datasets** (same distribution in the training, validation, and test set).

A. Statnikov
SoFi San Francisc, California, USA

W.-W. Tu
4Paradigm, Beijing, Republic of China

E. Viegas
Microsoft Research, Redmond, WA, USA

- **Medium size datasets** of less than 200 MBytes.
- **Limited computer resources** with execution times of less than 20 min per dataset on an 8 core $x86\_64$ machine with 56 GB RAM.

We excluded unsupervised learning, active learning, transfer learning, and causal discovery problems, which are all very dear to us and have been addressed in past ChaLearn challenges [31], but which require each a different evaluation setting, thus making result comparisons very difficult. We did not exclude the treatment of video, images, text, and more generally time series and the selected datasets actually contain several instances of such modalities. However, they were first preprocessed in a feature representation, thus de-emphasizing feature learning. Still, learning from data pre-processed in feature-based representations already covers a lot of grounds and a fully automated method resolving this restricted problem would already be a major advance in the field.

Within this constrained setting, we included a variety of difficulties:

- **Different data distributions:** the intrinsic/geometrical complexity of the dataset.
- **Different tasks:** regression, binary classification, multi-class classification, multi-label classification.
- **Different scoring metrics:** AUC, BAC, MSE, F_1, etc. (see Sect. 10.4.2).
- **Class balance:** Balanced or unbalanced class proportions.
- **Sparsity:** Full matrices or sparse matrices.
- **Missing values:** Presence or absence of missing values.
- **Categorical variables:** Presence or absence of categorical variables.
- **Irrelevant variables:** Presence or absence of additional irrelevant variables (distractors).
- **Number P_{tr} of training examples:** Small or large number of training examples.
- **Number N of variables/features:** Small or large number of variables.
- **Ratio P_{tr}/N of the training data matrix:** $P_{tr} \gg N$, $P_{tr} = N$ or $P_{tr} \ll N$.

In this setting, the participants had to face many modeling/hyper-parameter choices. Some other, equally important, aspects of automating machine learning were not addressed in this challenge and are left for future research. Those include data "ingestion" and formatting, pre-processing and feature/representation learning, detection and handling of skewed/biased data, inhomogeneous, drifting, multi-modal, or multi-view data (hinging on transfer learning), matching algorithms to problems (which may include supervised, unsupervised, or reinforcement learning, or other settings), acquisition of new data (active learning, query learning, reinforcement learning, causal experimentation), management of large volumes of data including the creation of appropriately-sized and stratified training, validation, and test sets, selection of algorithms that satisfy arbitrary resource constraints at training and run time, the ability to generate and reuse workflows, and generating meaningful reports.

This challenge series started with the NIPS 2006 "model selection game"[1] [37], where the participants were provided with a machine learning toolbox based on the Matlab toolkit CLOP [1] built on top of the "Spider" package [69]. The toolkit provided a flexible way of building models by combining preprocessing, feature selection, classification and post-processing modules, also enabling the building of ensembles of classifiers. The goal of the game was to build the best hyper-model: the focus was on model selection, not on the development of new algorithms. All problems were feature-based binary classification problems. Five datasets were provided. The participants had to submit the schema of their model. The model selection game confirmed the effectiveness of cross-validation (the winner invented a new variant called cross-indexing) and emphasized the need to focus more on search effectiveness with the deployment of novel search techniques such as particle swarm optimization.

New in the 2015/2016 AutoML challenge, we introduced the notion of "task": each dataset was supplied with a particular scoring metric to be optimized and a time budget. We initially intended to vary widely the time budget from dataset to dataset in an arbitrary way. We ended up fixing it to 20 min for practical reasons (except for Round 0 where the time budget ranged from 100 to 300 s). However, because the datasets varied in size, this put pressure on the participants to manage their allotted time. Other elements of novelty included the freedom of submitting any Linux executable. This was made possible by using automatic execution on the open-source platform Codalab.[2] To help the participants we provided a starting kit in Python based on the scikit-learn library [55].[3] This induced many of them to write a wrapper around scikit-learn. This has been the strategy of the winning entry "auto-sklearn" [25–28].[4] Following the AutoML challenge, we organized a "beat auto-sklearn" game on a single dataset (madeline), in which the participants could provide hyper-parameters "by hand" to try to beat auto-sklearn. But nobody could beat auto-sklearn! Not even their designers. The participants could submit a json file which describes a sklearn model and hyper-parameter settings, via a GUI interface. This interface allows researchers who want to compare their search methods with auto-sklearn to use the exact same set of hyper-models.

A large number of satellite events including bootcamps, summer schools, and workshops have been organized in 2015/2016 around the AutoML challenge.[5] The AutoML challenge was part of the official selection of the competition program of IJCNN 2015 and 2016 and the results were discussed at the AutoML and CiML workshops at ICML and NIPS in 2015 and 2016. Several publications accompanied these events: in [33] we describe the details of the design of the AutoML challenge.[6]

---

[1] http://clopinet.com/isabelle/Projects/NIPS2006/

[2] http://competitions.codalab.org

[3] http://scikit-learn.org/

[4] https://automl.github.io/auto-sklearn/stable/

[5] See http://automl.chalearn.org

[6] http://codalab.org/AutoML

In [32] and [34] we review milestone and final results presented at the ICML 2015 and 2016 AutoML workshops. The 2015/2016 AutoML challenge had 6 rounds introducing 5 datasets each. We also organized a follow-up event for the PAKDD conference 2018[7] in only 2 phases, with 5 datasets in the development phase and 5 datasets in the final "blind test" round.

Going beyond the former published analyses, this chapter presents systematic studies of the winning solutions on all the datasets of the challenge and conducts comparisons with commonly used learning machines implemented in scikit-learn. It provides unpublished details about the datasets and reflective analyses.

This chapter is in part based on material that has appeared previously [32–34, 36]. This chapter is complemented by a 46-page online appendix that can be accessed from the book's webpage: http://automl.org/book.

10.2 Problem Formalization and Overview

10.2.1 Scope of the Problem

This challenge series focuses on supervised learning in ML and, in particular, solving classification and regression problems, without any further human intervention, within given constraints. To this end, we released a large number of datasets preformatted in given feature representations (i.e., each example consists of a fixed number of numerical coefficients; more in Sect. 10.3).

The distinction between input and output variables is not always made in ML applications. For instance, in recommender systems, the problem is often stated as making predictions of missing values for every variable rather than predicting the values of a particular variable [58]. In unsupervised learning [30], the purpose is to explain data in a simple and compact way, eventually involving inferred latent variables (e.g., class membership produced by a clustering algorithm).

We consider only the strict supervised learning setting where data present themselves as identically and independently distributed input-output pairs. The models used are limited to fixed-length vectorial representations, excluding problems of time series prediction. Text, speech, and video processing tasks included in the challenge have been preprocessed into suitable fixed-length vectorial representations.

The difficulty of the proposed tasks lies in the data complexity (class imbalance, sparsity, missing values, categorical variables). The testbed is composed of data from a wide variety of domains. Although there exist ML toolkits that can tackle all of these problems, it still requires considerable human effort to find, for a given dataset, task, evaluation metric, the methods and hyper-parameter settings that maximize performance subject to a computational constraint. The participant challenge is to create the *perfect black box* that removes human interaction, alleviating the shortage of data scientists in the coming decade.

[7] https://www.4paradigm.com/competition/pakdd2018

10.2.2 Full Model Selection

We refer to participant solutions as *hyper-models* to indicate that they are built from simpler components. For instance, for classification problems, participants might consider a hyper-model that combines several classification techniques such as nearest neighbors, linear models, kernel methods, neural networks, and random forests. More complex hyper-models may also include preprocessing, feature construction, and feature selection modules.

Generally, a predictive model of the form $y = f(\mathbf{x}; \boldsymbol{\alpha})$ has:

- a set of parameters $\boldsymbol{\alpha} = [\alpha_0, \alpha_1, \alpha_2, \ldots, \alpha_n]$;
- a learning algorithm (referred to as trainer), which serves to optimize the parameters using training data;
- a trained model (referred to as predictor) of the form $y = f(\mathbf{x})$ produced by the trainer;
- a clear objective function $J(f)$, which can be used to assess the model's performance on test data.

Consider now the model hypothesis space defined by a vector $\boldsymbol{\theta} = [\theta_1, \theta_2, \ldots, \theta_n]$ of hyper-parameters. The hyper-parameter vector may include not only parameters corresponding to switching between alternative models, but also modeling choices such as preprocessing parameters, type of kernel in a kernel method, number of units and layers in a neural network, or training algorithm regularization parameters [59]. Some authors refer to this problem as *full model selection* [24, 62], others as the CASH problem (Combined Algorithm Selection and Hyperparameter optimization) [65]. We will denote hyper-models as

$$y = f(\mathbf{x}; \boldsymbol{\theta}) = f(\mathbf{x}; \boldsymbol{\alpha}(\boldsymbol{\theta}), \boldsymbol{\theta}), \qquad (10.1)$$

where the model parameter vector $\boldsymbol{\alpha}$ is an implicit function of the hyper-parameter vector $\boldsymbol{\theta}$ obtained by using a trainer for a fixed value of $\boldsymbol{\theta}$, and training data composed of input-output pairs $\{\mathbf{x}_i, y_i\}$. The participants have to devise algorithms capable of training the hyper-parameters $\boldsymbol{\theta}$. This may require intelligent sampling of the hyper-parameter space and splitting the available training data into subsets for both training and evaluating the predictive power of solutions—one or multiple times.

As an optimization problem, model selection is a bi-level optimization program [7, 18, 19]; there is a lower objective J_1 to train the parameters $\boldsymbol{\alpha}$ of the model, and an upper objective J_2 to train the hyper-parameters $\boldsymbol{\theta}$, both optimized simultaneously (see Fig. 10.1). As a statistics problem, model selection is a problem of multiple testing in which error bars on performance prediction ϵ degrade with the number of models/hyper-parameters tried or, more generally, the complexity of the hyper-model $C_2(\boldsymbol{\theta})$. A key aspect of AutoML is to avoid overfitting the upper-level objective J_2 by regularizing it, much in the same way as lower level objectives J_1 are regularized.

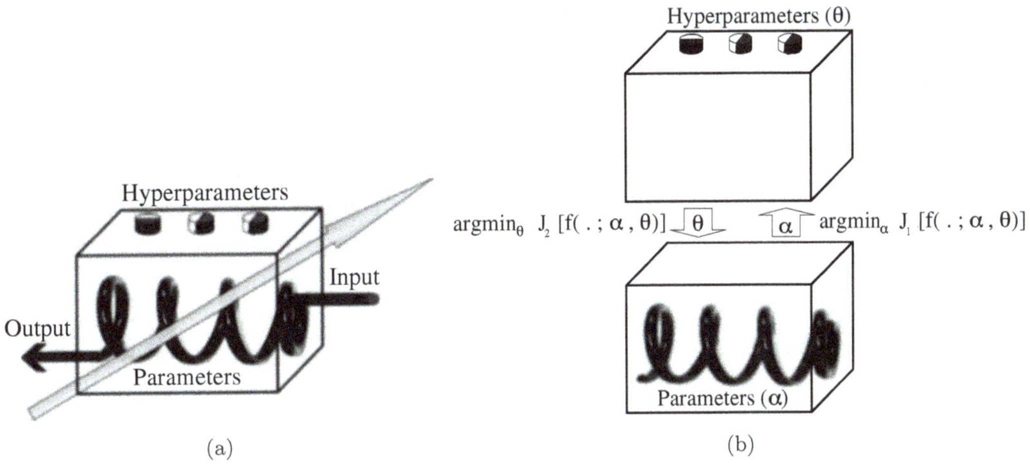

Fig. 10.1 Bi-level optimization. (**a**) Representation of a learning machine with parameters and hyper-parameters to be adjusted. (**b**) De-coupling of parameter and hyper-parameter adjustment in two levels. The upper level objective J_2 optimizes the hyper-parameters $\boldsymbol{\theta}$; the lower objective J_1 optimizes the parameters $\boldsymbol{\alpha}$

The problem setting also lends itself to using ensemble methods, which let several "simple" models vote to make the final decision [15, 16, 29]. In this case, the parameters $\boldsymbol{\theta}$ may be interpreted as voting weights. For simplicity we lump all parameters in a single vector, but more elaborate structures, such as trees or graphs can be used to define the hyper-parameter space [66].

10.2.3 Optimization of Hyper-parameters

Everyone who has worked with data has had to face some common modeling choices: scaling, normalization, missing value imputation, variable coding (for categorical variables), variable discretization, degree of nonlinearity and model architecture, among others. ML has managed to reduce the number of hyper-parameters and produce *black-boxes* to perform tasks such as classification and regression [21, 40]. Still, any real-world problem requires at least some preparation of the data before it can be fitted into an "automatic" method, hence requiring some modeling choices. There has been much progress on end-to-end automated ML for more complex tasks such as text, image, video, and speech processing with deep-learning methods [6]. However, even these methods have many modeling choices and hyper-parameters.

While producing models for a diverse range of applications has been a focus of the ML community, little effort has been devoted to the optimization of hyper-parameters. Common practices that include *trial and error* and grid search may lead to overfitting models for small datasets or underfitting models for large datasets. By overfitting we mean producing models that perform well on training data but perform poorly on unseen data, i.e., models that do not generalize. By underfitting we mean selecting too simple a model, which does not capture the complexity of the data, and hence performs poorly both on training and test data. Despite well-optimized off-the-shelf algorithms for optimizing parameters, end-users are still responsible for organizing their numerical experiments to identify the best of a number of models under consideration. Due to lack of time and resources, they often perform model/hyper-parameter selection with ad hoc techniques. Ioannidis and Langford [42, 47] examine fundamental, common mistakes such as poor construction of training/test splits, inappropriate model complexity, hyper-parameter selection using test sets, misuse of computational resources, and misleading test metrics, which may invalidate an entire study. Participants must avoid these flaws and devise systems that can be blind-tested.

An additional twist of our problem setting is that code is tested with limited computational resources. That is, for each task an arbitrary limit on execution time is fixed and a maximum amount of memory is provided. This places a constraint on the participant to produce a solution in a given time, and hence to optimize the model search from a computational point of view. In summary, participants have to jointly address the problem of over-fitting/under-fitting and the problem of efficient search for an optimal solution, as stated in [43]. In practice, the computational constraints have turned out to be far more challenging to challenge participants than the problem of overfitting. Thus the main contributions have been to devise novel efficient search techniques with cutting-edge optimization methods.

10.2.4 Strategies of Model Search

Most practitioners use heuristics such as grid search or uniform sampling to sample $\boldsymbol{\theta}$ space, and use k-fold cross-validation as the upper-level objective J_2 [20]. In

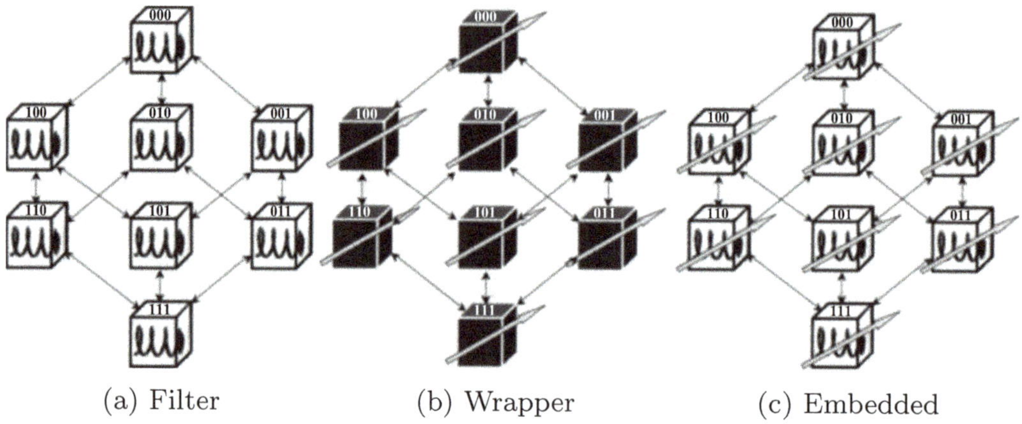

Fig. 10.2 Approaches to two-level inference. (**a**) **Filter methods** select the hyper-parameters without adjusting the learner parameters. (No arrows indicates no parameter training.) (**b**) **Wrapper methods** select the hyper-parameters using trained learners, treating them as black-boxes. (**c**) **Embedded methods** use knowledge of the learner structure and/or parameters to guide the hyper-parameter search

this framework, the optimization of $\boldsymbol{\theta}$ is not performed sequentially [8]. All the parameters are sampled along a regular scheme, usually in linear or log scale. This leads to a number of possibilities that exponentially increases with the dimension of $\boldsymbol{\theta}$. k-fold cross-validation consists of splitting the dataset into k folds; $(k-1)$ folds are used for training and the remaining fold is used for testing; eventually, the average of the test scores obtained on the k folds is reported. Note that some ML toolkits currently support cross-validation. There is a lack of principled guidelines to determine the number of grid points and the value of k (with the exception of [20]), and there is no guidance for regularizing J_2, yet this simple method is a good baseline approach.

Efforts have been made to optimize continuous hyper-parameters with bilevel optimization methods, using either the k-fold cross-validation estimator [7, 50] or the leave-one-out estimator as the upper-level objective J_2. The leave-one-out estimator may be efficiently computed, in closed form, as a by-product of training only one predictor on all the training examples (e.g., virtual-leave-one-out [38]). The method was improved by adding a regularization of J_2 [17]. Gradient descent has been used to accelerate the search, by making a local quadratic approximation of J_2 [44]. In some cases, the full $J_2(\boldsymbol{\theta})$ can be computed from a few key examples [39, 54]. Other approaches minimize an *approximation* or an *upper bound* of the leave-one-out error, instead of its exact form [53, 68]. Nevertheless, these methods are still limited to specific models and continuous hyper-parameters.

An early attempt at full model selection was the *pattern search* method that uses k-fold cross-validation for J_2. It explores the hyper-parameter space by steps of the same magnitude, and when no change in any parameter further decreases J_2, the step size is halved and the process repeated until the steps are deemed sufficiently small [49]. Escalante et al. [24] addressed the full model selection problem using Particle Swarm Optimization, which optimizes a problem by having a population of candidate solutions (particles), and moving these particles around the hyper-parameter space using the particle's position and velocity. k-fold cross-validation is also used for J_2. This approach retrieved the winning model in $\sim$76% of the cases. Overfitting was controlled heuristically with early stopping and the proportion of training and validation data was not optimized. Although progress has been made in experimental design to reduce the risk of overfitting [42, 47], in particular by splitting data in a principled way [61], to our knowledge, no one has addressed the problem of optimally splitting data.

While regularizing the second level of inference is a recent addition to the frequentist ML community, it has been an intrinsic part of Bayesian modeling via the notion of hyper-prior. Some methods of multi-level optimization combine importance sampling and Monte-Carlo Markov Chains [2]. The field of Bayesian hyper-parameter optimization has rapidly developed and yielded promising results, in particular by using Gaussian processes to model generalization performance [60, 63]. But Tree-structured Parzen Estimator (TPE) approaches modeling $P(\mathbf{x}|y)$ and $P(y)$ rather than modeling $P(y|\mathbf{x})$ directly [9, 10] have been found to outperform GP-based Bayesian optimization for structured optimization problems with many hyperparameters including discrete ones [23]. The central idea of these methods is to fit $J_2(\boldsymbol{\theta})$ to a smooth function in an attempt to reduce variance and to estimate the variance in regions of the hyper-parameter space that are under-sampled to guide the search towards regions of high variance. These methods are inspirational and some of the ideas can be adopted in the frequentist setting. For instance, the random-forest-based SMAC algorithm [41], which has helped speed up both local search and tree search algorithms by orders of magnitude on certain instance distributions, has also been found to be very effective for the hyper-parameter optimization of machine learning algorithms, scaling better to high dimensions and discrete input dimensions than other algorithms [23]. We also notice that Bayesian optimization methods are often combined with other techniques such as meta-learning and ensemble methods [25] in order to gain advantage in some challenge settings with a time limit [32]. Some of these methods consider jointly the two-level optimization and take time cost as a critical guidance for hyper-parameter search [45, 64].

Besides Bayesian optimization, several other families of approaches exist in the literature and have gained much attention with the recent rise of deep learning. Ideas borrowed from *reinforcement learning* have recently been used to construct optimal neural network architectures [4, 70]. These approaches formulate the hyper-parameter optimization problem in a reinforcement learning flavor, with for example states being the actual hyper-parameter setting (e.g., network architecture), actions being adding or deleting a module (e.g., a CNN layer or a pooling layer), and reward being the validation accuracy. They can then apply off-the-shelf reinforcement learning algorithms (e.g., RENFORCE, Q-learning, Monte-Carlo Tree Search) to solve the problem. Other architecture search methods use *evolutionary* algorithms [3, 57]. These approaches consider a set (population) of hyper-parameter settings (individuals), modify (mutate and reproduce) and eliminate unpromising settings according to their cross-validation score (fitness). After several generations, the global quality of the population increases. One important common point of reinforcement learning and evolutionary algorithms is that they both deal with the exploration-exploitation trade-off. Despite the impressive results, these approaches require a huge amount of computational resources and some (especially evolutionary algorithms) are hard to scale. Pham et al. [56] recently proposed weight sharing among child models to speed up the process considerably [70] while achieving comparable results.

Note that splitting the problem of parameter fitting into two levels can be extended to more levels, at the expense of extra complexity—i.e., need for a hierarchy of data splits to perform multiple or nested cross-validation [22], insufficient data to train and validate at the different levels, and increase of the computational load.

Table 10.1 shows a typical example of multi-level parameter optimization in a frequentist setting. We assume that we are using an ML toolbox with two learning machines: Kridge (kernel ridge regression) and Neural (a neural network a.k.a. "deep learning" model). At the top level we use a test procedure to assess the performance of the final model (this is not an inference level). The top-level inference algorithm Validation({GridCV(Kridge, MSE), GridCV(Neural, MSE)}, MSE) is decomposed into its elements recursively. Validation uses the data split $D = [D_{Tr}, D_{Va}]$ to compare the learning machines Kridge and Neural (trained

Table 10.1 Typical example of multi-level inference algorithm. The top-level algorithm Validation({GridCV(Kridge, MSE), GridCV(Neural, MSE)}, MSE) is decomposed into its elements recursively. Calling the method "train" on it using data D_{TrVa} results in a function f, then tested with test(f, MSE, D_{Te}). The notation $[.]_{CV}$ indicates that results are averages over multiple data splits (cross-validation). NA means "not applicable". A model family $\mathcal{F}$ of parameters $\boldsymbol{\alpha}$ and hyper-parameters $\boldsymbol{\theta}$ is represented as $f(\boldsymbol{\theta}, \boldsymbol{\alpha})$. We derogate to the usual convention of putting hyper-parameters last, the hyper-parameters are listed in decreasing order of inference level. $\mathcal{F}$, thought of as a bottom level algorithm, does not perform any training: $train(f(\boldsymbol{\theta}, \boldsymbol{\alpha}))$ just returns the function $f(\mathbf{x}; \boldsymbol{\theta}, \boldsymbol{\alpha})$

		Parameters			
Level	Algorithm	Fixed	Varying	Optimization performed	Data split
NA	f	All	All	Performance assessment (no inference)	D_{Te}
4	Validation	None	All	Final algorithm selection using validation data	$D = [D_{Tr}, D_{Va}]$
3	GridCV	Model index i	$\boldsymbol{\theta}, \gamma, \boldsymbol{\alpha}$	10-fold CV on regularly sampled values of $\boldsymbol{\theta}$	$D_{Tr} = [D_{tr}, D_{va}]_{CV}$
2	Kridge($\boldsymbol{\theta}$) Neural($\boldsymbol{\theta}$)	$i, \boldsymbol{\theta}$	$\gamma, \boldsymbol{\alpha}$	Virtual LOO CV to select regularization parameter γ	$D_{tr} = [D_{tr}^{\backslash\{d\}}, d]_{CV}$
1	Kridge($\boldsymbol{\theta}, \gamma$) Neural($\boldsymbol{\theta}, \gamma$)	$i, \boldsymbol{\theta}, \gamma$	$\boldsymbol{\alpha}$	Matrix inversion of gradient descent to compute $\boldsymbol{\alpha}$	D_{tr}
0	Kridge($\boldsymbol{\theta}, \gamma, \boldsymbol{\alpha}$) Neural($\boldsymbol{\theta}, \gamma, \boldsymbol{\alpha}$)	All	None	NA	NA

using D_{Tr} on the validation set D_{Va}, using the mean-square error) (MSE) evaluation function. The algorithm GridCV, a grid search with 10-fold cross-validation (CV) MSE evaluation function, then optimizes the hyper-parameters $\boldsymbol{\theta}$. Internally, both Kridge and Neural use virtual leave-one-out (LOO) cross-validation to adjust γ and a classical L_2 regularized risk functional to adjust $\boldsymbol{\alpha}$.

Borrowing from the conventional classification of feature selection methods [11, 38, 46], model search strategies can be categorized into filters, wrappers, and embedded methods (see Fig. 10.2). **Filters** are methods for narrowing down the model space, without training the learner. Such methods include preprocessing, feature construction, kernel design, architecture design, choice of prior or regularizers, choice of noise model, and filter methods for feature selection. Although some filters use training data, many incorporate human prior knowledge of the task or knowledge compiled from previous tasks. Recently, [5] proposed to apply collaborative filtering methods to model search. **Wrapper methods** consider learners as a black-box capable of learning from examples and making predictions once trained. They operate with a search algorithm in the hyper-parameter space (grid search or stochastic search) and an evaluation function assessing the trained learner's performance (cross-validation error or Bayesian evidence). **Embedded methods** are similar to wrappers, but they exploit the knowledge of the machine learning algorithm to make the search more efficient. For instance, some embedded methods compute the leave-one-out solution in a closed form, without leaving anything out, i.e., by performing a single model training on all the training data (e.g., [38]). Other embedded methods jointly optimize parameters and hyper-parameters [44, 50, 51].

In summary, many authors focus only on the efficiency of search, ignoring the problem of overfitting the second level objective J_2, which is often chosen to be k-fold cross-validation with an arbitrary value for k. Bayesian methods introduce techniques of overfitting avoidance via the notion of hyper-priors, but at the expense of making assumptions on how the data were generated and without providing guarantees of performance. In all the prior approaches to full model selection we know of, there is no attempt to treat the problem as the optimization of a regularized functional J_2 with respect to both (1) modeling choices and (2) data split. Much remains to be done to jointly address statistical and computational issues. The AutoML challenge series offers benchmarks to compare and contrast methods addressing these problems, free of the inventor/evaluator bias.

10.3 Data

We gathered a first pool of 70 datasets during the summer 2014 with the help of numerous collaborators and ended up selecting 30 datasets for the 2015/2016 challenge (see Table 10.2 and the online appendix), chosen to illustrate a wide variety of domains of applications: biology and medicine, ecology, energy and sustainability management, image, text, audio, speech, video and other sensor data processing, internet social media management and advertising, market analysis and financial prediction. We preprocessed data to obtain feature representations (i.e., each example consists of a fixed number of numerical coefficients). Text, speech, and video processing tasks were included in the challenge, but not in their native variable-length representations.

For the 2018 challenge, three datasets from the first pool (but unused in the first challenge) were selected and seven new datasets collected by the new organizers and sponsors were added (see Table 10.3 and the online appendix).

Some datasets were obtained from public sources, but they were reformatted into new representations to conceal their identity, except for the final round of the 2015/2016 challenge and the final phase of the 2018 challenge, which included completely new data.

In the 2015/2016 challenge, data difficulty progressively increased from round to round. Round 0 introduced five (public) datasets from previous challenges illustrating the various difficulties encountered in subsequent rounds:

Novice Binary classification problems only. No missing data; no categorical features; moderate number of features (<2,000); balanced classes. Challenge

Table 10.2 Datasets of the 2015/2016 AutoML challenge. *C* number of classes, *Cbal* class balance, *Sparse* sparsity, *Miss* fraction of missing values, *Cat* categorical variables, *Irr* fraction of irrelevant variables, *Pte, Pva, Ptr* number of examples of the test, validation, and training sets, respectively, *N* number of features, *Ptr/N* aspect ratio of the dataset

Rnd	DATASET	Task	Metric	Time	C	Cbal	Sparse	Miss	Cat	Irr	Pte	Pva	Ptr	N	Ptr/N
0	1 ADULT	multilabel	F1	300	3	1	0.16	0.011	1	0.5	9768	4884	34,190	24	1424.58
0	2 CADATA	regression	R2	200	0	NaN	0	0	0	0.5	10,640	5000	5000	16	312.5
0	3 DIGITS	multiclass	BAC	300	10	1	0.42	0	0	0.5	35,000	20,000	15,000	1568	9.57
0	4 DOROTHEA	binary	AUC	100	2	0.46	0.99	0	0	0.5	800	350	800	100,000	0.01
0	5 NEWSGROUPS	multiclass	PAC	300	20	1	1	0	0	0	3755	1877	13,142	61,188	0.21
1	1 CHRISTINE	binary	BAC	1200	2	1	0.071	0	0	0.5	2084	834	5418	1636	3.31
1	2 JASMINE	binary	BAC	1200	2	1	0.78	0	0	0.5	1756	526	2984	144	20.72
1	3 MADELINE	binary	BAC	1200	2	1	1.2e-06	0	0	0.92	3240	1080	3140	259	12.12
1	4 PHILIPPINE	binary	BAC	1200	2	1	0.0012	0	0	0.5	4664	1166	5832	308	18.94
1	5 SYLVINE	binary	BAC	1200	2	1	0.01	0	0	0.5	10,244	5124	5124	20	256.2
2	1 ALBERT	binary	F1	1200	2	1	0.049	0.14	1	0.5	51,048	25,526	425,240	78	5451.79
2	2 DILBERT	multiclass	PAC	1200	5	1	0	0	0	0.16	9720	4860	10,000	2000	5
2	3 FABERT	multiclass	PAC	1200	7	0.96	0.99	0	0	0.5	2354	1177	8237	800	10.3
2	4 ROBERT	multiclass	BAC	1200	10	1	0.01	0	0	0	5000	2000	10,000	7200	1.39
2	5 VOLKERT	multiclass	PAC	1200	10	0.89	0.34	0	0	0	7000	3500	58,310	180	323.94
3	1 ALEXIS	multilabel	AUC	1200	18	0.92	0.98	0	0	0	15,569	7784	54,491	5000	10.9
3	2 DIONIS	multiclass	BAC	1200	355	1	0.11	0	0	0	12,000	6000	416,188	60	6936.47
3	3 GRIGORIS	multilabel	AUC	1200	91	0.87	1	0	0	0	9920	6486	45,400	301,561	0.15
3	4 JANNIS	multiclass	BAC	1200	4	0.8	7.3e-05	0	0	0.5	9851	4926	83,733	54	1550.61
3	5 WALLIS	multiclass	AUC	1200	11	0.91	1	0	0	0	8196	4098	10,000	193,731	0.05
4	1 EVITA	binary	AUC	1200	2	0.21	0.91	0	0	0.46	14,000	8000	20,000	3000	6.67
4	2 FLORA	regression	ABS	1200	0	NaN	0.99	0	0	0.25	2000	2000	15,000	200,000	0.08
4	3 HELENA	multiclass	BAC	1200	100	0.9	6e-05	0	0	0	18,628	9314	65,196	27	2414.67
4	4 TANIA	multilabel	PAC	1200	95	0.79	1	0	0	0	44,635	22,514	157,599	47,236	3.34
4	5 YOLANDA	regression	R2	1200	0	NaN	1e-07	0	0	0.1	30,000	30,000	400,000	100	4000
5	1 ARTURO	multiclass	F1	1200	20	1	0.82	0	0	0.5	2733	1366	9565	400	23.91
5	2 CARLO	binary	PAC	1200	2	0.097	0.0027	0	0	0.5	10,000	10,000	50,000	1070	46.73
5	3 MARCO	multilabel	AUC	1200	24	0.76	0.99	0	0	0	20,482	20,482	163,860	15,299	10.71
5	4 PABLO	regression	ABS	1200	0	NaN	0.11	0	0	0.5	23,565	23,565	188,524	120	1571.03
5	5 WALDO	multiclass	BAC	1200	4	1	0.029	0	1	0.5	2430	2430	19,439	270	72

Table 10.3 Datasets of the 2018 AutoML challenge. All tasks are binary classification problems. The metric is the AUC for all tasks. The time budget is also the same for all datasets (1200 s). Phase 1 was the development phase and phase 2 the final "blind test" phase

Phase	DATASET	Cbal	Sparse	Miss	Cat	Irr	Pte	Pva	Ptr	N	Ptr/N
1	1 ADA	1	0.67	0	0	0	41,471	415	4147	48	86.39
1	2 ARCENE	0.22	0.54	0	0	0	700	100	100	10,000	0.01
1	3 GINA	1	0.03	0.31	0	0	31,532	315	3153	970	3.25
1	4 GUILLERMO	0.33	0.53	0	0	0	5000	5000	20,000	4296	4.65
1	5 RL	0.10	0	0.11	1	0	24,803	0	31,406	22	1427.5
2	1 PM	0.01	0	0.11	1	0	20,000	0	29,964	89	224.71
2	2 RH	0.04	0.41	0	1	0	28,544	0	31,498	76	414.44
2	3 RI	0.02	0.09	0.26	1	0	26,744	0	30,562	113	270.46
2	4 RICCARDO	0.67	0.51	0	0	0	5000	5000	20,000	4296	4.65
2	5 RM	0.001	0	0.11	1	0	26,961	0	28,278	89	317.73

lies in dealing with sparse and full matrices, presence of irrelevant variables, and various Ptr/N.

Intermediate Binary and multi-class classification problems. Challenge lies in dealing with unbalanced classes, number of classes, missing values, categorical variables, and up to 7,000 features.

Advanced Binary, multi-class, and multi-label classification problems. Challenge lies in dealing with up to 300,000 features.

Expert Classification and regression problems. Challenge lies in dealing with the entire range of data complexity.

Master Classification and regression problems of all difficulties. Challenge lies in learning from completely new datasets.

The datasets of the 2018 challenge were all binary classification problems. Validation partitions were not used because of the design of this challenge, even when they were available for some tasks. The three reused datasets had similar difficulty as those of rounds 1 and 2 of the 2015/2016 challenge. However, the seven new data sets introduced difficulties that were not present in the former challenge. Most notably an extreme class imbalance, presence of categorical features and a temporal dependency among instances that could be exploited by participants to develop their methods.[8] The datasets from both challenges are downloadable from http://automl.chalearn.org/data.

10.4 Challenge Protocol

In this section, we describe design choices we made to ensure the thoroughness and fairness of the evaluation. As previously indicated, we focus on supervised learning tasks (classification and regression problems), without any human intervention,

[8]In RL, PM, RH, RI and RM datasets instances were chronologically sorted, this information was made available to participants and could be used for developing their methods.

within given time and computer resource constraints (Sect. 10.4.1), and given a particular metric (Sect. 10.4.2), which varies from dataset to dataset. During the challenges, the identity and description of the datasets is concealed (except in the very first round or phase where sample data is distributed) to avoid the use of domain knowledge and to push participants to design fully automated ML solutions. In the 2015/2016 AutoML challenge, the datasets were introduced in a series of rounds (Sect. 10.4.3), alternating periods of code development (Tweakathon phases) and blind tests of code without human intervention (AutoML phases). Either results or code could be submitted during development phases, but code had to be submitted to be part of the AutoML "blind test" ranking. In the 2018 edition of the AutoML challenge, the protocol was simplified. We had only one round in two phases: a development phase in which 5 datasets were released for practice purposes, and a final "blind test" phase with 5 new datasets that were never used before.

10.4.1 Time Budget and Computational Resources

The Codalab platform provides computational resources shared by all participants. We used up to 10 compute workers processing in parallel the queue of submissions made by participants. Each compute worker was equipped with 8 cores $x86\_64$. Memory was increased from 24 to 56 GB after round 3 of the 2015/2016 AutoML challenge. For the 2018 AutoML challenge computing resources were reduced, as we wanted to motivate the development of more efficient yet effective AutoML solutions. We used 6 compute workers processing in parallel the queue of submissions. Each compute worker was equipped with 2 cores $x86\_64$ and 8 GB of memory.

To ensure fairness, when a code submission was evaluated, a compute worker was dedicated to processing that submission only, and its execution time was limited to a given time budget (which may vary from dataset to dataset). The time budget was provided to the participants with each dataset in its *info* file. It was generally set to 1200 s (20 min) per dataset, for practical reasons, except in the first phase of the first round. However, the participants did not know this ahead of time and therefore their code had to be capable to manage a given time budget. The participants who submitted results instead of code were not constrained by the time budget since their code was run on their own platform. This was potentially advantageous for entries counting towards the Final phases (immediately following a Tweakathon). Participants wishing to also enter the AutoML (blind testing) phases, which required submitting code, could submit both results and code (simultaneously). When results were submitted, they were used as entries in the on-going phase. They did not need to be produced by the submitted code; i.e., if a participant did not want to share personal code, he/she could submit the sample code provided by the organizers together with his/her results. The code was automatically forwarded to the AutoML phases for "blind testing". In AutoML phases, result submission was not possible.

The participants were encouraged to save and submit intermediate results so we could draw learning curves. This was not exploited during the challenge. But we study learning curves in this chapter to evaluate the capabilities of algorithms to quickly attain good performances.

10.4.2 Scoring Metrics

The scores are computed by comparing submitted predictions to reference target values. For each sample $i, i = 1 : P$ (where P is the size of the validation set or of the test set), the target value is a continuous numeric coefficient y_i for regression problems, a binary indicator in $\{0, 1\}$ for two-class problems, or a vector of binary indicators $[y_{il}]$ in $\{0, 1\}$ for multi-class or multi-label classification problems (one per class l). The participants had to submit prediction values matching as closely as possible the target values, in the form of a continuous numeric coefficient q_i for regression problems and a vector of numeric coefficients $[q_{il}]$ in the range $[0, 1]$ for multi-class or multi-label classification problems (one per class l).

The provided starting kit contains an implementation in Python of all scoring metrics used to evaluate the entries. Each dataset has its own scoring criterion specified in its *info* file. All scores are normalized such that the expected value of the score for a random prediction, based on class prior probabilities, is 0 and the optimal score is 1. Multi-label problems are treated as multiple binary classification problems and are evaluated using the average of the scores of each binary classification subproblem.

We first define the notation $\langle \cdot \rangle$ for the average over all samples P indexed by i. That is,

$$\langle y_i \rangle = (1/P) \sum_{i=1}^{P} (y_i). \tag{10.2}$$

The score metrics are defined as follows:

R² The coefficient of determination is used for regression problems only. The metric is based on the mean squared error (MSE) and the variance (VAR), and computed as

$$R^2 = 1 - MSE/VAR, \tag{10.3}$$

where $MSE = \langle (y_i - q_i)^2 \rangle$ and $VAR = \langle (y_i - m)^2 \rangle$, with $m = \langle y_i \rangle$.

ABS This coefficient is similar to R^2 but based on the mean absolute error (MAE) and the mean absolute deviation (MAD), and computed as

$$ABS = 1 - MAE/MAD, \tag{10.4}$$

where $MAE = \langle \text{abs}(y_i - q_i)\rangle$ and $MAD = \langle \text{abs}(y_i - m)\rangle$.

BAC Balanced accuracy is the average of class-wise accuracy for classification problems—and the average of *sensitivity* (true positive rate) and *specificity* (true negative rate) for binary classification:

$$BAC = \begin{cases} \frac{1}{2}[\frac{TP}{P} + \frac{TN}{N}], & \text{for binary} \\ \frac{1}{C}\sum_{i=1}^{C} \frac{TP_i}{N_i}, & \text{for multi-class} \end{cases} \tag{10.5}$$

where P (N) is the number of positive (negative) examples, TP (TN) is the number of well classified positive (negative) examples, C is the number of classes, TP_i is the number of well classified examples of class i and N_i the number of examples of class i.

For binary classification problems, the class-wise accuracy is the fraction of correct class predictions when q_i is thresholded at 0.5, for each class. For multi-label problems, the class-wise accuracy is averaged over all classes. For multi-class problems, the predictions are binarized by selecting the class with maximum prediction value $\arg\max_l q_{il}$ before computing the class-wise accuracy.

We normalize the metric as follows:

$$|BAC| = (BAC - R)/(1 - R), \tag{10.6}$$

where R is the expected value of BAC for random predictions (i.e., $R = 0.5$ for binary classification and $R = (1/C)$ for C-class problems).

AUC The area under the ROC curve is used for ranking and binary classification problems. The ROC curve is the curve of *sensitivity* vs. *1-specificity* at various prediction thresholds. The AUC and BAC values are the same for binary predictions. The AUC is calculated for each class separately before averaging over all classes. We normalize the metric as

$$|AUC| = 2AUC - 1. \tag{10.7}$$

F1 score The harmonic mean of precision and recall is computed as

$$F1 = 2 * (precision * recall)/(precision + recall), \tag{10.8}$$

$$precision = true\ positive/(true\ positive + false\ positive) \tag{10.9}$$

$$recall = true\ positive/(true\ positive + false\ negative) \tag{10.10}$$

Prediction thresholding and class averaging is handled similarly as in BAC. We normalize the metric as follows:

$$|F1| = (F1 - R)/(1 - R), \tag{10.11}$$

where R is the expected value of F1 for random predictions (see BAC).

PAC Probabilistic accuracy is based on the cross-entropy (or log loss) and computed as

$$PAC = \exp(-CE), \tag{10.12}$$

$$CE = \begin{cases} average \sum_l \log(q_{il}), & \text{for multi-class} \\ -\langle y_i \log(q_i), & \\ +(1 - y_i)\log(1 - q_i)\rangle, & \text{for binary and multi-label} \end{cases} \tag{10.13}$$

Class averaging is performed after taking the exponential in the multi-label case. We normalize the metric as follows:

$$|PAC| = (PAC - R)/(1 - R), \tag{10.14}$$

where R is the score obtained using $q_i = \langle y_i \rangle$ or $q_{il} = \langle y_{il} \rangle$ (i.e., using as predictions the fraction of positive class examples, as an estimate of the prior probability).

Note that the normalization of R^2, ABS, and PAC uses the average target value $q_i = \langle y_i \rangle$ or $q_{il} = \langle y_{il} \rangle$. In contrast, the normalization of BAC, AUC, and F1 uses a random prediction of one of the classes with uniform probability.

Only R^2 and ABS are meaningful for regression; we compute the other metrics for completeness by replacing the target values with binary values after thresholding them in the mid-range.

10.4.3 Rounds and Phases in the 2015/2016 Challenge

The 2015/2016 challenge was run in multiple phases grouped in six rounds. Round 0 (Preparation) was a practice round using publicly available datasets. It was followed by five rounds of progressive difficulty (Novice, Intermediate, Advanced, Expert, and Master). Except for rounds 0 and 5, all rounds included three phases that alternated AutoML and Tweakathons contests. These phases are described in Table 10.4.

Submissions were made in Tweakathon phases only. The results of the latest submission were shown on the leaderboard and such submission automatically migrated to the following phase. In this way, the code of participants who abandoned before the end of the challenge had a chance to be tested in subsequent rounds and phases. New participants could enter at any time. Prizes were awarded in phases marked with a * during which there was no submission. To participate in phase AutoML[n], code had to be submitted in Tweakathon[n-1].

Table 10.4 Phases of round n in the 2015/2016 challenge. For each dataset, one labeled training set is provided and two unlabeled sets (validation set and test set) are provided for testing

Phase in round [n]	Goal	Duration	Submissions	Data	Leader-board scores	Prizes
* AutoML[n]	Blind test of code	Short	NONE (code migrated)	New datasets, not downloadable	Test set results	Yes
Tweakathon[n]	Manual tweaking	Months	Code and/ or results	Datasets downloadable	Validation set results	No
* Final[n]	Results of Tweakathon revealed	Short	NONE (results migrated)	NA	Test set results	Yes

In order to encourage participants to try GPUs and deep learning, a GPU track sponsored by NVIDIA was included in Round 4.

To participate in the Final[n], code or results had to be submitted in Tweakathon[n]. If both code and (well-formatted) results were submitted, the results were used for scoring rather than rerunning the code in Tweakathon[n] and Final[n]. The code was executed when results were unavailable or not well formatted. Thus, there was no disadvantage in submitting both results and code. If a participant submitted both results and code, different methods could be used to enter the Tweakathon/Final phases and the AutoML phases. Submissions were made only during Tweakathons, with a maximum of five submissions per day. Immediate feedback was provided on the leaderboard on validation data. The participants were ranked on the basis of test performance during the Final and AutoML phases.

We provided baseline software using the ML library scikit-learn [55]. It uses ensemble methods, which improve over time by adding more base learners. Other than the number of base learners, the default hyper-parameter settings were used. The participants were not obliged to use the Python language nor the main Python script we gave as an example. However, most participants found it convenient to use the main python script, which managed the sparse format, the any-time learning settings and the scoring metrics. Many limited themselves to search for the best model in the scikit-learn library. This shows the importance of providing a good starting kit, but also the danger of biasing results towards particular solutions.

10.4.4 Phases in the 2018 Challenge

The 2015/2016 AutoML challenge was very long and few teams participated in all rounds. Further, even though there was no obligation to participate in previous rounds to enter new rounds, new potential participants felt they would be at a disadvantage. Hence, we believe it is preferable to organize recurrent yearly events, each with their own workshop and publication opportunity. This provides a good balance between competition and collaboration.

In 2018, we organized a single round of AutoML competition in two phases. In this simplified protocol, the participants could practice on five datasets during the first (development) phase, by either submitting code or results. Their performances were revealed immediately, as they became available, on the leaderboard.

The last submission of the development phase was automatically forwarded to the second phase: the AutoML "blind test" phase. In this second phase, which was the only one counting towards the prizes, the participants' code was automatically evaluated on five new datasets on the Codalab platform. The datasets were not revealed to the participants. Hence, submissions that did not include code capable of being trained and tested automatically were not ranked in the final phase and could not compete towards the prizes.

We provided the same starting kit as in the AutoML 2015/2016 challenge, but the participants also had access to the code of the winners of the previous challenge.

10.5 Results

This section provides a brief description of the results obtained during both challenges, explains the methods used by the participants and their elements of novelty, and provides the analysis of post-challenge experiments conducted to answer specific questions on the effectiveness of model search techniques.

10.5.1 Scores Obtained in the 2015/2016 Challenge

The 2015/2016 challenge lasted 18 months (December 8, 2014 to May 1, 2016). By the end of the challenge, practical solutions were obtained and open-sourced, such as the solution of the winners [25].

Table 10.5 presents the results on the test set in the AutoML phases (blind testing) and the Final phases (one time testing on the test set revealed at the end of the Tweakathon phases). Ties were broken by giving preference to the participant who submitted first. The table only reports the results of the top-ranking participants. We also show in Fig. 10.3a comparison of the leaderboard performances of all participants. We plot in Fig. 10.3a the Tweakathon performances on the final test set vs. those on the validation set, which reveals no significant overfitting to the validation set, except for a few outliers. In Fig. 10.3b we report the performance in AutoML result (blind testing) vs. Tweakathon final test results (manual adjustments possible). We see that many entries were made in phase 1 (binary classification) and then participation declined as the tasks became harder. Some participants put a lot of effort in Tweakathons and far exceeded their AutoML performances (e.g. Djajetic and AAD Freiburg).

There is still room for improvement by manual tweaking and/or additional computational resources, as revealed by the significant differences remaining between Tweakathon and AutoML (blind testing) results (Table 10.5 and Fig. 10.3b). In

Table 10.5 Results of the 2015/2016 challenge winners. $< R >$ is the average rank over all five data sets of the round and it was used to rank the participants. $< S >$ is the average score over the five data sets of the round. UP is the percent increase in performance between the average performance of the winners in the AutoML phase and the Final phase of the same round. The GPU track was run in round 4. Team names are abbreviated as follows: *aad* aad_freiburg, *djaj* djajetic, *marc* marc.boulle, *tadej* tadejs, *abhi* abhishek4, *ideal* ideal.intel.analytics, *mat* matthias.vonrohr, *lisheng* lise_sun, *asml* amsl.intel.com, *jlr44* backstreet.bayes, *post* postech.mlg_exbrain, *ref* reference

	AutoML				Final				
Rnd	Ended	Winners	$< R >$	$< S >$	Ended	Winners	$< R >$	$< S >$	UP (%)
0	NA	NA	NA	NA	02/14/15	1. ideal	1.40	0.8159	NA
						2. abhi	3.60	0.7764	
						3. aad	4.00	0.7714	
1	02/15/15	1. aad	2.80	0.6401	06/14/15	1. aad	2.20	0.7479	15
		2. jrl44	3.80	0.6226		2. ideal	3.20	0.7324	
		3. tadej	4.20	0.6456		3. amsl	4.60	0.7158	
2	06/15/15	1. jrl44	1.80	0.4320	11/14/15	1. ideal	2.00	0.5180	35
		2. aad	3.40	0.3529		2. djaj	2.20	0.5142	
		3. mat	4.40	0.3449		3. aad	3.20	0.4977	
3	11/15/15	1. djaj	2.40	0.0901	02/19/16	1. aad	1.80	0.8071	481
		2. NA	NA	NA		2. djaj	2.00	0.7912	
		3. NA	NA	NA		3. ideal	3.80	0.7547	
4	02/20/16	1. aad	2.20	0.3881	05/1/16	1. aad	1.60	0.5238	31
		2. djaj	2.20	0.3841		2. ideal	3.60	0.4998	
		3. marc	2.60	0.3815		3. abhi	5.40	0.4911	
GPU	NA	NA	NA	NA	05/1/16	1. abhi	5.60	0.4913	NA
						2. djaj	6.20	0.4900	
						3. aad	6.20	0.4884	
5	05/1/16	1. aad	1.60	0.5282	NA	NA	NA	NA	NA
		2. djaj	2.60	0.5379					
		3. post	4.60	0.4150					

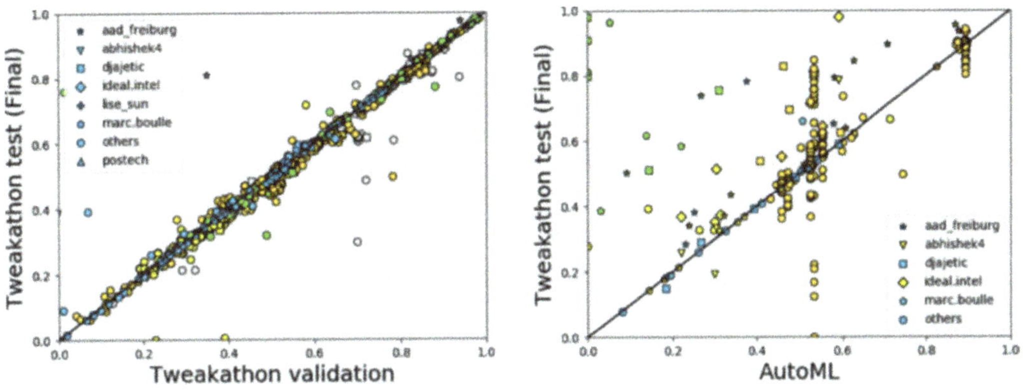

(a) Leaderboard overfitting? (b) Gap AutoML/Tweakathon?

Fig. 10.3 Performances of all participants in the 2015/2016 challenge. We show the last entry of all participants in all phases of the 2015/2016 challenge on all datasets from the competition leaderboards. The symbols are color coded by round, as in Table 10.5. (**a**) **Overfitting in Tweakathons?** We plot the performance on the final test set vs. the performance on the validation set. The validation performances were visible to the participants on the leaderboard while they were tuning their models. The final test set performances were only revealed at the end of the Tweakathon. Except for a few outliers, most participants did not overfit the leaderboard. (**b**) **Gap between AutoML and Tweakathons?** We plot the Tweakathons vs. AutoML performance to visualize improvements obtained by manual tweaking and additional computational resources available in Tweakathons. Points above the diagonal indicate such improvements

Round 3, all but one participant failed to turn in working solutions during blind testing, because of the introduction of sparse datasets. Fortunately, the participants recovered, and, by the end of the challenge, several submissions were capable of returning solutions on all the datasets of the challenge. But learning schemas can still be optimized because, even discarding Round 3, there is a 15–35% performance gap between AutoML phases (blind testing with computational constraints) and Tweakathon phases (human intervention and additional compute power). The GPU track offered (in round 4 only) a platform for trying Deep Learning methods. This allowed the participants to demonstrate that, given additional compute power, deep learning methods were competitive with the best solutions of the CPU track. However, no Deep Learning method was competitive with the limited compute power and time budget offered in the CPU track.

10.5.2 Scores Obtained in the 2018 Challenge

The 2018 challenge lasted 4 months (November 30, 2017 to March 31, 2018). As in the previous challenge, top-ranked solutions were obtained and open sourced. Table 10.6 shows the results of both phases of the 2018 challenge. As a reminder, this challenge had a feedback phase and a blind test phase, the performances of the winners in each phase are reported.

Performance in this challenge was slightly lower than that observed in the previous edition. This was due to the difficulty of the tasks (see below) and the fact that data sets in the feedback phase included three deceiving datasets (associated to tasks from previous challenges, but not necessarily similar to the data sets used in the blind test phase) out of five. We decided to proceed this way to emulate a realistic AutoML setting. Although harder, several teams succeeded at returning submissions performing better than chance.

The winner of the challenge was the same team that won the 2015/2016 AutoML challenge: AAD Freiburg [28]. The 2018 challenge helped to incrementally improve the solution devised by this team in the previous challenge. Interestingly, the second-placed team in the challenge proposed a solution that is similar in spirit to that of the winning team. For this challenge, there was a triple tie in the third place, prizes

Table 10.6 Results of the 2018 challenge winners. Each phase was run on five different datasets. We show the winners of the AutoML (blind test) phase and for comparison their performances in the Feedback phase. The full tables can be found at https://competitions.codalab.org/competitions/17767

2. AutoML phase				1. Feedback phase			
Ended	Winners	$<R>$	$<S>$	Ended	Performance	$<R>$	$<S>$
03/31/18	1. aad_freiburg	2.80	0.4341	03/12/18	aad_freiburg	9.0	0.7422
	2. narnars0	3.80	0.4180		narnars0	4.40	0.7324
	3. wlWangl	5.40	0.3857		wlWangl	4.40	0.8029
	3. thanhdng	5.40	0.3874		thanhdng	14.0	0.6845
	3. Malik	5.40	0.3863		Malik	13.8	0.7116

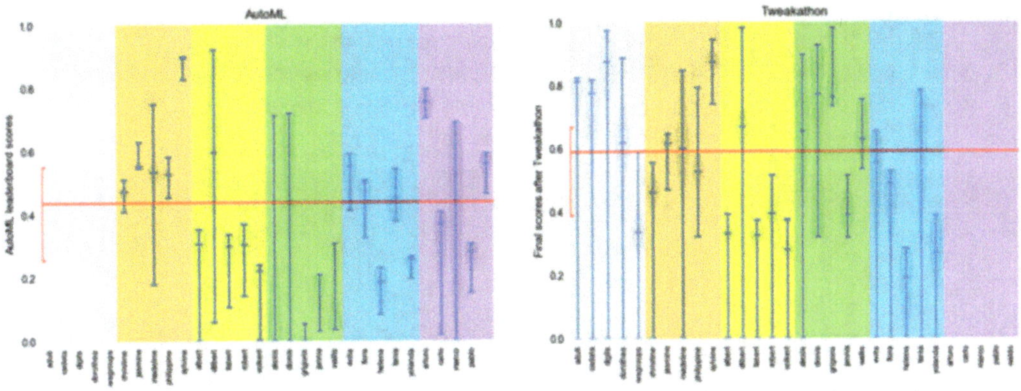

(a) AutoML (test set) (b) Tweakathon (test set)

Fig. 10.4 Distribution of performance on the datasets of the 2015/2016 challenge (violin plots). We show for each dataset the performances of participants at the end of AutoML and Tweakathon phases, as revealed on the leaderboard. The median and quartiles are represented by horizontal notches. The distribution profile (as fitted with a kernel method) and its mirror image are represented vertically by the gray shaded area. We show in red the median performance over all datasets and the corresponding quartiles. (**a**) **AutoML (blind testing).** The first 5 datasets were provided for development purpose only and were not used for blind testing in an AutoML phase. In round 3, the code of many participants failed because of computational limits. (**b**) **Tweakathon (manual tweaking).** The last five datasets were only used for final blind testing and the data were never revealed for a Tweakathon. Round 3 was not particularly difficult with additional compute power and memory

were split among the tied teams. Among the winners, two teams used the starting kit. Most of the other teams used either the starting kit or the solution open sourced by the AAD Freiburg team in the 2015/2016 challenge.

10.5.3 Difficulty of Datasets/Tasks

In this section, we assess dataset difficulty, or rather *task difficulty* since the participants had to solve prediction problems for given datasets, performance metrics, and computational time constraints. The tasks of the challenge presented a variety of difficulties, but those were not equally represented (Tables 10.2 and 10.3):

- **Categorical variables and missing data.** Few datasets had categorical variables in the 2015/2016 challenge (ADULT, ALBERT, and WALDO), and not very many variables were categorical in those datasets. Likewise, very few datasets had missing values (ADULT and ALBERT) and those included only a few missing values. So neither categorical variables nor missing data presented a real difficulty in this challenge, though ALBERT turned out to be one of the most difficult datasets because it was also one of the largest ones. This situation changed drastically for the 2018 challenge where five out of the ten datasets included categorical variables (RL, PM, RI, RH and RM) and missing values

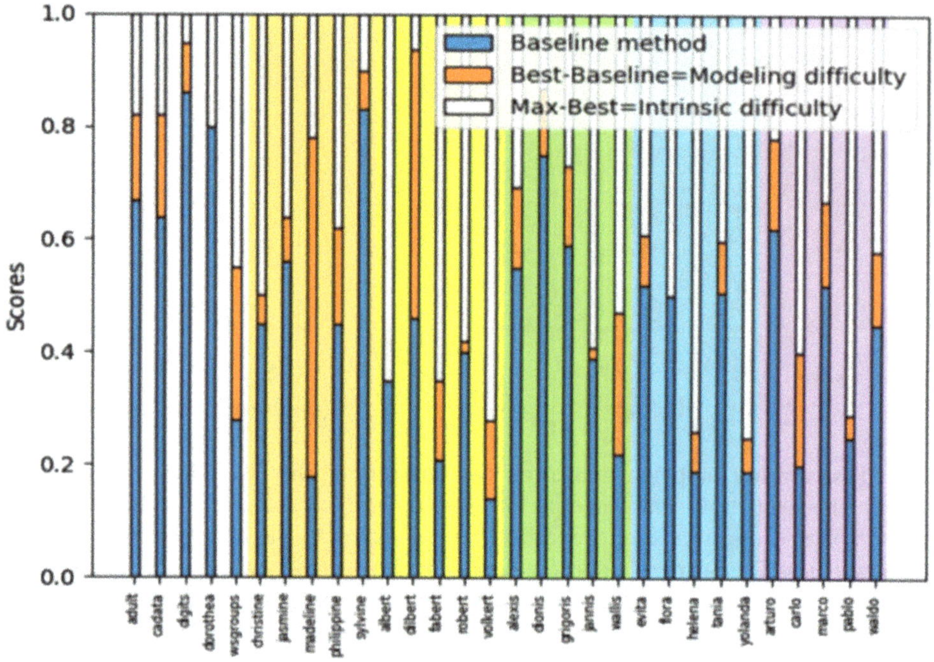

Fig. 10.5 Difficulty of tasks in the 2015/2016 challenge. We consider two indicators of task difficulty (dataset, metric, and time budget are factored into the task): intrinsic difficulty (estimated by the performance of the winners) and modeling difficulty (difference between the performance of the winner and a baseline method, here Selective Naive Bayes (SNB)). The best tasks should have a relatively low intrinsic difficulty and a high modeling difficulty to separate participants well

(GINA, PM, RL, RI and RM). These were among the main aspects that caused the low performance of most methods in the blind test phase.

- **Large number of classes.** Only one dataset had a large number of classes (DIONIS with 355 classes). This dataset turned out to be difficult for participants, particularly because it is also large and has unbalanced classes. However, datasets with large number of classes are not well represented in this challenge. HELENA, which has the second largest number of classes (100 classes), did not stand out as a particularly difficult dataset. However, in general, multi-class problems were found to be more difficult than binary classification problems.
- **Regression.** We had only four regression problems: CADATA, FLORA, YOLANDA, PABLO.
- **Sparse data.** A significant number of datasets had sparse data (DOROTHEA, FABERT, ALEXIS, WALLIS, GRIGORIS, EVITA, FLORA, TANIA, ARTURO, MARCO). Several of them turned out to be difficult, particularly ALEXIS, WALLIS, and GRIGORIS, which are large datasets in sparse format, which cause memory problems when they were introduced in round 3 of the 2015/2016 challenge. We later increased the amount of memory on the servers and similar datasets introduced in later phases caused less difficulty.
- **Large datasets.** We expected the ratio of the number N of features over the number P_{tr} of training examples to be a particular difficulty (because of the risk

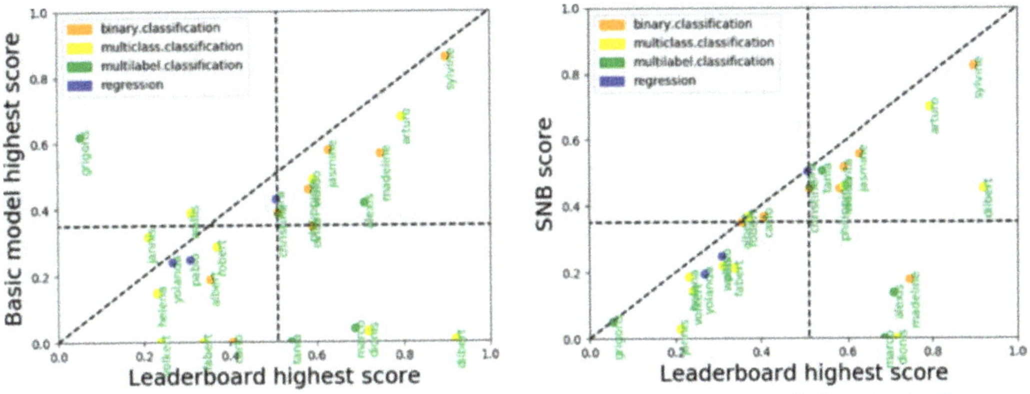

(a) Leaderboard overfitting? (b) Gap AutoML/Tweakathon?

Fig. 10.6 Modeling Difficulty vs. intrinsic difficulty. For the AutoML phases of the 2015/2016 challenge, we plot an indicator of modeling difficulty vs. and indicator of intrinsic difficulty of datasets (leaderboard highest score). (**a**) Modeling difficulty is estimated by the score of the best untuned model (over KNN, NaiveBayes, RandomForest and SGD (LINEAR)). (**b**) Modeling difficulty is estimated by the score of the Selective Naive Bayes (SNB) model. In all cases, higher scores are better and negative/NaN scores are replaced by zero. The horizontal and vertical separation lines represent the medians. The lower right quadrant represents the datasets with low intrinsic difficulty and high modeling difficulty: those are the best datasets for benchmarking purposes

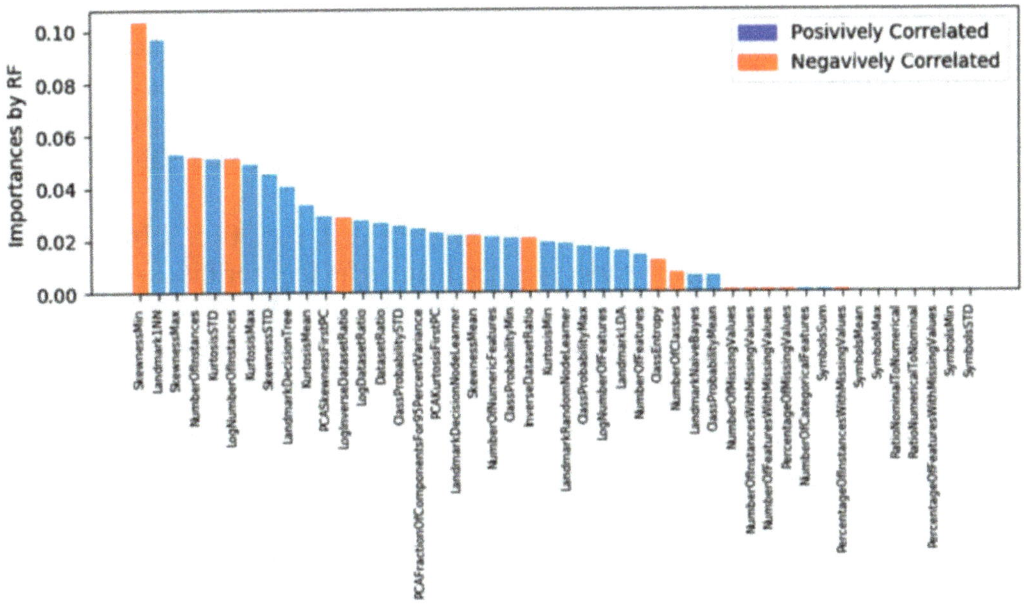

Fig. 10.7 Meta-features most predictive of dataset intrinsic difficulty (2015/2016 challenge data). Meta-feature GINI importances are computed by a random forest regressor, trained to predict the highest participant leaderboard score using meta-features of datasets. Description of these meta-features can be found in Table 1 of the supplementary material of [25]. Blue and red colors respectively correspond to positive and negative correlations (Pearson correlations between meta features and score medians)

of overfitting), but modern machine learning algorithm are robust against overfitting. The main difficulty was rather the PRODUCT $N * P_{tr}$. Most participants attempted to load the entire dataset in memory and convert sparse matrices into full matrices. This took very long and then caused loss in performances or program failures. Large datasets with $N * P_{tr} > 20.10^6$ include ALBERT, **ALEXIS**, DIONIS, **GRIGORIS, WALLIS, EVITA, FLORA, TANIA, MARCO**, GINA, GUILLERMO, PM, RH, RI, RICCARDO, RM. Those overlap significantly with the datasets with sparse data (in bold). For the 2018 challenge, all data sets in the final phase exceeded this threshold, and this was the reason of why the code from several teams failed to finish within the time budget. Only ALBERT and DIONIS were "truly" large (few features, but over 400,000 training examples).

- **Presence of probes:** Some datasets had a certain proportion of distractor features or irrelevant variables (probes). Those were obtained by randomly permuting the values of real features. Two-third of the datasets contained probes ADULT, CADATA, DIGITS, DOROTHEA, CHRISTINE, JASMINE, MADELINE, PHILIPPINE, SYLVINE, ALBERT, DILBERT, FABERT, JANNIS, EVITA, FLORA, YOLANDA, ARTURO, CARLO, PABLO, WALDO. This allowed us in part to make datasets that were in the public domain less recognizable.
- **Type of metric:** We used six metrics, as defined in Sect. 10.4.2. The distribution of tasks in which they were used was not uniform: BAC (11), AUC (6), F1 (3), and PAC (6) for classification, and R2 (2) and ABS (2) for regression. This is because not all metrics lend themselves naturally to all types of applications.
- **Time budget:** Although in round 0 we experimented with giving different time budgets for the various datasets, we ended up assigning 1200 s (20 min) to all datasets in all other rounds. Because the datasets varied in size, this put more constraints on large datasets.
- **Class imbalance:** This was not a difficulty found in the 2015/2016 datasets. However, extreme class imbalance was the main difficulty for the 2018 edition. Imbalance ratios lower or equal to 1–10 were present in RL, PM, RH, RI, and **RM** datasets, in the latter data set class imbalance was as extreme as 1–1000. This was the reason why the performance of teams was low.

Fig. 10.4 gives a first view of dataset/task difficulty for the 2015/2016 challenge. It captures, in a schematic way, the distribution of the participants' performance in all rounds on test data, in both AutoML and Tweakathon phases. One can see that the median performance over all datasets improves between AutoML and Tweakathon, as can be expected. Correspondingly, the average spread in performance (quartile) decreases. Let us take a closer look at the AutoML phases: The "accident" of round 3 in which many methods failed in blind testing is visible (introduction of sparse matrices and larger datasets).[9] Round 2 (multi-class classification) appears to have also introduced a significantly higher degree of difficulty than round 1 (binary

[9]Examples of sparse datasets were provided in round 0, but they were of smaller size.

classification). In round 4, two regression problems were introduced (FLORA and YOLANDA), but it does not seem that regression was found significantly harder than multiclass classification. In round 5 no novelty was introduced. We can observe that, after round 3, the dataset median scores are scattered around the overall median. Looking at the corresponding scores in the Tweakathon phases, one can remark that, once the participants recovered from their surprise, round 3 was not particularly difficult for them. Rounds 2 and 4 were comparatively more difficult.

For the datasets used in the 2018 challenge, the tasks' difficulty was clearly associated with extreme class imbalance, inclusion of categorical variables and high dimensionality in terms of $N \times P_{tr}$. However, for the 2015/2016 challenge data sets we found that it was generally difficult to guess what makes a task easy or hard, except for dataset size, which pushed participants to the frontier of the hardware capabilities and forced them to improve the computational efficiency of their methods. Binary classification problems (and multi-label problems) are intrinsically "easier" than multiclass problems, for which "guessing" has a lower probability of success. This partially explains the higher median performance in rounds 1 and 3, which are dominated by binary and multi-label classification problems. There is not a large enough number of datasets illustrating each type of other difficulties to draw other conclusions.

We ventured however to try to find summary statistics capturing overall takes difficulty. If one assumes that data are generated from an *i.i.d.*[10] process of the type:

$$y = F(\mathbf{x}, noise)$$

where y is the target value, $\mathbf{x}$ is the input feature vector, F is a function, and $noise$ is some random noise drawn from an unknown distribution, then the difficulty of the learning problem can be separated in two aspects:

1. **Intrinsic difficulty**, linked to the amount of noise or the signal to noise ratio. Given an infinite amount of data and an unbiased learning machine $\hat{F}$ capable of identifying F, the prediction performances cannot exceed a given maximum value, corresponding to $\hat{F} = F$.
2. **Modeling difficulty**, linked to the bias and variance of estimators $\hat{F}$, in connection with the limited amount of training data and limited computational resources, and the possibly large number or parameters and hyper-parameters to estimate.

Evaluating the intrinsic difficulty is impossible unless we know F. Our best approximation of F is the winners' solution. **We use therefore the winners' performance as an estimator of the best achievable performance.** This estimator may have both bias and variance: it is possibly biased because the winners may be under-fitting training data; it may have variance because of the limited amount of

[10] Independently and Identically Distributed samples.

test data. Under-fitting is difficult to test. Its symptoms may be that the variance or the entropy of the predictions is less than those of the target values.

Evaluating the modeling difficulty is also impossible unless we know F and the model class. In the absence of knowledge on the model class, data scientists often use generic predictive models, agnostic with respect to the data generating process. Such models range from very basic models that are highly biased towards "simplicity" and smoothness of predictions (e.g., regularized linear models) to highly versatile unbiased models that can learn any function given enough data (e.g., ensembles of decision trees). To indirectly assess modeling difficulty, we resorted to use the difference in performance between *the method of the challenge winner* and that of (a) the best of four "untuned" basic models (taken from classical techniques provided in the scikit-learn library [55] with default hyper-parameters) or (b) Selective Naive Bayes (SNB) [12, 13], a highly regularized model (biased towards simplicity), providing a very robust and simple baseline.

Figs. 10.5 and 10.6 give representations of our estimates of intrinsic and modeling difficulties for the 2015/2016 challenge datasets. It can be seen that the datasets of round 0 were among the easiest (except perhaps NEWSGROUP). Those were relatively small (and well-known) datasets. Surprisingly, the datasets of round 3 were also rather easy, despite the fact that most participants failed on them when they were introduced (largely because of memory limitations: scikit-learn algorithms were not optimized for sparse datasets and it was not possible to fit in memory the data matrix converted to a dense matrix). Two datasets have a small intrinsic difficulty but a large modeling difficulty: MADELINE and DILBERT. MADELINE is an artificial dataset that is very non-linear (clusters or 2 classes positioned on the vertices of a hyper-cube in a 5 dimensional space) and therefore very difficult for Naïve Bayes. DILBERT is an image recognition dataset with images of objects rotated in all sorts of positions, also very difficult for Naïve Bayes. The datasets of the last 2 phases seem to have a large intrinsic difficulty compared to the modeling difficulty. But this can be deceiving because the datasets are new to the machine learning community and the performances of the winners may still be far from the best attainable performance.

We attempted to predict the intrinsic difficulty (as measured by the winners' performance) from the set of meta features used by AAD Freiburg for meta-learning [25], which are part of OpenML [67], using a Random Forest classifier and ranked the meta features in order of importance (most selected by RF). The list of meta features is provided in the online appendix. The three meta-features that predict dataset difficulty best (Fig. 10.7) are:

- LandmarkDecisionTree: performance of a decision tree classifier.
- Landmark1NN: performance of a nearest neighbor classifier.
- SkewnessMin: min over skewness of all features. Skewness measures the symmetry of a distribution. A positive skewness value means that there is more weight in the left tail of the distribution.

10.5.4 Hyper-parameter Optimization

Many participants used the scikit-learn (sklearn) package, including the winning group AAD Freiburg, which produced the auto-sklearn software. We used the auto-sklearn API to conduct post-challenge systematic studies of the effectiveness of hyper-parameter optimization. We compared the performances obtained with default hyper-parameter settings in scikit-learn and with hyper-parameters optimized with auto-sklearn,[11] both within the time budgets as imposed during the challenge, for four "representative" basic methods: k-nearest neighbors (KNN), naive Bayes (NB), Random Forest (RF), and a linear model trained with stochastic gradient descent (SGD-linear[12]). The results are shown in Fig. 10.8. We see that hyper-parameter optimization usually improves performance, but not always. The advantage of hyper-parameter tuning comes mostly from its flexibility of switching the optimization metric to the one imposed by the task and from finding hyper-parameters that work well given the current dataset and metric. However, in some cases it was not possible to perform hyper-parameter optimization within the time budget due to the data set size (score ≤ 0). Thus, there remains future work on how

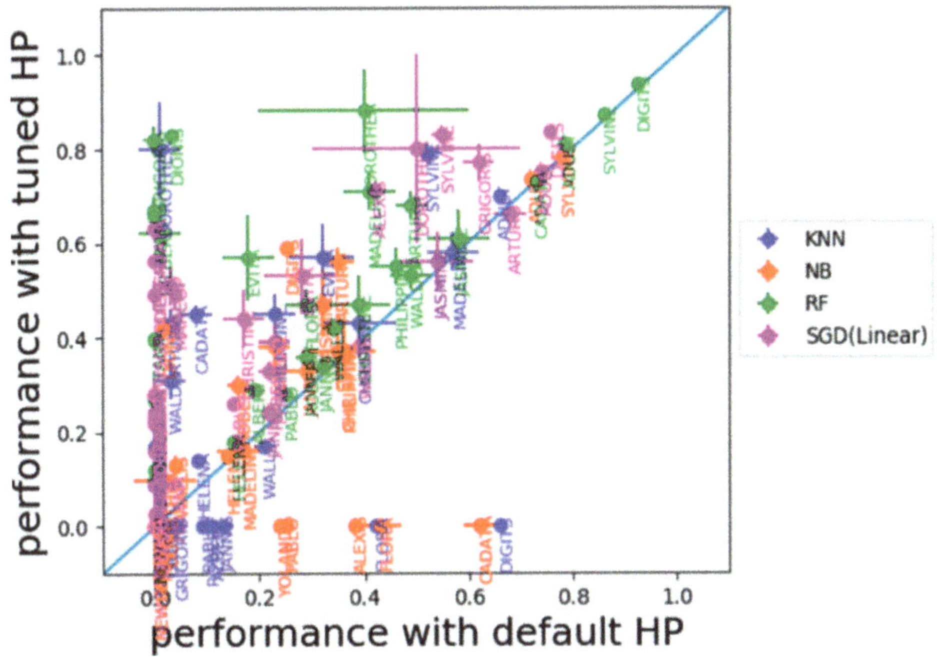

Fig. 10.8 Hyper-parameter tuning (2015/2016 challenge data). We compare the performances obtained with default hyper-parameters and those with hyper-parameters optimized with auto-sklearn, within the same time budgets as given during the challenge. The performances of predictors which failed to return results in the allotted time are replaced by zero. Note that returning a prediction of chance level also resulted in a score of zero

[11]We use sklearn 0.16.1 and auto-sklearn 0.4.0 to mimic the challenge environment.

[12]We set the loss of SGD to be 'log' in scikit-learn for these experiments.

to perform thorough hyper-parameter tuning given rigid time constraints and huge datasets (Fig. 10.8).

We also compared the performances obtained with different scoring metrics (Fig. 10.9). Basic methods do not give a choice of metrics to be optimized, but auto-sklearn post-fitted the metrics of the challenge tasks. Consequently, when "common metrics" (BAC and R^2) are used, the method of the challenge winners, which is not optimized for BAC/R^2, does not usually outperform basic methods. Conversely, when the metrics of the challenge are used, there is often a clear gap between the basic methods and the winners, but not always (RF-auto usually shows a comparable performance, sometimes even outperforms the winners).

10.5.5 Meta-learning

One question is whether meta-learning [14] is possible, that is learning to predict whether a given classifier will perform well on future datasets (without actually training it), based on its past performances on other datasets. We investigated whether it is possible to predict which basic method will perform best based on the meta-learning features of auto-sklearn (see the online appendix). We removed the "Landmark" features from the set of meta features because those are performances of basic predictors (albeit rather poor ones with many missing values), which would lead to a form of "data leakage".

We used four basic predictors:

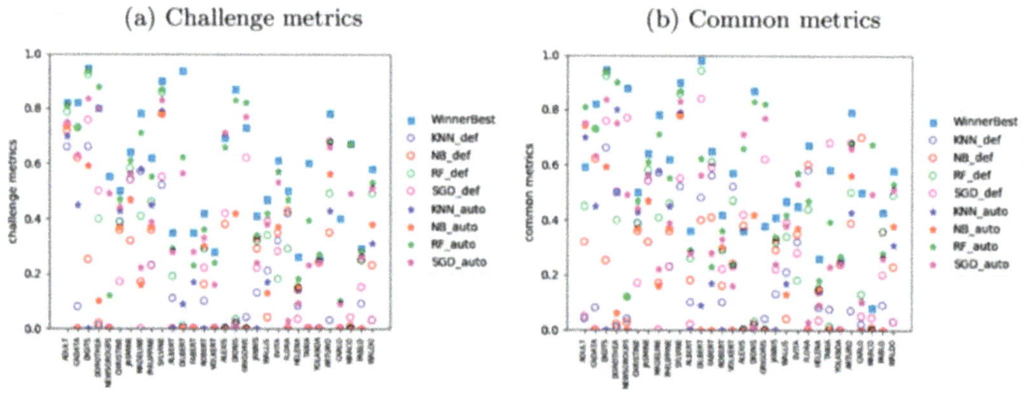

Fig. 10.9 Comparison of metrics (2015/2016 challenge). (**a**) We used the metrics of the challenge. (**b**) We used the normalized balanced accuracy for all classification problems and the R^2 metric for regression problems. By comparing the two figures, we can see that the winner remains top-ranking in most cases, regardless of the metric. There is no basic method that dominates all others. Although RF-auto (Random Forest with optimized HP) is very strong, it is sometimes outperformed by other methods. Plain linear model SGD-def sometimes wins when common metrics are used, but the winners perform better with the metrics of the challenge. Overall, the technique of the winners proved to be effective

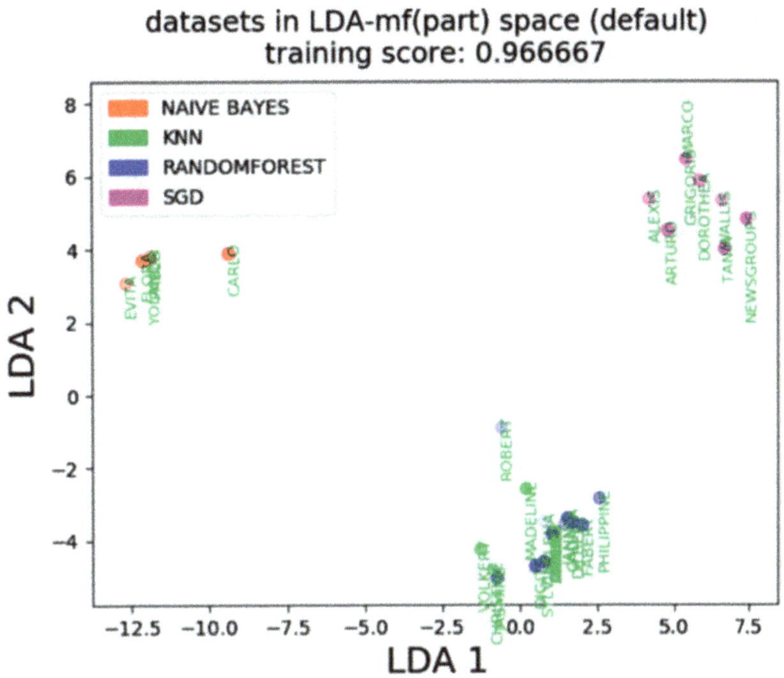

(a)

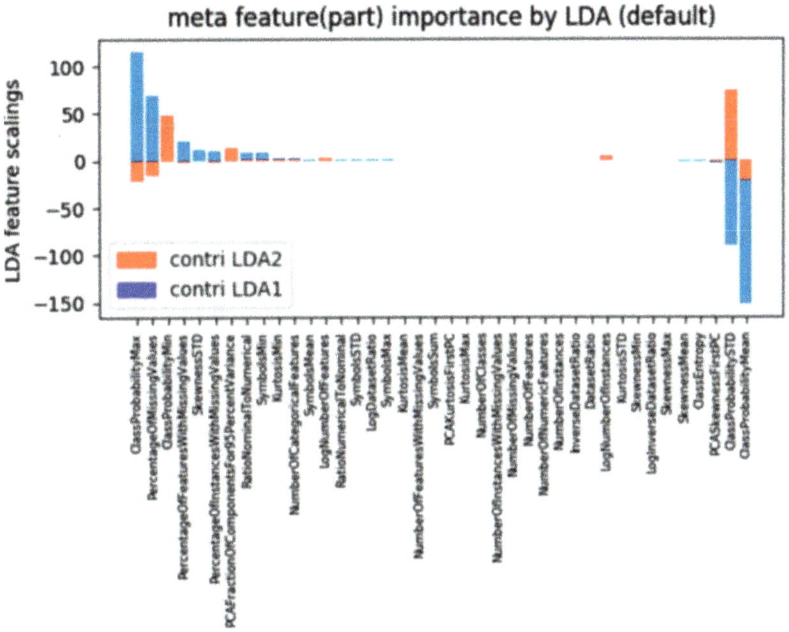

(b)

Fig. 10.10 Linear discriminant analysis. (**a**) **Dataset scatter plot in principal axes**. We have trained a LDA using X = meta features, except landmarks; y = which model won of four basic models (NB, SGD-linear, KNN, RF). The performance of the basic models is measured using the common metrics. The models were trained with default hyper-parameters. In the space of the two first LDA components, each point represents one dataset. The colors denote the winning basic models. The opacity reflects the scores of the corresponding winning model (more opaque is better). (**b**) **Meta feature importances** computed as scaling factors of each LDA component

- NB: Naive Bayes
- SGD-linear: Linear model (trained with stochastic gradient descent)
- KNN: K-nearest neighbors
- RF: Random Forest

We used the implementation of the scikit-learn library with default hyper-parameter settings. In Fig. 10.10, we show the two first Linear Discriminant Analysis (LDA) components, when training an LDA classifier on the meta-features to predict which basic classifier will perform best. The methods separate into three distinct clusters, one of them grouping the non-linear methods that are poorly separated (KNN and RF) and the two others being NB and linear-SGD.

The features that are most predictive all have to do with "ClassProbability" and "PercentageOfMissingValues", indicating that the class imbalance and/or large number of classes (in a multi-class problem) and the percentage of missing values might be important, but there is a high chance of overfitting as indicated by an unstable ranking of the best features under resampling of the training data.

10.5.6 Methods Used in the Challenges

A brief **description of methods** used in both challenges is provided in the online appendix, together with the results of a survey on methods that we conducted after the challenges. In light of the overview of Sect. 10.2 and the results presented in the previous section, we may wonder whether a dominant methodology for solving the AutoML problem has emerged and whether particular technical solutions were widely adopted. In this section we call "model space" the set of all models under consideration. We call "basic models" (also called elsewhere "simple models", "individual models", "base learners") the member of a library of models from which our hyper-models of model ensembles are built.

Ensembling: dealing with over-fitting and any-time learning Ensembling is the big AutoML challenge series winner since it is used by over 80% of the participants and by all the top-ranking ones. While a few years ago the hottest issue in model selection and hyper-parameter optimization was over-fitting, in present days the problem seems to have been largely avoided by using ensembling techniques. In the 2015/2016 challenge, we varied the ratio of number of training examples over number of variables (Ptr/N) by several orders of magnitude. Five datasets had a ratio Ptr/N lower than one (dorothea, newsgroup, grigoris, wallis, and flora), which is a case lending itself particularly to over-fitting. Although Ptr/N is the most predictive variable of the median performance of the participants, there is no indication that the datasets with $Ptr/N < 1$ were particularly difficult for the participants (Fig. 10.5). Ensembles of predictors have the additional benefit of addressing in a simple way the "any-time learning" problem by growing progressively a bigger ensemble of predictors, improving performance over time. All trained predictors are usually incorporated in the ensemble. For instance, if cross-validation is used, the predictors of all folds are directly incorporated in the ensemble, which saves the computational time of retraining a single model on the best HP selected and may yield more robust solutions (though slightly more biased due to the smaller sample size). The approaches differ in the way they weigh the contributions of the various predictors. Some methods use the same weight for all predictors (this is the case of bagging methods such as Random Forest and of Bayesian methods that sample predictors according to their posterior probability in model space). Some methods assess the weights of the predictors as part of learning (this is the case of boosting methods, for instance). One simple and effective method to create ensembles of heterogeneous models was proposed by [16]. It was used successfully in several past challenges, e.g., [52] and is the method implemented by the *aad_freibug* team, one of the strongest participants in both challenges [25]. The method consists in cycling several times over all trained model and incorporating in the ensemble at each cycle the model which most improves the performance of the ensemble. Models vote with weight 1, but they can be incorporated multiple times, which de facto results in weighting them. This method permits to recompute very fast the weights of the models if cross-validated predictions are saved. Moreover, the method allows optimizing the ensemble for any metric by post-fitting the predictions of the ensemble to the desired metric (an aspect which was important in this challenge).

Model evaluation: cross-validation or simple validation Evaluating the predictive accuracy of models is a critical and necessary building block of any model selection of ensembling method. Model selection criteria computed from the predictive accuracy of basic models evaluated from training data, by training a single time on all the training data (possibly at the expense of minor additional calculations), such as performance bounds, were not used at all, as was already the case in previous challenges we organized [35]. Cross-validation was widely used, particularly K-fold cross-validation. However, basic models were often "cheaply" evaluated on just one fold to allow quickly discarding non-promising areas of model space. This is a technique used more and more frequently to help speed up search. Another speed-up strategy is to train on a subset of the training examples and monitor the learning curve. The "freeze-thaw" strategy [64] halts training of models that do not look promising on the basis of the learning curve, but may restart training them at a later point. This was used, e.g., by [48] in the 2015/2016 challenge.

Model space: Homogeneous vs. heterogeneous An unsettled question is whether one should search a large or small model space. The challenge did not allow us to give a definite answer to this question. Most participants opted for searching a relatively large model space, including a wide variety of models found in the scikit-learn library. Yet, one of the strongest entrants (the Intel team) submitted results simply obtained with a boosted decision tree (i.e., consisting of a homogeneous set of weak learners/basic models). Clearly, it suffices to use just one machine learning approach that is a universal approximator to be able to learn anything, given enough training data. So why include several? It is a question of rate of convergence: how fast we climb the learning curve. Including stronger basic models is one way to climb the learning curve faster. Our post-challenge experiments (Fig. 10.9) reveal that the scikit-learn version of Random Forest (an ensemble of homogeneous basic models—decision trees) does not usually perform as well as the winners' version, hinting that there is a lot of know-how in the Intel solution, which is also based on ensembles of decision tree, that is not captured by a basic ensemble of decision trees such as RF. We hope that more principled research will be conducted on this topic in the future.

Search strategies: Filter, wrapper, and embedded methods With the availability of powerful machine learning toolkits like scikit-learn (on which the starting kit was based), the temptation is great to implement **all-wrapper methods** to solve the CASH (or "full model selection") problem. Indeed, most participants went that route. Although a number of ways of optimizing hyper-parameters with **embedded methods** for several basic classifiers have been published [35], they each require changing the implementation of the basic methods, which is time-consuming and error-prone compared to using already debugged and well-optimized library version of the methods. Hence practitioners are reluctant to invest development time in the implementation of embedded methods. A notable exception is the software of *marc.boulle*, which offers a self-contained hyper-parameter free solution based on Naive Bayes, which includes re-coding of variables (grouping or discretization) and variable selection. See the online appendix.

Multi-level optimization Another interesting issue is whether multiple levels of hyper-parameters should be considered for reasons of computational effectiveness or overfitting avoidance. In the Bayesian setting, for instance, it is quite feasible to consider a hierarchy of parameters/hyper-parameters and several levels of priors/hyper-priors. However, it seems that for practical computational reasons, in the AutoML challenges, the participants use a shallow organization of hyper-parameter space and avoid nested cross-validation loops.

Time management: Exploration vs. exploitation tradeoff With a tight time budget, efficient search strategies must be put into place to monitor the exploration/exploitation tradeoff. To compare strategies, we show in the online appendix learning curves for two top ranking participants who adopted very different methods: *Abhishek* and *aad_freiburg*. The former uses heuristic methods based on prior human experience while the latter initializes search with models predicted to be best suited by meta-learning, then performs Bayesian optimization of hyper-parameters. *Abhishek* seems to often start with a better solution but explores less effectively. In contrast, *aad_freiburg* starts lower but often ends up with a better solution. Some elements of randomness in the search are useful to arrive at better solutions.

Preprocessing and feature selection The datasets had intrinsic difficulties that could be in part addressed by preprocessing or special modifications of algorithms: sparsity, missing values, categorical variables, and irrelevant variables. Yet it appears that among the top-ranking participants, preprocessing has not been a focus of attention. They relied on the simple heuristics provided in the starting kit: replacing missing values by the median and adding a missingness indicator variable, one-hot-encoding of categorical variables. Simple normalizations were used. The irrelevant variables were ignored by 2/3 of the participants and no use of feature selection was made by top-ranking participants. The methods used that involve ensembling seem to be intrinsically robust against irrelevant variables. More details from the fact sheets are found in the online appendix.

Unsupervised learning Despite the recent regain of interest in unsupervised learning spurred by the Deep Learning community, in the AutoML challenge series, unsupervised learning is not widely used, except for the use of classical space dimensionality reduction techniques such as ICA and PCA. See the online appendix for more details.

Transfer learning and meta learning To our knowledge, only *aad_freiburg* relied on meta-learning to initialize their hyper-parameter search. To that end, they used datasets of OpenML.[13] The number of datasets released and the diversity of tasks did not allow the participants to perform effective transfer learning or meta learning.

Deep learning The type of computations resources available in AutoML phases ruled out the use of Deep Learning, except in the GPU track. However, even in that track, the Deep Learning methods did not come out ahead. One exception is *aad_freiburg*, who used Deep Learning in Tweakathon rounds three and four and found it to be helpful for the datasets Alexis, Tania and Yolanda.

Task and metric optimization There were four types of tasks (regression, binary classification, multi-class classification, and multi-label classification) and six scoring metrics (R2, ABS, BAC, AUC, F1, and PAC). Moreover, class balance and number of classes varied a lot for classification problems. Moderate effort has been put into designing methods optimizing specific metrics. Rather, generic methods were used and the outputs post-fitted to the target metrics by cross-validation or through the ensembling method.

Engineering One of the big lessons of the AutoML challenge series is that most methods fail to return results in all cases, not a "good" result, but "any" reasonable result. Reasons for failure include "out of time" and "out of memory" or various other failures (e.g., numerical instabilities). We are still very far from having "basic models" that run on all datasets. One of the strengths of auto-sklearn is to ignore those models that fail and generally find at least one that returns a result.

Parallelism The computers made available had several cores, so in principle, the participants could make use of parallelism. One common strategy was just to rely on numerical libraries that internally use such parallelism automatically. The *aad_freiburg* team used the different cores to launch in parallel model search for different datasets (since each round included five datasets). These different uses of computational resources are visible in the learning curves (see the online appendix).

[13] https://www.openml.org/

10.6 Discussion

We briefly summarize the main questions we asked ourselves and the main findings:

1. **Was the provided time budget sufficient to complete the tasks of the challenge?** We drew learning curves as a function of time for the winning solution of *aad_freiburg* (auto-sklearn, see the online appendix). This revealed that for most datasets, performances still improved well beyond the time limit imposed by the organizers. Although for about half the datasets the improvement is modest (no more that 20% of the score obtained at the end of the imposed time limit), for some datasets the improvement was very large (more than 2× the original score). The improvements are usually gradual, but sudden performance improvements occur. For instance, for Wallis, the score doubled suddenly at 3× the time limit imposed in the challenge. As also noted by the authors of the auto-sklearn package [25], it has a slow start but in the long run gets performances close to the best method.
2. **Are there tasks that were significantly more difficult than others for the participants?** Yes, there was a very wide range of difficulties for the tasks as revealed by the dispersion of the participants in terms of average (median) and variability (third quartile) of their scores. Madeline, a synthetic dataset featuring a very non-linear task, was very difficult for many participants. Other difficulties that caused failures to return a solution included large memory requirements (particularly for methods that attempted to convert sparse matrices to full matrices), and short time budgets for datasets with large number of training examples and/or features or with many classes or labels.
3. **Are there meta-features of datasets and methods providing useful insight to recommend certain methods for certain types of datasets?** The *aad_freiburg* team used a subset of 53 meta-features (a superset of the simple statistics provided with the challenge datasets) to measure similarity between datasets. This allowed them to conduct hyper-parameter search more effectively by initializing the search with settings identical to those selected for similar datasets previously processed (a form of meta-learning). Our own analysis revealed that it is very difficult to predict the predictors' performances from the meta-features, but it is possible to predict relatively accurately which "basic method" will perform best. With LDA, we could visualize how datasets recoup in two dimensions and show a clean separation between datasets "preferring" Naive Bayes, linear SGD, or KNN, or RF. This deserves further investigation.
4. **Does hyper-parameter optimization really improve performance over using default values?** The comparison we conducted reveals that optimizing hyper-parameters rather than choosing default values for a set of four basic predictive models (K-nearest neighbors, Random Forests, linear SGD, and Naive Bayes) is generally beneficial. In the majority of cases (but not always), hyper-parameter optimization (hyper-opt) results in better performances than default values.

Hyper-opt sometimes fails because of time or memory limitations, which gives room for improvement.

5. **How do winner's solutions compare with basic scikit-learn models?** They compare favorably. For example, the results of basic models whose parameters have been optimized do not yield generally as good results as running auto-sklearn. However, a basic model with default HP sometimes outperforms this same model tuned by auto-sklearn.

10.7 Conclusion

We have analyzed the results of several rounds of AutoML challenges.

Our design of the first AutoML challenge (2015/2016) was satisfactory in many respects. In particular, we attracted a large number of participants (over 600), attained results that are statistically significant, and advanced the state of the art to automate machine learning. Publicly available libraries have emerged as a result of this endeavor, including auto-sklearn.

In particular, we designed a benchmark with a large number of diverse datasets, with large enough test sets to separate top-ranking participants. It is difficult to anticipate the size of the test sets needed, because the error bars depend on the performances attained by the participants, so we are pleased that we made reasonable guesses. Our simple rule-of-thumb "N = 50/E" where N is the number of test samples and E the error rate of the smallest class seems to be widely applicable. We made sure that the datasets were neither too easy nor too hard. This is important to be able to separate participants. To quantify this, we introduced the notion of "intrinsic difficulty" and "modeling difficulty". Intrinsic difficulty can be quantified by the performance of the best method (as a surrogate for the best attainable performance, i.e., the Bayes rate for classification problems). Modeling difficulty can be quantified by the spread in performance between methods. Our best problems have relatively low "intrinsic difficulty" and high "modeling difficulty". However, the diversity of the 30 datasets of our first 2015/2016 challenge is both a feature and a curse: it allows us to test the robustness of software across a variety of situations, but it makes meta-learning very difficult, if not impossible. Consequently, external meta-learning data must be used if meta-learning is to be explored. This was the strategy adopted by the AAD Freiburg team, which used the OpenML data for meta training. Likewise, we attached different metrics to each dataset. This contributed to making the tasks more realistic and more difficult, but also made meta-learning harder. In the second 2018 challenge, we diminished the variety of datasets and used a single metric.

With respect to task design, we learned that the devil is in the details. The challenge participants solve exactly the task proposed to the point that their solution may not be adaptable to seemingly similar scenarios. In the case of the AutoML challenge, we pondered whether the metric of the challenge should be the area under the learning curve or one point on the learning curve (the performance obtained after a fixed maximum computational time elapsed). We ended up favoring the second solution for practical reasons. Examining after the challenge the learning curves of some participants, it is quite clear that the two problems are radically different, particularly with respect to strategies mitigating “exploration” and “exploitation”. This prompted us to think about the differences between “fixed time” learning (the participants know in advance the time limit and are judged only on the solution delivered at the end of that time) and “any time learning” (the participants can be stopped at any time and asked to return a solution). Both scenarios are useful: the first one is practical when models must be delivered continuously at a rapid pace, e.g. for marketing applications; the second one is practical in environments when computational resources are unreliable and interruption may be expected (e.g. people working remotely via an unreliable connection). This will influence the design of future challenges.

The two versions of AutoML challenge we have run differ in the difficulty of transfer learning. In the 2015/2016 challenge, round 0 introduced a sample of all types of data and difficulties (types of targets, sparse data or not, missing data or not, categorical variables of not, more examples than features or not). Then each round ramped up difficulty. The datasets of round 0 were relatively easy. Then at each round, the code of the participants was blind-tested on data that were one notch harder than in the previous round. Hence transfer was quite hard. In the 2018 challenge, we had 2 phases, each with 5 datasets of similar difficulty and the datasets of the first phase were each matched with one corresponding dataset on a similar task. As a result, transfer was made simpler.

Concerning the starting kit and baseline methods, we provided code that ended up being the basis of the solution of the majority of participants (with notable exceptions from industry such as Intel and Orange who used their own “in house” packages). Thus, we can question whether the software provided biased the approaches taken. Indeed, all participants used some form of ensemble learning, similarly to the strategy used in the starting kit. However, it can be argued that this is a “natural” strategy for this problem. But, in general, the question of providing enough starting material to the participants without biasing the challenge in a particular direction remains a delicate issue.

From the point of view of challenge protocol design, we learned that it is difficult to keep teams focused for an extended period of time and go through many challenge phases. We attained a large number of participants (over 600) over the whole course of the AutoML challenge, which lasted over a year (2015/2016) and was punctuated by several events (such as hackathons). However, it may be preferable to organize yearly events punctuated by workshops. This is a natural way of balancing competition and cooperation since workshops are a place of exchange. Participants are naturally rewarded by the recognition they gain via the system of scientific publications. As a confirmation of this conjecture, the second instance of the AutoML challenge (2017/2018) lasting only 4 months attracted nearly 300 participants.

One important novelty of our challenge design was code submission. Having the code of the participants executed on the same platform under rigorously similar conditions is a great step towards fairness and reproducibility, as well as ensuring the viability of solution from the computational point of view. We required the winners to release their code under an open source licence to win their prizes. This was good enough an incentive to obtain several software publications as the "product" of the challenges we organized. In our second challenge (AutoML 2018), we used Docker. Distributing Docker images makes it possible for anyone downloading the code of the participants to easily reproduce the results without stumbling over installation problems due to inconsistencies in computer environments and libraries. Still the hardware may be different and we find that, in post-challenge evaluations, changing computers may yield significant differences in results. Hopefully, with the proliferation of affordable cloud computing, this will become less of an issue.

The AutoML challenge series is only beginning. Several new avenues are under study. For instance, we are preparing the NIPS 2018 Life Long Machine Learning challenge in which participants will be exposed to data whose distribution slowly drifts over time. We are also looking at a challenge of automated machine learning where we will focus on transfer from similar domains.

Acknowledgements Microsoft supported the organization of this challenge and donated the prizes and cloud computing time on Azure. This project received additional support from the Laboratoire d'Informatique Fondamentale (LIF, UMR CNRS 7279) of the University of Aix Marseille, France, via the LabeX Archimede program, the Laboratoire de Recheche en Informatique of Paris Sud University, and INRIA-Saclay as part of the TIMCO project, as well as the support from the Paris-Saclay Center for Data Science (CDS). Additional computer resources were provided generously by J. Buhmann, ETH Zürich. This work has been partially supported by the Spanish project TIN2016-74946-P (MINECO/FEDER, UE) and CERCA Programme/Generalitat de Catalunya. The datasets released were selected among 72 datasets that were donated (or formatted using data publicly available) by the co-authors and by: Y. Aphinyanaphongs, O. Chapelle, Z. Iftikhar Malhi, V. Lemaire, C.-J. Lin, M. Madani, G. Stolovitzky, H.-J. Thiesen, and I. Tsamardinos. Many people provided feedback to early designs of the protocol and/or tested the challenge platform, including: K. Bennett, C. Capponi, G. Cawley, R. Caruana, G. Dror, T. K. Ho, B. Kégl, H. Larochelle, V. Lemaire, C.-J. Lin, V. Ponce López, N. Macia, S. Mercer, F. Popescu, D. Silver, S. Treguer, and I. Tsamardinos. The software developers who contributed to the implementation of the Codalab platform and the sample code include E. Camichael, I. Chaabane, I. Judson, C. Poulain, P. Liang, A. Pesah, L. Romaszko, X. Baro Solé, E. Watson, F. Zhingri, M. Zyskowski. Some initial analyses of the challenge results were performed by I. Chaabane, J. Lloyd, N. Macia, and A. Thakur were incorporated in this paper. Katharina Eggensperger, Syed Mohsin Ali and Matthias Feurer helped with the organization of the Beat AutoSKLearn challenge. Matthias Feurer also contributed to the simulations of running auto-sklearn on 2015–2016 challenge datasets.

Bibliography

1. Alamdari, A.R.S.A., Guyon, I.: Quick start guide for CLOP. Tech. rep., Graz University of Technology and Clopinet (May 2006)
2. Andrieu, C., Freitas, N.D., Doucet, A.: Sequential MCMC for Bayesian model selection. In: IEEE Signal Processing Workshop on Higher-Order Statistics. pp. 130–134 (1999)
3. Assunção, F., Lourenço, N., Machado, P., Ribeiro, B.: Denser: Deep evolutionary network structured representation. arXiv preprint arXiv:1801.01563 (2018)

4. Baker, B., Gupta, O., Naik, N., Raskar, R.: Designing neural network architectures using reinforcement learning. arXiv preprint arXiv:1611.02167 (2016)
5. Bardenet, R., Brendel, M., Kégl, B., Sebag, M.: Collaborative hyperparameter tuning. In: 30th International Conference on Machine Learning. vol. 28, pp. 199–207. JMLR Workshop and Conference Proceedings (May 2013)
6. Bengio, Y., Courville, A., Vincent, P.: Representation learning: A review and new perspectives. IEEE Transactions on Pattern Analysis and Machine Intelligence 35(8), 1798–1828 (2013)
7. Bennett, K.P., Kunapuli, G., Jing Hu, J.S.P.: Bilevel optimization and machine learning. In: Computational Intelligence: Research Frontiers, Lecture Notes in Computer Science, vol. 5050, pp. 25–47. Springer (2008)
8. Bergstra, J., Bengio, Y.: Random search for hyper-parameter optimization. Journal of Machine Learning Research 13(Feb), 281–305 (2012)
9. Bergstra, J., Yamins, D., Cox, D.D.: Making a science of model search: Hyperparameter optimization in hundreds of dimensions for vision architectures. In: 30th International Conference on Machine Learning. vol. 28, pp. 115–123 (2013)
10. Bergstra, J.S., Bardenet, R., Bengio, Y., Kégl, B.: Algorithms for hyper-parameter optimization. In: Advances in Neural Information Processing Systems. pp. 2546–2554 (2011)
11. Blum, A.L., Langley, P.: Selection of relevant features and examples in machine learning. Artificial Intelligence 97(1–2), 273–324 (December 1997)
12. Boullé, M.: Compression-based averaging of selective naive bayes classifiers. Journal of Machine Learning Research 8, 1659–1685 (2007), http://dl.acm.org/citation.cfm?id=1314554
13. Boullé, M.: A parameter-free classification method for large scale learning. Journal of Machine Learning Research 10, 1367–1385 (2009), https://doi.org/10.1145/1577069.1755829
14. Brazdil, P., Carrier, C.G., Soares, C., Vilalta, R.: Metalearning: Applications to data mining. Springer Science & Business Media (2008)
15. Breiman, L.: Random forests. Machine Learning 45(1), 5–32 (2001)
16. Caruana, R., Niculescu-Mizil, A., Crew, G., Ksikes, A.: Ensemble selection from libraries of models. In: 21st International Conference on Machine Learning. pp. 18–. ACM (2004)
17. Cawley, G.C., Talbot, N.L.C.: Preventing over-fitting during model selection via Bayesian regularisation of the hyper-parameters. Journal of Machine Learning Research 8, 841–861 (April 2007)
18. Colson, B., Marcotte, P., Savard, G.: An overview of bilevel programming. Annals of Operations Research 153, 235–256 (2007)
19. Dempe, S.: Foundations of bilevel programming. Kluwer Academic Publishers (2002)
20. Dietterich, T.G.: Approximate statistical test for comparing supervised classification learning algorithms. Neural Computation 10(7), 1895–1923 (1998)
21. Duda, R.O., Hart, P.E., Stork, D.G.: Pattern Classification. Wiley, 2nd edn. (2001)
22. Efron, B.: Estimating the error rate of a prediction rule: Improvement on cross-validation. Journal of the American Statistical Association 78(382), 316–331 (1983)
23. Eggensperger, K., Feurer, M., Hutter, F., Bergstra, J., Snoek, J., Hoos, H., Leyton-Brown, K.: Towards an empirical foundation for assessing bayesian optimization of hyperparameters. In: NIPS workshop on Bayesian Optimization in Theory and Practice (2013)
24. Escalante, H.J., Montes, M., Sucar, L.E.: Particle swarm model selection. Journal of Machine Learning Research 10, 405–440 (2009)
25. Feurer, M., Klein, A., Eggensperger, K., Springenberg, J., Blum, M., Hutter, F.: Efficient and robust automated machine learning. In: Proceedings of the Neural Information Processing Systems, pp. 2962–2970 (2015), https://github.com/automl/auto-sklearn
26. Feurer, M., Klein, A., Eggensperger, K., Springenberg, J., Blum, M., Hutter, F.: Methods for improving bayesian optimization for automl. In: Proceedings of the International Conference on Machine Learning 2015, Workshop on Automatic Machine Learning (2015)
27. Feurer, M., Springenberg, J., Hutter, F.: Initializing bayesian hyperparameter optimization via meta-learning. In: Proceedings of the AAAI Conference on Artificial Intelligence. pp. 1128–1135 (2015)

28. Feurer, M., Eggensperger, K., Falkner, S., Lindauer, M., Hutter, F.: Practical automated machine learning for the automl challenge 2018. In: International Workshop on Automatic Machine Learning at ICML (2018), https://sites.google.com/site/automl2018icml/
29. Friedman, J.H.: Greedy function approximation: A gradient boosting machine. The Annals of Statistics 29(5), 1189–1232 (2001)
30. Ghahramani, Z.: Unsupervised learning. In: Advanced Lectures on Machine Learning. Lecture Notes in Computer Science, vol. 3176, pp. 72–112. Springer Berlin Heidelberg (2004)
31. Guyon, I.: Challenges in Machine Learning book series. Microtome (2011–2016), http://www.mtome.com/Publications/CiML/ciml.html
32. Guyon, I., Bennett, K., Cawley, G., Escalante, H.J., Escalera, S., Ho, T.K., Macià, N., Ray, B., Saeed, M., Statnikov, A., Viegas, E.: AutoML challenge 2015: Design and first results. In: Proc. of AutoML 2015@ICML (2015), https://drive.google.com/file/d/0BzRGLkqgrI-qWkpzcGw4bFpBMUk/view
33. Guyon, I., Bennett, K., Cawley, G., Escalante, H.J., Escalera, S., Ho, T.K., Macià, N., Ray, B., Saeed, M., Statnikov, A., Viegas, E.: Design of the 2015 ChaLearn AutoML challenge. In: International Joint Conference on Neural Networks (2015), http://www.causality.inf.ethz.ch/AutoML/automl_ijcnn15.pdf
34. Guyon, I., Chaabane, I., Escalante, H.J., Escalera, S., Jajetic, D., Lloyd, J.R., Macía, N., Ray, B., Romaszko, L., Sebag, M., Statnikov, A., Treguer, S., Viegas, E.: A brief review of the ChaLearn AutoML challenge. In: Proc. of AutoML 2016@ICML (2016), https://docs.google.com/a/chalearn.org/viewer?a=v&pid=sites&srcid=Y2hhbGVhcm4ub3JnfGF1dG9tbHxneDoyYThjZjhhNzRjMzI3MTg4
35. Guyon, I., Alamdari, A.R.S.A., Dror, G., Buhmann, J.: Performance prediction challenge. In: the International Joint Conference on Neural Networks. pp. 1649–1656 (2006)
36. Guyon, I., Bennett, K., Cawley, G., Escalante, H.J., Escalera, S., Ho, T.K., Ray, B., Saeed, M., Statnikov, A., Viegas, E.: Automl challenge 2015: Design and first results (2015)
37. Guyon, I., Cawley, G., Dror, G.: Hands-On Pattern Recognition: Challenges in Machine Learning, Volume 1. Microtome Publishing, USA (2011)
38. Guyon, I., Gunn, S., Nikravesh, M., Zadeh, L. (eds.): Feature extraction, foundations and applications. Studies in Fuzziness and Soft Computing, Physica-Verlag, Springer (2006)
39. Hastie, T., Rosset, S., Tibshirani, R., Zhu, J.: The entire regularization path for the support vector machine. Journal of Machine Learning Research 5, 1391–1415 (2004)
40. Hastie, T., Tibshirani, R., Friedman, J.: The elements of statistical learning: Data mining, inference, and prediction. Springer, 2nd edn. (2001)
41. Hutter, F., Hoos, H.H., Leyton-Brown, K.: Sequential model-based optimization for general algorithm configuration. In: Proceedings of the conference on Learning and Intelligent OptimizatioN (LION 5) (2011)
42. Ioannidis, J.P.A.: Why most published research findings are false. PLoS Medicine 2(8), e124 (August 2005)
43. Jordan, M.I.: On statistics, computation and scalability. Bernoulli 19(4), 1378–1390 (September 2013)
44. Keerthi, S.S., Sindhwani, V., Chapelle, O.: An efficient method for gradient-based adaptation of hyperparameters in SVM models. In: Advances in Neural Information Processing Systems (2007)
45. Klein, A., Falkner, S., Bartels, S., Hennig, P., Hutter, F.: Fast bayesian hyperparameter optimization on large datasets. In: Electronic Journal of Statistics. vol. 11 (2017)
46. Kohavi, R., John, G.H.: Wrappers for feature selection. Artificial Intelligence 97(1–2), 273–324 (December 1997)
47. Langford, J.: Clever methods of overfitting (2005), blog post at http://hunch.net/?p=22

48. Lloyd, J.: Freeze Thaw Ensemble Construction. https://github.com/jamesrobertlloyd/automl-phase-2 (2016)
49. Momma, M., Bennett, K.P.: A pattern search method for model selection of support vector regression. In: In Proceedings of the SIAM International Conference on Data Mining. SIAM (2002)
50. Moore, G., Bergeron, C., Bennett, K.P.: Model selection for primal SVM. Machine Learning 85(1–2), 175–208 (October 2011)
51. Moore, G.M., Bergeron, C., Bennett, K.P.: Nonsmooth bilevel programming for hyperparameter selection. In: IEEE International Conference on Data Mining Workshops. pp. 374–381 (2009)
52. Niculescu-Mizil, A., Perlich, C., Swirszcz, G., Sindhwani, V., Liu, Y., Melville, P., Wang, D., Xiao, J., Hu, J., Singh, M., et al.: Winning the kdd cup orange challenge with ensemble selection. In: Proceedings of the 2009 International Conference on KDD-Cup 2009-Volume 7. pp. 23–34. JMLR. org (2009)
53. Opper, M., Winther, O.: Gaussian processes and SVM: Mean field results and leave-one-out, pp. 43–65. MIT (10 2000), massachusetts Institute of Technology Press (MIT Press) Available on Google Books
54. Park, M.Y., Hastie, T.: L1-regularization path algorithm for generalized linear models. Journal of the Royal Statistical Society: Series B (Statistical Methodology) 69(4), 659–677 (2007)
55. Pedregosa, F., Varoquaux, G., Gramfort, A., Michel, V., Thirion, B., Grisel, O., Blondel, M., Prettenhofer, P., Weiss, R., Dubourg, V., Vanderplas, J., Passos, A., Cournapeau, D., Brucher, M., Perrot, M., Duchesnay, E.: Scikit-learn: Machine learning in Python. Journal of Machine Learning Research 12, 2825–2830 (2011)
56. Pham, H., Guan, M.Y., Zoph, B., Le, Q.V., Dean, J.: Efficient neural architecture search via parameter sharing. arXiv preprint arXiv:1802.03268 (2018)
57. Real, E., Moore, S., Selle, A., Saxena, S., Suematsu, Y.L., Le, Q., Kurakin, A.: Large-scale evolution of image classifiers. arXiv preprint arXiv:1703.01041 (2017)
58. Ricci, F., Rokach, L., Shapira, B., Kantor, P.B. (eds.): Recommender Systems Handbook. Springer (2011)
59. Schölkopf, B., Smola, A.J.: Learning with Kernels: Support Vector Machines, Regularization, Optimization, and Beyond. MIT Press (2001)
60. Snoek, J., Larochelle, H., Adams, R.P.: Practical Bayesian optimization of machine learning algorithms. In: Advances in Neural Information Processing Systems 25, pp. 2951–2959 (2012)
61. Statnikov, A., Wang, L., Aliferis, C.F.: A comprehensive comparison of random forests and support vector machines for microarray-based cancer classification. BMC Bioinformatics 9(1) (2008)
62. Sun, Q., Pfahringer, B., Mayo, M.: Full model selection in the space of data mining operators. In: Genetic and Evolutionary Computation Conference. pp. 1503–1504 (2012)
63. Swersky, K., Snoek, J., Adams, R.P.: Multi-task Bayesian optimization. In: Advances in Neural Information Processing Systems 26. pp. 2004–2012 (2013)
64. Swersky, K., Snoek, J., Adams, R.P.: Freeze-thaw bayesian optimization. arXiv preprint arXiv:1406.3896 (2014)
65. Thornton, C., Hutter, F., Hoos, H.H., Leyton-Brown, K.: Auto-weka: Automated selection and hyper-parameter optimization of classification algorithms. CoRR abs/1208.3719 (2012)
66. Thornton, C., Hutter, F., Hoos, H.H., Leyton-Brown, K.: Auto-weka: Combined selection and hyperparameter optimization of classification algorithms. In: 19th ACM SIGKDD International Conference on Knowledge Discovery and Data Mining. pp. 847–855. ACM (2013)
67. Vanschoren, J., Van Rijn, J.N., Bischl, B., Torgo, L.: Openml: networked science in machine learning. ACM SIGKDD Explorations Newsletter 15(2), 49–60 (2014)

68. Vapnik, V., Chapelle, O.: Bounds on error expectation for support vector machines. Neural computation 12(9), 2013–2036 (2000)
69. Weston, J., Elisseeff, A., BakIr, G., Sinz, F.: Spider (2007), http://mloss.org/software/view/29/
70. Zoph, B., Le, Q.V.: Neural architecture search with reinforcement learning. arXiv preprint arXiv:1611.01578 (2016)

Correction to: Neural Architecture Search

Thomas Elsken, Jan Hendrik Metzen, and Frank Hutter

Correction to:
Chapter 3 in: F. Hutter et al. (eds.), *Automated Machine Learning*, The Springer Series on Challenges in Machine Learning, https://doi.org/10.1007/978-3-030-05318-5_3

The original version of this chapter was inadvertently published without the author "Thomas Elsken" primary affiliation. The affiliation has now been updated as below.

Bosch Center for Artificial Intelligence, Robert Bosch GmbH, Renningen, Baden-Württemberg, Germany

Department of Computer Science, University of Freiburg, Freiburg, Baden-Württemberg, Germany

The updated version of this chapter can be found at
https://doi.org/10.1007/978-3-030-05318-5_3

F. Hutter et al. (eds.), *Automated Machine Learning*, The Springer Series on Challenges in Machine Learning, https://doi.org/10.1007/978-3-030-05318-5_11

www.ingramcontent.com/pod-product-compliance
Lightning Source LLC
LaVergne TN
LVHW082227200926
848484LV00008B/2311